RAJASTHAN

THE QUEST FOR SUSTAINABLE DEVELOPMENT

PUBLISHED BY ACADEMIC FOUNDATION
IN ASSOCIATION WITH THE
INSTITUTE OF DEVELOPMENT STUDIES,
JAIPUR, RAJASTHAN

RAJASTHAN

THE QUEST FOR SUSTAINABLE DEVELOPMENT

EDITORS

VIJAY S. VYAS

SARTHI ACHARYA

SURJIT SINGH

VIDYA SAGAR

ACADEMIC FOUNDATION

NEW DELHI

ACADEMIC FOUNDATION

First published in 2007
by

ACADEMIC FOUNDATION
4772-73 / 23 Bharat Ram Road, (23 Ansari Road),
Darya Ganj, New Delhi - 110 002 (India).
Phones : 23245001 / 02 / 03 / 04.
Fax : +91-11-23245005.
E-mail : academic@vsnl.com
www. academicfoundation.com

in association with:

Institute of Development Studies, Jaipur
www.idsj.org

Cataloging in Publication Data--DK
Courtesy: D.K. Agencies (P) Ltd. <docinfo@dkagencies.com>

Rajasthan: the quest for sustainable development / editors, V.S. Vyas ... [et al.].
p. cm.
Contributed articles.
ISBN-13: 9788171886210
ISBN-10: 8171886213

1. Sustainable development--India--Rajasthan. 2. Rajasthan (India)--Economic conditions. 3. Rajasthan (India)--Social conditions. I. Vyas, V. S. (Vijay Shankar), 1931-

DDC 333.709 544 22

Typeset by Italics India, New Delhi.
Printed and bound in India.

Contents

II

Dimensions of Economic Growth

III

Beyond Economics

List of Tables, Figures and Boxes

TABLES

FIGURES

BOXES

FIGURES

BOXES

Editors/Contributors

Sarthi Acharya was educated at the Indian Institute of Technology Kanupur and Central School of Planning and Statistics, Warsaw. He is a former Director of the Institute of Development Studies, Jaipur. His areas of specialisation are: agrarian issues and labour economy.

Anita is Professor at Indira Gandhi Panchayati Raj Gramin Vikas Sansthan, Jaipur. She is Ph.D in Sociology from University of Rajasthan, Jaipur. Her areas of specialisation are: *panchayati raj*, human development, human rights and gender issues.

Pradeep Bhargava is Professor, Institute of Development Studies, Jaipur and adviser to the Commissioners of the Supreme Court in the PUCL case on Right to Food. He has Ph.D in Economics from University of Rajasthan. His research interests include: poverty, education and public policy.

K.N. Joshi is Professor in the Institute of Development Studies, Jaipur. He has a Ph.D in Geography from Jai Naryan Vyas University, Jodhpur. His current research interests include: application of remote sensing in national resource and environment management.

Varsha Joshi is Associate Professor at Institute of Development Studies, Jaipur. She is Ph.D in Cultural History from University of London, London. She specialises in cultural studies, nutrition and gender issues.

Devendra Kothari is the Director and Professor, Population Programme Management, Parivar Seva Sanstha, a NGO working in the area of reproductive health. He has Ph.D in demography from the Australian University. His area of specialisation is demography and health systems.

Kanchan Mathur is Professor at the Institute of Development Studies, Jaipur and Coordinator of the Women's/Gender Studies, Unit. She is Ph.D in Sociology from the University of Rajasthan. Her areas of interest include: gender based violence, women's empowerment, education, sexual and reproductive health, poverty, gender and livelihoods, child labour and childhood poverty

Shobhita Rajagopal is Associate Professor at the Institute of Development Studies, Jaipur. She has a Ph.D in Sociology from the University of Rajasthan. Her areas of research include: gender and education, childhood poverty, gender, poverty and livelihoods and violence against women.

Jyotsana Rajvanshi is Associate Professor and Coordinator of NGO Unit in Institute of Development Studies, Jaipur. She has a Ph.D in Sociology from University of Rajasthan. Her current research interests are: panchayati raj institutions, gender studies and child rights.

M.S. Rathore is Professor at the Institute of Development Studies, Jaipur. He has Ph.D in Agricultural Economics from University of Himachal Pradesh & ICRISAT. His current research includes: environment and natural resource management with special reference to water resource management.

Sunil Ray is Professor at the Institute of Development Studies, Jaipur. He obtained Ph.D from University of Mysore through Institute for Social Economic Change, Bangalore. His current area of interest is management of natural resource through development of local institutions.

Vidya Sagar is Visiting Professor at the Institute of Development Studies, Jaipur. He has a Ph.D in Economics from the University of Rajasthan. His current research interest include issues related to poverty and human development besides agriculture.

P.R. Sharma is Assistant Professor at the Institute of Development Studies, Jaipur. He is Ph.D. in Political Science from M.D.S University, Ajmer. His areas of specialisation are decentralised planning, panchayati raj institution and human development.

Surjit Singh is a Professor of Economics at the Institute of Development Studies, Jaipur. He has a Ph.D in Economics from Gujarat University through Sardar Patel Institute of Economic and Social Research, Ahmedabad. His areas of interest are economic policies, labour markets and rural financial sector.

V.S. Vyas is Professor Emeritus at the Institute of Development Studies, Jaipur. He has a Ph.D in Economics from University of Bombay. His current research interests are public policies for agricultural growth and rural development.

Introduction

The Journey, Milestones and Destinations

V.S. VYAS

Rajasthan started its quest for development with several handicaps and a few advantages. It is the largest state in the country, and a land locked state. Nearly two-third of its area is arid or semi-arid, with low and irregular rainfall characterised with extremes of climate. For a predominantly agrarian economy these conditions prove a major handicap in ensuring sustainable growth. A good monsoon can bolster up production, which can crash down very next year with a drought. The uncertainty of such magnitude leads to sub-optimal resource allocation in its primary, agricultural sector with repercussions in other sectors of the economy.

For the reasons, which are not fully understood, despite a hostile climate and unfavourable geographical features, population growth in the state is one of the highest in the country. The growth is even faster in the arid northwestern districts. This is exerting high pressure on the states' fragile ecosystem. Due to rapid rate of growth of population and vast gaps in the provision of social services and basic infrastructure, expenditure on the basic services such as education and health, and for creation of infrastructure, has to be increased in a commensurate measure. Weak economic base of the state makes the task of resource mobilisation extremely difficult.

If geography of the state is proving a stumbling block, the history—especially, the recent history—makes the task of sustainable growth all the more daunting. The state came into being after the merger of a number of princely states, big and small, and few enclaves of former British India. The feudal tendencies had a deep sway over social organisation, which was characterised by hierarchical outlook, paternalistic institutions, low status of women and sharp social and economic discrimination against certain sections of population. The princely states, with very few exceptions, made no systematic efforts to improve agriculture, or attract industry and commerce in their territories. Fewer still showed any concern for social development of their citizens. The general picture presented at the time of the formation of Rajasthan was that of under developed economies, neglected population and autocratic rulers.

It will be wrong, however, to conclude that the state has not got any intrinsic advantages. A part of the state is relatively well watered and fertile. It has enviable deposits of minerals, with the prospect of abundant reserves of oil and gas. It has natural advantages for attracting tourists, and rich tradition of handicrafts. Its hardy stock of peasantry is capable of facing adversities. A large animal husbandry sector, as an important part of the farming systems, not only adds to the income of the farmers, makes them better prepared to face weather-induced uncertainties. Feudal past has also contributed to the inculcation of the values of bravery, fortitude and charity. Above all it encouraged a spirit of adventure, which in the modern context was transformed in economic and social entrepreneurship. Task of transforming such a society into a modern, egalitarian, democratic society, and to put it on a path of sustainable development is not easy. Following chapters in this volume address this task in all its complexities.

First four chapters in the book deal with key determinants of sustainable development, i.e. use (or misuse) of natural resources and qualitative and quantitative aspect of population and labour force. First two chapters, respectively by M.S. Rathore and K.N. Joshi, deal with use and abuse of natural resources, i.e. land and water, in the state and indicate the directions in which efforts have to be mounted to reverse the trend in deterioration of these resources.

With the fragile natural resource base of the state one should expect a more careful management of these resources. Unfortunately, the record suggests just the opposite. Village common lands are dwindling with seriously upsetting ecological balance, disturbing the symbiotic relationship between agriculture and animal husbandry, and adversely impacting the economy of the poor households. Agricultural land has expanded mainly with the introduction of irrigation and extension of the intensive cultivation. This, as the authors suggest, has taken place in the regions, which are not suited for intensive agriculture. As in other parts of the country, in Rajasthan also, non-agricultural uses of land has expanded significantly and this, in several regions of the state, has encroached upon fertile agricultural land. Misuse of urban land is equally glaring. Degradation of land manifested in a variety of ways is weakening the production base of state's agriculture and posing serious long-term consequences. Efforts of land improvements have not touched even the fringe of the problem.

Situation in regard to water resources is, if anything, worse. The state has nearly 10 per cent of the country's land surface with nearly 6 per cent of its population, but less than 1.5 per cent of the water resources. There are only two perennial rivers flowing in the state. Major part of the state comprise arid and semi-arid regions. In these parts rainfall is scanty and highly fluctuating. With paucity of surface water there is progressively larger dependence on groundwater. In most blocks withdrawal of groundwater exceeds the recharge, leading to deepening of wells. These blocks known as dark zones are becoming all pervasive. As a consequence economic cost of water is increasing. Impurity of water both from surface as well as groundwater sources is posing another serious problem. Water related disputes between regions, within the regions, and between the rural and urban areas are becoming rampant.

Some of the handicaps faced by the state in terms of natural resources are due to its geographical location and topography. Vast expanse of arid region, extremes in climate, fragile soil cover, scanty water resources, absence of perennial rivers, etc., are given by Nature. However, the situation is exacerbated due to man-made follies. Two major culprits are, a) unregulated mining activities, and b) unplanned expansion and tardy management of irrigation resources. Both have contributed heavily in the deterioration of the natural resource base. In the quest for sustainable development these two areas will deserve prior attention.

There is an absence of a proper land and water use policy for the state. Only recently a draft on Water Policy, largely based on the recommendations of the Expert Committee on Development and Management of the Water Resources, is being circulated. A lot of damage is done because of the absence of a coherent and consistent policy on the use of natural resources. Inconsistencies among various policy measures defeat the objective of sustainable use of natural resources. Policies on water use and power supply, for example, give conflicting signals, former aiming at economic use of water, while latter making the extraction of water easier.

It is becoming clear that useable land and water resources in the state cannot be augmented to any remarkable extent. There is need, therefore, to give high priority to demand management. This is particularly true for water resources. There is, for example, large scope to economise use of water in irrigation without sacrificing productivity. For achieving this objective, appropriate technological, economic as well as legal measures will have to be devised. At the same time, public opinion for justifying such measures has to be created. Negative externalities arising from the present mode of ownership and use have to be made explicit, and lessons to be learnt from some successful experiments, within the state and elsewhere in the country, in conserving land and water resources have to be popularised.

Contrary to prevailing thinking on 'demographic dividend', Devendra Kothari highlights the problems associated with the pressure of population on fragile ecosystem of the state and points out the link between rapid increase in the workforce and rising phenomenon of unemployment. Over the period of time there is hardly any improvement in the health indicators. Rate of population growth in Rajasthan is not only one of the highest among the states of India; the population dynamics is such that every successive census is recording a phenomenal increase in the number of people. The situation is rather intriguing as a large 'unmet' demand for family planning is revealed in scientifically conducted surveys.

According to the author the demographic transition, from high death-rate high birth-rate stage to low death-rate low birth–rate stage, is stalled as death rate has declined but the birth rate has not. The reason for that is ascribed mainly to the mis-management of the family planning programme. There are other contributing factors as well, e.g. low age of marriage. However, the main factor, which needs emphasis in this context, is the issue of women empowerment, as an earlier report on Population Policy had also underlined. It is important to observe that increase in women's literacy rate—which in the recent past was rather satisfactory—is, what may be called, an essential but not a sufficient condition for women empowerment. Raising the status of women and empowering them has social as well as economic content. This is reflected in author's 'action plan', which includes preventing early marriages, improving utilisation of reproductive health services, placing still greater emphasis on women literacy and enlarging women's role in formal economic activities.

Demographic as well as social and economic factors are reflected in the composition of work force, extent of workers participation, sectoral deployment of workers, extent of employment and unemployment and, earning of workers. Sarthi Acharya and Vidya Sagar have discussed all these aspects in their chapter. Some of their conclusions are quite significant. It seems that workers participation rate has declined only marginally, may be because of higher enrolment in the schools in the school going age group, but a more significant fact is higher participation of women, especially in agriculture. The phenomenon of progressive feminisation of agriculture, which is evident at the all-India level, is also getting reflected in Rajasthan. The sectoral distribution of the workforce has not changed much, yet the phenomenon of out-migration among male workers seems to be getting stronger. This might have increased family's economic resources, it has at the same time put additional burden on the women folk.

Earnings from labour seem to have increased, but there is no consistent trend in this regard. This is not surprising in an economy where the production and productivity in the largest sector, i.e., agriculture, fluctuates from year to year. What is more surprising is that the investment in education, as reflected in the years of schooling, has not got any substantial impact on the earning of the self employed persons, at least in the rural area. This is an indicator of the traditional mode of production in agriculture.

A welcome feature of Rajasthan's economy is the low level of poverty compared to the country as a whole. Even more remarkable is the fact that for a considerable period of time, from the early eighties to the mid-nineties, the pace of decline was fairly high. This was made possible mainly due to high rate of growth in agricultural production during that period. With the slackness in agricultural growth, decline in poverty rate also decelerated. Yet if the average level of poverty is low it is mainly because of larger agricultural holdings, diversification of the household economy—the more prominent being livestock agricultural combination—and out-migration, both long term and seasonal. An important feature of Rajasthan's economy, especially its rural sector is that the 'asset less' households are numerically not significant. The asset base of land, howsoever small and infertile, which a large majority possess, provides not only a safety cushion, it also throws opens options for adding household income by supplementary enterprises to agriculture. The task before the state is to create conditions where the complementarity between different enterprises is maximised and fuller employment and larger incomes are ensured.

It is instructive in this context to review the pace and pattern of industrialisation in the state, a task addressed by Surjit Singh. Over a period of time the pattern of economic growth followed the country's example in an important respect, i.e., the service sectors growth was faster than that of primary sector or for that matter secondary sector. However, the nature of service sector was much different. It was the traditional service sector with petty trade and hospitality related activities dominating this sector. Only lately tourism is getting a boost in the organised sector. In the secondary sector there was, and continues, preponderance of household enterprises (i.e., own account manufacturing enterprises) operating at a low level of technology and employing, in large majority of cases one or two workers, mainly family members. There is a nascent construction sector in the organised fold.

The primary sector is identified with two major activities, agriculture and mining. However, neither agro-based industries nor mineral-based industries are significant at this stage. Rajasthan continues to be identified as supplier of raw materials. The state has comparative advantages in certain sectors and activities. These include agro-processing industries, mineral-based industries, tourism and handicrafts. Textile industry, both cotton and woolen has some intrinsic advantages, which are yet to be exploited fully. Certain agricultural products, especially the spices and condiments, herbs and medicinal plants can form a base for viable industrial activities. Agro-processing in general is acquiring greater importance with consumers preference for more processed food. The state has not taken advantage of this shift in consumer preference, except in the preparation of certain snack foods, mainly in unorganised sector.

The reasons for stalled industrialisation have to be sought in parts in the historical legacy characterised by lack of infrastructure, lack of skill enhancing facilities and absence of a vision for diversifying economy of the state. Industrial policy statement, the current one as well as the previous one recognises that these gaps have to be filled in. However, the results so far are not very encouraging. The state could not attract large industrial units, or significant inflow of capital. Small and cottage industry sector which has some inherent advantages such as low capital intensity, high employment potential and niche market for several products could not, by and large, graduate to surplus generating, forward looking, enterprises, an achievement which, for example, China's township enterprises could register. Two important links are missing in the state's industrial policy: a clear strategy for technology upgradation, and institutional support in the areas of credit and marketing. From a long-term point of view industrial growth has to be harmonised with its natural resource endowment, especially water. There cannot, therefore, be an unqualified support to industrialisation irrespective of its demand on natural resources of the state.

For quite some time to come, agriculture will retain its importance in Rajasthan's economy and society. This despite the fact that share of agriculture in the State Domestic Product is declining and its role to influence economic growth in non-agricultural sectors is diminishing. The overwhelming dependence of the state's workforce on agriculture has remained more or less in tact. Vidya Sagar in his chapter has examined the process of growth of the sector in the eighties and the nineties, later coinciding with the initiation of economic reform in the country and in the state. The performance is poor in the later period by any standard of efficiency and equity.

It will be instructive to understand reasons for the deceleration of growth. An important development in the nineties was, as the author calls 'over active price policy' which subsumed the role of the non-price factors such as technology and infrastructure. The problem was compounded, especially from the state's point of view, because of tilting of relative prices from water saving, and environmentally better suited, crops of oilseeds (rape and mustard) to wheat. The resultant shift in area from oilseeds to wheat was not helpful to either of the crops. Growth of oilseeds production was further compromised with the liberal imports of oilseeds as a part of economic reform package. The lesson is inescapable. All regions do not share gains from international trade uniformly. Unless a compensatory mechanism is put in place the net loss in welfare for a region can exceed whatever may be the over all gains.

A large part of Rajasthan's agriculture, especially in the western arid and semi-arid region, growing *bajra* (pearl millet) is a loser not because the crop is not grown efficiently, but because of the shift in the consumer tastes from coarse cereals to wheat. The market for this crop is shrinking. Unfortunately, there are no easily adaptable substitute crops. The alternative that the author has advocated is to make *bajra* a 'value added' crop by making it more suitable for animal fodder or in other uses. Also, addition of pulses as a mixed crop can improve the economy of *bajra* growing farmers. On a smaller scale newer crops like Jatropha hold some promise. But success of these alternatives is predicated on availability of the market and suitable infrastructure and required support services. Rajasthan's agriculture is at crossroad. It requires bold and imaginative initiatives in state policy, investment strategy and institutional support to resolve its predicaments.

Sunil Ray's chapter in this volume discusses another vital component of Rajasthan's rural economy in detail, i.e., sustainable livestock development. In large part of the state the farming system is characterised as mixed farming with important place accorded to animal husbandry along with crop raising. This feature of the farming system has helped in ensuring fuller employment of family labour, augmentation of household income and an effective devise to face weather-induced uncertainties. Livestock economy of the state is also becoming as vulnerable as the crops component of agriculture. The major threat to animal husbandry is caused due to weakening of the natural resource base, mainly the common pasture lands on which this segment of rural economy was mainly relying.

There is noticeable shrinking of the village commons to which the authors in the section on "Land and Labour" have also drawn attention. Simultaneously, there is rapid deterioration in the quality of the grazing lands. The livestock economy, especially of the poorer sections heavily depend on this 'free' resource. The major culprit for these developments is the state's burgeoning population, but the disintegration of the communal institutions which were evolved to manage these resources in a sustainable manner, have exacerbated the situation. It is quite clear that, as Ray emphasises, livestock development in the state cannot ignore deteriorating carrying capacity of its renewable natural resources.

Imbalance between natural grazing resources and stock of animals is reflected in the changes in the composition of livestock, although there were other contributing factors leading to the observed changes. Proportion of buffaloes in the animal herds has increased and that of cattle has gone down. Former depend more on stall-feeding. Factors such as the development of milk market with heavier premium on fat content, and mechanisation of agricultural operations reducing the need for bullock labour, have hastened the pace of such change. Buffaloes require heavier initial investment and larger working capital, as a result the poorer sections are at a disadvantage. There is also a change in the composition of small ruminants with goats receiving greater preference compared to sheeps. In this case, apart from the hardiness of goats as animals, the deteriorating market conditions for wool has made sheep rearing less attractive for the poor.

Major initiatives at the policy and organisational level are needed to rejuvenate animal husbandry sector of the state. First and foremost, as Ray points out, is to improve the natural resource base, i.e., common grazing lands. This can be achieved only by encouraging community-based institutions. Another direction in which change is needed is to emphasise selective breeding to reduce the burden of non-descript animals. The strategy of popularising hybrid animals has not succeeded; popularising improved local breeds offer better alternative. There is also a need to re-look at the delivery system for veterinary services with concerted efforts to promote public private partnership. Equally important is to strengthen the marketing infrastructure and relevant institutions. The development of the dairy segment and deterioration of the wool segment can largely be ascribed to the functioning of the markets in these products. Today a large part of the animal husbandry sector is becoming non-viable. This trend has to be reversed, and can be reversed.

Development to be sustainable would necessitate action beyond the narrow confines of Economics. The holistic approach to development presupposes a just society, democratic polity and cultural effervescence. Chapters in the third section of the book address some of these questions in the context of Rajasthan.

In his chapter on civil society, Pradeep Bhargava traces the history of the civil society movements in the states, distinguishes between the institutions, which help people to 'do' things, i.e. to develop their potential capability, and the institutions which help them to 'be' through increasing their welfare and happiness. The type of civil society institutions, which emerged in many parts of the country in the years following Independence carried the legacy of the national movement with emphasis on equality and justice while recognising the importance of social reforms. In Rajasthan the civil society had to carry the burden of its feudal past. This made socially inclusive institutions difficult to take roots but ensured autonomy at the level of particular groups i.e. castes, clans or tribes. The latter also degenerated into extremely conservative institutions lead by ill-informed and opportunist individuals. A fresh beginning was made in the seventies and the eighties by some enlightened individuals and groups, mostly well educated and reasonably well connected. Many of whom came from outside the state.

This new breed of institutions took two distinct paths. While some emphasised social mobilisation and stressed on a larger degree of self-reliance for developing their economy and the resources, other took a more confrontalist approach and asserted the rights of people, especially the marginalised sections, to have food security, employment opportunities and access to education and health. We have good example of both types of institutions, and in contrast also a plethora of organisations, which are performing just the service function as agents of the state or some other outside entities.

Picture is not as bleak as it is occasionally presented. Civil society institutions in Rajasthan have been in the forefront in advocating right to information, employment guarantee, fair wages, food security, and in other similar areas. Some of these institutions are doing exemplary work in natural resource conservation, especially in the conservation and management of water resources, forests and village commons, in education and skill upgradation, and in health and nutrition. In achieving all this emphasis has been on social mobilisation. Another unique feature of Rajasthan is the active support extended by the academics in people's movements. Institute of Development Studies has a truly enviable record in this respect and its role is documented in the chapters in this section. A section of bureaucracy has also distinguished itself by supporting the cause of social justice and fair play. With all the positive results the civil society has not been able to redress injustice to women and to Dalits.

Another worrisome feature is that in all civil society movements as well as in civil society organisations soon 'fatigue' sets in once the prime movers leave the scene. Need to institutionalise people's movements on the one hand and sensitise various organs of state has become evident. This suggests an important role for the statutory organisations at the village level, namely *Panchayats*.

Rajasthan was pioneer in the establishment of *Panchayati Raj*. In fact, even before the formation of the state, some princely states had introduced devolution of power at the local level. However, such examples were few, and there too the efforts were more in terms of decentralisation of administration rather than devolution of power of governance. It goes to the credit of Balwant Rai Mehta Committee, which drawing inspirations from Gandhian concept of *Gram Swaraj*, advocated a model of decentralised governance at the vllage, block and district level. Rajasthan was the first state to start this experiment in right earnest. *Panchayati Raj* system was introduced in the state on 2nd October (Gandhi's birthday), 1954.

As P.R. Sharma and Anita report in their chapter, since then the state has witnessed swings of activities and apathy. After 20 years of experimentation panchayati raj institution (PRI) system was more or less abandoned in Rajasthan (and in the country as a whole), as much greater importance was attached to the various government sponsored schemes for development and welfare. In administering these schemes, much less in their formulation, PRI had hardly any role to play. In this state even the formal elections to these bodies were deferred under one pretext or other.

New era of *panchayati raj* started with the constitutional amendments affected in 1998, which made these institutions constitutional entities, prescribed a list of functions to be delegated to these institutions and, made their election mandatory and under independent supervision. A new wave of enthusiasm to devolve power was witnessed all over the country. Unfortunately this enthusiasm was not translated into concrete actions. The authors of the chapter on *panchayati raj* give enough evidence to support this conclusion. In nutshell, the effort to devolve power was half-hearted and incomplete. Both the bureaucracy and the local level politicians interpreted these institutions as threat to their authority. Leadership at the state level more or less connived with these entrenched interests. In several instances the civil society institutions whose role should have been to strengthen these institutions, unwittingly projected themselves as alternative to elected bodies of the people.

Apart from unfavourable external environment, the elected members, in most of the cases, did not prove equal to their tasks. It goes to the credit of the state government that a massive campaign to strengthen capabilities of the *panchayat* leaders at all levels was launched. The Institute of Development Studies (IDS) played a significant role in designing syllabi and advising on the pedagogy of teaching PRI representatives. A few NGOs also joined in the training programme. The evaluation studies suggest that this training contributed to capability enhancement and, more importantly, in empowerment of the elected representatives, a large number being women and members of the scheduled caste and scheduled tribes.

The constitutional amendments have provided framework for people's participation at the grass root level, and decentralised and responsive system of governance. For translating it in reality a lot more efforts will be needed. This will be possible only if a coalition of like-minded people from different walks of life, especially those who contribute in opinion making, is formed in support of panchayati raj institutions.

The next two chapters in the volume narrate the experience of the researchers in IDS in two critical areas, in womens studies, and in support of NGOs. For an equitable and sustainable development in Rajasthan, one of the major handicaps is the low status of women in society, which is still largely governed by feudal and patriarchal norms. Institute of Development Studies played a pioneering role in organising these studies in a systematic way in its Women Studies Unit (WSU) under leadership of one of the most respected scholars in this area, Dr. Sharda Jain. Two of the early participants in this endeavour

Kanchan Mathur and Shobhita Rajagopal delineate the scope and the history of these studies in Rajasthan's context. They outline the challenges and suggest future direction these studies may take.

As a unit located in an academic institution, WSU had a significant influence in raising women's issues and suggesting programmes and activities to resolve them. This was mainly because of the approach to these studies adopted right from the beginning. Experience of WSU in this respect has lessons for other similar initiatives. The studies in this Unit adopted holistic approach to examine the issues, tried to bridge the gap between action and research, took state functionaries with them to the extent possible, and most importantly, focused on the recipient system more than on delivery mechanisms. They soon earned credibility among their peers, and confidence of the stakeholders. The 'twining' arrangement entered by IDS, Jaipur, with the Institute of Development Studies of the University of Sussex put them in touch with the internationally renowned scholars in this area.

A distinguishing feature of these activities was an active involvement with the protest movement against exploitation of women, especially the marginalised sections. In all the notorious cases of violence against women, exemplified, for instance, by rape, *Sati* or economic exploitation, WSU was in the forefront of the protest movement. At the same time the researchers in this Unit made significant contributions in the design and formulation of institutions and programme for women's development in the state and the Centre. Another area in which the Unit distinguished itself was in monitoring and evaluation of various programmes where they adopted the approach of 'shared reflections'.

Women's studies in the IDS, as in several other institutions of research and training in this area are at a crossroad. On the one hand, it seems that despite a large number of training and sensitising exercises basic attitude towards women in the society is not changing. Some of the indicators such as destruction of female embryo, dowry deaths and, neglect of girl child in education and nutrition, suggest that situation rather than improving might have worsened. Internally, the transition from women's studies to 'gender studies' has created confusion about the exact nature of these studies, as many scholars fear that it might distance these efforts from women's movement against exploitation and oppression. A state like Rajasthan can ill afford such regression.

Just as WSU, another pioneering initiative, at least in the context of Rajasthan, is a full-fledged unit to study Non-Governmental Organisations (which now has been expanded to study panchayati raj institutions as well), commonly known as NGO Centre of the Institute of Development Studies. The Institute's mandate enjoined on it to study programmes and activities of relevance to the poor conducted by government or non-government organisation. (At one stage the mission of the IDS was defined as "working as a link between macro policies and micro realities"). Jyotsana Rajvanshi who traces the history and activity profile of NGO Centre in her chapter in this volume gives an account of evolution of this activity in IDS from occasional seminars and workshops, and a few evaluation type of studies, to an integral part of the Institutes activities. The Centre took its present shape as a unit of the Institute with initial support from the Ford Foundation and IDRC. It goes to the credit of these institutions that they never tried to influence the Centre's agenda.

Strength of this initiative is in adapting to the changing scene of NGO activities in this state. Its major contribution has been to provide a platform for collaborative work between NGOs and academics. For academics the main advantage was a better understanding of the social processes. In turn, they could contribute in building capacity of the NGO partners; research in the problems faced by them and do the policy advocacy. A whole variety of activities were undertaken comprising issue specific researches, training programmes, seminars and workshops, publication of directories and compilations of relevant information. Colleagues in the institute were not passive spectators, they also participated in movements organised by NGOs in areas of food security, right to information, employment guarantee, etc. The Centre was also involved in a major way in the programme pertaining to nutrition and childcare etc. In these areas also the Centre took an active role in designing innovative approaches. The result has been a fund of goodwill and credibility for the NGO Centre.

Both the internal and external environment facing the Centre have changed in recent years. The internal problems of lack of adequate resources, legitimacy in a disciplined based setup, dearth of dedicated and competent staff is real but not intractable. The external environment poses the major problems. A large number of NGO partners have adopted the 'rights' mode in their activities, giving secondary importance to the service aspect of their activities. This obviously results in confrontational situation, not only *vis-a-vis* state but also with the community, especially the wasted interest. An academic institution is handicapped in becoming a full-fledged partner in people's struggle. At the same time, it cannot remain a silent spectator. A lot depends on the composition and orientation of the faculty, but there is undeniably a built in tension in the situation. Nor it is easy to deal with other types of NGOs who are basically social contractors, or worse. To work with them is to compromise with the basic values informing the Centre.

A major cause for concern is the conflict with the PRI and the NGOs, both having rather jaundiced view about the other. The Centre wants to serve both the entities. There have been a few attempts to bring them on the same platform and create an understanding about their respective roles, but not with great deal of success. The difficulties are compounded as the politicians start playing one against the other, and thus weakening both.

For sustainable development at the grass root level, it is important to recognise that PRI have greater accountability to the people and the NGOs, in most of the cases, have greater skills. From NGOs point of view it is important to recognise that they have three-fold function, of advocacy on behalf of the marginalised sections, of delivering service in an efficient manner and starting innovative and scalable development programme. Academician can clarify these roles and help NGOs in equipping them to perform these roles.

They (the academic institutions) in turn have an advocacy role, in ensuring right set of policies and programmes, a service role, in equipping NGO functionaries to perform their tasks more efficiently and catalytic role in organisational and human resource development. Rajasthan is fortunate to have a sound tradition of viable NGOs manned by dedicated leadership, and academicians who are prepared to help the civil society institutions as well as PRIs. A few among political leadership as well as bureaucracy recognise the positive role, which these institutions can play. With this constellation of favourable features the state is favourably placed to meet these challenges.

For a holistic development the cultural aspects need to be taken into account. Varsha Joshi in her chapter looks into the cultural facets of Rajasthan. Generally, Rajasthan culture is identified as the feudal culture and its inhibiting factors are highlighted. There is much substance in that criticism. However, there are positive aspects, which also need to be recognised and encouraged. For example, Rajasthan has strong tradition of secularism. Several deities of one community are worshipped by other community. Many religious festivals are celebrated jointly; there are place of worship of one community where *pujari* belongs to other community. In the region, the prevailing notion is 'live and let live'. Unfortunately, these traditions are threatened with the spread of sectarian ideas.

As in many other rural societies joys and sorrows are shared by all in a community. They are expressed in songs, dance, folk theatre, fairs and social gathering. An equally important aspect is the creativity of the common people expressed in songs, stories, idioms and proverbs. Participation of the common people in these creative activities cements their bonds of fellowship. It also shows the liveliness of the society and creativity of its people. In all these respects, as in case of clothing and food, there is a rich diversity representing strong and vibrant sub-cultures.

Inter-personal relations, though governed by customs and social norms, ensured a fixed but respectful place for every member of society, and practitioner of every craft. There is also a long and strong tradition of preserving flora and fauna of the vicinity, to the extent that people were prepared to lay down their lives to save trees, animals and birds. Their respect for earth and water is legendary. It is true that most of these practices, and the values supporting them, are fast eroding, yet the fact that this region has a valuable heritage need to be recognised and preserved. There are equally obnoxious features, such as subjugation of women, discrimination against the Dalits, undue importance to status and hierarchical positioning of societal relationship, which need to be discouraged. Conscious efforts will be needed by the opinion makers to contribute to the preservation and enhancement of the healthier features of our traditions and discouragement of the ideas and behaviour patterns, which are corrupting the social systems.

Preceding discussion covering the key aspects of development in Rajasthan has narrated the progress, or lack of progress, in different field and suggested certain directions for future growth. It can be surmised from above that sustainable development in Rajasthan, though will be vitally affected by what happens in the country as a whole, has to meet certain priorities. It has to be based on four major premises.

In the first place, the development has to be multi-faceted. In a state where a large section of population is faced with severe social handicaps as much as economic deprivation emphasis on the growth of the State Domestic Product alone will not be helpful. The second premise for a sustainable growth is that we will have to give much larger attention to natural resources of land and water than in the present. Rajasthan's natural resource base is weak and fragile. Activities of last few years have worsened the situation. An emphasis on proper land utilisation and water conservation is a high priority for the state. The third requirement is to plan for an inclusive growth, which in other words means that each able bodied person should have access to some assets, be that the physical assets, useful skills or stamina to put in labour. Without some asset they will remain marginalised and will not be able to take advantage of the growth process or contribute to it. Finally, for equitable and sustainable growth there is distinct role for the state, for the market and for the civil society institutions. They cannot abdicate their respective roles nor can usurp others role.

I

Land and Labour in Rajasthan

1

Natural Resource Use

Environmental Implications

M.S. RATHORE

Around three quarters of our total relevant area is in need of urgent attention and a third is so sick that it is almost completely unproductive.

— Vohra, 1982: 4

The changes in natural resources (land water and vegetation) usage affect the ecosystem of an area in terms of local weather effects, land quality, vegetation and quality of life of people and livestock that can be sustained. The shifts in land use, water use and vegetation use can be attributed to the urban and industrial expansion, agricultural growth and expansion of irrigation networks, roads, market and other infrastructures. A balance needs to be maintained in sectoral land use, water use and biomass use to avoid short and long term negative ecological consequences. Despite enough evidences of land degradation, water shortages and quality issues, land use and water policy lack environmental and sustainability concern. This chapter attempts to examine the land and water use dynamics in the state of Rajasthan and its development and ecological implications.

Land Use in Rajasthan

Land is a vital and natural gift to mankind/living being, it needs to be passed on to the succeeding generations without impoverishing. Land use pattern and agrarian expansions in the semi-arid and arid areas were influenced by: (i) demographic; (ii) market related; (iii) technology related, and (iv) infrastructure related factors. An analysis of structural changes in land use pattern over a period of time is needed for planned and judicious management of land for sustainable development.

The way in which our land resources are being used is far from satisfactory. Even allowing for any possible inaccuracies and overlaps, the fact remains that despite much of investment in soil conservation, watershed development, and other land development the situation did not improve as 52.8 per cent of the total geographical area of the country is still categorised as problem area (IAB January, 2000). Of these total problem areas, 83 per cent is subjected to water and wind erosion and 17 per cent area is degraded because of special problems. In the case of Rajasthan, 373.94 lakh hectare area is classified as problem area and till 1996-97 only 19.94 lakh hectare (5.3 per cent) area got treated. The National Remote Sensing Agency (NRSA) has come out with a Wasteland Atlas of India and classified wastelands into 28 categories. The wastelands of Rajasthan are reported in Table 1.1. The categorised problem areas in Rajasthan can be grouped into two types as: (i) soil erosion affected and (ii) degraded lands. They account for 50.4 and 49.6 per cent respectively.

The major threat to the land is the erosion of the fertile topsoil. Erosion can be caused either by water or wind action. It is the direct result of the over-exploitation of non-agricultural lands by way of excessive felling and grazing and extension of agriculture on marginal lands. Once the erosion sets in, the land is caught in a vicious circle because the loss of topsoil renders it increasingly less capable of sustaining vegetation to save it from further damage. In this chapter, the water and wind erosion issues are deliberately set aside and impact of change in land use is discussed.

Land Use Dynamics

The land use in Rajasthan, as per the nine-fold classification used by the state government for publication of land use statistics, is reported in Table 1.2 and 1.3. The changes in each category are discussed below.

Forest Land

The area under forest land category in Rajasthan increased from 1355 (4%) in 1971 to 2651 (7.7%) thousand hectares in 2002. This doubling of forest area can be ascribed to: (i) forest lands got properly demarcated; (ii) state and national level awareness about

Table 1.1

Category-wise and Region-wise Wasteland in Rajasthan

(Area in sq. km.)

Category	*Jaipur Region*	*Bharatpur Region*	*Kota Region*	*Jodhpur Region*	*Ganganagar Region*	*Bhilwara Region*	*Udaipur Region*	*State Total*
Gullied and/Ravinous Land (Shallow)	633.42	1116.22	1850.77	226.96	48.46	88.5	3.69	3968.02
Gullied and/Ravinous Land (Medium)	81.27	875.99	96.56	9.20	30.98	0.00	0.00	1094.00
Gullied and/Ravinous Land (Deep)	373.62	425.13	735.77	4.29	0.00	0.00	0.00	1538.81
Land with Scrub	1636.79	2301.30	742.94	16193.98	1909.00	4047.01	3179.57	30010.59
Land without Scrub	120.64	147.07	592.70	4716.66	384.98	348.35	535.84	6846.24
Waterlogged and Marshy Land (Permanent)	10.37	37.35	0.00	2.19	66.01	0.00	0.00	115.92
Waterlogged and Marshy Land (Seasonal)	0.00	0.00	0.76	35.35	107.95	0.00	0.00	144.06
Land Affected by Salinity/ Alkalinity (Strong)	74.05	80.56	0.00	472.87	6.12	0.00	0.00	633.60
Land Affected by Aalinity/ Alkalinity (Moderate)	122.14	131.24	0.00	390.99	13.67	0.00	0.00	658.04

Contd. ...

...Contd. ...

Category	*Jaipur Region*	*Bharatpur Region*	*Kota Region*	*Jodhpur Region*	*Ganganagar Region*	*Bhilwara Region*	*Udaipur Region*	*State Total*
Land Affected by Salinity/ Alkalinity (Slight)	66.52	624.16	1254.96	379.46	7.93	140.94	0.11	2474.08
Shifting Cultivation Area (Abandoned *jhum*)	0.00	0.00	0.00	0.00	0.00	0.00	0.00	0.00
Shifting Cultivation Area (Current *jhum*)	0.00	0.00	0.00	0.00	0.00	0.00	0.00	0.00
Under Utilised/Degraded Notified Forest Land	1263.94	1715.51	2574.93	1334.76	135.28	675.48	1210.02	8909.92
Under Utilised/Degraded Notified Forest Land (Agricultural)	229.28	82.13	199.76	47.89	1.97	44.49	104.78	710.30
Degraded Pastures/Grazing Land	972.21	182.84	773.51	4453.24	1067.68	1312.24	4.77	8766.49
Degraded Land under Plantation Crops	48.28	11.73	61.74	43.58	0.00	5.07	10.87	181.27
Sands (Flood/Plain)	111.60	4.73	62.30	0.00	0.00	0.00	0.00	178.63
Sands (Levees)	10.92	0.00	0.00	0.00	0.00	0.00	0.00	10.92

Contd. ...

...Contd. ...

Category	*Jaipur Region*	*Bharatpur Region*	*Kota Region*	*Jodhpur Region*	*Ganganagar Region*	*Bhilwara Region*	*Udaipur Region*	*State Total*
Sands (Coastal sand)	0.00	0.00	0.00	0.00	0.00	0.00	0.00	0.00
Sands (Semi stab-stab > 40 m)	0.00	0.00	0.00	2593.82	79.06	0.00	0.00	2672.88
Sands (Semi stab-stab. moder. high 15-40 m)	10.78	0.00	0.00	13347.71	3022.21	0.00	0.00	16380.70
Sands (Semi stab to-stab low < 15 m)	161.79	12.88	1.35	5566.66	2776.41	9.97	0.00	8529.06
Sands (Closely spaced inter-dun area)	91.27	0.08	3.24	1545.70	105.74	0.00	0.00	1746.03
Mining Wasteland	27.63	7.51	36.81	64.20	31.28	61.03	5.31	233.77
Industrial Wasteland	6.82	364.54	12.95	14.37	0.00	0.00	0.00	398.68
Barren Rocky/Stone Waste/Sheet Rocky	566.42	1064.12	665.35	2281.10	4.61	445.68	12.7	5039.98
Steep Sloping Area	24.38	109.53	40.22	0.39	0.00	0.02	37.27	211.81
Snow Covered and/ or Glacial Area	0.00	0.00	0.00	0.00	0.00	0.00	0.00	0.00
Total Wasteland Area	6644.11	9294.70	9706.63	53725.36	9799.34	7178.76	5104.93	101453.83
Total Geographical Area (TGA)	36209.00	27007.00	31399.00	135519.00	64706.00	25980.00	21397.00	342217.00
% TGA	17.90	34.18	30.98	31.98	12.85	30.45	28.53	29.64

Source: Wastelands Atlas of India, NRSA, page 74.

Table 1.2

Region-wise Land Use Pattern in Rajasthan—1972-2001

(Percentages)

Region	Geographical According to Village Papers	Forest	Not Available for Cultivation	Other Uncultivated Excluding Fallow Land	Fallow Land	Net Area Sown
			(1971-1973)			
Jaipur Region	100.0	3.6	12.2	13.9	9.8	60.5
Bharatpur Region	100.0	8.8	20.0	10.2	2.8	58.2
Ganganagar Region	100.0	0.2	4.5	34.8	11.5	49.1
Jodhpur Region	100.0	1.1	20.7	22.2	16.4	39.6
Kota Region	100.0	10.7	18.2	17.5	5.3	48.3
Udaipur Region	100.0	15.8	33.4	20.0	6.3	24.5
Bhilwara Region	100.0	4.5	22.4	34.7	6.8	31.5
Rajasthan	**100.0**	**4.1**	**17.6**	**22.9**	**11.3**	**44.1**
			(1999-2001)			
Jaipur Region	100.0	7.0	10.8	11.0	12.3	59.0
Bharatpur Region	100.0	14.4	15.9	6.1	5.6	57.9
Ganganagar Region	100.0	2.5	7.5	14.7	16.4	59.0
Jodhpur Region	100.0	2.4	10.9	27.4	17.8	41.4
Kota Region	100.0	19.8	11.2	11.4	8.1	49.5
Udaipur Region	100.0	24.6	28.9	13.7	8.0	24.8
Bhilwara Region	100.0	11.3	19.3	28.0	8.6	32.8
Rajasthan	**100.0**	**7.6**	**12.5**	**19.2**	**13.8**	**46.8**

Source: Government of Rajasthan (1992). *Trends in Land Use Statistics*, Directorate of Agriculture (Statistical Wing) and Government of Rajasthan, *Statistical Abstract-2002*.

environmental issues, Supreme Court directives to check deforestation etc., and (iii) external and internal funding for afforestation and State's special efforts to improve conditions of forest lands. All these factors jointly contributed to this increase in area under forests. This positive change was observed in all the seven administrative regions in the state (Table 1.2).

Lands Not Available for Cultivation

These lands are of two types: (A) land put to non-agricultural use and (B) barren and uncultivated lands. The first category lands are used for building industry, road, school, urban housing, etc. Overall decline in the area under this category was observed. The area got

Table 1.3

Land Use Pattern and Percentage Share in Total Reported Area—(1971-2002)

Region/Items	*Area ('000 Hectare)*					*Percentage Share*				
	1971	*1980*	*1990*	*2000*	*2002*	*1971*	*1980*	*1990*	*2000*	*2002*
1. Geographical Area According to Village Papers	34109	34110	34252.9	34264.8	34266.4	100.0	100.0	100.0	100.0	100.0
2. Forest	1355	2089	2353.4	2606.1	2651.0	4.0	6.1	6.9	7.6	7.7
3. Not Available for Cultivation										
(A) Land put to non-agricultural use	1162	1507	1490.4	1739.6	1764.6	3.4	4.4	4.4	5.1	5.1
(B) Barren & uncultivated	4716	2917	2789.6	2566.1	2514.4	13.8	8.6	8.1	7.5	7.3
Total (A+B)	5878	4424	4280.0	4305.6	4279.0	17.2	13.0	12.5	12.6	12.5
4. Other Uncultivated Excluding Fallow Land										
(C) Permanent pasture & other grazing land	1807	1834	1912.2	1707.2	1703.3	5.3	5.4	5.6	5.0	5.0
(D) Land under misc. tree crops & groves not included in net area sown	9	24	22.4	13.6	12.4	0.0	0.1	0.1	0.0	0.0
(E) Culturable Waste	6112	6417	5566.4	4907.8	4866.4	17.9	18.8	16.3	14.3	14.2
Total (C+D+E)	7928	8275	7501.0	6628.6	6582.1	23.2	24.3	21.9	19.3	19.2

Contd. ...

...Contd. ...

Region/Items	*Area ('000 Hectare)*					*Percentage Share*				
	1971	*1980*	*1990*	*2000*	*2002*	*1971*	*1980*	*1990*	*2000*	*2002*
5. Fallow Land										
(F) Old fallow land	2326	2089	1927.3	2444.4	3259.1	6.8	6.1	5.6	7.1	9.5
(G) Current fallow land	1443	2085	1814.1	2415.1	6688.1	4.2	6.1	5.3	7.0	19.5
Total (F+G)	3769	4174	3741.5	4859.5	9947.2	11.0	12.2	10.9	14.2	29.0
6. Net Area Sown	15179	15148	16377	15864.9	10807.1	44.5	44.4	47.8	46.3	31.5
7. Total Cropped Area	16729	17350	19379.5	19230.2	13217.5	49.0	50.9	56.6	56.1	38.6
8. Area Sown More Than Once	1550	2202	3002.5	3365.3	2410.4	10.2	14.5	18.3	21.2	22.3

Source: Government of Rajasthan, *Statistical Abstract-2002*, Directorate of Economics and Statistics.

reduced from 5878 (17.2%) thousand hectares in 1971 to 4279 (12.5%) thousand hectares in 2002. But, between the two types of land under this category area under (A) increased from 1162 to 1765 thousand hectares while the area under (B) declined from 4716 (13.8%) to 2514 (7.3%) thousand hectares since 1971. It indicates that barren lands were put to other uses.

Other Uncultivated Excluding Fallow Land

This category comprises three types of land: (C) permanent pasture and other grazing land; (D) miscellaneous tree crops and groves; and (E) culturable waste. These lands play important role in the village ecosystem. They are the catchment areas of traditional water harnessing structures, source of fodder for animals, and fuel and livelihood source for human population, particularly economically poor households. Any major shift in use or decline in productivity of these lands result in adverse ecological and livelihood impact. These are also the source of biodiversity in the ecosystem.

Pasture and grazing lands and culturable wastelands declined from 1807 (5.3%) and 6112 (17.9%) thousand hectares in 1971 to 1703 (5%) and 4866 (14.2%) in 2001 respectively. The wasteland data reported in the Table 1.1 are sum total of the two land use categories, *viz.* land not available for cultivation and other uncultivated excluding fallow lands. Of the 28 categories the most prominent category is of sands, that account for 29 per cent of the total wastelands and these are mostly in the western Rajasthan, i.e. Jodhpur region and Sri Ganganagar region, and less than 1 per cent in Jaipur and Kota regions.

The ecologically sensitive category of wastelands are mining and industrial wastelands, degraded pasture and grazing lands, under utilised/degraded notified wasteland, waterlogged and marshy land, and land affected by salinity/alkalinity. All these categories combined account for 22.79 of the total identified wasteland. These problem areas are sensitive because of their economically active areas rather than historical natural wastelands, i.e. problem emerging because of mismanagement of land and/or water resources. Regional analysis shows that waterlogging problem is mostly in canal irrigated area of Ganganagar region while salinity/alkalinity problem is in all the regions. Mining and industrial wastelands are also in all the regions.

As per NRSA, 29.64 per cent of total geographical area in the state is classified as wasteland, based on remote sensing data. Bharatpur region has got the highest (34.18%) and the lowest is in Ganganagar region (12.85%). Increasing activity in and around Aravalli range, particularly unscientific mining and quarrying, is an issue of future concern. So far, the State is in favour of livelihood and employment rather than environment and sustainability, i.e., heavilly discounting the future gains.

Fallow Land

The fallow lands are also classified into two types: (F) old fallow land and (G) current fallow land. Cultivable land kept unused for more than five years is classified as old fallow land. In Rajasthan area under both the types of fallow land increased from 3769 (11%) thousand hectares in 1971 to 4859 (29%) thousand hectares in 2002. This trend is serious both from the agricultural production in the State and also for ecological concern. Increase in area under current fallow can be for following reasons, such as: (i) variation in rainfall, as agriculture in the state is most by rainfed and frequent droughts are very common (Rathore, 2001) consequently seasonal fallow and current fallow may vary significantly across years, for example, in the year 2002, which was a severe drought year, current fallow increased from 7.1 per cent to 19.5 per cent. But the long-term trend shows increase in area under this category is problematic; and (ii) increase in the number of marginal and small holdings, decline in productivity of land by over/under or inappropriate use of agricultural inputs, and misuse of water creating either water logging conditions or increase in salinity or alkalinity.

In the above context, it is necessary to examine changing size of holding in Rajasthan. Table 1.4 shows that average size of holding has declined from 5.46 hectares in 1970-71 to 3.96 hectares in 1995-96 (the last census data available). The area owned by marginal and small holdings increased from 14.6 to 23.5 lakh hectares. Arid and semi-arid area are known for their low productivity and dominance of rainfed agriculture, increase in number of small and marginal holding will push more area under current and old fallow categories. The other factor that will further worsen the situation is the high human population growth rate in Rajasthan that will force further

Table 1.4

Distribution of Land by Ownership and Size in Rajasthan

Items	*All Social Groups*					
	1970-71	*1976-77*	*1980-81*	*1985-86*	*1990-91*	*1995-96*
Size of Farms (No. in Lakhs)						
Marginal (Below 1 ha.)	9.4	13.2	13.17	13.58	15.17	16.11
Small (1 to 2 ha.)	6.91	7.99	8.78	9.2	10.19	10.85
Semi-medium (2 to 4 ha.)	7.72	8.67	9.17	9.79	10.61	11.17
Medium (4 to 10 ha.)	8.03	8.74	8.85	9.86	10.17	10.64
Large (10 ha. to above)	5.21	5.05	4.9	5	4.93	4.87
Total	**37.27**	**43.65**	**44.87**	**47.43**	**51.07**	**53.64**
Size of Farms (Area in Lakh Hectares)						
Marginal (Below 1 ha.)	4.59	5.84	6.33	6.41	7.25	7.8
Small (1 to 2 ha.)	10.04	11.48	12.7	13.26	14.69	15.66
Semi-medium (2 to 4 ha.)	22.35	24.83	26.21	27.91	30.21	21.85
Medium (4 to 10 ha.)	50.22	54.93	55.24	61.52	63.34	66.17
Large (10 ha. to above)	116.21	105.93	98.84	96.79	94.22	91.02
Total	**203.41**	**203.01**	**199.32**	**205.98**	**209.71**	**212.50**
Average Size of Holding (Hectares)						
Marginal (Below 1 ha.)	0.49	0.44	0.48	0.47	0.48	0.48
Small (1 to 2 ha.)	1.45	1.44	1.45	1.44	1.44	1.44
Semi-medium (2 to 4 ha.)	2.9	2.86	2.86	2.85	2.85	2.85
Medium (4 to 10 ha.)	6.25	6.28	6.24	6.24	6.23	6.22
Large (10 ha. to above)	22.31	20.98	20.17	19.36	19.11	18.69
Total	**5.46**	**4.65**	**4.44**	**4.34**	**4.11**	**3.96**

Source: Agriculture Census of Rajasthan 1995-96.

sub-division of holdings, to make landholdings non-viable and force to be kept fallow. Land reforms in the state need to be revisited in the context of changing livelihood pattern.

For similar reasons the area under old fallow lands is also increasing.

Net Area Sown (NAS)

The Green Revolution, mechanisation of agricultural operation and energised pumps for water lifting in the State has resulted in changes in land use pattern and intensity of use. All possible expansion on the area under cultivation has mostly been accomplished. Areas that are not strictly suitable for crop cultivation such as degraded forest land, grazing land and other wasteland are being brought under cultivation (may not be found on record). Cultivable lands are put to different kind of pressures. Productivity per unit of land has to be increased to meet the requirement of growing population hence resulted into input intensification. This change was facilitated by energisation of wells and tube wells, drilling technology facilitating deeper and faster digging and the government policy of input subsidy. Deepening of wells and digging of new wells and tube wells resulted into intensification of agriculture, extension of cultivation on marginal lands and fast depletion of groundwater. This was followed by heavy use of chemicals which led to both reversible and irreversible environmental damages to the cultivated land areas.

Despite the State being categorised as arid and semi-arid, as large part of it is covered under Thar Desert, the Net Area Sown (NAS) account for more than 44 per cent of total geographical area. NAS increased from 15179 (44.3%) thousand hectare in 1971 to 15864.9 (46.3%) thousand hectares in 2000. It declined in the year 2002 as it was a severe drought year. Canal and groundwater irrigated area increased and more areas were brought under plough. Mechanisation of agricultural operation particularly in western region facilitated utilisation of the limited moisture available during monsoon season. This enhanced the quantum of NAS in the State. Regional analysis shows that NAS is highest in Jaipur region followed by Bharatpur region and lowest in Udaipur region. The cropping intensity is an indicator of efficient use of agricultural lands (Table 1.5). The overall trend is that cropping intensity is increasing in the state.

Livestock occupies an important place particularly in the rural economy. In the traditionally evolved farming system livestock was important component contributing to agriculture (crop husbandry) as manure and draught power and to household milk, meat and fibre. In the post Green Revolution period with the introduction of mechanisation of agricultural operation and new crop technology based on inorganic inputs the symbiotic relationship between crops and livestock in the rural economy has undergone major change. Further, the White Revolution also affected the composition of livestock as state policies favoured milch (bovine) animals. The composition of livestock is also governed by the available land mass and land use pattern. The land use-livestock issues are not covered in the chapter for lack of space and also being covered by some other chapter in the volume.

Table 1.5

Region-wise Cropping Intensity in Rajasthan

Region	*Cropping Intensity*				
	1971	*1980*	*1990*	*2000*	*2002*
Jaipur	112.5	120.4	126.9	135.3	129.6
Bharatpur	124.4	125.5	134.8	142.8	137.9
Ganganagar	104.2	111.8	111.7	116.3	124.2
Jodhpur	102.9	104.3	106.2	110.0	113.1
Kota	110.6	115.8	125.2	136.7	121.9
Udaipur	134.9	162.2	143.8	114.8	117.0
Bhilwara	130.1	132.1	146.4	121.7	114.7
Rajasthan	**110.2**	**114.5**	**118.3**	**121.2**	**122.3**

Source: Government of Rajasthan (1999). *50 Years of Agricultural Development in Rajasthan*, Directorate of Agriculture, Jaipur and Government of Rajasthan, *Statistical Abstract 2002*.

Ecosystem Impact of Land Use

The total geographical area of the State is demarcated and is treated as fixed. For land use statistics purpose the reported area is generally less than the geographical area. The changes in land use and water use affects the ecosystem of an area in terms of change in vegetation, local weather effects, land quality, and livelihood of human and livestock. The ecosystem impact of land use can be studied by observing quantitative and qualitative changes in the land and its use pattern.

The total geographical area of the state as reported in village papers and the different categories on land can be represented as:

$$R = F_r + P + M + N + B + W + C + F_c + F_o$$

Where

R is total geographical area as reported in the village papers, i.e., Reported area,

F_r – Forest Area,

P – Permanent Pasture and Grazing Lands,

M – Miscellaneous Trees and Groves,

N – Non-agricultural Uses,

B – Barren and Uncultivated Lands,

W – Culturable Wastelands,

C – Net Area Sown,

F_c – Current Fallow Land, and

F_o – Old Fallow Land.

As the total land area of the state is fixed the land use changes can occur only through inter-class transfers, hence, the land use changes over time are linearly additive. The accounting identity for land use changes can be expressed as:

$$\Delta R = \Delta F_r + \Delta P + \Delta M + \Delta N + \Delta B + \Delta W + \Delta C + \Delta F_c + \Delta F_o$$

To study ecological impacts, these land use categories can be further grouped into three broad classes. First, land area under forest, permanent pastures and grazing lands, miscellaneous tree crops and groves, and barren and uncultivated lands. This category can be named as ecologically sensitive lands (E). Second, Land put to non-agricultural use (N) and can be termed as economic lands. Third, NAS, fallow lands (old and current fallow) and culturable wastelands, lands which can be used for agriculture and labelled as agricultural/livelihood lands (A). Change in these categories can be expressed as;

$$\Delta E = (\Delta F_r + \Delta P + \Delta M) + (\Delta B), \qquad \Delta N \text{ and}$$

$$\Delta A = \Delta C + \Delta F_c + \Delta F_o + \Delta W$$

The overall change $\Delta R = \Delta E + \Delta A + \Delta N$

The ecological impact of observed changes in each category, i.e., ΔE, ΔN, and ΔA can be positive as well as negative. This is also true for changes within the three above defined broad groups and between or amongst the groups. For example, positive or desirable ecological change will be, if in the first category the area under forest increases by shift from barren and uncultivated lands or grazing lands categories. But shift of forest lands to any other category in the group will have adverse ecological effects.

Similarly, net changes in the agricultural/livelihood groups can be either positive or negative. Shift in area from Culturable Wasteland category to NAS will be positive change, and reverse obviously shall be negative change. Increase in area under category Land put to non-agricultural use can also be negative if the area comes from agricultural land or forest lands for the purpose of urbanisation, mining and quarrying, etc. Mismanagement of new agricultural technology and water resources may lead to decline in net sown area, either becoming waterlogged, saline or alkaline lands and ultimately classified as fallow lands or culturable wastelands will be counted as negative impact.

From land use policy point of view it is important to identify these changes and explicitly lay down social preference function for the trade off between ecological balance and economic development in the state.

In order to estimate positive and negative impact of land use changes, data related to the period of 1970-71 to 2001-02 for Rajasthan was used to find out annual rates of change in various land use classes. Both linear and log-linear time trend equations were estimated for the State as a whole and for different agro-climatic and socioeconomic regions. The compound growth rates in different land use classes are estimated from the trend equations.

The region-wise compound growth rate for various land use classes in Rajasthan indicates that area under forest increased by 1.05 per cent and it was highest in Bhilwara region (3.1%) and lowest in Kota region (0.39%). Land put to non-agricultural use increased by 0.95 per cent with highest increase in Jaipur region (1.27%) and lowest in Bharatpur region (0.18%). It is mainly due to: firstly, increasing pressure of human population leading to urbanisation; and secondly, infrastructure development, such as roads, marketing facilities, industries, etc. The most noticeable negative growth in land use categories is barren and uncultivated lands and all the three categories under other uncultivated lands excluding fallow lands. This decline is registered in all the regions except Bhilwara. This is the cause of concern and will be discussed later. The other major notable fact is the declining growth in NAS in the State. It is declining by 1.42 per cent as a whole with highest declining growth rate in Kota region (-1.08%). Except Jaipur and Bhilwara regions, net sown area has shown declining growth rate over the 30 years. Even the total cropped area has registered negative growth rate but the area sown more than once is growing at the rate of 1.73 per cent per annum with high growth in Jodhpur and Sri Ganganagar region. This is in the regions where irrigated agriculture is being practiced and is compensating for the area loss in NAS.

The increase in fallow lands, in general and current fallow in particular, that too at fairly high rates is causing a serious concern from the view point of both agricultural growth and ecological balance in the state. It is mostly high in the Bharatpur, Kota and Sri Ganganagar regions.

The growth in forest area across the State might be due to demarcation of forest lands and afforestation programmes with the support of external funding agencies across the Aravalli Range and along the Indira Gandhi Nahar Project (IGNP) and other Canal systems.

The region-wise estimates of annual rate of change in the land use classes shows that in the last 30 years positive change in the area under forest is evident in Rajasthan and the trend is same in all the regions. The shift in land use is mostly from barren and uncultivated land and culturable waste categories of land. There is pressure on these lands for allotment for development activities such as, RICCO industrial areas, educational structure, land allotment to below poverty line households for housing and other purpose, roads etc. Region-wise analysis of change shows that barren and uncultivated land had negative change in all the regions except Bhilwara. While land put to non-agricultural use increased in all the regions except Udaipur. It is difficult to analyse contribution of the factors affecting shift in land use in the absence of disintegrated or more detailed data on land use in industries, roads, urbanisation, etc. For example it is difficult to find area covered by 183 urban town and cities in Rajasthan. Attempt is made to cull out data from Population Census Handbooks and reported in Table 1.3. It is interesting to note that against the general belief that urban areas are increasing fast the table shows decline in area in many districts. It may be because of problem in notification of area as urban or some other reason. But factually the population in the urban towns and cities has grown, particularly much faster in the last decade. This growth in urban areas is at the cost of prime agricultural lands, water bodies, forestlands, etc., which is directly affecting environment. Similar is the case of area under the other economic activities in the state.

The sectoral land use changes are reported in Table 1.6. The annual rate of change is used to examine the inter-sectoral as well as intra-sectoral dynamics of land use. It is observed that substantial land shifts have taken place from ecologically sensitive categories (ΔE), *viz.* barren and uncultivated land and culturable wastelands. The use category of these lands has changed to agricultural and non-agricultural sector. In agriculture sector there has been overall increase in the area at the State level. However, the regional analysis reveals that in Bhilwara (12.8) and Jodhpur region (24.6) there is a positive gain while in rest of the regions it is otherwise. In non-agriculture sector there is a positive shift in the area in all the regions except Udaipur where there is a negative change. This change is mainly confined to increase in area under urbanisation, industry, road and other infrastructure facilities, etc. There has been reorganisation of districts in the State. Increase or decrease in the geographical area affected the two regions namely Bhilwara and Udaipur. To address this issue, both these regions data set was merged and analysis on combined set of data was made. It shows that there is marginal positive shift in ΔE but negative shift in agriculture and non-agriculture sectors.

Table 1.6

Sectoral Land Use Changes in Rajasthan (1970-71–2001-02)

Region	*Annual Rate of Change ('000 hectares)*		
	Ecological Sector (ÄE)	*Agricultural Sector (ÄA)*	*Non-agriculture Sector (ÄN)*
Jaipur	0.1	0.0	2.2
Bharatpur	-1.8	-1.0	1.2
Kota	-0.5	-0.6	1.0
Udaipur	-8.5	-7.6	-2.1
Bhilwara	11.0	12.8	1.7
Udaipur-Bhilwara	0.3	2.2	-0.7
Jodhpur	-30.5	24.6	3.9
Sri Ganganagar	-4.3	-2.3	6.0
Rajasthan	**-24.8**	**10.9**	**14.3**

The phenomenon of declining area under agricultural sector, i.e., NSA and increase in fallow lands is threat to agriculture in the state. Decrease in NSA will affect agricultural production and food availability in the state. So far this decrease is compensated by increase in area sown more than once. It is mainly because of the irrigation facilities created in the state. However, the increase in fallow land indicates that either the size of holding are turning out to be uneconomical because of sub-division of lands or mismanagement of land has caused decline in productivity of existing lands. Consequently people are compelled to keep land as fallow. The culturable wastelands that are partly being brought under cultivation are also a cause of concern. It shows that in some areas people are encroaching wastelands for cultivation, which are of low productivity. It will ultimately reflect upon the overall production and productivity in the state. Culturable wastelands are also used for economic developmental activities without understanding their role in the ecosystem.

To conclude, the observed direction and magnitude of land use changes is not in the larger environmental health of the state. The high negative annual rate of change in ecological sector calls for review of sectoral policies from environmental point of view. Regional analysis also confirm that except for Bhilwara region all regions are experiencing negative environmental impact. In agriculture sector the positive annual rate of change at state level is mainly influenced by changes in the Jodhpur and Bhilwara region. Rest of the regions shows negative changes. Increase in agricultural land in the Jodhpur region is at the cost of environment as it has also got the highest negative change in ecological sector. Shift in area under non-agriculture sector is positive at state-level as well as in all the regions except Udaipur region. There is need to review economic policies to control negative environmental impact on account of high rate of change in favour of this sector. Regional analysis indicates Udaipur region as most sensitive to the emerging trends in land use changes as it has shown negative rate of change in all the three category of land.

Water Resources

Water resource development and management is the challenge before all nations and all regions in the world. The challenge is severe in case of Rajasthan as it has large area under arid and semi-arid conditions. Growth in human and livestock population along with economic development has increased the water demand many fold. The water availability and utilisation in Rajasthan is reported in Table 1.7. Total water resouruces i.e., surface, ground and interstate transfer account for 45.09 BCM. Against this availability the utilisation is 35.78 BCM, which is 81 per cent of the total available water. The share of surface and groundwater is 33.94 BCM and 11.15 BCM respectively. Of the total surface water 52.7 per cent is received from outside the state. The groundwater availability is 11.15 BCM, against that the utilisation is 11.83 (104%), i.e., over utilisation of groundwater in the state.

Table 1.7

Water Resource Availability and Utilisation in Rajasthan—2000

Source	*Availability (in BCM)*	*Utilisation (in BCM)*
Surface Water		
Internal	16.05	11.29
Inter-state	17.89	12.66
Total	33.94	23.95 (71%)
Groundwater	11.15	11.83 (104%)
Grand Total	**45.09**	**35.78 (81%)**

Source : *Report of the Expert Committee on Integrated Development and Management of Water Resource in Rajasthan*, June 2005, p.5.

The assessment of surface water resources is made by dividing the state into 13 River Basins and a Basin called 'Out of basin', which covers the entire area of Western Rajasthan. River Basin-wise total surface water available is reported in Table 1.8. It shows that there is 15.86 MAF runoff in the state of that 51.6 per cent is being harvested by existing and ongoing schemes. There is a proposal for harnessing 4.64 MAF and the remaining 3.02 MAF to be identified and utilised in future. Chambal and Mahi are the only two river basins where there is a potential for harnessing surface water.

The demand for water from different sectors for 2005, 2015 and 2045 was estimated and reported by the Vyas Committee (2005) as shown in Table 1.9. The gap between the supply and demand for water is likely to increase every year. Analysis of sector-wise demand shows that of the total demand, 89.5 per cent is from irrigation sector, 6.5 per cent domestic, 2.2 per cent livestock drinking water, and 1.8 per cent industry and other use. If the aggregate demand is analysed by source then of the total demand 52 per cent is met from surface sources and 48 per cent from groundwater. And, if analysed by sector than domestic water demand 80.7 per cent, livestock 88.9 per cent, irrigation 44.3 per cent, and industrial 57.1 per cent demand is met from groundwater.

To revalidate the irrigation demand using the land use statistics providing information on area irrigated by source (Table 1.10) shows that in 1960 the area irrigated by source was 58.5 per cent from tube wells and wells, 25.2 per cent from canals and 15.2 per cent from tanks. The composition changed in the year 2001 to 64.7 per cent from tube well and wells, 33.4 per cent from canals and only 1.2 per cent from tanks. If compared with estimated demand for the year 2005 given in Table 1.9 it shows a gap of 14.3 per cent excess groundwater demand for irrigation. This clearly indicates increasing dependence on groundwater for irrigation, and also domestic and industrial use. The regional analysis shows that in the year 2001 Jaipur, Bharatpur, Jodhpur and Bhilwara region area irrigated by tube wells and wells was 99 per cent, 94.2 per cent, 90.4 per cent and 88.6 per cent respectively. These changes are to be taken seriously as they are at the cost of environment in the state.

Development of groundwater has led to increased drought proofing of Rajasthan agricultural economy. It is a significant source of drinking water and irrigation. The changing status of groundwater in Rajasthan is reported in Table 1.11 under four categories namely, Safe (withdrawal is less than recharge), Semi-critical, Critical and Overexploited (dark) (withdrawal more than recharge). Rajasthan is divided into 237 groundwater blocks and water table is regularly monitored. The number of safe blocks was 162 (74.4%) in 1984 that declined to only 32 (13.6%) in 2004, while the blocks turned into dark zone increased from 22 (10.1%) to 140 (59.3%). If the number under critical zones is also added to dark zone, it comes out to be 80.5 per cent. This is a very serious problem. The regional analysis shows that except Kota and Udaipur regions all other regions have attained danger level, i.e., point of no return. The Jaipur and Bhilwara regions are in most critical stage as more than 84 per cent of

Table 1.8

Internal Surface Water: Basin-wise Runoff and Utilisation in Rajasthan (MAF)

River Basin	*Runoff*	*Runoff Harvested by Exisiting and Ongoing Schemes*	*Balance Runoff*	*Runoff to be Harnessed by Proposed Schemes*	*Total Runoff*	*Balance Available at Present for Utilisation in Future to be Identified*	*Existing Schemes (CCA in '000 ha.)*	*Ongoing Schemes*
Chambal	8052.79	1587.34	6465.46	4404.61	5991.94	2060.85	89.34	93.43
Banas	3451.92	3117.15	334.78	334.77	3451.92	0	517.93	134.77
Luni	789.84	658.72	131.12	71.93	730.66	59.19	151.11	13.48
Mahi	4530.07	3063.09	1466.98	112.15	3175.24	1354.83	71.14	205.94
Shekhawati	183.51	87.91	95.6	45.77	133.67	49.84	11.05	5.23
Sabarmati	512.62	183.09	329.53	260.26	443.35	69.27	11.25	9.11
Parbati	248.37	225.51	22.85	22.84	248.37	0	40.46	0.00
Sabi	213.87	121.8	92.07	74.96	196.77	17.1	14.87	5.99
Banganga	448.31	406.02	42.28	42.28	448.3	0	97.04	5.46
Ruparel	183.63	153.15	30.47	17.64	170.8	12.83	50.82	0.00
Gambhir	531.42	353.32	178.1	91.9	445.22	86.21	63.57	0.83
Western Banas	279.8	88.02	191.78	166.52	254.54	25.26	13.29	2.02
Sukhali	87.23	22.68	64.54	64	86.69	0.54	3.74	0.57
Other Nala	55.23	39.36	15.86	11.67	51.03	4.19	2.93	1.82
Total Rajasthan	19568.61	10107.18	9461.43	5721.32	15828.5	3740.11	1138.53	478.59
MAF	15.86	8.19	7.67	4.64	12.84	3.02		

Note: CCA: Culturable Command Area, MAF: Million Acre Feet.

Source: *Working Group on Irrigation for Ninth Five Year Plan*, Department of Irrigation, GoR, 1997.

groundwater blocks fall in dark zone. The Jhunjhunu and Jalore districts have attained worst level where 100 per cent blocks have turned into dark zone followed by Chittor and Alwar districts were it is above 92 per cent. State planners and politicians still hope that the water harnessing initiatives can rectify the situation. These hopes seem to be misplaced. Average rainfall in the state is low and varies between 100 mm in west to 700 mm in south and with high inter-annual variation. Also, because of continuous over exploitation of groundwater the water table has gone deep. Droughts are common hence given these conditions there are very little chances of natural recharge to fill the gap caused by over exploitation. The present initiatives will take very long time to revert the situation provided simultaneously other measures to check groundwater extraction are taken. The only option left is regulating groundwater demand and that too agricultural demand on priority basis.

Table 1.9

Demand and Supply of Water and Water Balance in Rajasthan

(in BCM)

Purpose	*2005*			*2015*			*2045*		
	SW	*GW*	*Total*	*SW*	*GW*	*Total*	*SW*	*GW*	*Total*
Demand									
Domestic	0.5	2.1	2.6	1.0	2.2	3.2	2.5	2.2	4.7
Livestock	0.1	0.8	0.9	0.3	0.8	1.1	0.5	0.8	1.3
Irrigation	20.0	15.9	35.9	26.0	14.0	40.0	36.0	13.1	49.1
Others	0.3	0.4	0.7	0.4	0.4	0.8	1.0	1.0	2.0
Total	**20.9**	**19.2**	**40.1**	**27.7**	**17.4**	**45.1**	**40.0**	**17.1**	**57.1**
Availability									
Intrastate	5.8	7.5		8.0	7.5		16.9	7.5	
Interstate	12.2	-		13.0	-		15.0	-	
			25.5			**28.5**			**39.4**
Recycled water									
Domestic	0.8	-		1.1	-		1.1	-	
Irrigation	-	6.0		-	6.5		-	7.2	
			6.8			**7.6**			**8.3**
Total Supply	**18.8**	**13.6**	**32.4**	**22.1**	**14.0**	**36.1**	**33.0**	**14.7**	**47.7**
Shortage			**7.7**			**9.0**			**9.4**

Source: *Report of Expert Committee on Integrated Development and Management of Water Resource,* June 2005, p.6.

Note: SW-Surface Water, GW-Goundwater.

Table 1.10

Region-wise and Source-wise Area under Irrigation–1961-2001

(Percentages)

Years/Source	Region							
	Jaipur	Bharatpur	Ganganagar	Jodhpur	Kota	Udaipur	Bhilwara	Rajasthan
1960								
Canals	0.0	0.0	99.9	0.0	0.0	0.0	0.0	25.2
Tanks	15.3	34.6	0.0	14.5	25.7	18.8	19.2	15.2
Tube Well & Wells	84.6	63.3	0.0	84.4	73.1	78.4	80.7	58.8
Other Sources	0.1	2.1	0.1	1.1	1.2	2.8	0.1	0.8
Total	100.0	100.0	100.0	100.0	100.0	100.0	100.0	100.0
1970								
Canals	0.0	18.6	99.4	0.1	47.9	0.0	0.0	37.0
Tanks	8.8	14.6	0.0	0.6	12.4	22.9	20.2	11.7
Tube Well & Wells	91.0	64.1	0.2	98.8	38.8	75.0	79.4	50.6
Other Sources	0.1	2.8	0.4	0.4	0.9	2.1	0.4	5.9
Total	100.0	100.0	100.0	100.0	100.0	100.0	100.0	100.0
1980								
Canals	3.2	7.2	99.6	0.8	56.2	0.0	0.4	33.6
Tanks	3.3	0.8	0.0	2.9	4.9	18.6	14.4	4.0
Tube Well & Wells	93.2	83.6	0.2	96.2	37.9	77.8	84.9	60.8
Other Sources	0.2	8.3	0.2	0.1	1.0	3.5	0.3	1.6
Total	100.0	100.0	100.0	100.0	100.0	100.0	100.0	100.0

Contd. ...

...contd. ...

Years/Source	*Region*							
	Jaipur	*Bharatpur*	*Ganganagar*	*Jodhpur*	*Kota*	*Udaipur*	*Bhilwara*	*Rajasthan*
1990								
Canals	0.7	8.1	99.2	2.6	51.4	26.7	3.4	38.0
Tanks	2.0	0.4	0.0	7.8	2.4	19.4	17.0	4.3
Tube Well & Wells	97.3	91.2	0.8	89.5	44.5	50.3	79.0	57.1
Other Sources	0.0	0.4	0.0	0.1	1.7	3.6	0.7	0.6
Total	100.0	100.0	100.0	100.0	100.0	100.0	100.0	100.0
2001								
Canals	0.6	5.2	93.5	8.2	38.4	42.1	3.7	33.4
Tanks	0.4	0.4	0.0	1.3	1.2	12.7	6.0	1.2
Tube Well & Wells	99.0	94.2	6.5	90.4	57.8	37.1	88.6	64.7
Other Sources	0.1	0.1	0.0	0.0	2.6	8.0	1.7	0.7
Total	100.0	100.0	100.0	100.0	100.0	100.0	100.0	100.0

Source: Trends in Land Use Statistics, Directorate of Agriculture (Statistical Wing), Jaipur, Rajasthan.

Table 1.11

Region-wise and District-wise Status of Groundwater in Rajasthan—1984 and 2004

(Percentages)

Region/District	Status of Groundwater (Category of Block)									
	1984					2004				
	S	SC	C	OE	Total No. of Blocks	S	SC	C	OE	Total No. of Blocks
Ajmer	62.5	0.0	12.5	25.0	8 (100)	0.0	0.0	25.0	75.0	8 (100)
Jaipur	46.2	23.1	7.7	23.1	13(100)	0.0	0.0	15.4	84.6	13 (100)
Sikar	87.5	0.0	0.0	12.5	8 (100)	12.5	0.0	0.0	87.5	8 (100)
Jhunjhunu	75.0	12.5	0.0	12.5	8 (100)	12.5	0.0	0.0	87.5	8 (100)
Dousa						0.0	0.0	0.0	100.0	5 (100)
Jaipur Region	64.9	10.8	5.4	18.9	37 (100)	4.8	-	9.5	85.7	42 (100)
Alwar	42.9	21.4	14.3	21.4	14 (100)			7.1	92.9	14 (100)
Bharatpur	77.8	11.1	11.1	0.0	9 (100)	55.6	11.1	0.0	33.3	9 (100)
Dholpur	100.0	0.0	0.0	0.0	4 (100)	25.0	0.0	25.0	50.0	4 (100)
S. Madhopur	80.0	20.0	0.0	0.0	5 (100)	0.0	0.0	60.0	40.0	5 (100)
Karauli						0.0	20.0	20.0	60.0	5 (100)

Contd. ...

...Contd. ...

Region/District	*Status of Groundwater (Category of Block)*									
	1984					*2004*				
	S	*SC*	*C*	*OE*	*Total No. of Blocks*	*S*	*SC*	*C*	*OE*	*Total No. of Blocks*
Bharatpur Region	65.6	15.6	9.4	9.4	32 (100)	16.2	5.4	16.2	62.2	37 (100)
Bikaner	100.0	0.0	0.0	0.0	5 (100)	40.0	0.0	20.0	40.0	5 (100)
Churu	100.0	0.0	0.0	0.0	6 (100)	60.0	0.0	20.0	20.0	5 (100)
S. Ganganagar	85.7	14.3	0.0	0.0	7 (100)	100.0	0.0	0.0	0.0	7 (100)
Hanumangarh						100.0	0.0	0.0	0.0	3 (100)
Ganganagar Region	94.4	5.6	0.0	0.0	18 (100)	75.0	0.0	10.0	15.0	20 100)
Jodhpur	66.7	33.3	0.0	0.0	9 (100)	11.1	11.1	22.2	55.6	9 (100)
Jaisalmer	100.0	0.0	0.0	0.0	3 (100)	33.3	0.0	0.0	66.7	3 (100)
Jalore	71.4	0.0	0.0	28.6	7 (100)	0.0	0.0	0.0	100.0	7 (100)
Barmer	62.5	25.0	0.0	12.5	8 (100)	12.5	0.0	25.0	62.5	8 (100)
Nagaur	90.9	9.1	0.0	0.0	11 (100)	9.1	9.1	18.2	63.6	11 (100)
Pali	80.0	10.0	0.0	10.0	10 (100)	0.0	0.0	50.0	50.0	10 (100)
Sirohi	100.0	0.0	0.0	0.0	5 (100)	0.0	0.0	60.0	40.0	5 (100)
Jodhpur Region	79.2	13.2		11.3	53 (100)	7.5	3.8	26.4	62.3	53 (100)
Kota	100.0	0.0	0.0	0.0	5 (100)	0.0	0.0	20.0	80.0	5 (100)
Baran	100.0	0.0	0.0	0.0	7 (100)	42.9	14.3	14.3	28.6	7 (100)
Bundi	100.0	0.0	0.0	0.0	4 (100)	0.0	0.0	50.0	50.0	4 (100)

Contd. ...

...Contd. ...

Region/District	*Status of Groundwater (Category of Block)*									
	1984					*2004*				
	S	*SC*	*C*	*OE*	*Total No. of Blocks*	*S*	*SC*	*C*	*OE*	*Total No. of Blocks*
Jhalawar	100.0	20.0	0.0	0.0	5 (100)	0.0	0.0	66.7	33.3	6 (100)
Tonk	100.0	0.0	0.0	0.0	6 (100)	0.0	0.0	83.3	16.7	6 (100)
Kota Region	96.4	3.6			28 (100)	10.7	3.6	46.4	39.3	28 (100)
Banswara	100.0	0.0	0.0	0.0	8 (100)	12.5	75.0	12.5	0.0	8 (100)
Dungarpur	100.0	0.0	0.0	0.0	5 (100)	20.0	40.0	40.0	0.0	5 (100)
Udaipur	27.3	0.0	9.1	63.6	11 (100)	0.0	0.0	27.3	72.7	11 (100)
Rajsamand						0.0	0.0	28.6	71.4	7 (100)
Udaipur Region	66.7		4.2	29.2	24 (100)	6.5	25.8	25.8	41.9	31 (100)
Bhilwara	45.5	54.5	0.0	0.0	11 (100)	0.0	0.0	27.3	72.7	11 (100)
Chittor	71.4	21.4	0.0	7.1	14 (100)	0.0	7.1	0.0	92.9	14 (100)
Bhilwara Region	60.0	36.0	0.0	4.0	25 (100)	0.0	4.0	12.0	84.0	25 (100)
Rajasthan	**74.7**	**12.4**	**2.8**	**10.1**	**217 (100)**	**13.6**	**5.9**	**21.2**	**59.3**	**236 (100)**

Note : S = Safe; SC = Semi-critical; C = Critical; OE = Overexploitation (dark).

Source : *Report of the Group on the Estimation of Groundwater Resource and Irrigation Potential from Groundwater in Rajasthan*, July 1986, Table 7(a); *Report on Dynamic Groundwater Resources of Rajasthan*, March 2004, p. 23.

The Challenge of Management

Access to water can be a major engine for poverty alleviation and economic development in rural areas. There is a large social value in increasing rural agricultural incomes and slowing migration of the poor to urban areas. The basic challenges before the managers of water resources in the state are:

(i) Maintaining balance between surface and groundwater use. Presently the balance between the two is disturbed as there is over exploitation of groundwater resources. Surface water availability and storage facilities are unevenly distributed and are highly dependent on annual rainfall. Being a arid and semi-arid state there is high degree of variability in inter-temporal and spatial occurrence of rainfall. Meeting drinking water needs of areas sparsely populated and scattered settlements in desert and hilly areas poses further challenge before the managers/planners. The other important feature of surface water supply is that 52 per cent of it is received from out of state. Given the political economy of water and status of inter-state water disputes in the country ensuring sustainable supply of committed quantities is also a challenging task.

(ii) The other issue is inter-sectoral allocation of water. Developing rational basis for prioritising allocation of water among different usage is a major issue. Meeting drinking water demand of rural and urban population is always a top priority in the state, which is well justified. Despite drinking water demand accounts for only 8 to 9 per cent of total demand, there is always a shortage of supply in urban and rural areas. Quality of water supplied is an added issue. Presently there is need for economic or scientific basis for allocation and sustainable supply of water among different uses, i.e., domestic, agricultural, industry, etc.

(iii) Competition between agricultural and domestic water users is increasing. With economic development industrial and other sector demand for water is also increasing. Urbanisation has increased domestic water demand many folds. The nature of urban water demand is different than rural demand as these areas require too large quantity (bulk supply) in concentrated area with lot of distribution losses and have almost no local sources. Hence, meeting urban water demand by transfer/ diversion of water from rural areas at the cost of agricultural/livelihood becomes source of conflict. How to establish balance between sectoral and/or rural-urban demand with least conflict is a challenge.

(iv) Efficient and effective control and management of surface and groundwater pollution is a yet another challenge. Pollution poses a serious threat to all groundwater aquifers in Rajasthan that is virtually irreversible. Also, the industrial and municipal effluents have caused major pollution problems in many towns/cities and streams. Non-point source pollution from agricultural fertilisers and pesticides, however, may be even greater issue (particularly in sandy soils) but for authentic information and continuous monitoring the increase in intensity of non-point source pollution is not known. The problem is believed to be increased and widespread.

Reallocation of water among different usage based on economic and social consideration has to be worked out on long-term basis for sustainable development of different sectors in the state. While doing so, priority has to be given to environmentally sustainable management rather than economic development alone.

Environmental Issues

Given the statue of surface and groundwater in the state, particularly over exploitation of groundwater, it is essential to look into the environmental impacts of groundwater extraction. Groundwater and surface water are integral parts of the same hydrologic system. The need for maintaining in-stream flows is a critical though often unrecognised component of groundwater management. Depleting water tables due to groundwater extraction often have major implications for the base flows of streams. Unless base flows are maintained, downstream users can lose access to water at critical times and pollution of both ground and surface water is likely to increase. Both problems of stream flow and groundwater pollution is today being observed in Rajasthan. Unless groundwater situation is improved the state is going to face serious environmental crisis, as it will directly affect health of human population and growth of surface vegetation communities.

Water resource development and management policies/ approaches must respond to the environmental implications of surface and groundwater development. It is because the water development has implication for the environment beyond those directly associated with agriculture or domestic uses (both in urban and rural areas). Surface water mismanagement leads to water logging, salinity and alkalinity problems mostly in the surface irrigation command areas. While overexploitation of groundwater leads to major environmental impacts on flows in surface streams, which in turn affect the quality of the aquifer and the ecology in the contiguous areas of the streams. The other environmental impact of groundwater overexploitation is on the groundwater quality, as they are strongly related. This correlation is even more striking when one compares blocks classified as 'critical' and 'over exploited (dark)' with those where quality is poor. The quality problem is widespread across Rajasthan and is discussed below.

The district and region-wise villages and habitations suffering from chemical problem in drinking water in the state is reported in Table 1.12 In the year 2001, 61.3 per cent of villages and habitation were found affected by chemical in drinking water. The percentage was higher in habitations (68.6) compared to main village settlements (53.3), as main villages are covered by multiple or alternative sources. The situation if compared with 1996 shows that the water quality deteriorated over time, as in 1996 only 25.10 per cent villages and habitations were affected and it increased to 61.3 per cent in 2001. The regional analysis shows that problem was more serious in Sri Ganganagar region followed by Jodhpur and Jaipur regions, as the affected village and habitation were 90.1, 84.9 and 71 per cent respectively. Fluoride is found to be the major problem and it is directly related to depleting groundwater table in the state. The fluoride affected villages and habitation in 1996 were 25 per cent and 15 per cent respectively, and if both combined 19.9 per cent, the number affected increased in 2001 to 32, 22.4 and 27.5 per cent respectively. The regional analysis shows that it is highest in Jodhpur

Table 1.12

District-wise and Region-wise Number of Villages and Habitation Suffering from Chemical Problem in Drinking Water in Rajasthan, 1996-2001

District/Region	Total Village	No. of HAB	Total	Percentages of Chemically Affected Villages					
				1996			2001		
				Total Village	No. of HAB	Total	Total Village	No. of HAB	Total
Ajmer	985	952	1937	46.9	39.7	43.4	71.9	98.0	85.8
Jaipur/Dausa	3140	7618	10758	25.7	49.2	42.4	56.3	70.9	67.3
Sikar	931	2401	3332	23.1	50.7	43.0	30.4	78.7	66.9
Jhunjhunu	824	208	1032	9.0	68.3	20.9	64.4	62.4	63.9
Jaipur Region	5880	11179	17059	26.2	52.0	37.4	55.8	77.5	71.0
Alwar	1946	2449	4395	16.1	32.5	25.3	54.2	63.4	59.8
Bharatpur	1345	549	1894	42.5	24.8	37.3	53.2	85.7	66.1
Dholpur	551	983	1534	10.2	31.7	24.0	47.7	39.5	42.0
Sawai Madhopur/ Karauli	1464	2191	3655	19.3	29.7	25.5	35.0	70.8	57.9
Bharatpur Region	5306	6172	11478	22.0	29.7	28.0	47.5	64.8	56.5
Bikaner	580	366	946	8.6	24.6	14.8	73.6	100.0	84.5
Churu	926	199	1125	36.2	77.4	43.5	96.9	100.0	97.6
Ganganagar/ Hanumangarh	4437	4190	8627	21.7	38.6	29.9	75.8	100.0	88.3

Contd. ...

...Contd. ...

District/Region	*Total Village*	*No. of HAB*	*Total*	*Percentages of Chemically Affected Villages*					
				1996			*2001*		
				Total Village	*No. of HAB*	*Total*	*Total Village*	*No. of HAB*	*Total*
Ganganagar Region	5943	4755	10698	22.2	46.9	29.4	82.1	100.0	90.1
Jodhpur	860	2801	3661	19.9	54.5	46.4	60.6	89.8	84.9
Jaisalmer	518	1172	1690	37.1	71.2	60.7	88.8	97.0	95.1
Jalore	666	823	1489	32.9	68.5	52.6	67.7	88.6	80.3
Barmer	1623	2780	4403	66.9	99.6	87.5	94.5	98.8	97.6
Nagaur	1374	1972	3346	42.5	58.5	51.9	82.7	89.5	87.0
Pali	904	651	1555	13.7	45.5	27.0	66.2	80.8	73.3
Sirohi	446	92	538	13.9	23.9	15.6	63.7	94.1	76.0
Jodhpur Region	6391	10291	16682	32.4	60.2	48.8	74.9	91.2	84.9
Kota/Baran	1881	288	2169	4.5	15.3	5.9	65.0	69.4	65.7
Bundi	826	332	1158	6.8	20.8	10.8	27.2	6.7	20.5
Jhalawar	1448	124	1572	3.7	5.6	3.9	21.2	51.0	24.0
Tonk	1019	881	1900	10.2	26.7	17.8	82.6	85.8	84.3
Kota Region	5174	1625	6799	6.3	17.1	9.6	49.0	53.2	48.6
Banswara	1431	3175	4606	0.4	4.1	2.9	37.5	44.9	42.6
Dungarpur	846	681	1527	4.8	18.2	10.8	5.3	59.3	30.2

Contd. ...

...Contd. ...

District/Region	*Total Village*	*No. of HAB*	*Total*	*Percentages of Chemically Affected Villages*					
				1996			*2001*		
				Total Village	*No. of HAB*	*Total*	*Total Village*	*No. of HAB*	*Total*
Udaipur/ Rajasamand	3179	5561	8740	4.7	27.8	19.4	49.2	54.8	52.8
Udaipur Region	5456	9417	14873	3.3	16.7	11.0	30.6	53.0	41.9
Bhilwara	1565	968	2533	9.8	26.1	16.0	43.6	46.3	44.8
Chittorgarh	2173	904	3077	2.0	16.0	6.1	22.9	34.6	27.1
Bhilwara Region	3738	1872	5610	5.9	21.1	11.1	33.3	40.5	36.0
Rajasthan	**37888**	**45311**	**83199**	**16.9**	**34.8**	**25.1**	**53.3**	**68.6**	**61.3**

Note: HAB: Habitation.

Source: Rathore, M.S. (1997). "Strategies for Managing Drinking Water Crises in Rajasthan", *Working Paper*, IDS Jaipur, August. Reference-Source: *Groundwater Quality Status of Rajasthan 2001*, Public Health Engineering Department, GoR, Jaipur.

region followed by Jaipur and Sri Ganganagar region. In Jodhpur region, the districts Nagaur and Barmer are worst affected, as 75.2 and 66.6 per cent villages are affected respectively. In Jaipur region district Ajmer and in Sri Ganganagar region district Churu are worst affected.

Nitrate affected villages and habitations are also high in fluoride affected regions. The number has increased since 1991. The total dissolved substances (TDS) in groundwater is also increasing and the major affected regions are Jodhpur, Ganganagar, Bharatpur and Jaipur.

A study by HEDCON (Malik, *et al.*, 2002) on water quality in IGNP area shows that 60 per cent of the disease and routine human ailments is caused by water quality. It is affecting human health and also source of high annual household expenditure on healthcare. The deteriorating groundwater quality in the state is a serious problem to be attended on top priority.

Rajasthan is home to some of the prime mineral resources of the country and ranked first in minerals namely, marble (Block), chips and powder, serpentine, and sand stone. Important minerals found within the state are lead, zinc and copper (non-ferrous metals), tungsten (ferrous mineral) and a number of other industrial minerals. Rajasthan is also the sole producer of jasper and wollastonite and a leading producer of cement and steel grade lime stone, soapstone, ball clay, calcite, feldspar, natural gypsum, kaolin, rock phosphate, ochre and building stones. On one hand the mineral availability reflects a sign of prosperity, on other hand it is also a major source of environmental disaster within the state. A very large area of the state is under mining and quarrying and related activities. There are 12175 number of legal licences and leases of major and minor mineral extraction covering 238.4 thousand hectares of area in the state. The number of illegal extraction may be much for more than this. The direct impact of such excessive extraction can be seen on the natural resource base of the state, which is being degraded in an exponential manner.

The mineral industries often have to go deep into the ground to extract minerals and during the process pump out large quantities of groundwater. While such a process has a profound negative impact on the groundwater table, it also results in a large amount of precious groundwater being wasted. In addition, large amounts of water are needed for the processing of the minerals extracted, for example, one tonne marble require 120 litres, one tonne zinc ore extraction require 1.7 cum and then one tonne concentrate require 13.6 cum of water. The processing units are generally located far from the mining sites, and water for processing these minerals is being purchased by the industries at a high cost. The waste generated from the processing of minerals is not disposed appropriately. For example, numerous marble and soapstone slurry dumps are visible in different parts of the state, which not only degrade the soil but also block natural drains and interfere in the groundwater infiltration process. Thus, while calculating the industrial requirement of water for the state, the portion of groundwater that has been drawn as part of mineral extraction and wasted is not considered. Vyas Committee report provides estimates of industrial demand (including other demand) as 1.8 per cent, which appears to be much lower than reality in Rajasthan's case, especially when the indirect impact of mining of groundwater and the effects of industrial activity on groundwater recharge is also taken into account. Other than mining, the cloth dyeing industries located in Sanganer (Jaipur), Bhilwara, and Pali are polluting the underground aquifers over many kilometres. Although the groundwater has been rendered unfit even for irrigation, it is still being used in crop cultivation impacting human health. Presently the seriousness of the problem is not recognised, as there is no evidence of commitment of the concerned departments to address these problems in a time bound manner.

Conclusions and Suggestions

The gaps in land use database and its limitations are discussed at length in Iyengar (2003) that is also true for Rajasthan. The existing system of land use classification as created by British Administration for their purpose need to be changed in the today's development planning context particularly to study the environmental impact of land use. First and foremost action required is to change the name of the government department looking after land issues from Revenue Department to Land Resource Management Department, as was done in the case of water sector by creating Water Resource Department in the state. The existing nine-fold classification need to be changed by adding few more categories namely, mining and quarry lands, urban lands, industrial lands, water bodies, etc., for better land use planning and understanding the environmental impact. This will help reduce litigations particularly based on environmental issues, delaying many development projects and wasting time and energy of large number of people in the country/ state. Presently, lots of efforts are being made to change the nomenclature of land by all means to get land allotted for various purposes without worrying about the environmental consequences. The state has gone to the extent to appoint a committee to redefine Aravali Hills to allot land for marble mining, such moves be checked in the larger interest of the state and people.

Encroachment and allotment of common lands is statewide problem, particularly grazing lands and catchment areas of water bodies. Even today these lands provide livelihood to the poorest of the poor and are also environmentally most sensitive areas. The state land use policy needs review, particularly the long term lease/ allotment of land in the name of social forestry or production of bio-fuel, etc., and laws to check encroachment of public land in urban and rural areas. Encroachment of lands that are catchment area of water bodies has to be checked on priority basis.

Western Rajasthan covering more than 50 per cent of geographical area needs special attention in terms of land use planning. Unless this part is developed, the state will never be at the top 10 developed states in the country. Reclamation of the desert through development of pasture lands (enclosures and controlled grazing), planting wind breaks and shelter belts would make the lands suitable for vastly expended programmes of scientific animal husbandry and dairying and make the marginal agriculture that is practiced and expending in such areas today, much less attractive. A deliberate policy of diverting land from agriculture to forestry and animal husbandry therefore needs to be followed for sustainable development in the western Rajasthan.

Extension and intensification of agriculture on the marginal lands because of fast growing population and increasing rural unemployment has generated substantial demand for groundwater in the state. Besides initiating new agricultural policy addressing efficiency in crop water use the need is for creating more jobs in non-farm sector, i.e., diversification of occupation. Alternative livelihood options should be created to reduce water demand in agriculture, presently consuming 85 to 90 per cent of total water demand. This will also help attaining drinking water security in the state.

The phenomenon of declining area under agricultural sector, i.e., net sown area and increase in fallow lands will have long term impact on the agricultural production in the state. Review of state land tenancy policy, land consolidation policy should be undertaken to check increase in area under current fallow and old fallow category. Appropriate measures be taken to check further sub division of land in the state.

The increase in area under forest is a welcome sign. This trend has to be maintained with special emphasis on quality of forestlands.

The state water policy, land use policy, agricultural policy, industrial policy, urban area development policy should strongly address the surface and groundwater pollution by urban sewerage, industrial waste, effluent and solid waste disposal in water bodies, high or improper use of fertilisers and pesticides in agriculture, etc. and should have time bound commitment to deal with each environmental issue.

Over the past three decades, state policies that subsidise credit and rural energy, electrification of wells and tube wells have encouraged rapid development (extraction) of groundwater resources. These polices needs review in the light of the above discussed environmental consequences of over exploitation of groundwater in the state.

The state's development objective of, 'universal access to safe drinking water covering all villages and habitations' can be met only if the status of groundwater is improved. The state's initiative has to go beyond water literacy movement and take serious steps to check groundwater demand and initiate community based groundwater recharge movement using existing traditional wisdom, research and technical knowledge.

The districts and regions suffering from chemical problem in drinking water in the state need immediate measures, such as, (i) search for alternative source, (ii) change from groundwater to surface water by reviving traditional drinking water systems, particularly in western areas, (iii) state investment and initiative in development of economically viable defluoridation and desalination techniques, (iv) provide medical and livelihood support to affected population, etc.

Ground and surface water pollution by industry or any economic enterprise should be treated as criminal act and strong laws for punishment should be made and suitable institutions be created to execute them. Zero discharge principal should be made compulsory for all the industries. The specific measures to control water pollution in urban areas can be; reducing polluting load; introduction of sanitary waste disposal facilities based on environmentally sound, low-cost, and upgradeable technologies.

References

Basavaraja, H. and S.D. Dbali (1999). "Land Use Dynamics in India: An Agricultural Perspective", *Agricultural Situation in India*, Vol. 56, No. 4, p.199.

Borthakur, N. and K.C. Heromba (1999). "An Intra-Regional Analysis of Changes and Trends in Agricultural Productivity in Assam", *Agricultural Situation in India*, November, p.519.

Chadha, G.K., S. Sen and H.R. Sharma (2004). "Land Resources", in *State of the Indian Farmer—A Millennium Study*, Vol. 2, Department of Agriculture and Cooperation, Ministry of Agriculture, GoI, New Delhi, published by Academic Foundation, New Delhi.

Dinkar, V.S. (1990). "Integration of Land and Water Use Efforts to Realise Optimum Benefits from Irrigation", *Agricultural Situation in India*, Vol. 45, No. 8, November, p.53.

Goswami, S.N. and O. Challa (2004). "Indian Land Use Scenario: An Overview", *Agricultural Situation in India*, Vol. 60, No. 12, March, p.783.

Hooja, B. (1982), "Land Use Pattern in Rajasthan: A Plea to Change the Priorities" *Prashasnika*, Vol. 9, No.1-2, Jan-June, pp.79-90.

———. (1983). "Some Challenges and Strategies of Agricultural Development and Land Water Management for Rajasthan in the 1980s" *Prashasnika*, Vol. 12, No.1-2, Jan-June, pp.95-129.

Hooja, R. and B. Hooja (1982). " Land-Water Management and Productivity", *Indian Journal of Public Administration*, Vol.28. No.3, pp.633-50.

Iyengar, S. (1989). "Common Property Land Resources in Gujarat: Some Findings About their Size, Status and Use", *Economic and Political Weekly*, Vol. 24, No. 25, p.A-67.

———. (2003). "Environmental Damage to Land Resource–Need to Improve Land Use Data Base", *Economic and Political Weekly*, Vol. 38, No. 34, August 23, p.3586.

Joseph, K.V. (2002). "Migration and the Changing Pattern of Land Use in Malabar", *Journal of Indian School of Political Economy*, Vol. 14, No. 1, January-March, p.63.

Malik, D., M.S. Rathore and M. Bagoria (2002). "Water and Health-Study of IGNP", Health Environment and Development Consortium (HEDCON), Jaipur (mimeograph).

Pandey, V.K. and S.K. Tewari (1987). "Some Ecological Implication of Land Use Dynamics in Uttar Pradesh", *Indian Journal of Agricultural Economics*, Vol.42, No.3, July-Sept., pp.388-94.

Puri, K.S. (1987). "Problems and Prospects of Land Use and Soil Conservation in India: An Overview", *Agricultural Situation in India*, Vol. 42, No. 4, p.267.

Rao, G.N. and D. Rajasekhar (1994). "Land Use Pattern and Agrarian Expansion in a Semi-Arid Region: Case of Rayalaseema in Andhra, 1886-1939", *Economic and Political Weekly*, June 25.

Rathore, M.S. (2001). "Droughts and State Failure: Unwilling to Learn and Unwilling to Distribute", IDS, Jaipur.

Swaminathan, M. (1993). "Changes in Land Distribution in an Agrarian Economy: Measurement of Household Mobility", *Economic and Political Weekly*, Vol. 28, No. 21, p.1067.

Vohra, B.B. (1982). *Land and Water Management Problems in India*, Training Division, Department of Personnel and Administrative Reforms, Ministry of Home Affairs, New Delhi, Jan.

World Bank (1998). "India–Water Resources Management Sector Review", *Groundwater Management Report*, March 27.

2

Land Use and Land Degradation in Rajasthan

K.N. JOSHI

Introduction

The pressure on the land is increasing every year due to rapid increase in human and animal population and economic developmental activities. Thus, increasing demand for land for various purposes force conversion of productive agricultural lands into non-agricultural uses. The constraint on the land is more in the rural areas on account of greater land based activities and demand for fuel, fodder and small timber. As a result, large tracts of agricultural land, particularly around urban areas and forests in the rural areas, are being or have been destroyed. Secondly, introduction of irrigation facility in the desert without considering suitability of topography, geology and appropriate land use planning, has increased the agricultural area but bringing about unforeseen ecological crisis at the same time. It has been, of late, recognised that the increasing efforts to raise agricultural growth particularly in the Indira Gandhi canal region have cost us dearly in the form of land and water degradation. Large scale ecological losses were reported in crop land, grass land, such as soil erosion, soil alkalinity and salinity, water logging and fast depletion of groundwater. These factors limit future gains from the land and water resources. In the lack of suitable land use policy in the state, improper utilisation of water and poor maintenance and management of canal irrigation system have contributed significantly to the soil degradation problem.

Spatial Profile of the Physical Landscape of Rajasthan

Rajasthan stretches two of India's major physiographic divisions, namely the Great Plains (Indian Desert) and the Central Highlands. The Aravalli range of hills intersects the state diagonally from southwest to northeast, extending right up to Delhi. While the area east of the Aravalli falls in the northern part of the Central Highlands. The Aravalli forms the watershed line between catchment streams flowing into Arabian Sea and Bay of Bengal respectively. It has a steep but discontinuous front to the Thar Plains in the west and a relatively gentle slope to the alluvial basins in the north and the east. The central part of Aravalli, consists of an important basin of interior drainage, is gifted with Sambhar lake. This area is full of sand hills and typical landscape with several low depressions.

The climate of Rajasthan, west of the Aravalli as of other desert and semi-desert regions, which rapidly gets heated during the day and cool down quickly after dusk, notes variations of as much as 22^0 c in the maximum and minimum temperature. In the east and south of Aravallis there is considerable variation in the temperature and amount of rainfall. Climatically Rajasthan is the driest State in the country.

The rainfall is the only source of water in the State, which is received from southwest monsoon which usually arrives by the middle of June and continues with intervening breaks till almost September end. The annual rainfall varies from less than 100 mm to 1000 mm. As one moves from southwest to northeast, the rainfall goes on decreasing. It is maximum on the Aravalli near Mt. Abu where it exceeds 1000 mm. The average rainfall in north-western parts of Jaisalmer district ranges between 1 to 100 mm while in Banswara, Chittorgarh and Jhalawar districts it varies between 901 to 1000 mm. The state has about 528 mm of average rainfall.

Land Use of Rajasthan

The existing land use in the State potrays a dismal picture. The present geographical area of 34,236,936 hectares for a population of 5,65,07,188 (2001) provides an availability of about 0.060 hectare of land per capita. With expected population of people in 2010 the per capita availability is likely to fall further, demanding better management of existing land. It is observed from Table 2.1 that 48.92 per cent of net cultivated area is used for various types of agricultural products including food grain, oilseeds, pulses, cash crops and fodder. Forests that are highly degraded and mostly in the form of scrubs, constitute only 7.71 per cent which is highly insufficient in view of the ecological requirements and the country's accepted policy of keeping 33 per cent area under forest cover. Permanent pasture constitutes only 4.95 per cent of the total land use which is very less to sustain 54.34 million cattle heads of the state. The percentage of orchards and gardens is also very low. The land unsuitable for agriculture which is put under the category of 'barren and un-culturable land' is 7.35 per cent.

Finally, it is cultivable waste and other fallow land, which constitute a major share, 13.80 and 6.77 per cent respectively, useful for cultivation. It needs to be harnessed for agriculture to raise the food resources and economy. It is observed that Rajasthan occupying nearly 10 per cent of the land area of the country has more than 20 per cent of the waste lands awaiting their utilisation for agriculture, forestry and pasture development. This land has to be examined at micro level and reclamation measures applied for development, which varies from area to area depending upon the local conditions.

Table 2.1

Land Use in Rajasthan (2001-02)

S. No.	*Land Use*	*Area in ha.*	*Percentage*
	Reported area	34265309	100.00
(i)	Forest	2645097	7.72
(ii)	Land Put to Non-agricultural Uses	1751549	5.11
(iii)	Barren and Un-culturable Land	2520654	7.36
(iv)	Permanent Pasture & Other Grazing Land	1698554	4.96
(v)	Land Under Misc. Tree Crops & Groves	13180	0.04
(vi)	Culturable Waste	4730528	13.80
(vii)	Current Fallow	1819241	5.32
(viii)	Other Fallow Land	2321424	6.77
(ix)	Net Area Sown	16765082	48.92
Area Sown More Than Once		4033229	11.77
Total Cropped Area		20798311	60.70

Source: Statistical Abstract of Rajasthan, 2004.

Spatial Distribution of Agricultural Land

Due to variability in physiographic conditions, fertility of soil and irrigation facilities, large disparities have been noticed in the inter-district distribution of cultivable land. As the entire population is dependent on the productivity of land for its food requirements and other agrarian needs, this land is more significant. Nearly 48.92 per cent of the land of the entire state is utilised for agricultural production. With large variations every year, it depends upon the onset of the southwest monsoon and the rainfall variability. It may be noticed that most of the central part of hilly districts like Ajmer, Pali, Kota, Jhalawar, Swai Madhopur and Banswara districts attain the state average (Table 2.2). The lowest percentages of area under cultivation are found in Jaisalmer (12.64 per cent), Udaipur (16.44 per cent) and Rajsamand districts (20.06 per cent) on account of sand dunes/hilly terrain, hostile climate, rugged terrain and greater depths of the water table. Highest percentage of cultivable land is found in Hanumangarh (80.14 per cent) forming part of north western irrigated plain of the state, where alluvial fertile soils, availability of canal water for irrigation made the area more cultivable. The second largest area of cultivable land is found in the 'flood prone eastern plain' located in east of Rajasthan. This region consists of Alwar, Bharatpur, Dholpur and Sawai Madhopur districs, where 71.06 per cent of the total geographical area of the region is endowed with good agro-climatic condition. The highest percentage of the agricultural area is found in Bharatpur district (77.16%). The third region is 'transitional plain of inland drainage' which has 69.35 per cent area under cultivation. The area consists of Churu, Jhunjhunu, Sikar and Nagaur districts, where in the absence of surface irrigation facility, the groundwater is extremely being used for irrigation. The south sub-humid region of South Aravalli has 27.65 per cent of minimum agricultural area in the state as the entire topography is hilly. This part is rich in forest and also in mineral deposits.

Area under Forests

The recorded forest area of the State is 32,488 sq. km (9.40% of the total area of the State) as reported by the State Forest Departments (SFR, 2003). This area has been classified into reserved,

Table 2.2

Distribution of Land under Cultivation in Rajasthan (2001-02)

Agro-Climatic Regions	*Total Area*	*Area under Cultivation*	*% Area under Cultivation*
Arid Western Plain			
Bikaner	2735946	1477979	54.02
Jaisalmer	3839154	485475	12.64
Jodhpur	2256405	1265944	56.10
Barmer	2817332	1649224	58.54
Total	**11648837**	**4878622**	**41.88**
Irrigated North Western Plain			
Ganganagar	1093352	698293	63.87
Hanumangarh	970315	778027	80.14
Total	**2063667**	**1476320**	**71.53**
Transitional Plain of Inland Drainage			
Churu	168598	1151220	68.28
Jhunjhunu	591683	433249	73.22
Sikar	774244	518399	66.96
Nagaur	1764383	1237480	70.13
Total	**4816208**	**3340348**	**69.35**
Transitional Plain of Luni Basin			
Pali	1233079	576225	46.73
Jalore	1056602	648625	61.38
Sirohi	517947	147368	28.45
Total	**2807628**	**1372218**	**48.87**
Semi-Arid Eastern Plain			
Jaipur	1105494	622237	56.29
Dausa	340467	209999	61.69
Tonk	717960	397385	55.35
Ajmer	842345	3894413	46.23
Total	**3006266**	**1619034**	**53.85**
Flood Prone Eastern Plain			
Alwar	782897	509107	65.02
Bharatpur	507073	391287	77.16
Dholpur	300905	145684	48.41
Karauli	505217	181844	35.99
S. Madhopur	499424	261539	52.37
Total	**2096092**	**1489461**	**71.06**

contd. ...

...contd. ...

Agro-Climatic Regions	*Total Area*	*Area under Cultivation*	*% Area under Cultivation*
Sub-Humid Southern Plain and Aravalli			
Bhilwara	1047451	370341	35.36
Rajsamand	455093	91286	20.06
Udaipur	1462109	240384	16.44
Chittorgarh	1035704	404301	39.03
Total	**4000357**	**1106312**	**27.65**
Humid Southern Plain			
Banswara	506279	230725	45.57
Dungarpur	385593	121005	31.38
Total	**891872**	**351730**	**39.43**
Humid Southern Eastern Plain			
Bundi	581938	240506	41.33
Baran	699652	316335	45.21
Kota	521133	261382	50.16
Jhalawar	6322355	312814	49.48
Total	**24349958**	**1131037**	**46.45**
G.Total	**34265309**	**16765082**	**48.92**

Source: *Statistical Abstract*, Rajasthan, 2002.

protected and un-classed forest,[1] which constitute 36.51, 54.33 and 9.16 of the forest area respectively. The other statistics available based on the remote sensing technique reveal that only 16,367 sq. km. (4.78 per cent of the total geographical area of the State) is estimated under actual forest cover as of 2001. This discrepancy is basically due to differences in methods of data interpretation. First category represents the administrative area irrespective of the actual tree cover on the ground where as other represents the actual green cover (*Forest Survey of India*, 2001) (Table 2.3).

1. Reserved Forest: An area notified under the provisions of Indian Forest Act having full degree of protection. In reserved forest, all activities are prohibited unless permitted.
Protected Forest: An area notified under the provisions of the Indian Forest Acts having limited degree of protection. In protected forests, all activities are permitted unless prohibited.
Unclassed Forest: An area recorded as forest but not included in reserved or protected forest category.

Table 2.3

Forest Area Statistics

Class	*Area in Sq.Km*	*Percentage of Geographical Area*
Dense Forest	6,322	1.85
Open Forest	10.045	2.93
Total	**16,368**	**4.78**

Source: Forest Survey of India, 2001.

The ownership of forest rests mainly with the Government. The per capita available forest area is only 0.05 hectares in comparison to India, which is 0.08 hectares. From the consumption requirement point of view, it is estimated that each Indian would require at least 0.47 hectares of forest to meet his basic needs (SOE, 1995). Hence, the state is very much lacking behind the normal needs of the people. The potential areas for expansion of forest cover are culturable wastelands covering 4.73 m.ha. and part of fallow land and land other than current fallows, covering 4.14 m.ha.

Under Utilised Land

This category of land, excludes current fallows, covers areas classified under permanent pastures and grazing lands, the areas under miscellaneous tree crops and culturable wasteland. About 6.44 m.ha. of land in the state (18.80%) is recorded under this category. Rajasthan constitutes a major share of culturable waste and other fallow land (20.57%) useful for cultivation. It needs to be harnessed for agriculture to raise the food resources and economy.

These lands are in community use. Jaisalmer district at 70.62 per cent has the highest area in the state under this category whereas Bharatpur has minimum of 0.86 per cent area left for grazing. If we look at the distribution from the agro-climatic zone point of view, it presents much more rationale picture. Out of nine zones, four zones have area ranging from 12 per cent to 16 per cent which is almost near the state average whereas arid western plain has maximum of 31.31 per cent area under this category. The transitional plain of inland drainage which consists of Churu, Jhunjhunu, Sikar, and Nagaur has minimum of 4.67 per cent area under this category. The distribution shows that whereever the water is available whether surface or ground the common area has been shrinking.

Recent past, in the year 1981, a new classification of this, considering permanent pasture and grazing land, land under miscellaneous tree, culturable wasteland, current fallow and other fallowland have been made by National Remote Sensing Agency. It was renamed as wasteland. The definition says, "Wastelands are lands which are economically unproductive, ecologically unstable and are subject to severe environmental deterioration." Further, wasteland have been divided into two classes *viz.* culturable wasteland and unculturable wasteland. New classification reflects the qualitative nature of land as well as biological potential of land. It includes all the lands that are salt affected, gullied or ravenous, waterlogged or marshy, undulating upland with or without shrub, jhum or forest blank and sandy area. These lands can be put to productive use after proper treatment and reclamation measures. Latter includes barren lands on hilly ridges, mined out area, etc.

Considering all the above classifications of land use, the best classification of wasteland is based on the characteristics of the wasteland i.e. culturable and unculturable wasteland. It is further classified as follows:

Culturable Wastelands

1. Gullied/or ravenous land.
2. Undulating upland with or without scrub.
3. Surface waterlogged land.
4. Salt affected land.
5. Shifting cultivation.
6. Degraded forest.
7. Degraded pastures/grazing land.
8. Degraded non-forest plantation.
9. Strip land.
10. Sands.
11. Mining/industrial wasteland.

Table 2.4

Distribution of Under Utilised Land

Agro-Climatic Regions	*Culturable Wasteland*	*Fallow and Other Than Current Fallow*	*Total Area*	*Total of Culturable Fallow Land*	*% of Total Geographical Area of District*
Arid Western Plain					
Bikaner	777482	210675	2735946	988157	36.11
Jaisalmer	2579464	131709	3839154	2711173	70.61
Jodhpur	11676	365444	2356405	377120	16.71
Barmer	217687	330770	2817332	548457	19.46
Total	**3586309**	**1038598**	**11648837**	**4624907**	**39.70**
Irrigated North West Plain (Ghaggar Belt)					
Ganganagar	35500	112602	1093352	148102	13.54
Hanumangarh	10451	41574	970315	52025	5.36
Total	**45951**	**154176**	**2063667**	**200127**	**9.69**
Transitional Plain of Inland Drainage					
Churu	9501	53181	1685898	62682	3.72
Jhunjhunu	6367	19770	591683	26137	4.41
Sikar	10009	47286	774244	57295	7.40
Nagaur	13294	89503	1764383	102797	5.82
Total	**39171**	**209740**	**4816208**	**248911**	**5.16**
Transitional Plain of Luni Basin					
Pali	46011	133008	1233079	179019	14.52
Jalore	24394	108123	1056602	132517	12.54
Sirohi	8621	43513	517947	52134	10.06
Total	**79026**	**284644**	**2807628**	**363670**	**12.95**
Semi-Arid Eastern Plain					
Jaipur	32702	85619	1105494	118321	10.70
Dausa	9385	14961	340467	24346	7.15
Tonk	45611	45277	717960	90888	12.66
Ajmer	74238	53555	842345	127793	15.17
Total	**161936**	**199412**	**3006266**	**361348**	**12.02**
Flood Prone Eastern Plain					
Alwar	7814	15999	782897	23813	3.04
Bharatpur	3040	1314	507073	4354	0.86
Dhaulpur	12583	11456	300905	24039	7.99
Kararuli	14064	13869	505217	27933	5.53
S. Madhopur	10289	18398	499424	28687	5.74
Total	**47790**	**61036**	**2096092**	**108826**	**5.19**

contd. ...

...contd. ...

Agro-Climatic Regions	*Culturable Wasteland*	*Fallow and Other Than Current Fallow*	*Total Area*	*Total of Culturable Fallow Land*	*% of Total Geographical Area of District*
Sub-Humid Southern Plain and Aravalli Hills					
Bhilwara	156858	68052	1047451	224910	21.47
Rajsamand	121577	27724	455093	149301	32.80
Udaipur	133722	74502	1462109	208224	14.24
Chittor	166770	27785	1035704	194555	18.78
Total	**578927**	**198063**	**4000357**	**776990**	**19.42**
Humid Southern Plain					
Banswara	31695	38255	506279	69950	13.81
Dungarpur	23138	35620	385593	58758	15.24
Total	**54833**	**73875**	**891872**	**128708**	**14.43**
Humid South Eastern Plain					
Bundi	33430	29806	581938	63236	10.86
Baran	23771	24001	699652	47772	6.82
Kota	26612	16980	521133	43592	8.36
Jhalawar	52772	23093	632235	75865	12.00
Total	**136585**	**93880**	**2434958**	**230465**	**9.46**
Grand Total	**4730528**	**2313424**	**34265309**	**7043952**	**20.57**

Source: Computed from *Ravira*, Rajasthan Revenue Board, Ajmer, 2004.

These can be clubbed into two groups i.e., cultivable waste and old fallow. The cultivable wasteland includes all lands which are cultivable but at present lying waste due to numerous limitations. This includes ravenous, undulating upland with or without scrub, waterlogged, degraded lands containing plantations outside the notified forest-area, degraded pastures, eroded and soil fertility loss coupled with moderate slope and rough surface, high soil *ph* value, thin layer of soil, erratic and low rainfall areas etc. On the other hand, the genesis of old-fallow is traceable in lands left uncultivated for two consecutive years for maintaining soil fertility status. When current fallow is not bought under cultivation for two years, it marks the initial stage of the development of old fallows. The large size of holding of the cultivators contributes towards this cause, as they can afford it so. Thus, the middle stage is characterised by the loss of the loose soil being washed off through water. Such continuous degradation of the top soil structure, added with the human mismanagement and paucity of water justifies land being left out of cultivation even for more than five years, and re-categorised as culturable waste.

Unculturable Wastelands

1. Barren rocky/stony waste/sheet rock area.
2. Steep sloping area.

Unculturable wastelands appears to be related with physical factors like high slope, high drainage density and high *ph* value of water and soil on one hand and excess of evaporation over precipitation amount on the other. The rocky, stony and gravelly wastes have high slope, rough topography and high drainage density characterising continuous erosional process. Moreover, the exploitation of minerals, rocks and building limestones has led to extensive mining and quarrying, aggravating the condition towards the process of barrenness in the area. This category includes all such lands that are practically unproductive, unfit for cultivation, barren and uncultivable may provide space for industries or settlements etc.

Table 2.5 shows that 29.60 per cent of total geographical area of the state is under diffrent category of wastelands. Out of which, 94.31 per cent (95,60,652 ha) is culturable and 5,87,544 ha (5.79%) is un-culturable waste. The maximum wastelands area lies in arid western plain and flood prone eastern plain which is 44.34 and 44.03 per cent respectively whereas the minimum is 9.59 per cent in the irrigated north west plain. The culturable is a maximum of 99.87 per cent in the irrigated north west plain, whereas un-culturable wasteland is a maximum of 16.62 per cent in the flood prone eastern plain. The minimum area of 83.38 and 0.13 per cent of culturable and un-culturable land is in flood prone zone and area under irrigated northwest plain respectively.

Out of the total wasteland, 35.66 per cent of wasteland in culturable falls under the category of gullied, ravines and sand (Table 2.6) followed by degraded forest, pasture and land with scrub. Under un-culturable category, the highest 5.17 per cent of land is barren and rocky which can hardly be reclaimed.

Table 2.5

Distribution of Wasteland in Rajasthan

(Based on Remote Sensing Data)

S. No.	*Agro-Climatic Zones*	*Culturable Wasteland*		*Unculturable Wasteland*		*Total Wasteland*	*% to Total Geographical Area of the District*
		Area in Sq.km	*%*	*Area in Sq.km*	*%*		
I	Arid Western Plain	49654.62	96.80	1641.39	3.20	51296.01	44.03
II	Irrigated North West Plain	1977.32	99.87	2.61	0.13	1979.93	9.59
III	Transitional Plain of Inland Drainage	5541.08	91.78	495.79	8.22	6036.87	12.53
IV	Transitional Plain of Luni River Basin	5411.52	89.79	615.14	10.21	6026.66	21.46
V	Semi-Arid Eastern Plain	5688.63	90.65	586.07	9.35	6274.70	20.87
VI	Flood Prone Eastern Plain	7749.00	83.38	1545.70	16.62	9292.70	44.34
VII	Sub-Humid Southern Plain and Aravali	8713.23	94.46	510.99	5.54	9224.24	23.06
VIII	Humid Southern Plain	3008.43	98.34	42.22	1.66	3059.45	34.30
IX	Humid Southern Eastern Plain	7755.64	94.68	435.58	5.32	8191.30	33.64
	Total	**95499.47**	**94.31**	**5875.49**	**5.79**	**101374.96**	**29.60**

Note: Culturable Wasteland: Gullied ravinous land, Land with scrub, Land without scrub, Waterlogged area, Land affected by salinity/alkalinity.

Un-culturable Wasteland: Degraded notified forest area, Degraded pasture/grazing land, Degraded land under plantation, Sand mining wasteland, Industrial wasteland, Barren/Rocky/Stony wasteland.

Source: Compiled from *Wasteland Atlas of India*, 2005.

Table 2.6

Type of Wastelands in Rajasthan

		Area in Sq.km	*% to Total Wasteland*
	Culturable Wasteland		
I	Gullied/Ravinous Land	6581.41	6.49
II	Land with Scrub	30010.59	29.60
III	Land without Scrub	6846.16	6.74
IV	Waterlogged Land	259.98	0.24
V	Land Affected by Salinity/Alkalinity	3765.72	3.70
VI	Degraded Notified Forest Land	9620.22	9.47
VII	Degraded Pasture/Grazing Land	8766.41	8.63
VIII	Degraded Land under Plantation	181.27	0.17
IX	Sand	29574.76	29.17
	Un-Culturable Land		
1	Mining Wasteland	233.77	0.23
II	Industrial Wasteland	398.68	0.39
III	Barren/Rocky/Sandy Waste	5242.99	5.17

Source: Complied from *Wasteland Atlas of India 2005*. NRSA Hyderabad.

Land–Man Ratio

This is a suitable index to measure the pressure of population upon the land. The density of population in various districts varies from 9 sq. km in Jaisalmer to 427 sq. km in Jaipur (Table 2.7).

It is noticeable that population density in Rajasthan is directly related to the average annual rainfall, meaning hereby that those districts which receive higher rains are more densely populated and *vice-versa*. It is further discernible that as the rainfall goes on decreasing from east to west the population density also depicts proportionate decrease to the extent that the western most districts of Jaisalmer, Bikaner and Barmer have the density of 13, 61 and 69 respectively.

Due to less people in the northwestern parts, the per capita availability of land is high while in the southeastern and eastern parts it is low on account of high population density. The state average is 165 people per sq. km. Exceptionally high ratio of availability of land per person is noticed in Jaisalmer (0.075), followed by Bikaner (0.016) and Barmer (0.014) where large deposit of sand makes the cultivation difficult. The overall state average is 0.06 sq. km. per person.

Table 2.7

Population Density and Per Capita Availability of Land

Districts	*Total Area in Sq. Km*	*Population*	*Density*	*Per Capita Land in Sq. Km*
Jaipur	14068	6568134	466	0.002
Bharatpur	5066	2101142	414	0.002
Alwar	8380	2992592	357	0.002
Jhunjhunu	5928	1913689	323	0.003
Dholpur	3034	983258	324	0.003
Sikar	7732	2287788	296	0.003
Dungarpur	3770	1107643	294	0.003
Banswara	5037	1501589	298	0.003
Ajmer	6219	1180323	257	0.003
Swai Madhopur	10527	2326732	221	0.004
Udaipur	17279	3620336	209	0.004
Kota	12436	2590178	208	0.004
Jhalawar	6219	1180323	190	0.005
Bhilwara	10455	2013789	192	0.005
Bundi	5550	962620	173	0.005
Chittorgarh	10856	1803524	166	0.006
Tonk	7194	1211671	168	0.005
Sirohi	5136	851107	166	0.006
Ganganagar	20634	3307428	160	0.008
Nagaur	17718	2775058	157	0.006
Pali	12387	1820251	147	0.006
Jalore	10640	1448940	136	0.007
Jodhpur	22850	2886505	126	0.008
Churu	16830	1923878	114	0.008
Barmer	28387	1964835	69	0.014
Bikaner	27244	1674271	61	0.016
Jaisalmer	38401	508247	13	0.075
Rajasthan State	342239	56507198	165	0.006

Source: *Statistical Abstract*, Rajasthan, 2004.

The highest density of population and the consequent lowest per capita availability of land are noticeable in Jaipur, Alwar, Bharatpur, Jhunjhunu, Sikar, Jaipur, Dholpur, Dungarpur and Banswara districts. In these districts the availability of per capita land is low but it is so fertile that it can sustain high population pressure. On the other hand, Churu, Jodhpur, Jalore district have nearly more than double the per capita land available and low population density. It is because the land is not fertile and also it is un-irrigated and has hostile climatic conditions. In remaining districts, the distribution is nearly same as the state's average.

Land Degradation in Rajasthan

The term land degradation refers to the decline in the productive capacity of an ecosystem due to processes induced mainly by anthropogenic activities. The processes leading to land degradation are generally triggered by increasing demand for food from the growing population, which results in overexploitation of natural resources. Human activities such as firewood cutting in rural areas and around main cities, deforestation for commercial use, urbanisation and industrialisation, overtaxed gangland carrying capacity and overgrazing by ever-expanding herds, cultivation in ecologically marginal areas and agricultural overexploitation, low level of agricultural technology, reduced fallow time, deep well construction, etc., lead to various land degradation processes, including increasing soil degradation through salinisation, flooding, drought, waterlogging, etc. These processes in turn reduce biological productivity.

Causes of Land Degradation

Factors contributing to degradation of land are several. Most important factor is the indiscriminate and over utilisation of natural resources. Both natural and anthropogenic pressures contribute to land degradation. Among the natural factors, landslides, floods, wind and water erosion, drought, mudflows, etc. are the important driving forces. The anthropogenic factors responsible are: inappropriate agricultural practices, improper irrigation techniques, shifting cultivation and unscientific land management by putting the areas to improper land use. The process of development *viz.*, construction of dams and reservoir, building of roads in fragile mountain areas, setting up of industries, laying of railway lines, waterlogged areas formed due to seepage of canal water, and mine overburdens also results in the formation of wastelands.

Deforestation

On account of the phenomenal increase in population of the state from 3.42 million in 1901 to 56.50 million in 2001, heavy demands are being placed on the tree-lands. The demand in rural areas is met by felling of trees standing on the private agricultural farms, government forests and wasteland, community pasturelands etc. Another important demand on forest and pasturelands is uncontrolled grazing. The livestock population of the state is about 49 million as per 2003 census. They are rarely stall-fed, they are allowed to graze in village wastelands or the government forests which results into further degradation of vegetation cover.

Forests that are highly degraded and mostly in the form of scrubs, constitute a bare 7.71 per cent which is highly insufficient in view of the ecological requirements and the country's accepted National Forest Policy, 1952 of keeping 33 per cent area under forest cover. The satellite data mapping done by the Forest Survey of India, during 2001, indicates that only 4.78 per cent of the area of the state was under good forest. The average annual loss of the forest cover was to the tune of one-lakh hectares in the country, which was alarming to the entire society. According to a recent assessment by the Rajasthan State Forest Department, 9.49 per cent of the state area is under different types of forest. Another recent estimate in the year 2000 based on the satellite data by National Remote Sensing Agency, Hyderabad (*Wasteland Atlas of India*), reported that the Rajasthan holds 1.25 million hectares of degraded notified forest.

Improper Agriculture Land Use

Intensive agriculture in arid areas has led to extension of area under irrigation. Much of this increase has come from Indira Gandhi Canal region (which is of arid topography) and water extracted from the fast depleting groundwater resources. Improper use and maintenance of canal irrigation has contributed significantly to the soil degradation problem. Extension of canal irrigation to arid and semi-arid areas has resulted in waterlogging and salination.

According to the National Remote Sensing Agency and Forest Survey of India, 60 per cent of the total area under cultivation is substantially degraded. Most of this damage is in the form of loss of topsoil. According to National Remote Sensing Agency, Hyderabad, the physical deterioration of the soil due to waterlogging has affected about 29 thousand hectares in Rajasthan. This is mostly due to over irrigation and linkage from canal in the Western Rajasthan. According to a study conducted by the State Groundwater Board, in the year 1981 about 19.75 sq. km. area was waterlogged that was increased up to 609.37 sq. km. by the year 1998 under the Indira Gandhi Canal Command area.

Mining

Mining has been a very critical issue for the last two decades. Rajasthan ranks second to Bihar in mineral deposits. Some minerals like wollastozite and jespar are found only in Rajasthan. It has 97 per cent of zinc, 93 per cent of gypsum, 96 per cent of fluorite, 70 per cent of sandstone and limestone, 89 per cent of asbestos, 90 per cent of marble, 70 per cent of calcite, 80 per cent of lead, 65 per cent of tungsten and 75 per cent of soapstone deposits of India. Most of these occur scattered and in small areas. Their mining does not contribute much in terms of the area under land use at the state-level but the way mining areas are being tackled and managed, environmentally it damages much more areas than it is allotted for mining many activities. The building and construction stones like sandstone, limestone and marble occupy large area and shallow depth. Excavation of these has constituted a major hazard to ecology and environment.

Mining despoliation (spoiling of land) is a major factor in blocking the natural drainage as a consequence of dumping waste, overburden material across them. In addition, it destroys and removes the vegetation, increasing erosion in cleared areas. Overburden, when removed and dumped in unplanned manner, causes the chain reaction of enhanced run-off, sedimentation. It causes drastic and often irreversible damage. The uncultivable land that is created by the excavation of the earth is more serious a problem because it can not be brought under cultivation or use for biological production purpose by any means. To arrest increasing incidence of the uncultivable wasteland, state as well as central government has made the provisions for reclamation of mined out area in various acts. Besides, the mine owners morally or by law are supposed to reclaim the land and maintain the ecological balance. Despite these provisions the satellite data shows a fast increasing trends in wasteland. The *Wasteland Atlas of India* prepared for 2000 and 2005 by National Remote Sensing Agency, Hyderabad, reported that the mined out area in Rajasthan has increased by double within five years. During 2000 the mined out area was 128.65 sq. km which increased to 233.77 sq. km in 2005. The more pronounced degradation of land in recent years in Rajasthan appears mainly due to the increased open cast mining as indicated in Table 2.8.

Table 2.8

Forest Land Diverted under Forest (Conservation) Act, 1980 for Non-forest Purpose up to 2001

S.No.	*Purpose*	*Area in Hect.*	*Percentage*
1.	Irrigation Projects	169.86	01.36
2.	Hydel Projects	24.50	0.20
3.	Mining Projects	2,916.39	23.40
4.	Railways/Roads	1,210.36	09.70
5.	Transmission Line	815.11	06.54
6.	Other	7,327.69	58.80

Source: State of Forest Report, 2003.

Table 2.8 reveals that maximum forest land i.e. 23.40 per cent has been converted for a single cause of mining activity. Reckless mining and ineffective implementation of environmental rules and regulations are main cause of degradation of land. Presently, there is no scientific mechanism through which one may know the extent to which both legal and illegal mining takes place across the state. Besides one does not know the geographical extent of degraded land due to mining activities. Even to implement the environmental laws, one has to monitor the area on regular basis and keep watch from time to time on mining right from the starting of its operation. Hence, a scientific monitoring system which provides low cost data at regular interval on various scale is required.

Lack of Land Use Policy

There is no clear-cut land use policy formulated in India so far, mainly due to the fragmented handling of different components of agriculture like land and soil. However, a Land Resource Management Policy and Approach was attempted in consultation with FAO, the Lal Bahadur Shastri National Academy of Administration and the National Institute of Rural Development (NIRD) but it was not finalised. The policy is intended to have dynamic conservation, sustainable development and equitable access to the benefits of intervention as its thrust. Land being a State subject, many States have enacted legislation on land. The basic objectives of the National Land Use Policy: Outline and Action Points are given below.

Objectives of the National Land Use Policy: Outline and Action Points (1988)

1. To meet the consumption needs of a growing population by increasing productivity of the integrated land resource of the country.
2. To prevent any further deterioration of land resource by appropriate preventive measure.
3. To restore the productivity of degraded land by appropriate package of practices.
4. To provide the necessary technological and extension support to all concerned and to the farming community in particular for obtaining maximum production through increased productivity.
5. To allocate land for different uses based upon land capability, land productivity and national production goals.
6. To install an efficient and effective administrative structure for prescribing and regulating land by all concerned, including the government department and to revitalise the land use boards in this respect.
7. To involve the community for adoption of appropriate land use for increased productivity, by ensuring that the land use policy provides adequately for the consumption and energy needs and generally improves their income levels and provides them a better quality of life.

8. To create greater awareness of advantages of national land use policy at all levels through appropriate educational, extension and training programmes.
9. To restructure the livestock production programme in such a manner that the livestock population is gradually limited to economically productive stock and to prevent degradation of grassland by promoting measures of increasing stall feeding of livestock in rural areas.
10. To provide for optimum use of land under agriculture by promoting mixed farming systems in which the production programme will include the production of fodder and tree crops also on marginal and sub-marginal farm land.
11. To motivate farmers by organising input supplies and marketing support for encouraging them to cultivate the appropriate crop or fodder or trees in conformity with the land use policy.
12. To take up, on priority basis the completion of land and soil surveys and to complete the inventory of land resources on the basis of the prescribed land use classification so that allocation is based on a reliable database.
13. To examine the legal support available for enforcement of land use policy in the form of existing State and Central laws and to consider the need for comprehensive legislation to provide some teeth to any machinery entrusted with implementation of the national land use policy.

Government Strategies for Reclamation

Reclamation of degraded land is a big challenge for the government yet it cannot be deferred or ignored. To augment the food resources of the state and to restore the ecology, it is essential to transform the arid swathes into fertile green belts. Hence, in 1985, realising the importance of reclamation of wastelands, the then Prime Minister, Mr. Rajiv Gandhi, had announced to reclaim five million hectares of wasteland every year in the country. He took new initiative and set up the National Wastelands Development Board under the Ministry of Environment and Forests and the National Land Use Conservation Board under the Ministry of Agriculture and

Rural Development to fulfil the above target. The functions of the board were: policy formulation, coordination, awareness raising, monitoring and evaluation, and conduct pilot studies. Later the government abolished the Wastelands Development Board and merged it with the Ministry of Rural Development. There are a number of departments involved in different ways in the programme of waste lands development. These are: the Forestry Department and its social forestry programme, the Rural Development Department with its programmes of rural development, social forestry and rural development, especially Integrated Rural Development Programme, and National Rural Employment Programme, the Department of Agriculture and Cooperation with its soil conservation measures and animal husbandry programmes including fodder development, Tribal Welfare Division of Ministry of Home Affairs, etc.

Policy Suggestions

Need to Improve Land Use Classification System

Till 1949-50, the land area in the country was classified into five categories known as the five-fold land-utilisation classification. This five-fold land utilisation classification was, however, a very broad outline of land use in the country and was not found adequate enough to meet the needs of agricultural planning in the country. The states were also finding it difficult to present comparable data according to this classification, owing to the lack of uniformity in the definition and scope of classification covered by these five broad categories. To remove the non-comparability and to break up the broad categories into smaller constituents for better comprehension, the Technical Committee on Co-ordination of Agricultural Statistics, set up by the Ministry of Food and Agriculture, recommended a nine-fold land use classification replacing the old five-fold classification. The existing database on land use is classified in nine categories of land use classification system: (1) forests, (2) area under non-agricultural use, (3) barren and unculturable land, (4) permanent pature and other grazing land, (5) miscellaneous tree crops, (6) culturable wasteland (7) fallow land other than current fallows, (8) current fallows, and (9) net area sown (NAS). This data fulfils very limited objectives of keeping records of the land collection of revenue mainly from agriculture and forest. It does not provide much useful information regarding different use or misuse of land by anthropogenic activities and natural occupancy. Also, qualitative assessment of the land is not possible in this system. The National Remote Sensing Agency, Hyderabad has developed the land use classification system based on remote sensing data and has been mapping the nation. They have developed four levels of land use classification. It includes qualitative, quantitative and spatial information about the land use as well as land cover. For estimation of land degradation, the wasteland, which has only two categories in the old system, the NRSA has 25 categories. It gives better understanding and valuable information from the point of view of land use planning and management. In addition, the system is fully mechanised for data analysis, storage, manipulation, retrieval and display. Such advanced technology should be adopted that can go a long way in helping generation of more information on different dimensions of land use and land degradation. Adequate changes in the classification of land use statistics are needed in order to study environmental impact of land use.

Selection of Appropriate Land Use

Wrong policy choices have aggravated the problem of land degradation in Rajasthan. Nowhere in any desert of the world is water wasted over extensive cultivation by flood irrigation method. The geo-physical character of land in the desert areas of Rajasthan is of margin origin. Also, there are a large deposits of gypsum at many places in the Indira Gandhi Canal Command areas below a sand sheet ranging from one to three meters of depth from surface. In such condition, if intensive irrigation is done for continuous 10 to 15 years the area is bound to be waterlogged. Moreover, there is hard rock beneath the surface at many places which does not allow water to penetrate. Hence, the intensive irrigation over extensive agriculture is all the more inadvisable in particularly desert areas of Rajasthan. After 10 years of intensive irrigation in the command area of Indira Gandhi Canal, most of the area is in the process of turning brackish and saline. Another problem is of waterlogging. Earlier there was no danger of waterlogging as such in the desert, but with the introduction of canal, the problem of land degradation has been cropped up due to seepage from canals. It is now suggested that the land, which is not suitable for intensive irrigation, should be used for pasture land development and hence, the animal husbandry should be promoted in the desert rather than agriculture which is not sustainable.

Urban-Rural Land Use

The urban population is increasing very fast so are the urban areas. Presently almost all urban areas are expanding at the cost of peripheral agricultural land, quite often very fertile and productive. For example the Jaipur city which has experienced its expansion at the cost of peripheral agricultural land. The city, when founded had a total area of about 4.81 sq. km. In 1951 due to rapid increase in population, the city area further expanded to 40 sq. km. In 1972, it had reached up to 385 sq. km. In the year 1995, the Master Plan was revised targeting the need for the year 2011. Additional 6 towns and 342 revenue villages have been identified for inclusion in the urban areas for city planning purpose. Now the total geographical area of Jaipur city is spread in 1464 sq. km. This process has resulted in the conversion of agricultural lands into non-agricultural uses. Apart from the diversion of lands for non-agricultural uses, the extensive damage to ecology and environment due to industrial waste, pollution, and misuse of land can also be seen in the urban areas and its periphery. One other important impact noticed is on the natural hydrological system of the city. As the urban areas spread, the natural hydrological features like rivers, *nallah* and water bodies come in the heart of the city. The people subject them to encroachment. These results in either completely or partly block of the system. This process on one hand breaks the hydrological system and on other hand creates a permanent recurrent flood damage zone in the city area.

There are as many as 518 rivulets originating from the hill ranges. Out of these, 398 are of first order, 92 second order, 25 third order and 3 are of fourth order streams. In early stages, the city expansion was restricted to foot hills only and no drainage system was disturbed. But as the expansion took place, people started filling, diverting and blocking the stream. At many places the natural streams were used to dump the garbage. As a result, 160 streams (out of which 113 are first order, 37 second order and 10 are of third order) are blocked or filled. It has a direct bearing on the availability of surface as well as groundwater.

No data is being collected on urban land use. Hence, there is a need to collect the extensive data of urban as well as rural land use separately covering environmental aspects.

Legislation

There are a number of legislations protecting and conserving natural resources like water, air, forest and bio-diversity, etc. But there is no direct legislation which protects the quality of soil or helps in conservation of soil, however there are soil conservation programmes that are mostly confined to Agriculture Departments, and the aim is to educate the farmers with various conservation practices. But so far, these programmes have not been successful due to inadequate approach of implementation.

References

Department of Economics and Statistics (2004). *Statistical Abstract of Rajasthan*, Jaipur.

Department of Forest (2003). *Rajasthan Forest Statistics*, Jaipur

Dhawan, C.L. (1964). *Land Reclamation*, Publication Vol. No. 48, Central Board of Irrigation and Power.

Directorate of Livestock (2004-05). *Administrative Report*, GoR.

Government of Rajasthan (undated). *Report on Watershed Development Programme in Rajasthan*, Directorate of Watershed and Soil Conservation, Jaipur.

Joshi K.N. (1993). "Drought in Semi-Arid" in *Land Studies in Arid Land Management*, Scientific Publisher, Jodhpur.

———. (2002). "Changing Urban Land use and its Impact on the Environment", Proc. Con. of 23rd *Asian Conference on Remote Sensing*, Kathmandu, Nepal November 26-29.

———. (2003). "Changing Urban Sprawl and its Impact on Hydrological Regime", *Nagarlok*, Vol. XXXV, No. 4.

Ministry of Agriculture and Irrigation (1976). "Part V: Resource Development", *Report of the National Commission of Agricultural.*

National Remote Sensing Agency (1985). *Mapping of Wastelands in India from Satellite Imagery*, Department of Space, Govt. of India, Hyderabad.

National Wastelands Development Board (1986). *Report of the Technical Task Group on Wastelands*, Ministry of Environment and Forests, New Delhi.

Planning Commission (1963). "Study on Wastelands including Saline, Alkaline and Waterlogged Lands and their Reclamation Measures", *Committee Report on Natural Resource*, Government of India, New Delhi.

Rajasthan Revenue Board (2004). *Ravira*, Ajmer.

Shaffi, M. (1968). "Problems of Wastelands in India", *The Geographer*, Vol. XV.

Singh, A.L. (1978). *Economics and Geography of Agricultural Land Reclamation*, D.K. Publishers, New Delhi.

Yadav, H.R. (1987). *Wastelands: Diagnosis and Treatment*, Concept, New Delhi.

3

Stalled Demographic Transition

Implications for Sustainable Development

DEVENDRA KOTHARI

Population and Development

From Adam Smith onward, economists have recognised important linkages between population and socioeconomic development. Yet, the attention given to these linkages in the current development thinking is not very clear. This is because one can argue that it is not rapid population growth but rather weak government, corruption and social injustices that are preventing economic and social development. The counter argument is that rapid population growth exacerbates the problems of weak government, corruption and social injustice. However, one has to recognise that population is an important factor in development, especially when it is growing seemingly out of control (Gavin, 2005). While delivering the Eighth J.R.D. Tata Memorial Oration, Dr. Manmohan Singh said, "Human population is an important constituent of the sustainable development agenda. However, a fast growing population is leading to a significant diversion of national investable resources to consumption which could otherwise be used for increasing investment and productivity and for improving the quality of public social services such as education, health, sanitation, provision of safe drinking water and for control of environmental degradation."[1]

---

1. Dr. Manmohan Singh delivered the Eighth J.R.D. Tata Memorial Oration on February 3, 2003 at India Habitat Centre, New Delhi. At that time, Dr. Singh was the Leader of the Opposition, Rajya Sabha. For details, see: *Focus: Population Environment Development*, A Bulletin of Population Foundation of India, New Delhi, Vol. XVIII, No. 1, 2003, pp.1-2.

'Demographic transition' is a model that describes population change over time. It defines four clear stages of population growth that nations/regions often traverse in tandem with their socioeconomic development. This transition from a stable population with high mortality and high fertility to a stable population with low mortality and low fertility is called demographic transition. Rajasthan has been in the middle of demographic transition over the past few decades where the death rate has fallen sharply because of preventable causes like improved public health as well as sanitation; but the birth rate has remained high due to poor socioeconomic development as well as limited access to quality reproductive health and contraceptive services. That is a major cause of a spurt in population as well as slow progress in attaining demographic transition in Rajasthan.

Figure 3.1

Rajasthan: Stalled Demographic Transition

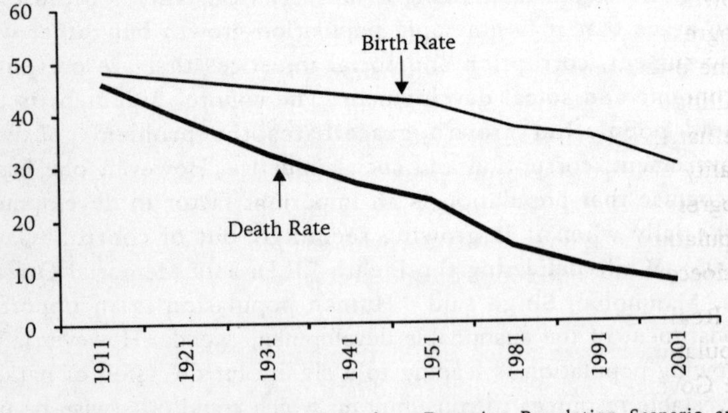

Source: Kothari, Devendra (2002). "Rajasthan: Emerging Population Scenario and Agenda for Population Stabilisation", *FPA Occasional Paper* No.1, Forum for Population Action, Jaipur.

The demographic transition in Rajasthan, stalled midway, is adversely impacting various development parameters like per capita income, poverty, employment, food security, environment, health and education as well as the quality of governance. Higher levels of total fertility and infant and maternal mortality in Rajasthan, as compared to the other States, show a large gap, which needs to be covered to reach the levels already achieved elsewhere in India. Interestingly enough, over the past few decades, the contribution of natural increase in population growth has been alarmingly high, ranging from 92 to 95 per cent (Kothari, 2002b). It appears that the impact of the Family Welfare Programme (FWP) has not been significant in Rajasthan. If this trend continues, the State will have to use up a substantial part of all additional income to feed the increased mouths, as it is happening currently. Further, due to two-thirds area of the State being arid or semi-arid, the growing population is leading the State towards a man-made ecological disaster with extreme water shortage.

The population issue has not been given due recognition in the development debate in Rajasthan. This neglect of the population factor in sustainable development has come at the time when Rajasthan is speaking of development and investment to attain the status of a modern and progressive state. Although a long journey of development lies ahead, if the State can bring down the population growth as well as maternal and infant mortality in the next few years, progress in this direction will be smooth, as has been observed in some other states of India with similar socioeconomic background.[2] Stalling demographic transition will exert an enormous pressure on the natural resources and could frustrate all attempts to improve the quality of life of the people and to achieve the goal of a modern and progressive state. Therefore, there is an urgent need to stabilise the population at a level consistent with the requirements of the State's socioeconomic development and protection of the environment.

Realising the seriousness of the consequences of the rapid population growth which the State might face in the coming years, the Government of Rajasthan constituted a high level Committee under the chairmanship of the Chief Secretary to suggest measures for achieving replacement level fertility by 2011 in order to get a stable population by the middle of the century (GoR, 2003). Is it

2. Andhra Pradesh (population: 76 million) is one such state where the level of education is equivalent to that of Rajasthan (61 per cent as compared to 60 per cent) and the proportion of people living below the poverty line is much more than in Rajasthan (23 per cent as compared to 12 per cent). Even then, Andhra Pradesh has, by improving the management of family planning services, brought down the population growth rate from 24.2 per cent in 1981-1991 to 14.6 per cent in 1991-2001, while there is no change in the growth rate of Rajasthan (24.4 per cent).

possible to achieve this goal in the stipulated time frame? Though it sounds ambitious, it is possible to achieve it even before the stipulated time looking at the prevailing favourable conditions. There is a widespread feeling among experts that Rajasthan has all the ingredients to achieve the initial breakthrough on the population front and that it can be the first state to break free from the club of the 4 large North Indian States of Bihar, Madhya Pradesh, Rajasthan and Uttar Pradesh (generally, referred to as 'Bimaru' or 'sick' states). These States share common poor development indicators. The breakthrough requires a steady political as well as administrative will, which sadly has been waxing and waning so far.

Situated in the northwest of India, Rajasthan has become the largest state in the country in terms of area (342,239 sq. km) after the bifurcation of the erstwhile state of Madhya Pradesh into Madhya Pradesh and Chhattisgarh. The present state of Rajasthan was formed in 1956 by integrating the erstwhile Rajasthan and the centrally administrated territory of Ajmer-Marwara. The State is divided into 7 administrative divisions and 32 districts. The districts are further divided into 241 *tehsils*. About 23 per cent of its total population of 56.5 million resides in 222 cities and towns, while the remaining 77 per cent live in 39,753 villages. More than half of the total inhabited villages in the state, have fewer than 500 inhabitants each. The economy of the state reflects not only its geographical diversity but also its historical legacy of feudal social norms. Water is indeed a critical resource because the state, which occupies 10.4 per cent of the total area of the country and has about 5.5 per cent of its population, is endowed with only 1 per cent of the total surface water resources of the country. The groundwater table, owing to scanty and erratic rainfall, is getting deeper and deeper. Agriculture is, thus, still dependent on the vagaries of the monsoon. In terms of Human Development Index (HDI), the State lags behind the country as a whole, with an index value of 37 out of 100 compared to 45 for the country. In short, Rajasthan marked by a complex social structure, a predominantly agrarian economy, difficult and inaccessible terrain, and scattered settlements over a vast area—poses several formidable problems to the population stabilisation efforts.

The main purpose of this chapter is to argue that population dynamics matter in the development agenda of the State and to suggest a mechanism to bring the fertility to replacement level, at the earliest to achieve a stable population before the middle of the century. The discussion may also help the State Government in formulating a comprehensive action plan that addresses issues related to population and development including women's empowerment, gender equity, urbanisation and migration, work participation and growing young population, provision of quality reproductive and child health services, etc.

Apart from the census data on total population, estimates of vital rates derived from the Sample Registration System (SRS) of the Office of the Registrar General, India have also been made use of. The SRS is an annual survey conducted in 350 rural-urban sample units spread all over Rajasthan. The paper has also used the data provided by the National Family Health Surveys conducted in 1992-1993 and 1998-99 (NFHS-1: 1995; NFHS-2: 2001), as well as District Reproductive and Child Health (RCH) Surveys conducted during 2002-2004. The findings of the Coverage Evaluation Survey 2002 (GoI, 2002) are also being made use of.

Emerging Population Scenario

In the last few years, Rajasthan has made remarkable progress in the fields of female literacy, supply of water and electricity and availability of roads and schools. But, its impact is not clearly visible, as the population of the State has increased rapidly. Table 3.1 provides some basic demographic information about India and Rajasthan. With an estimated population of 56.5 million on March 1, 2001, the State has added more than 1.3 million people in the year 2000-01, compared to less than 0.4 million in the year 1956-57 when the present state of Rajasthan came into existence. Rapid population growth in Rajasthan is, thus, a relatively recent phenomenon. After decades of very slow or minimal population growth, the state's population began to increase rapidly in the 1950's as a result of improvements in public health, which contributed to a steep decline in the death rate without a corresponding decline in the birth rate. The pace of population growth since Independence can be gauged by the fact that while it took around six decades to increase from one crore in 1898 to two crore in 1961 (63 years), each successive crore took 16 years (1977), 11 years (1988), 8 years

(1996) and 7 years (2003), respectively. The next crore is expected to be added in 8 years by the year 2011 (Kothari, 1990).

Table 3.1

Socio-Demographic Profile of India and Rajasthan, 2001

Item	*India*	*Rajasthan*
Population (in million)	10,28.6	56.5
Decadal Population Growth Rate 1991-01 (per cent)	21.5	28.4
Sex Ratio (females per thousand males)	933	921
Population Density (persons per sq.km)	324	165
Per cent Urban	27.8	23.4
Literacy Rate Total (per cent)	64.8	60.4
Literacy Rate Male (per cent)	75.3	75.7
Literacy Rate Female (per cent)	53.7	43.9
Crude Birth Rate (births/1000 population)	25.4	31.1
Crude Death Rate (deaths/1000 population)	8.4	8.0
Infant Mortality Rate (infant deaths/1000 births)	66	80

Source: Registrar General of India, Government of India, New Delhi.

The state's population growth is much higher than the national average and this gap has widened in the last few decades. Its population growth rate of 28.4 per cent during the 1990s was around 32 per cent higher than recorded for the country as a whole (21.5 per cent). Out of the 32 districts, only 3 had a lower population growth rate than the national average in the nineties. These are Rajsamand (19.9%), Jhunjhunu (20.9%) and Chittaurgarh (21.5). Further, no change was noticed in the growth rates between the 1981-1991 and the 1991-2001 decades (28.4 per cent versus 28.4 per cent). Furthermore, the population of the State is doubling in less than 28 years. During the first 30 years after the formation of Rajasthan (1951-1981), the population of the state was doubling in 27.5 years; this period came down to 26.8 years in the next 30 years (1981-2001), and this is a worrisome scenario. Also, no significant decline was observed in infant and maternal mortality during the 1990s. In short, no significant improvement was observed on the demographic front in Rajasthan during the nineties in spite of the sizeable increase recorded in female literacy in the corresponding period, as shown in

Table 3.2. As such, the 1990s may be labelled as 'the decade of demographic stability' at an undesirably high level. These emerging trends portend, further, massive increase in population, which Rajasthan appears ill-equipped to deal with. This has serious implications for sustainable development of the State.

Table 3.2

Rajasthan: 'Nineties-Decade (1991-2001) of Demographic Stability' at an Undesirable High Level

Item	*Year*			
	1981	*1991*	*2001*	*2004*
Decadal Population Growth (per cent)	32.4	28.4	28.4	NA
Infant Deaths per 1000 Births (IMR)	108	79	80	67
Births per 1000 Population (CBR)	40	35	31	29
Female Literacy Rate (per cent)	14	20	44	NA

Source: Registrar General of India, GoI.

Reasons behind Demographic Stability

The major reason behind the emerging demographic scenario in Rajasthan may be related to the low utilisation of RCH and Family Planning (FP) services. As per the Coverage Evaluation Survey, 2002 (GoI, 2002), the use of antenatal and postnatal services is very low. Less than 20 per cent of infants were fully immunised, and only 9 per cent of pregnant women received required antenatal care (ANC) in 2002. The corresponding figures for Andhra Pradesh were 72 and 73 per cent, respectively (Table 3.3). Further, around 26 per cent of eligible couples are currently protected by terminal methods (that is, sterilisation), whereas the corresponding figure for Andhra Pradesh is more than 55 per cent. Another important indicator of reproductive healthcare is institutional deliveries. The proportion of institutional deliveries in Rajasthan has increased from 12 per cent in 1992 to 23 per cent in 2002. On the other hand, more than 60 per cent deliveries in Andhra Pradesh were conducted in health institutions. And this had an impact on resulting reproductive health status of population, as shown in Table 3.3.

Table 3.3

Utilisation of RCH and FP Services and Reproductive Health Indicators, 2002

	Rajasthan	Madhya Pradesh	Andhra Pradesh	India
Service Indicators (%)	9	52	73	44
Received Required ANC	9	52	73	44
Fully Immunised Children	20	37	72	57
Institutional Deliveries	23	36	63	49
Couple Protection Rate (1999)	38	42	59	43
Impact Indicators				
Infant Mortality Rate	78	85	62	63
Maternal Mortality Rate (1998)	670	408	159	407
Crude Birth Rate	31	30	21	25
Decadal Growth Rate (1991-2001)	28.4	24.3	14.6	21.5

Source: Coverage Evaluation Survey, 2002 and *SRS*, 2002, GoI.

There are four primary reasons behind the low utilisation of RCH services in Rajasthan. First, the Family Welfare Programme has not been effectively managed. It continues to be a diffused programme, not providing area-specific, need-based and quality services as well as timely follow-up on a large enough scale. Second, not a single Primary Health Centre is providing basic RCH services like abortion, sterilisation and 24-hour delivery services.[3] Third, no systematic efforts have been made to involve NGOs and the private sector in the delivery of services. Finally, the many-faceted population programme, which is impacted by women's literacy status, empowerment, age at marriage, etc. has not been properly implemented and monitored, and thus, is lacking in inter-departmental cooperation. No serious efforts have been made to tackle these issues, although they have been widely discussed.

An effort has been made here to investigate some of the causes behind the poor functioning of the programme on the basis of discussions with officials as well as field level workers and the data collected in recent surveys. During the 1990s, especially after the International Conference on Population and Development (ICPD) in Cairo, many new innovative schemes like target-free approach,

3. There are more than 1,700 Primary Health Centres in Rajasthan as compared to only 1,200 in Andhra Pradesh.

revised RCH package, etc. have been introduced into the programme, but without adequate preparation. One senior programme manager has rightly said, "ICPD Plan of Action assumes that there is already a good service delivery system in place, but the system has many problems. Without trained health personnel and a proper work environment, they cannot effectively deliver reproductive health services to the people who need them." In addition to training, to ensure greater impact, the health workers need support through provision of logistics and supplies, supervision, monitoring and evaluation. One field worker stated, "We have a good infrastructure in the government system, but the weakest part concerns management issues, including supervision and monitoring."

Non-functional organisational structure: The organisational structure of the Department of Medical, Health and Family Welfare in general, and the Directorate of Medical and Health in particular, is hierarchical and vertical, and many of the administrative, programmatic and financial decisions that could be taken at the Zonal or District level are dealt with at the Secretariat or Directorate level in Jaipur. This creates problems at the field level. The existing organisational structure is too unwieldy and complex, and there is the problem of line of command. It also promotes centralisation in decision-making. A simplified organisational structure, based on the functional approach and managed by professionals, is needed to make it truly effective.[4]

Low involvement of panchayati raj institutions: The final responsibility of delivering basic RCH services rests, in particular on the ANM (Auxiliary Nurse Midwife), posted at the Sub-Centre level. The workload of the ANMs is extensive and heavy. It is reported that an ANM is required to perform an amazingly unwieldy number of tasks. In addition, she is supposed to do community work. After the introduction of the *Panchayati Raj* system, the ANMs are expected to work in close collaboration with and under the supervision of the *Gram Panchayats*. However, the jurisdictions of the *Gram Panchayat* and the Sub-Centre do not coincide. And, as such, the role of the *Panchayat* in the supervision of the programme is the minimum.

4. For details, see Kothari, Devendra (2004). "Revamping the Management of Family Welfare Programme in Rajasthan to Increase the Use of Services", *Working Paper*, Rajiv Gandhi Population Mission, Government of Rajasthan, June.

There are more than 9,000 *Gram Panchayats* in Rajasthan while the number of Sub-Centres is around 10,000. Further, frequent periodic campaigns like Pulse Polio generally disturb the daily work routine of the grassroot workers.

Lack of supportive supervision and under utilisation of human resources: It has been pointed out that there is very little supervision of the field workers. The Lady Health Visitor (LHV), posted at the PHC, is expected to supervise the field workers under its jurisdiction. However, her services are not being properly utilised and monitored. Apart from the ANMs, the State Government has initiated a scheme to train a local eligible couple to work as Jan Mangal Couple for 1000 population each. This couple is expected to provide spacing methods under its jurisdiction. A number of Jan Mangal Couples have been trained under the scheme. However, in the absence of proper guidance and supervision, they have not been able to make an effective contribution. As per the evaluation study carried out on behalf of UN Public-Private Alliance for Rural Development (UNPPA), it was found that one Jan Mangal Couple has been able to render services to only six couples in a year. Though the system has sufficient manpower, it is apparently not being properly used. This could be another reason for the limited creativity in decision making throughout the organisation responsible for RCH service delivery

Neglect of urban areas: The health service infrastructure in Rajasthan, as elsewhere in the country, is based on the norms recommended by Government of India (GoI). These norms are applied only to the rural and tribal areas. As such, the urban population does not enjoy the benefits of RCH and FP services as well as the preventive and promotional services provided by the Sub-Centres and PHCs. Since a sizeable population of the urban areas resides in slum areas, there is a need to develop a healthcare system for these areas on the lines of the primary healthcare provided in rural areas.[5] The RCH status in the urban areas of Rajasthan has deteriorated in recent times, as revealed by the findings of NFHS-2. This has been mainly due to the non-availability of services in urban slums. Another major weakness in the current policy framework is

---

5. Under the Urban RCH-II Project of National Rural Health Mission, one tier urban health institute covering a population of 50,000 is being proposed to deliver the basic RCH services in slum areas.

that it has not adequately mobilised the resources of the private sector for RCH care especially in the context of 75 per cent of the provision of general health services taking place in the private sector.

Lack of continuity at the policy making level: A number of innovative programmes were initiated during the nineties.[6] However, they were neither implemented effectively, nor were their continuity maintained and their evaluation done regularly. Further, many of these programmes are prematurely abandoned and, consequently, the desired goals remain unfulfilled. An important reason for this is that the policy makers and managers are frequently changed. Sometimes, they have to face transfers in the midst of a programme and this adversely affects implementation. For example, in the last 10 years, 12 Secretaries to the Government have been appointed to manage the FWP in Rajasthan, while in Andhra Pradesh, only 3 Secretaries have been managing and supervising the programme during the corresponding period. Every new officer tries to change the action plan/strategy according to his/her own thinking.[7] Consequently, these changes in the conduct of the programme and strategy adversely affect its success.

Some Critical Issues

The most important causes of the galloping population growth in Rajasthan are the nearly constant fertility and the rapidly declining mortality. This has a number of implications for Rajasthan's quest for development. Some basic issues are discussed in the following pages:

1. *Increasing role of migration in future population growth:* The population of an area grows or decreases as a result of both natural increase (births minus deaths) and net in-migration (in-migration minus out-migration). The role of in-migration has not been appreciable in Rajasthan in the past, since it was a net out-migration region. However, since 1981, migration

---

6. Some important programmes initiated by the Government of Rajasthan to strengthen the Family Welfare Programme during the nineties are: Raj Laxmi, Vikalp, Jan Mangal, Swastya Karmi, etc.

7. For details, see, "Rajasthan: Action Plan to Achieve Replacement Level Fertility by the Year 2011", Report of the Committee under Chairmanship of the Chief Secretary, Department of Medical, Health and Family Welfare, Government of Rajasthan, August 2003.

from outside has contributed to the growth of the population of the State to some extent. During the 1990s, the State's population increased by 12.5 million; out of this, 93 per cent was contributed by natural increase and the remaining 7 per cent was due to net in-migration. During the 1980s, net in-migration contributed only 5 per cent of the total increase of 9.7 million people, as shown in Table 3.4. It appears that the role of in-migration will be significant in any future population growth of the State. It is estimated that 10-15 per cent of total population growth in Rajasthan during 2001-2011 will be contributed by net in-migration.

Table 3.4

Components of Population Growth in Rajasthan

Item	*Number (in '000)*	*Per Cent*
Net Increase in Population (1981-1991)	9,744	100.0
Increase due to:		
* Natural Increase	9,266	95.1
* Net In-migration	478	4.9
Net Increase in Population (1991-2001)	12,467	100.0
Increase Due to:		
* Natural Increase	11,598	93.0
* Net In-migration	869	7.0

Source: Kothari (2002b).

2. *Baffling sex ratio*: Of the total population in 2001, 29.4 million were males and 27.1 million were females, giving a sex ratio of 921 females per 1000 males, which is lower than the sex ratio observed at the national level (933). The sex ratio has been adverse to females, and it has declined from 921 in 1951 to 910 in 1991. Thus, an increase in the sex ratio was one of the positive findings of the 2001 Census. However, the sudden rise of 11 females for every 1000 males needs critical analysis. On the other hand, the sex ratio of the child population in the age group of 0-6 years has declined from 916 female children for every 1000 male children in 1991 to 909 in 2001. Thus, out of a little over 10.6 million children in the age group of 0-6 years, the number of girls is less by almost half a million.

Though it may be a welcome sign that the number of females for every 1000 males has gone up in the total population, it is baffling to note that the number of young girls has gone down. It is interesting to note that the juvenile sex ratio has declined much more in the relatively developed and literate districts of the State as compared to the less developed ones. For example, the sex ratio declined sharply in the developed and relatively more literate district of Sri Ganganagar from 895 in 1991 to 850 in 2001. On the other hand, it declined from 975 to 964 in Banswara—the least literate district in the State.

3. *Significant increase in female literacy but slow progress in women's autonomy*: The State registered the highest growth in literacy among the major States of the country with its literacy rate going up from 38 per cent in 1991 to 60 per cent in 2001. An impressive hike of 24 percentage points in female literacy from 20 per cent in 1991 to 44 per cent in 2001 was also reported. The increase in the overall literacy rate is due to persistent efforts by the State Government to enroll and retain children in schools and to effectively implement adult education programmes. Rajasthan has made significant progress in literacy in recent years, as has also been reported by the 53rd Round of NSSO in 1997 and National Family Health Survey conducted in the year 1998-99.

   In spite of a significant jump in the female literacy, its impact has not been seen in the improvement in women's autonomy measured in terms of decision-making roles within the family and community. Women's autonomy can have a significant impact on the health seeking behaviour of women by altering their relative control over fertility and contraceptive use, and by influencing their attitudes and abilities. To measure women's autonomy and empowerment more directly, the National Family Health Survey, conducted in the State as part of the national exercise in 1998-99, asked about women's participation in household decision-making, their freedom of movement, and access to money that they could spend as they wished. As per the findings of NFHS-2, 82 per cent are involved in decisions about cooking, 41 per cent in decisions about their own health care, and 39 per cent in decisions about going to stay with parents. Regarding freedom of movement, 81 per cent of women need permission to go to the market, and 83 per cent need permission to visit relatives and friends. It is interesting to note that the proportion involved in any decision-making does not vary substantially by residence, education, religion or caste. Further, a comparison with other States of India indicates that Rajasthan has a consistently poor record on all the indicators of decision-making. In this connection, one should note that Rajasthan recorded the highest unwanted fertility in the country. High level of unwanted pregnancies leads to powerlessness and this, in turn, engenders lack of empowerment and autonomy.

4. *Slow but uneven progress in urbanisation*: Urbanisation is a process of great demographic significance. It transfers population to a very different physical, social and economic environment. The proportion of urban population to total population in Rajasthan is relatively low, as it is only 23.4 per cent. It is also increasing at a very slow pace. In 2001, more than 57 per cent of the urban population of Rajasthan lived in 20 Class I cities with 100,000 and more population. The proportion of the urban population living in the six regional urban centres was around 40 per cent. However, around 20 per cent of the State's urban population was enumerated in Jaipur alone. Except for Jaipur and Ajmer[8], the rate of population growth in the nineties as compared to eighties has declined significantly in the other regional urban centres, as shown in Table 3.5. This sort of urbanisation will create regional imbalances.

5. *Little change in early marriage regime*: Another important aspect of the demography of Rajasthan is the low age at marriage, though there is strong evidence of a rising age at first marriage. Marriage is virtually universal in Rajasthan and the marriages, especially in rural areas, take place at relatively young ages. About half of the married women aged 25-49 in 1999 had married before they were 15 and about four-fifths of them had married before reaching 18 years, the legal

8. The increased level of population growth in Ajmer city during the nineties was mainly due to the expansion of city boundaries.

Table 3.5

Imbalances in Population Growth of Major Regional Cities of Rajasthan

Cities	*Population (in lakh)*	*Decadal Population Growth (in per cent)*	
		1981-1991	*1991-2001*
Jaipur	23.2	50	60
Jodhpur	8.6	32	28
Kota	7.0	50	31
Bikaner	5.3	45	27
Ajmer	4.9	07	22
Udaipur	3.9	33	26

Source: Census of India 2001.

minimum age at marriage. In Rajasthan, the median age at first marriage is 15.1 years, and the median age at first cohabitation with husband is 16.4 years (NFHS-2: 2001). It is estimated that the child-wives in the State produced around 2 lakh children in 1998-99. This contributes not only to the high fertility rate but also to the risk associated with early childbearing as well as child survival. One important consequence of low age at marriage is the large proportion of married females in the reproductive age group (15-49). Over 90 per cent of females in these age groups are currently married as against only 70 per cent in Tamil Nadu. It means that the Family Welfare Programme has to serve more clients per worker in Rajasthan as compared to Tamil Nadu.

Although, there is a growing awareness of the risks and disadvantages of early marriages in Rajasthan, in many cases the mother's own sense of social and economic vulnerability leads her to conclude that her daughter's best chance in life depends on an 'early' marriage rather than a 'late' one. An increase in the age at marriage is possible only when there are major changes in social values and attitudes towards the girl child. If women in Rajasthan and elsewhere were afforded more rights and economic opportunities—allowing them to survive outside of marriage—parents might be more inclined to view alternative options to early marriage for their daughters. Girls' education should continue to be encouraged and supported economically, through scholarships and other kinds of assistance, especially for girls from the most disadvantage families. Microcredit and other programmes that create economic opportunities for women should be given priority. Continued efforts are needed to further support and legitimise women's presence in the public sector. In short, those programmes and activities should be promoted, which attempt to bring women out of their homes.[9]

6. *Growing young population and shrinking employment opportunities*: The age structure of Rajasthan's population is young. Around three-fifths of the total population is under 25 years of age and over 18 per cent are between 15 and 24 years. The proportion of the population in this age group is increasing fast. They have special needs for healthcare and education, including the very important area of sexual and reproductive health. In the year 2001, slightly less than one million young people reached the age of 21 and they need employment, etc. The corresponding figure for the year 2011 would be around 15 million (Table 3.6). The policy makers have to take this growing segment of the population into account while framing the socioeconomic policies of the state.

Table 3.6

Increasing Number of Young Persons in Rajasthan

(Figures in lakh)

Year	*Number of Persons in Age Group 20-24 Years*	*Number of Persons Attaining 21 Years of Age*
1961	26.2	05.2
1991	36.4	07.3
2001	47.2	09.4
2011*	74.3	14.9

Note : Calculations are based on data obtained from Census of India.
* Projected figure.

Source : For details see, Kothari (2002b).

9. Kothari, Devendra (2006). "Slow Progress at the Women Empowerment in Rajasthan: An Analysis", *FPA Working Paper*, Forum for Population Action.

The Census of India collects information about 'workers'[10] and 'non-workers'. The strength of the workers and the non-workers has a vital bearing on economic planning and development. Out of the total population of 56.5 million as per the 2001 Census, 30.9 per cent are main workers, 11.2 per cent are marginal workers and the remaining 57.9 per cent are non-workers. As between the two sexes, it is pertinent to note that among males, 43.8 per cent are main workers, 6.3 per cent marginal workers and the remaining 49.9 per cent the non-workers. Of the total female population of the state, 16.8 per cent constitute main workers and 16.6 per cent marginal workers. The bulk of the female population (66.5 per cent) constitutes non-workers. Thus, the participation of females in economic activity appears to be on a very modest scale.

The proportion of main workers has shown a fluctuating trend from 1981 to 2001. It increased from 30. 5 per cent in 1981 to 31.6 per cent and then declined to 30.9 per cent in 2001. Table 3.7 shows that male main workers have shown a continuous decreasing trend. From 49.9 per cent in 1981 they declined to 48.5 per cent in 1991 and further to 43.7 per cent in 2001. This sharp decline in the proportion of male workers in the nineties needs critical analysis. On the contrary, the proportion of female main workers has shown a continuously

Table 3.7

Trends in Work Participation of Main Workers in Rajasthan

Year	*Main Workers (Per Cent of Total Population)*		
	Total	*Males*	*Females*
1981	30.5	49.9	09.3
1991	31.6	48.5	13.0
2001	30.9	43.7	16.8

Source: Census of India 2001.

10. The *Census of India* has classified workers as Main and Marginal Workers. The main workers are those who had worked six month or more in a given reference year, while marginal workers are those who had worked for less than six months in the reference period.

increasing trend from 1981 to 2001. Recent trends in work participation rates indicate that Rajasthan may face an unemployment crisis in the coming years. As such, the repeated argument that the large young population is an asset to India or State like Rajasthan needs reexamination.

How to Forge Ahead

To address the issue of rapid population growth, the Government of Rajasthan formulated a State-specific Population Policy in 2000. It was launched on January 20, 2000 (GoR, 2000). The main aim of the policy is to attain the replacement level fertility by 2016. Even as efforts were being initiated to implement the policy, the results of the 2001 Census presented a dreadful scenario before the Government. These figures revealed that the population growth rate, which was 28.44 per cent in the decade 1981-1991, had remained 28.41 per cent in the decade 1991-2001, meaning thereby that there had been no decrease during the nineties. This situation puts a big question mark on the success of the efforts made for bringing down the population growth and other vital rates. Keeping in view this grim situation, and in order to achieve the goal of the population policy without any further delay, the State Government constituted the Rajiv Gandhi Population Mission in June 2001 under the Chairmanship of the Chief Minister. Under this Mission, the need for a detailed and time-bound action plan for improving the health of the people of the State and to achieve the goal of population stabilisation was recognised. In the first meeting of the Mission (20.8.2001), the results of the 2001 Census were discussed at length and it was decided to find out the reasons for the high population growth rate as well as the lack of decrease in the maternal and infant mortality rates. In the second meeting of the Mission (17.9.2002), the identified reasons for the population growth were discussed and it was decided that the total fertility rate of 2.1 children per woman should be achieved by 2011 and not by 2016, so that the process of population stabilisation might start earlier. The strategy to achieve this target was also discussed. New targets were put before the third meeting, and it was decided to achieve the new targets by 2011. For this purpose, it was decided to constitute a Committee under the chairmanship of the Chief

Secretary.[11] The Committee, comprising Secretaries of the concerned departments as members, was to evolve an action plan to achieve the goal of population stabilisation at the earliest (GoR, 2003). The revised goals are presented in Table 3.8. One can argue that the goals are ambitious. However, looking at the favourable prevailing conditions and recent efforts, the State can achieve the replacement level fertility by 2011, as will be discussed shortly.

Table 3.8

Rajasthan: Revised Population Policy Goals to be Achieved by 2011

Indicator	*1999*	*2002*	*2008*	*2011*
Total Fertility Rate	3.8	3.6	2.6	2.1
Crude Birth Rate	31.1	30.3	26.5	21.0
Maternal Mortality Rate	670	630	379	285
Infant Mortality Rate	80	78	62.	56
Contraceptive Prevalence Rate	38	39	53	65

Source : Government of Rajasthan (2003). *Rajasthan: Action Plan to Achieve Replacement Level Fertility.*

Knowledge of family planning is nearly universal in Rajasthan. The National Family Health Surveys (NFHS) and others have revealed that almost all women in the 15-49 years age group know about at least one modern family planning method. In spite of poverty and illiteracy, the prevailing unmet need for family planning services is surprising. The state has at present about 11 million eligible couples. Of these, about 2 million are such that they either not want any more children or want to wait for two or more years before having another child, and yet are not using any means of family planning. Further, the percentage of mothers giving birth to unplanned births in 1992-93 (NFHS-1, 1995) was 14 per cent and it increased to 16 per cent in 1998-99 (NFHS-2, 2001). This means around 0.3 million unplanned births take place every year in Rajasthan.[12] But,

11. At that time, the author was the Director of the Rajiv Gandhi Population Mission, Government of Rajasthan, and he was also appointed as the Member-Secretary of the Committee.

12. As per the latest estimates, around 1.75 million children are born each year in Rajasthan.

these figures do not reveal the complete picture as to what percentage of couples are having unwanted fertility, because the above figures are based on a questionnaire administered to only those couples that had newborn children during the previous three years. To cope with this problem, during the National Family Health Survey, all the eligible couples were asked as to how many children they have/had (total fertility or actual fertility) and how many children they wanted (wanted fertility or desired fertility). According to the survey, this percentage was 23 in 1992-93, but had increased to 32 per cent in 1998-99, and it is the highest in the country. This means that out of the total births in the State, 32 are unwanted. Some may not believe these figures, but the data on induced abortions in the State are equally surprising. Statistics of the Medical and Health Directorate of the Government of Rajasthan reveal that more than 50,000 MTP (Medical Termination of Pregnancy) cases are recorded each year. It is also true that for every legal termination of pregnancy (MTP), there are about 10 illegal ones (Khan *et al.*, 1999). People in the State are using termination of pregnancy as a means of family planning, which is reprehensible as illegal termination of pregnancy increases the chances of maternal mortality. Table 3.9 shows that Rajasthan has the highest unwanted fertility, the third highest unmet need for contraception and the fourth highest 4+ birth order mothers among the major States of India having population 25 million and more.

Thus, the strategic approach must focus on meeting the unmet need for family planning services and avoiding unwanted pregnancies. For this, there is an urgent need to revamp the management of service delivery system, especially that of the public health units. The experiences of countries, such as Bangladesh, Thailand, Indonesia, etc., support this argument. Even within the country, Tamil Nadu and Andhra Pradesh provide excellent examples where, in spite of a difficult socioeconomic climate, a breakthrough in fertility has been achieved by improving the management of the service delivery system. Rajasthan's own experience during the implementation of the Vikalp framework in Tonk and Dausa districts has revealed that by orienting the management of the Family Welfare Programme towards the needs of clients, desired results could be achieved (Kothari *et al.*, 1997; Lubhaya, 1998). Thus, an

Table 3.9

Levels of Unwanted Births, Unmet Need for Contraception and 4+ Births Order Mothers in Some Selected States of India, 1998-99

Major States	*Number of Unwanted Births per Woman*		*Per Cent of Couples with Unmet Need for Contraception*		*Per Cent of Mothers with Birth Order 4+*	
	Number	*All India Rank*	*Per cent*	*All India Rank*	*Per cent*	*All India Rank*
Rajasthan	1.21	1	17.6	3	34.8	4
Uttar Pradesh	1.16	2	25.1	1	39.9	1
Madhya Pradesh	0.91	3	16.2	4	35.0	3
Bihar	0.91	4	24.5	2	37.3	2
INDIA	0.72	-	15.8	-	27.5	
Karnatak	0.57	9	11.5	7	18.8	7
Tamil Nadu	0.48	10	13.0	5	09.1	11
Andhra Pradesh	0.37	11	07.7	9	15.0	10
Kerala	0.15	12	11.7	6	06.7	12

Source: NFHS-2 (2000).

essential requirement of the Family Welfare Programme is to ensure that RCH services, including contraceptive services, are available to the people, especially those who are interested, in terms of distance, convenience and quality.

In the current framework the public sector health units offer the best channel to reach men and women that need RCH care services in small towns and rural areas of Rajasthan as elsewhere in the country, as they exist throughout the State (Table 3.10). Most of these units, however, are grossly under-utilised. Reasons for this under-utilisation of services in particular, include non-availability of required medical and nursing staff, dearth of trained providers, non-availability/non functioning of essential equipment, instruments and operation theatres, poor quality of care and inadequate and limited availability of the required services in the rural settings. For example, the Community Health Centres provides specialised medical care in the form of facilities of Surgeons, Obstetricians & Gynecologists, Physicians and Pediatricians. Table 3.11 indicates that

Table 3.10

Average Population, Villages, and Radial Distance Covered by a Public Health Unit in Rajasthan and India, 2004

Public Health Unit	*Average Rural Population Covered by Per Unit*	*Average Number of Villages Covered by Per Unit*	*Average Radial Distance Covered by Per Unit (in kms.)*
Community Health Centres (CHCs)	145,277 (230,444)	139 (198)	18.9 (17.5)
Primary Health Centres (PHCs)	25,846 (32,123)	25 (28)	8.0 (6.5)
Sub-centres	4,361 (5,204)	4 (5)	3.3 (2.6)

Note: Figures in parentheses are for India

Source: Bulletin on Rural Health Statistics in India, 2005, MoHFW, GoI.

there is a shortfall of 606 specialists at the CHCs in 2005 in Rajasthan as compared to the requirement on the basis of existing norms. The problem is further compounded by social and cultural stigma as well as the fact that a sizeable proportion of the eligible couples remain unaware of the availability of the safe and legal services provided by such public health units. In addition, no systematic efforts have so far been made to involve NGOs and the private sector in strengthening public sector health units and service delivery system. As such, an earnest effort should be made in this direction.

Table 3.11

Manpower Shortfall at Community Health Centres in Rajasthan, 2004

Specialist	*Specialists at Community Health Centres**		
	Required	*In position*	*Shortfall*
Surgeons	298	196	102
Gynecologists	298	114	184
Physicians	298	198	100
Pediatricians	298	78	220
Total Specialists at CHCs	**1192**	**586**	**606**

Note: * Specialists include surgeons, Gynecologists, physicians, pediatricians, etc.

Source: Bulletin on Rural Health Statistics in India 2005, MoHFW, GoI.

Further, looking to the volume and nature of the efforts involved in achieving the replacement level fertility by 2011 and the State's fiscal situation, it is high time that the Government of Rajasthan recognises the role of the private and NGOs sectors in the delivery of RCH and family planning services. An effort should be made to develop an effective and equitable public-private mix in the delivery of RCH and family planning services. For this, the State Government should shift some of its expenditure from the public sector to the private sector. A number of legal, regulatory and quality assurance issues will also need to be resolved before the concept of such partnership could be developed and implemented successfully. In addition, there is an urgent need to take regional variations into account while developing the action plans to bridge the gap. This calls for comprehensive but sharply focused area-specific plans. If this is done, it will not be difficult to convert the existing and future unmet need into demand, thus paving the way for achieving the Replacement Level Fertility by 2011.

Discussion and Conclusion

As per the latest SRS figures, Rajasthan has achieved a significant breakthrough in fertility and infant mortality. The birth rate has declined from 30.3 births per 1000 population in 2003 to 29 in 2004. Similarly, infant mortality rate declined from 75 per 1000 births to 67 during the corresponding period. Such a sharpest decline has been recorded first time in the history of the Family Welfare Programme in the state. Table 3.12 indicates that the State of Rajasthan recorded the highest decline in birth and infant mortality rates in one-year period among the major states of India with special reference to BIMARU states. Though the rate of mothers dying per one lakh births in Rajasthan has reduced from 677 in the year 1997 to 445 in 2003, the State still has a high maternal mortality ratio as compared to the national average of 301.

If one can maintain the tempo, the target of achieving replacement level fertility that is Crude Birth Rate of 21 with infant mortality of 56 and maternal mortality ratio of 285, as targeted by the year 2011 does not look far-fetched. It is important, therefore, to design a suitable strategy to reach these goals. Achieving replacement level fertility is a prerequisite for promoting sustainable development

Table 3.12

Rajasthan and BIMARU States: Recent Trends in Vital Rates

State	Crude Birth Rate Per 1000 Population			Infant Mortality Rate Per 1000 Births		
	2003	2004	Difference	2003	2004	Differnce
Rajasthan	30.3	29.0	-1.3	75	67	-8
Bihar	30.7	30.2	-0.5	60	61	+1
MP	30.2	29.8	-0.4	82	79	-3
UP	31.3	30.8	-0.5	76	72	-4
India	24.8	24.1	-0.7	60	58	-2

Source: SRS Bulletin 2006, GoI.

with more equitable distribution. However, it is as much a function of making reproductive and child health (RCH) care accessible and affordable for all, as of increasing the provision and outreach of primary and secondary education, extending basic amenities including sanitation, safe drinking water and housing, besides empowering women and enhancing their employment opportunities as well as increasing their age at marriage. As such, any action plan has to place the major emphasis on the following:

- Preventing early marriages.
- Improving utilisation of RCH services, including promotion of institutional deliveries and follow ups.
- Placing greater emphasis on female literacy, and
- Enlarging representation of females in the wage employment.

All these will help Rajasthan to reduce the level of unmet need for contraception or level of unwanted fertility. In many states of India with high levels of demand satisfaction, unwanted fertility typically equals only around 0.5 birth per woman (Table 3.9). For example, total unwanted fertility in Tamil Nadu (0.48 per woman), Andhra Pradesh (0.37) and Kerala (0.15) is less than half, and this finding gives an indication of the proportion of reductions in unwanted fertility that is possible. If that is the case, unwanted fertility in Rajasthan (1.21 births per woman) could probably be reduced by more than half.

As such, action is urgently needed in expanding the use of services in order to reduce unwanted fertility as well as infant and maternal mortality. The use of services cannot be improved significantly unless these are easily available with quality. The way, the family welfare programme is being currently managed, is inadequate to meet the unmet need and the increasing demand for services. It may be possible to make some improvements through some cosmetic changes in the programme management, but achieving a breakthrough will be difficult with this network. We have to accept that the network/ system, which has failed to deliver results in the last 10 years or so, will not be able to face new challenges. Therefore, Rajasthan must address the overall management of its reproductive and child health care system. The key action areas, therefore, are:

- Reducing the travel barriers the clients face by providing comprehensive quality RCH services, including abortion, conventional sterilisation, twenty four-hour delivery services, etc., at least at one-third of the Primary health Centres[13] within one year by involving the private sector/NGOs as 'facilitator' on BOT (Build, Operate and Transfer) basis with financial assistance in a project mode.[14]
- Identifying couples that need services by name and providing services looking at their needs, and strengthening monitoring and accountability systems.
- Tailoring every policy response designed to address the population issue to the circumstances of the individual district in general and the levels of unwanted fertility in particular. That is preparing district-based annual action

13. Andhra Pradesh has achieved the breakthrough on demographic and reproductive and child health front by operationalising 470 PHCs known as Round-the-Clock Centers (RTC-PHC). In these Centres services like abortion, sterilisation, 24-hour delivery, etc., are available.

14. On the invitation of the Ministry of Health and Family Welfare, Government of India, the author along with his colleagues at the Parivar Seva Sanstha made a presentation at the Nirman Bhawan, New Delhi on May 26, 2006 as how to involve the private sector as 'facilitator' in improving the delivery of RCH and FP services at the public institutions like Primary Health Centres and Community Health Centres. For further details, see "Sajhedari (partnership) Framework: Improving the Utilisation of Reproductive and Child Health (RCH) Care Services in the Poor Performing States by 'Operationalising' the Public Sector Health Units."

plans by involving district officials and ensuring the participation of the District Collectors in monitoring the programme performance.

- Creating a positive atmosphere for a planned family and behavioural change by adopting area-specific communication policy.
- Generating political and administrative support for the programme in order to get the desired importance and visibility. Monitoring by the Chief Minister and the Chief Secretary will produce desirable results, as has been seen in Andhra Pradesh.

In conclusion, it is argued that there is a need to go beyond the prevailing notion that socioeconomic development is an essential precondition for fertility transition, since it provided only a partial explanation for the monumental changes taking place in fertility behaviour, especially in low-income economies. Evidence suggests the importance of management variables as well. Systematic application of modern management principles is, thus necessary in the implementation of population stabilisation programmes. In recent years, these have occupied a more prominent place in explanation of fertility decline (Kothari and Krishnaswamy, 2003). Although the population scenario in Rajasthan is not encouraging, population stabilisation is not impossible. By strengthening the programmes being conducted in the State at present and putting into practice the suggestions made above, the goal of replacement level fertility can be achieved by 2011. This does not require too much by way of resources, but reorientation of programme management. If we achieve this goal, the population of the State as per the 2051 Census will be around 85 million. Otherwise, it will be around 120 million, as shown in Table 3.13.

We now cite the examples of Tamil Nadu and Andhra Pradesh in the field of population stabilisation. In the same manner, Rajasthan can become a role model to other States, particularly in north India. Rajasthan can prove that, in spite of poverty and illiteracy, the goal of population stabilisation could be achieved by improving the reproductive health status with the help of a proper action plan with political, administrative and technical support. In short, the dream of

Table 3.13

Rajasthan: Expected Trends in Population

(Figures in million)

Year	*If Current Trends Continue*	*If Replacement Level Fertility is Achieved by 2011*
2001	56.5	56.5
2011	70.2	67.8
2021	84.3	76.3
2031	96.8	81.5
2041	107.5	84.5
2051	116.2	86.2

Source: Kothari (2002a).

bringing Rajasthan under the category of a 'modern state' can become a reality only when the process of socioeconomic development goes hand in hand with the goal of population stabilisation under the wider context of reproductive health.

References

Bongaarts, John (2006). "The Causes of Stalling Fertility", *Studies in Family Planning*, Vol. 37 (1), pp.1-16.

Gavin, W. Jones (2005). "Why are Population and Development Issues not Given Priority?" *Asia-Pacific Population Journal*, Vol. 20 (10), pp.5-9.

Government of India (GoI) (1996). "Population Projections for India and States, 1996-2016", *Report of the Technical Group on Population Projections*, Registrar General India, New Delhi.

———. (2000). *National Population Policy 2000*, Department of Family Welfare, Government of India, New Delhi.

———. (2002). *National Report: Coverage Evaluation Survey*, Department of Family Welfare, Government of India, New Delhi.

GoR (2000). *Population Policy for Rajasthan*, Government of Rajasthan.

———. (2003). *Rajasthan: Action Plan to Achieve Replacement Level Fertility*, Department of Medical, Health and Family Welfare Government of Rajasthan.

NFHS-1 (1995). *Rajasthan: National Family Health Survey, 1992-93*, International Institute for Population Sciences, Mumbai.

NFHS-2 (2001). *Rajasthan: National Family Health Survey, 1998-99*, International Institute for Population Sciences.

Khan, M.E. *et al.* (1999). "Abortion in India: Current Situation and Future Challenges", in Saroj Pauchori (ed.), *Implementing a Reproductive Health Agenda in India*, Population Council, New Delhi , pp.495-518.

Kothari, Devendra (1990). "Growing Population in Rajasthan: Some Emerging Issues", *IIHMR Occasional Paper* No. 1, Indian Institute of Health Management Research, Jaipur.

———. (2002a). "Rajasthan: Emerging Population Scenario and Agenda for Population Stabilisation", *FPA Occasional Paper* No. 1, Forum for Population Action, Jaipur.

———. (2002b). "Population Projections for Rajasthan and Districts: 2002-2011", *FPA Occasional Paper* No. 3, Indian Institute of Health Management Research and Forum for Population Action, Jaipur.

———. (2003). "The State of Population in Rajasthan", in C.D. Wadhva, B.N. Saxena and O.P. Sharma (eds.), *Population Stabilisation through District Action Plans*, APH Publishing House, New Delhi, pp.265-98.

———. (2004). "Revamping the Management of Family Welfare Programme in Rajasthan to Increase the Use of Services", *Working Paper*, Rajiv Gandhi Population Mission, Government of Rajasthan, pp.1-23.

Kothari, Devendra, R.M. Maru *et al.* (1997). "Vikalp: Managing Family Planning Programme in the Post-ICPD Era: An Experiment in Rajasthan", *IIHMR Occasional Paper* No.2, Indian Institute of Health Management Research, Jaipur.

Kothari, Devendra and S. Krishnaswamy (2003). "Poverty, Family Planning and Fertility vis-a vis Management of Family Planning Services in India: A Case Study", in Maria Eugenia Cosio-Zavala (ed.), *Poverty, Fertility and Family Planning*, CICRED, Paris. pp.335-58.

Lubhaya, Ram (1998). "Target-free Approach for Family Welfare: A Review of Experiences in Rajasthan", *Targets for Family Planning in India: An Analysis of Policy Change, Consequences, and Alternative Choices*, The Futures Group International, New Delhi.

4

Labour, Employment and Poverty

SARTHI ACHARYA and VIDYA SAGAR

Introduction

Up to the early-mid 1980s, Rajasthan exhibited slow progress on almost all economic and social indicators. A mere three per cent annual rise in gross state domestic product (GSDP) resulted in almost no growth in per capita income. Poverty levels were high and maintained above 40-45 per cent of the population for most part of these three decades. Naturally, one would not expect the structure of labour force or its quality to have improved.

Since the 1980s, the state began to improve upon its economic and social performance. Economic growth rates rose to about 5.5-6 per cent annually over 1980-2006 (per capita income has risen by more than twice in the last two decades), the share of agriculture in state GDP fell to about 20 per cent from 45-50 per cent earlier, poverty proportions noticeably reduced to less than 15 per cent in 1999-2000, infrastructure began to grow, urbanisation set in rapidly, and so on.[1]

Experiences from the Far Eastern and Southeast Asian countries, which have experienced relatively higher growth rates and greater penetration of market forces, suggest that with rapid and market-led growth, labour markets tend to mature. It implies that wage and salary earners tend to become proportionately larger and unpaid family labour progressively diminishes. Next, female labour participation increases as women get released from low productivity household activities. Third, excessive preponderance (underemployment) of workers in the peasant sector reduces. Finally, there is greater parity in productivity across sectors (Jose, 1989).

1. See Sagar (2005) for details.

Has the labour structure here too undergone some transformation and the labour market become more mature? This is the basic question that this paper tries to answer.

It must be borne in mind, however, that the East Asian experiences could be quite different from those in South Asia because the structural rigidity in the work force here (due to caste structure and higher conservativeness) and relatively high capital intensity, have permitted only a limited (and regionally concentrated) impact of economic dynamism on labour and society; hence, it might be difficult to expect a near parallel experience in the two settings. The question then is, to what extent has Rajasthan's work force structure been influenced?

The chapter is presented in five sections: the introduction describes the layout of the paper; section 2 explains labour participation rates in a temporal context as seen from NSS and census data; section 3 discusses the status and sectoral distribution of the work force, again at in temporal context; section 4 provides a brief on poverty trends; section 5 puts forth models for explaining trends in agricultural wages on the one hand, and individual earnings behaviour of wage and self-employed workers on the other; and section 6 concludes the paper with a note on changes and continuities.

Labour Participation Rates

The National Sample Survey Organisation (NSSO) deploys three methods to define labour participation rates. By the usual status (US), a person is defined to be in the work force—working or unemployed—if s/he has worked or is looking for work for a relatively long period of time (say, six months). If a person works or is available for a smaller period, say 120 days s/he is considered to be a subsidiary worker. The second definition is the current status: activity in the last one week (CWS). If a person works or is available for even one hour in the week preceding the interview, s/he is netted into the labour force. The third definition requires counting the number of days (actually, ½ days) worked (or for which a person is available), to determine the participation rate (CDS).

Table 4.1
Work Participation Rates by Years and Different Criteria, as seen from NSS

		Rural				*Urban*			
			Main +				*Main +*		
	Year	*US*	*Sub*	*CWS*	*CDS*	*US*	*Sub*	*CWS*	*CDS*
Men	1993-94	52.7	54.0	52.6	51.9	48.3	49.0	48.4	47.9
	1999-00	49.6	50.0	48.6	48.0	48.3	48.6	47.7	47.1
	2003-04	50.0	50.7	47.6	46.0	51.5	52.0	49.9	48.5
Women	1993-94	29.9	45.7	38.7	33.7	10.9	16.3	14.2	12.2
	1999-00	27.2	38.8	32.7	28.2	9.3	13.8	10.8	9.4
	2003-04	24.9	37.8	30.1	22.7	8.7	12.3	10.6	9.0

Source: NSS data, various round reports.

Table 4.1 shows work participation rates in Rajasthan obtained from the three rounds of NSS (50th, 55th and 60th)[2] for rural and urban areas according to the said three criteria. The usual status category is further divided into main and (main + subsidiary) work. Work participation rates of male workers, as per the usual status, have more or less remained unchanged overtime, though there appears to be a small drop in the participation rate between 1993-1994 and the later years (in rural areas), and a slight rise (in urban areas). For women workers, there is a visible drop in the work participation rate over time. When seen through the CWS criterion, fall in work participation rates is witnessed in rural areas (male and female). In urban areas, while male workers show no visible change in participation overtime, female workers do show a fall. Participation rates seen through CDS suggest similar trends as CWS.

Two points emerge from these data: one, proportions engaged as subsidiary workers, particularly among women workers are large—to the extent of 27-30 per cent in both rural and urban areas—though this proportion has been reducing over time. It is widely believed that subsidiary work results from seasonality in work—subsistence agriculture—and management of 'double burden'. When subsistence

2. The 60th Round (2003-04) is a based on thin sample, and as of now, only the first two round data have been published. However, since the thin sample this time is 40 per cent of the full sample and also that no major disaggregation is being made, it is believed that comparison is permissible.

agriculture begins to lose its centrality, the extent of subsidiary work tends to somewhat fall. This is probably what has been happening. Alternately, feminisation of agriculture, as has been discussed subsequently, may explain decline in female subsidiary workers. As men increasingly go out of agriculture, women get more opportunity to work regularly, thereby substituting their subsidiary worker status with the main worker status.

Next, there is a marginal reduction in participation rates, probably on account of some younger persons opting for a little more education.

Table 4.2

Work Participation Rates by Years, as seen from Census 1991 and 2001

	Year	*Main Workers*		*Main Plus Subsidiary Workers*	
		Male	*Female*	*Male*	*Female*
Rural	1991	48.91	15.59	49.88	32.77
	2001	43.70	19.99	50.82	30.71
Urban	1991	46.11	5.57	46.38	7.13
	2001	44.15	6.22	47.64	9.24

Source: Census of India, 1991 and 2001

Work participation rates, obtained from the Census of India for 1991 and 2001 (Table 4.2), show proportions similar to those obtained from NSS, as in Table 4.1. Three observations: work participation rates of workers have reduced in some categories while increased in others over 1991-2001, but in none of the categories is there a big change. Next, subsidiary workers are large in proportions, particularly females in rural areas, though this proportion has reduced somewhat over the decade. Finally, rural female work participation is considerably higher in rural areas compared to urban.

A comparison of work participation rates from the two data sets suggests that there is similarity of ratios and proportions obtained from the two, though the exact magnitudes might be somewhat dissimilar owing to definitional and coverage differences. Next, there is high volatility in the capture of women workers in the work force, a reflection of the amorphous nature of their work. Surely, if market conditions were more firmly set, this volatility would be smaller. Last, the rural-urban gap in female work participation is large. This is a reflection of large scale prevalence of subsistence-type work that women are occupied with, in rural areas; which they are unable to find in urban areas. Put alternatively, women choose to work or get work only in subsistence/peasant kinds of set-ups in rural areas, but their skills are not good enough for them to fetch similar jobs in urban areas; hence the rural-urban gap.

Age-specific participation in the work force, presented in Table 4.3, suggests that among women, maximum participation occurs in the age groups 35-49 years, peaking in the age group 40-44. This is the bracket in which women have crossed the reproductive and child care age, though are yet not too old to work—in rural areas women aged around 40 years often have grown-up children.

Table 4.3

Age-specific Usual Principal Worker to Population Ratios

	Age Groups												
	0-4	*5-9*	*10-14*	*15-19*	*20-24*	*25-29*	*30-34*	*35-39*	*40-44*	*45-49*	*50-54*	*55-59*	*60 & above*
Rural													
Female													
1999-00	-	3.5	18.3	33.1	41.8	45.6	49.8	48.0	52.0	49.4	40.8	38.0	17.7
1993-94	-	6.3	29.2	41.1	41.5	44.0	47.8	49.6	50.6	48.6	45.5	42.4	35.9
Male													
1999-00	-	1.4	11.0	49.0	89.7	95.8	98.9	98.2	98.8	99.1	95.8	93.6	63.0
1993-94	-	2.4	11.8	56.4	89.9	97.4	98.5	98.6	98.8	99.0	97.4	95.6	62.1
Urban													
Female													
1999-00	-	0.3	3.8	5.8	9.8	10.7	18.9	19.4	24.7	19.0	21.2	17.6	4.9
1993-94	-	1.1	5.4	7.3	11.8	16.4	17.8	19.8	28.8	24.4	20.1	16.7	12.5
Male													
1999-00	-	0.6	4.6	29.9	64.9	90.5	98.3	97.7	97.7	98.6	89.3	80.2	34.5
1993-94	-	0.2	4.3	34.5	70.0	91.8	98.6	98.3	98.0	96.7	94.0	81.6	67.6

Source: NSS, 50th and 55th Rounds.

A key observation pertains to the contrast of work participation rates between 1993-94 and 1999-00.[3] In rural areas, there has been a pronounced fall in participation in the age groups 10-14 and 15-19 years for women and in the age group 15-19, particularly for men.

While one might believe that consistent campaigns against child labour might have helped in some reduction in the younger age groups working, a reduction of more than 10 percentage points in five years is a bit intriguing. Equivalent numbers in urban areas also suggest reduction in participation rates, though the magnitudes are smaller.

It is possible to explain a part of such drop in participation rates due to a substantial increase in secondary school enrolment. The *Progress Report on Secondary Education in Rajasthan* shows an enrolment of 13 lakh boys and 5.7 lakh girls in the age group of 15-17 years. Projecting the 2001 age specific population of boys and girls to 2005 shows that 70 per cent of the boys and 40 per cent of the girls were enrolled.

Inference: Not much change seems to have occurred in the structure of the labour force consequent to the rapid economic growth since the early 1980s, as per these data. There is a definite fall in participation rates, which certainly could not have resulted as a consequence of economic growth. However, a significant part of the decline could be attributed to the secondary school enrolment.

Status and Industry Distribution of Workers

Status of Workers

NSS defines the status of workers as them being either self-employed, regular employees or casual workers. The first category includes unpaid family workers as well. In rural areas most self-employed (though not all, as some are engaged as rural non-farm workers) are engaged as cultivators on their own land, while in urban areas most are in (small) retail trade or service provision.

Table 4.4 suggests that in rural areas an overwhelmingly large proportion of workers is engaged in the capacity of self-employed;

3. Age-specific data for 2003-04 are yet not available in public domain.

many more female than male. In the recent years, though, this proportion has been coming down marginally for both male and female workers (2-3 per cent over 1993-94 to 2003-04, after an actual rise through 1993-94 to 1999-2000). In urban areas, though, this proportion is not as overwhelming; and while the proportion of female workers engaged in the capacity of self-employed has slightly reduced, for male workers there has been some increase.

On aggregate, despite the rapid rise in the labour force due to very high birth rates in the 1970s and 1980s, workers yet find some manoeuvrability in the labour market, permitting them to be in self-employment. This has happened because the population to land/resource ratio in the state is still favourable compared to, say in other states in the east.[4]

Table 4.4

Per Cent Distribution of Persons by Broad Usual Principal Activity Status

	Women			*Men*		
	Self-Employed	*Regular Wage*	*Casual Labour*	*Self-Employed*	*Regular Wage*	*Casual Labour*
Rural						
1993-1994	88.4	.9	10.7	71.8	7.4	20.8
1999-2000	89.0	1.0	10.0	73.3	7.8	18.9
2003-2004	85.9	2.0	12.5	68.8	9.1	21.9
Urban						
1993-1994	63.8	20.2	16.0	47.2	43.2	9.6
1999-2000	65.3	20.9	13.8	46.1	40.4	13.5
2003-2004	59.0	30.1	9.6	50.0	38.6	11.4

Source: NSS, different rounds.

There is little presence of female regular employees in rural areas: perhaps most of the two per cent (Table 4.4) would be government servants. This proportion among males is about nine

4. It is interesting to note that in Rajasthan, women's participation in the work force is higher when they work more in the capacity of self-employed. In contrast, in Maharashtra, women work more when they are in (casual) wage employment. Initial conditions of an agrarian system could explain these changes (Acharya and Panwalkar, 1989).

per cent, a small rise over 1993-2004. In urban areas, among females there has been a rapid rise in the proportion of regular employees while among males there has been a decline. Possible reason: regular jobs (akin to permanent jobs) have been fewer in the post-liberalisation era. Among female workers there is increase, possibly due to reservation for them in some regular jobs and increase in female education.[5]

Finally, casual labour proportions have been small in Rajasthan compared to most other major states, for reasons related to land/resource-ratios mentioned earlier. In rural areas, there has been a small increase in the proportions of casual labourers through the period 1993-94 to 2003-04 after a slight dip in 1999-2000 (both male and female workers). In urban areas, while for male workers the trend is similar, for female workers there is some unexplained dip.

'Casual workers' as an occupational group is economically the weakest link in the structure of work force in India (Visaria, 1981). This is because all they have to offer is physical labour, which is not at a premium; actually it is available in huge surplus. Labour demand situation is worsened by the relatively high capital intensity and rigid labour laws in India. The fact that Rajasthan has proportionately fewer casual labourers is the reason why the standards of living are not too low here (see next section).

Data presented in Table 4.4 suggest no significant change (on the aggregate) in the status of the work force over the period under study. This is again a reflection of economic growth making little impact on the structure of the work force—an aspect hinted at in the earlier table as well.

Distribution of Workers by Sectors

The 2001 census data on even a one-digit classification of industries are yet to be published. In this paper, therefore, data from the three NSS rounds (mentioned earlier) along with the limited census data are discussed.

---

5. The steep jump in regular wage employment of the urban female, at the cost of self-employment and casual wage employment, needs to be interpreted with caution for two reasons. One, the results come from the 'thin sample' and second, the base of urban female employment is small.

Table 4.5

Per Cent Distribution of Usually Working Persons

		Rural			*Urban*		
		Primary	*Secondary*	*Tertiary*	*Primary*	*Secondary*	*Tertiary*
Male	1993-94	71.6	16.5	11.9	9.0	31.5	59.4
	1999-00	69.2	17.6	13.2	9.3	32.9	57.9
	2003-04	59.1	22.9	18.0	6.7	30.4	62.9
Female	1993-94	92.6	4.7	2.7	31.5	24.5	44.1
	1999-00	92.7	5.2	2.0	39.3	30.0	30.5
	2003-04	88.5	8.2	3.3	36.8	24.6	38.7

Source: NSS, different rounds.

Table 4.5 suggests that over the 10 years 1993-94 to 2003-04, among rural male there has been a greater than 10 percentage point reduction in the share of the primary sector, almost all of it happening during the later quinquennium. For rural female workers, the fall has been less dramatic, but again all of it has happened in the later quinquennium. The corresponding gain for male workers appears in both secondary and tertiary sectors while for female workers it is mainly in the secondary sector. On the aggregate, workers in rural Rajasthan are still predominantly occupied in primary activities—agriculture, animal husbandry and to an extent, mining.

In urban areas, there is still a primary sector. For male workers, the proportion deployed in the primary sector is small and has fallen somewhat, which is compensated by a small rise in the service sector. The secondary sector has had virtually unchanged proportions engaged in it. Curiously, female engagement in the primary sectors has risen, which has been at the cost of the tertiary sector. These numbers, however, are small; as the female participation in the labour force is rather low in urban areas. Hence, not much should be deciphered from these numbers.

Do these tables also suggest that there has been little change in the said decade? There is a need to go into a little more data disaggregation, which NSS data do not permit, as they are best (though not exclusively) interpreted at the state level. NSS data are also not too accurate in determining absolute numbers: they are best interpreted as proportions. The limited census data available so far permit to identify, in which broad industry group have the new workers (who joined the work force between 1991 and 2001) gone to. A distribution of the incremental workers by absorption in agriculture (i.e. cultivators + agricultural labourers) and others is presented in Figure 4.1.

Figure 4.1

Distribution of Incremental Workers, 1991-2001 by Sectors

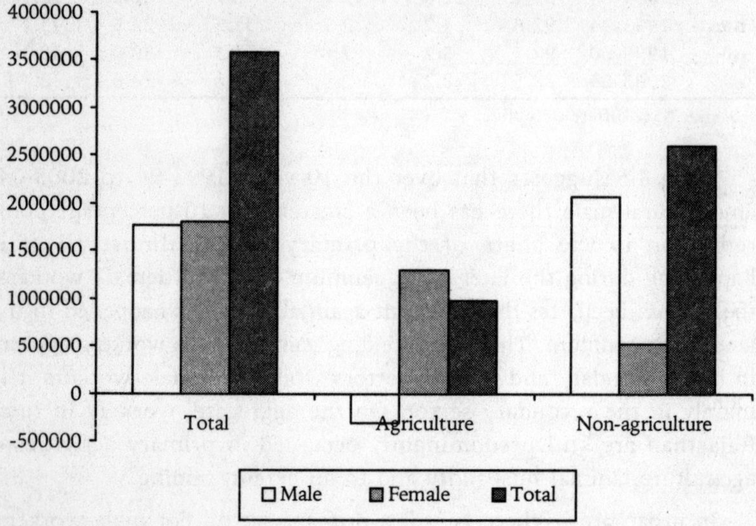

Source: Census of India, 1991 and 2001.

Figure 4.1 suggests that for the new workers (those added during 1991-2001), particularly male, the pattern of sectoral absorption has been somewhat unorthodox. There has been a reduction of male workers in agriculture, and from among the incremental workers, only women have joined this sector. There is thus, feminisation and ageing of the work force in agriculture. It is not that feminisation *per se* is undesirable; in the context of Rajasthan, however, women workers in agriculture are disempowered and low skilled, they do not own the land, and in many cases they represent the residual labour force. They have fewer occupational choices owing to lesser geographic mobility and lower education/skills; hence they stay back.

A more detailed break-up of data from Figure 4.1, given in Table 4.6, suggests that there is a net decrease of male cultivators, though female cultivators have increased. It implies that while male cultivators are shifting out of agriculture to more beneficial options, female workers stay back to tend the lands. Next, agricultural labourers are reducing among both sexes and locations. Keeping in view data from Table 4.3 (which shows that casual labourer proportions are not decreasing over time), one possibility is that workers are shifting out of being agricultural labourers and becoming labourers in non-agricultural activities. Construction, which has been expanding very rapidly in the recent years, is one sector where these workers, most probably, have been absorbed.

Table 4.6

Per Cent Distribution of Incremental Workers (1991-2001) by Sector/Activity

		Cultivators	*Agricultural Labourers*	*Household Industry*	*Other Workers*
Total	Persons	38.54	-11.08	3.02	69.51
	Male	-3.81	-13.42	2.40	114.83
	Female	80.23	-8.76	3.63	24.90
Rural	Persons	51.25	-11.87	2.90	57.72
	Male	0.57	-16.05	3.24	112.24
	Female	86.84	-8.93	2.67	19.42
Urban	Persons	-9.17	-8.10	3.47	113.80
	Male	-12.19	-8.41	0.81	119.79
	Female	3.63	-6.80	14.80	88.37

Source: Calculated from data obtained from Census of India, 1991 and 2001.

Prima facie, a trend of newer workers not joining agriculture is encouraging, as land frontiers are not increasing and agriculture in this arid state is already under severe strain. However, a district-wise disaggregated picture of workers' absorption in agriculture suggests that additional workers have primarily been absorbed in the northern and eastern districts. Absolute numbers of workers in agriculture (both sexes) have decreased in the southern districts (Dungarpur, Ajmer, Udaipur, Rajsamand, Jodhpur, Pali, Sirohi, Bhilwara, Kota, Baran), all of which other than Kota and Baran, have also performed badly in agriculture (zero or negative rates of growth in the 1990s). Zero or negative growth rates in agriculture, combined with reduction of workers, imply that workers have been 'pushed out' of this sector in these districts. This situation is problematic because none of these districts lies in the desert; it implies that factors other than natural conditions are causing this situation.

Inference: Data here suggest that at the aggregate level there is little change seen. A sectoral and incremental analysis, however, suggests that there is some dynamics taking place in terms of new workers quickly leaving agriculture for other options. In principle, young persons getting absorbed in non-agricultural occupations, is a welcome phenomenon. However, workers are leaving agriculture in areas where agriculture is decelerating, and this is not too happy a situation. This is not the classical path of rural transformation, where high growth in agriculture induces non-agricultural activities to come about, which is also accompanied by a sectoral transfer of workers away from agriculture.

Poverty Trends

Trends for 1970-2000 and Beyond

Rajasthan experienced rapid reduction in poverty in the last three decades: the per cent of population below the poverty line fell from an estimated 50 plus in the early 1970s (both rural and urban areas) to less than 15 (rural) and about 20 (urban) in 1999-00, the year when the last major survey was conducted (Table 4.7). In this context, Rajasthan is the third best achiever among major states in the country after Kerala and Tamil Nadu. During 1993/94-1999/2000, the number of people below the poverty line declined by 3.1 million. The (smaller-sized NSS) survey of 2003-04, however, shows that poverty proportions did not reduce further in the state during 1999-2000 till 2003-04.

Radhakrishna and Ray (2004) provide a distribution of poor workers by occupational groups (Table 4.8). Almost half of the poor in Rajasthan during 1999-2000 were self-employed in agriculture; 16 per cent were agricultural labour households and another 22 per cent were non-agricultural labour households. The share of the poor dependent on agriculture has increased from 56 per cent to 64 per cent during the nineties, while the share of the poor non-farm labourers declined from 28 per cent to 22 per cent. Predominance of small holdings (especially in south Rajasthan) and climatic

Table 4.7

Poverty Estimates for Rajasthan

	Rural		*Urban*	
	Planning Commission	*Expert Group*	*Planning Commission*	*Expert Group*
1970-1971	54.7	54.7		
1972-1973	47.1	-	39.3	-
1973-1974		44.8		53.2
1977-1978	33.5	35.9	33.9	46.4
1983	34.3	33.5	26.1	40.4
1987-1988	26.0	33.2	19.4	39.0
1993-1994	-	26.5		30.5
1999-2000		13.7		19.9

Source: Sagar (2005).

Table 4.8

Share of Various Occupational Groups in Poverty Population

Occupation Group	*Rural Rajasthan*		*Rural India*	
	1993-94	*1999-00*	*1993-94*	*1999-00*
Self Employed in Agriculture	42.4	47.8	33.2	28.1
Agricultural Labour	14.1	16.0	40.7	46.8
Non-agricultural Labour	27.9	22.3	8.4	7.6
Artisans	9.4	9.2	11.2	12.3
Others	6.2	4.7	6.5	5.3
Total	**100**	**100**	**100**	**100**

Source: Radhakrishna and Ray (2004).

vulnerability of dry land agriculture are among the reasons for workers in agriculture to be poor.

These data contrast with the distribution of poor at all-India level, where three-fourths of the poor belong to agriculture (mainly earning their living as agricultural labourers).[6]

---

6. However, the share of agricultural labour in the poverty population in Rajasthan has increased from 14.1 per cent in 1993-94 to 16 per cent in 1999-2000, while poverty among the self-employed in agriculture has declined by 5 per cent points (Table 4.8). Is Rajasthan slowly going to catch up with the rest of India?

Box 4.1

Some Key Features of Poverty in Rajasthan

First: There are larger proportions below poverty line in urban areas than rural, a feature unique to Rajasthan. Possible reason: The state has a large rural-urban migrant population, which has not fully integrated into the urban labour market.

Second: The extent of poverty among the scheduled group populations continues to be higher than that among the non-scheduled groups. Their comparative position, however, has improved over time.

Third: The poor are largely concentrated in the south and to a smaller extent in the west and eastern rim. Poverty in Rajasthan is mainly dependent upon the extent of agricultural growth, but factors like (tribal) land alienation, inequality, and social and geographic isolation matter.

While agricultural labourers might not be proportionately very large in the state—they being less than 20 per cent of the work force—trends in their wages are still an indication of levels of living of the wage-dependent populations. A slowdown in the growth of agricultural wages is indicated in the new millennium, most certainly due to the prolonged drought situation during 1998-99 to 2002-03. Next, in three out of the four regions, minimum wages were below the prescribed minimum during the triennium ending 2002-03 (Figure 4.2 and Table 4.9).

Table 4.9

Agriculture Wages in Rajasthan, 2001-02

	2001	*2002*
North Eastern	67	67
Southern	66	59
South Eastern	46	39
Western	61	53

Note : Minimum wage in this triennium period: Rs.65.

Source : Directorate of Economics and Statistics, Jaipur.

Figure 4.2

Agricultural Wages in Rajasthan

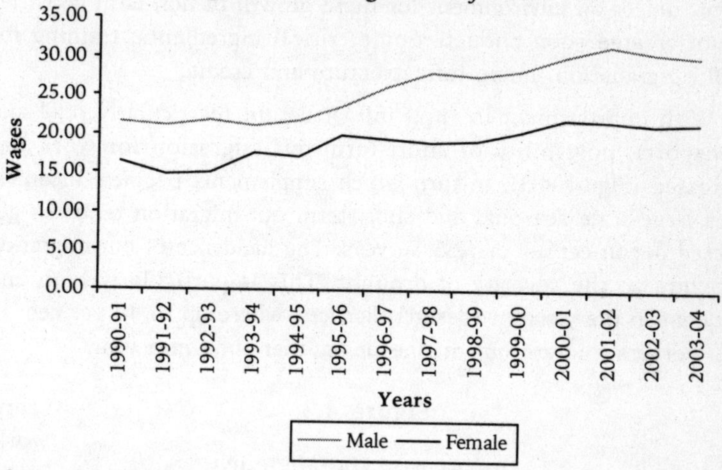

Source: GoR (2007).

A flattening of the poverty reduction trend, ebbing of agricultural wages, and in turn these two coinciding with a flattening of the growth in agriculture (GoR, 2006), all speak of how agriculture could affect standards of living even in the short run.

Explaining Poverty Reduction Trends

What explains the poverty reduction at such a brisk pace when the structure of the labour force and other variables do not suggest a major change for the better? One reason is the rapid growth in agriculture during 1980-1996. Next, people have devised alternative adaptation strategies to sustain their livelihoods since agriculture yields little in the face of repeated droughts. These include mixed cropping, animal husbandry, multiple-occupations (within a household) and short-term out-migration.

Since the proportion of rural labour households in the state is low and most of them possess some productive assets, it is possible even for labouring households to engage in more than one activity. Table 4.10 shows that the index of multiple job-holding in a household increased from about 1.8 in 1993-94 to more than 1.95 in 1999-2000. Multiple jobs help raise more incomes; hence permitting households a better standard of living. There might, however, be limitations to people diversifying occupations beyond a point, unless an environment for rapid growth of non-farm activities is not created soon enough. Some critical ingredients: training for skill up-gradation, micro-infrastructure and credit.

With improvement in rural infrastructure (particularly road and transport), possibility of short-term out-migration for work has increased (Figure 4.3), in turn which supplements people's incomes. This large-scale seasonal and short-term out-migration tends to get missed out in census or NSS surveys. The incidence of out-migration depends on the severity of drought. This is particularly high and frequent in the western (desert) districts, where up to 40 per cent of the workers migrate out at one or another time in a year.

Figure 4.3

District-wise Out-Migration

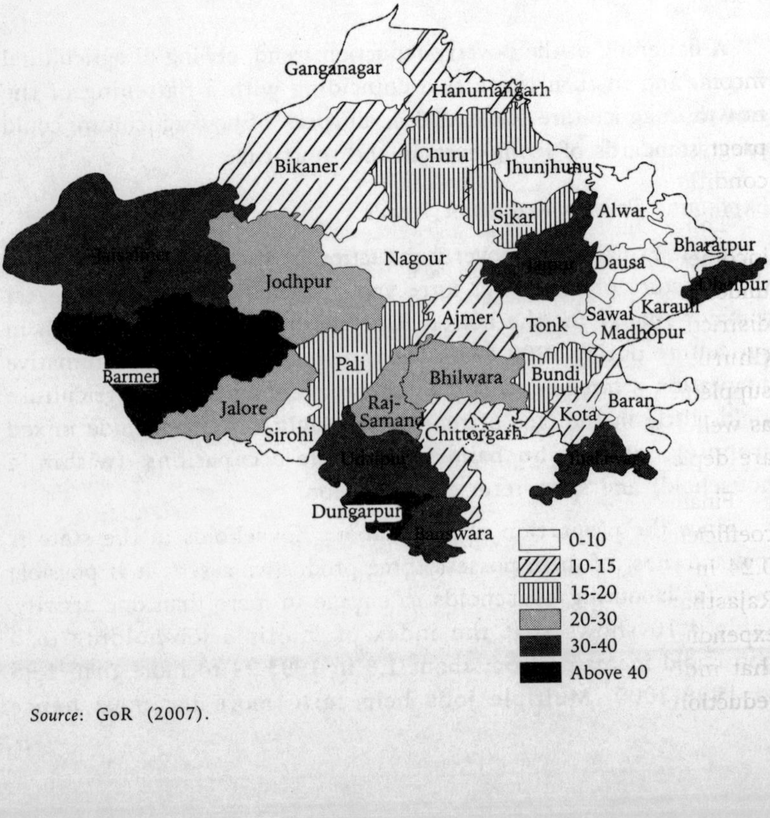

Source: GoR (2007).

Table 4.10

Distribution of Households by Household Type, Getting Income from Alternative Sources (1999-2000) in Rajasthan

Household Type	*Farm Income Cultivation*		*Wage/ Income*	*Non-farm Income Other*	*Others Sources*	*Index of Income Diversification**	
						1999-00	*1993-94*
Self-employed in Non-agricultural activity	543	251	146	915	127	1.98 (13)	1.87 (11)
Agriculture labour	542	267	937	60	158	1.96 (09)	1.76 (10)
Other labour	672	300	924	52	69	2.02 (15)	2.09 (16)
Self-employed in Agriculture	980	486	241	80	169	1.96 (53)	1.76 (54)
Others	452	203	498	46	597	1.80 (09)	1.41 (09)
All types	787	381	418	181	188	1.96 (100)	1.80 (100)

*Note** : Figures in parenthesis in the last column indicate per cent distribution of households.

Source : Sagar (2005).

A caution: Seasonal or short-term migration raises household incomes, but it also adversely affects some aspects of quality of life; not only does it thwart effective targeting of development programmes, there are other human implications as well, e.g. adverse conditions of female members left behind.

Third, there is distinct presence of child labour. This brings in incomes to households and helps alleviate poverty, though it is an undesirable practice. Patterns of child labour deployment in different districts suggest that the prevalence is highest in Alwar, Jalore and Churu. In rural areas, child workers' main work appears to be supplementing elders in economically meaningful activities in farms as well as in household and cottage industry. In urban areas, children are deployed in the informal tertiary sector.

Finally, reduction in inequality has mattered. In 1987-88, the Gini coefficient of consumption inequality was 0.28, which came down to 0.24 in 1993-94 and further reduced to 0.22 in 1999-2000 in rural Rajasthan; each of these implying that inequality in consumption expenditure is continuously becoming smaller. There is a possibility that more egalitarian distribution has been a reason for poverty reduction.

Unemployment

NSS measures unemployment within the same classification of how it measures work—usual status, current weekly status and current daily status.

Data on employment rate as a proportion of the total work force are presented in Table 4.11. Open unemployment rates in the later years are generally higher than those that prevailed in 1993-94, irrespective of the measures used. The highest rates are seen in urban areas in 2003-04. Unemployment rates have possibly risen in the later years because of an increase in casual work in Rajasthan (Table 4.3).[7] There is also a possibility of improved reporting on unemployment over time.

Table 4.11

Unemployment Rates as Seen from Different NSS Rounds

	Rural		*Urban*	
	Male	*Female*	*Male*	*Female*
1993-1994				
Usual Status	0.4	0.2	2.0	0.8
Current Weekly Status	1.0	0.2	2.4	1.2
Current Daily Status	1.5	0.4	2.6	1.5
1999-2000				
Usual Status	0.8	0.2	2.7	3.7
Current Weekly Status	2.6	1.5	4.0	2.7
Current Daily Status	3.3	1.9	4.7	3.5
2003-2004				
Usual Status	1.4	0.4	2.5	4.6
Current Weekly Status	3.8	1.3	3.5	3.6
Current Daily Status	4.8	2.2	4.0	4.4

Source: NSS, different rounds.

Unemployment here, is based on time disposition, a method by which many persons might not get netted, given the fact that quite a

7. Past researches have shown that unemployment is the highest among casual labourers.

few persons in poor agrarian economies might not be in a state of being openly unemployed (Acharya and Papanek 1995). One method to capture the extent of underemployment proposed in India is to calculate the difference between proportions of workers identified by the usual status and current daily status; it is postulated that workers usually in the labour force and not there on a specific day/week are the ones who tend to drop out in the face of no prospects in the market.[8] Whether this is underemployment or a 'discouraged worker' syndrome, is debatable, but numbers seen from Table 4.12 suggest that female underemployment (when subsidiary workers are included) is high, particularly in rural areas, and it has continued to be high over the decade.

Table 4.12

Underemployment Rates as Seen from Different Rounds of NSS

	Rural		*Urban*	
Year	*Male*	*Female*	*Male*	*Female*
1993-1994	2.2	11.9	1.1	4.1
1999-2000	2.0	10.6	1.5	4.4
2003-2004	4.7	15.1	3.5	3.3

Source: NSS, different rounds.

Inference: Poverty has been reducing, possibly for reasons that agricultural growth was strong at least until the late 1990s. Next, (consumption) inequality has been falling. Third, Rajasthan still permits some survival options: multiple job holding, out-migration, etc. However, not all survival options such as child labour or repeated out-migration (under some circumstances) are always desirable. Data on unemployment and underemployment do suggest some rise over time, but the numbers are not alarmingly high.

8. This explanation, though, is not free from controversy. For example, it has been stated earlier in this chapter that subsidiary workers are a product of seasonality, implying that the labour supply curve is shaped according to seasons. This is in contradiction to the postulation here, that subsidiary workers are underemployed in the off-seasons.

Explaining Earnings Behaviour

Trends in Agricultural Wages

Data in Figure 4.2 and trends in agricultural output (and GSDP) suggest that there is some association between wages and production. It might be instructive to find out, nevertheless, as to whether inflation and other factors also impact wages; and if yes, whether, and by what lag do wages catch up.

For this purpose, a regression equation has been fitted, using the functional form:

$$\text{Agr Wage}_t = a_0 + a_1\text{AgSDP}_{t-1} + \text{COL}_{t-1} + a_3 t$$

Monetary variables in this equation are at constant prices. Agr Wage_t = agricultural wage, GSDP_{t-1} = inflation-adjusted gross state domestic product (lagged one year) originating from agriculture, COL_{t-1} = one year lagged cost of living and t refers to 'time' introduced to account for a trend, which might capture the effects of missing variables. The period covered is 1990-91 to 2003-04 and the estimation method is OLS. The equation, in a double logarithmic transformation, is as below:

Table 4.13

Determinants of Real Agricultural Wages in Rajasthan

Variables	*Unstandardised Coefficients*		*Standardised Coefficients*	*t*	*Sig.*
	B	*Std. Error*	*Beta*		
(Constant)	2.080	1.266		1.64	0.13
Ln of Lagged AgSDP (1993-94 Constant Prices)	0.090	0.094	0.099	0.96	0.36
Ln of One year lagged CPIAL with 1960-61 base	0.039	0.207	0.077	0.19	0.85
TIME (t)	0.032	0.015	0.870	2.18	0.05

Note : Dependent Variable: LN_Real Wages with 1991 as base.

The results do not show impact of any of the real variables chosen for the analysis. All that is shown is that real agricultural wages have grown at around 3.2 per cent per annum during 1991-2004. No other factor appears to influence wages. The case of lagged AgSDP having a zero impact is obvious in a state with large weather induced fluctuations in agriculture. Part of the problem in interpreting this equation is multicollinearity: high correlation between independent variables and too small a sample.

Inference: For wages to rise external factors such as demand for labour (through urbanisation, and labour intensity in industrial activities, among others) must rise, for which creation of different skills would be a prerequisite. The wages in the state have been rising at a fair pace so far, thanks largely to the alternatives available to the labour households (Table 4.10). A sustained rise in wages however, would require further diversification of skills both for rural non-farm employment as well as urban and industrial employment.

A similar exercise attempted with the nominal variables shows a significant impact of current and lagged levels of agricultural income on agricultural wage. Wage elasticity with respect to the current and the lagged agricultural income is estimated at 0.35 and 0.19 respectively. A part of the explanation, as to why both current and lagged income affect nominal wage, lies in the way agricultural wage is defined. Agricultural wage is taken as the average of wage paid in ploughing/sowing and the harvesting operations. While the former would greatly depend on the size of last crop, agricultural wages paid for harvesting would be determined largely by the size of current crop.

Table 4.14

Determinants of Nominal Agricultural Wages in Rajasthan

Dependent Variables *Rsq=0.991*	*Unstandardised Coefficients*		*t*	*Sig.*
	B	*Std. Error*		
(Constant)	-1.818	0.736	-2.47	0.03
TIME	0.049	0.007	6.60	0.00
Ln Nominal Agsdp	0.193	0.072	2.67	0.02
Ln of Lagged Nominal AgSDP	0.348	0.065	5.32	0.00

Note : Dependent Variable: Ln of Nominal Wage.

Explaining Earnings Behaviour: Micro Level Analysis

Individual earnings are an outcome of both demand in a labour market and supply (individual attribute) conditions. However, since demand conditions are determined at the macro level, their being explained in a micro model appears infeasible. Hence, following the Mincer-Becker type formulation, effort has been made here to construct a human capital centred, supply-side model (with some variations). Unit record data from the NSS 55th Round for Rajasthan, pertaining to 1999-00, have been used for estimating the earnings functions.

The different variables—as per the Mincer-Becker model—which depict human capital are: education and work experience. For operationalising this model, it is necessary to statistically measure education and work experience. In this paper, the education variable has been quantified by (linear) years of education gone through by the workers (e.g. Class 1, 2 3,...); and the proxy for experience is age, as data on work experience are not available. Since the specification of experience is expected to be non-linear, 'age' is specified as: AGE + AGE^2 (SQAGE), where the sign of the coefficient of AGE^2 is expected to be negative, i.e. falling returns.

The other variables introduced in the equation are typically, demand elements or elements that signify the capacity to pay:

Industry (INDDUM): Primary sectors=0, else=1, is a dummy variable; under the assumption that primary sectors have lower capacity to pay (or alternatively, it could be stated that there is a slack in markets for agricultural workers);

Number of days worked (TOTAL-DAY): Typically, since large numbers work in not too formal settings, it matters as to how long are workers engaged for (the reverse of open unemployment);

Location (SECTOR): rural=1, urban=0, under the assumption that rural earnings would be lower) and,

Sex (SEX-DUMMY): males earn more (male=1, female=0).

The dependent variable is the logarithm of earnings of regular employees from hired work.

Coefficients of the regression equation, estimated for the status group Regular Employees (status category 31 of the NSS), are presented in Table 4.15.[9]

9. The reason why the model is estimated separately for regular employees is because the human capital model would be inapplicable for casual labourers.

Table 4.15

Regression Equation of Earnings Behaviour for Regular Employees

	Un-standardised Coefficients		*Standardised Coefficients*	*t*	*Sig.*
	B	*S.E.*	*Beta*		
Constant	1.75	0.24		7.15	0.00
Age	0.10	0.01	1.31	12.48	0.00
Sqage	0.00	0.00	-0.88	-8.40	0.00
General Education	0.09	0.01	0.37	18.95	0.00
Sex-dummy	0.32	0.05	0.11	6.14	0.00
Inddum2	0.18	0.06	0.06	3.16	0.00
Total-day	0.02	0.00	0.13	7.22	0.00
Sector (Rural/Urban)	-0.09	0.04	-0.05	-2.56	0.01

Note: Dependent Variable: ln (wage/salary earning); R2 = 0.491; F = 209.68; n = 1530.

Table 4.15 shows that all the coefficients are significant at 1 per cent confidence (two-tail test) and the overall explanation for a large sample like this one too is sufficiently high. In short, the equation is a good statistical fit.

Three observations: One, the coefficient of education suggests that the (private) rate of return on education for each year of education, on average, is about nine per cent; a figure which is higher than the all-India average of 5-8 per cent (World Bank, 1998). It is suggested thus, that investment into human capital in the state would contribute more than any other measure to raise incomes. Next, there is a distinct nine per cent gap between rural and urban incomes, after accounting for other factors. There is also a 10 per cent earnings gap between primary sector activities and others. Future remunerative jobs are, therefore, could best be obtained in urban, non-agricultural sectors. Last, there is a distinct 30 per cent gender-gap in earnings.[10]

The more difficult proposition is to estimate the earnings behaviour of the self-employed, since NSS authorities do not ask questions related to total incomes. There is, though, a question asked

10. Whether this has to do with the kind of job women do *versus* men do (self-selection), or pure discrimination, is a question that cannot be answered here (Acharya, 1995).

about total monthly household expenditure. Following Acharya (1999), effort is made to first (indirectly) estimate incomes of the self-employed, and then obtain their determinants–instrumental estimation.

Step 1: Estimate the equation:

Wage = a0 + a1(MPCE) + a2(MPCE^2)

Here, MPCE is per capita monthly expenditure. This equation is estimated only for the regular wage/salaried employees, for whom the data on wage are available. Estimates of the coefficients a0, a1 and a2 are then used for constructing an earnings series for the self-employed.

The explanatory variables for model are the same, with the exception that there is an additional variable, land owned, which figures as an additional explanatory variable.

Table 4.16

Regression Equation of Earnings Behaviour for the Self-Employed

	Un-standardised Coefficients		*Standardised Coefficients*	*t*	*Sig.*
	B	*S.E.*	*Beta*		
Constant	6.684	0.022		309.66	0.00
Age	0.003	0.001	0.16	3.45	0.00
Sqage	0.000	0.000	0.00	-0.03	0.98
General Education	0.025	0.001	0.31	24.35	0.00
Sex-dummy	-0.039	0.007	-0.07	-5.78	0.00
Inddum2	0.043	0.009	0.07	5.02	0.00
Total-day	-0.001	0.000	-0.06	-6.08	0.00
Sector (Rural/Urban)	-0.100	0.009	-0.15	-11.54	0.00
Land Owned	0.000	0.000	0.11	10.05	0.00

Note : Dependent Variable: ln (Earnings of self employed); R2 = 0.168; F = 210.195; n = 8295.

Table 4.16, which contains these estimates, suggests a few features: First, experience (age) appears to have a linear relationship with (log of) earnings, as the coefficient of SQAGE appears to be statistically insignificant. Next, the (private) rate of return on education for an extra year of education for the self-employed is low at 2.5 per cent, possibly because the nature of self employment in this sample does not require too much educational input; e.g. while basic education is essential for a petty shopkeeper, extra years of education might not be adding to his/her revenue. The same might hold for small farmers as well. These two worker-categories dominate the sample. Third, sector and sex dummies show remarkable similarity in the two equations (Table 4.11 and 4.12); this suggests the robustness of these results. Finally, the coefficient of land, while being highly statistically significant, is very small. Does it imply that the per cent increase in income with unit increase in land owned by a farmer—other factor kept constant—is small? This is possible in Rajasthan where falling returns to land are already setting in. Alternative reasoning: If larger land plots are less productive, incremental incomes with plot size increase would be low in the regression equation. In either case, the conclusion stays unchanged.

Inference: Private returns on education are high for regular employees (principally in non-agriculture). In land-based or the extant other self-employment activities, the (private) returns on education are not high. Incomes are low and rise poorly in agriculture and rural areas compared to non-agricultural and urban. Sectoral imbalances of labour allocation, along with falling returns in agriculture, are hinted at.

Conclusion

This chapter is an attempt to put together some evidence on changes that have occurred in the decade of the 1990s in the employment and standards of living in Rajasthan in response to the growth it has experienced.

Put succinctly, the impact of this growth has not been reflected on the aggregate structure of the labour force. Work participation rates have fallen, which could in part be attributed to the younger age groups opting for education. However, there has been no visible response (to raise work participation) in response to the growth.

This aspect is also reflected in the structure of the labour force: both the status and the industry distribution of workers have stayed largely unchanged on the aggregate. There is not even a major casualisation of the work force (the down side of rapid population growth) as has been witnessed in many other states. Since the land/resource to population ratio in the state is still favourable and mobility high, people have adopted a number of survival strategies like local occupational diversification and short-term out-migration for earning more. There is some movement of workers away from agriculture, particularly from agriculturally stagnant areas, either to areas that are agriculturally progressive or non-farm sectors (within the locale as well as outside). It appears that the latter is more dominant.

Poverty trends showed a decline during 1970s until 1999-2000. This is confirmed by the fact that agricultural wages rose during the 1990s; since casual wage workers are among the poorer sections, a rise in their wages is a progress. Three reasons why poverty reduced in that period were, possibly the four plus per cent rise in agricultural production during 1980-1996, public expenditure on anti-poverty and infrastructure programmes, and out-migration.

The modelling exercise suggests that agricultural wages rise more in response to external factors than those related to agriculture *per se*. Next, employees' individual earnings equations suggest that there is a strong case for expanding non-farm activities and spreading education, as both these help raise incomes. Third, the earnings equation for the self-employed, in contrast suggests that education as such matters, but little. Incremental incomes from additional land holding (land size) are also low. Instead, what matters more is whether the location of activity is in urban areas and whether it is non-agricultural. For employment and earnings growth, therefore, agriculture is not a favoured option.

The whole exercise suggests that the (so called rapid) growth has not been inclusive, it has been highly location specific, and it is probably pivoted on sectors that might not dent the state's labour structure.

References

Acharya, S. (1995). "Women in the Indian Labour Force: A Temporal and Spatial Analysis", in S. Horton (ed.) *Women and Industrialisation in Asia*, Routledge, London.

———. (1999). "Explaining Returns to Education Among the Self-Employed", *Indian Journal of Labour Economics*, Volume 42, No. 2.

Acharya, S. and V.G. Panwalkar (1989). "Labour Force Participation in Rural Maharashtra", in A.V. Jose (ed.) *Limited Options*, ILO-ARTEP, New Delhi.

Acharya S. and G.F. Papanek (1995). "Agricultural Wages and Rural Poverty in India", *Development Policy Review* (UK), Vol. 13, No. 1.

GoI (Government of India) (2001). "Sources of Household Income in India", *Report No.463, National Sample Survey*, New Delhi.

GoR (Government of Rajasthan) (2006). *Economic Survey*, Jaipur.

———. (2007). *Human Development Update of the State of Rajasthan.*

Jose, A.V. (ed.) (1989). *Limited Options*, ILO-ARTEP, New Delhi.

Radhakrishna R. and S. Ray (2004). "Poverty in India: Dimensions and Character", Indira Gandhi Institute of Development Studies, Mumbai (mimeo).

Sagar V. (2005). *Macroeconomics of Poverty Reduction in Rajasthan*, Paper prepared for IGIDR under a research programme funded by UNDP.

Visaria P. (1981). "Poverty and Unemployment in India", *World Development*, Vol. 9, No. 3.

World Bank (1998). *Primary Education in India*, Allied Publishers, New Delhi.

References

II

Dimensions of Economic Growth

5

Industrialisation in Rajasthan

Process and Pattern

SURJIT SINGH

Industrialisation plays a critical role in the process of economic development. Industrialisation is in one sense a process, which has invariably been the outcome or accompaniment of economic development. In 1947, India was an extremely backward economy and some of the states like Rajasthan, were totally agrarian. The economy of Rajasthan was mainly based on agriculture and livestock. In 1950-1951, there were six mills in Rajasthan, in addition to three in Ajmer-Marwar, which was merged in Rajasthan in 1956. Besides, the State had two factories each of cement and sugar. By early 1990s, the State had 30 textile mills and several powerloom units and about a dozen of processing units. There were five large scale and several mini cement factories, three sugar factories and half a dozen big engineering units (Government of Rajasthan, undated). The State, despite being rich in minerals especially nonferrous and non-metallic minerals and heritage of handicrafts, the manufacturing sector has a marginal role in the economy. Given this background, this chapter tries to map the industrial scene of Rajasthan using various sources of data. It also reflects on the changes that occurred overtime and the performance of organised and unorganised sectors. In the process it throws light on the informalisation of the economy. The chapter also briefly examines the recent policy announcements in this context.

Industrial Sector through the Plans

State has a major role to play in industrialisation. In Rajasthan, in the First Five-Year Plan industry and mineral sector hardly got any attention, only 0.85 per cent of total plan outlay was earmarked for this sector (Table 5.1). The Ninth Five-Year Plan observed a significant improvement in the outlay for this sector in both physical terms and proportionate terms (7.79%). However, the Tenth Five-Year Plan saw a decline in share as well as in absolute terms. This period stressed more on private initiative to deliver. This shows that industrial development did not receive the attention it deserved from the state. There is no doubt that since the First Plan, when less than half a crore of rupees were set aside it is a long tread to Rs. 2,154.09 crore by the Ninth Plan, the highest allocation ever. The targeted growth rate for industry during the Tenth Five-Year Plan was fixed at 10.06 per cent[1], when gross state domestic product (GSDP) was to grow at 8.3 per cent with agriculture growing at 4.50 per cent and services at 9.63 per cent. The corresponding national growth rates were 8.9 per cent for industry, 8.0 per cent for gross domestic product (GDP), 4.0 per cent for agriculture and 9.4 per cent for service sector respectively. Thus, the aims are high but allocations are poor.

Table 5.1

Industrial Outlays Over the Plans

(Rs. Crore)

Plan	*Industry & Minerals*	*Total Outlay*	*Share % of Industry & Minerals*
1951-1956	0.55	64.50	0.85
1956-1961	5.77	105.27	5.48
1961-1966	8.95	236.00	3.79
1966-1969	2.35	132.72	1.77
1969-1974	7.95	306.21	2.60
1974-1979	33.67	847.16	3.97
1980-1985	83.50	2025.00	4.12
1985-1990	190.52	3000.00	6.35
1992-1997	536.02	11500.00	4.66
1997-2002	2154.09	27650.00	7.79
2002-2007	1113.56	31831.75	3.50

Source: GoR, Various Plan Documents and GoR (2005; 2006).

1. During the Ninth Five-Year Plan, the yearly growth rates of manufacturing sector GSDP at 1993-94 prices were put at: 1997-98 (24.3 per cent); 1998-99 (-4.5 per cent); 1999-2000 (27.5 per cent); 2000-01 (-10.4 per cent); and 2001-02 (3.3 per cent) (GoR, 2006).

Industrial Structure

Given the trend in plan outlays for industry sector, it would be important to look at the structure of industry in Rajasthan. Industrial structure can be defined as the relative importance of individual industries or groups within an economy. Table 5.2 shows the sectoral division of gross state domestic product at constant prices. The primary sector comprising agriculture and allied activities, fisheries, forestry and mining lost ground since 1993-94; its share in 1993-94 was 33.98 that rose to 36.43 per cent by 1996-97, but declined thereafter, though fluctuating throughout, to 27.74 per cent in 2005-2006. On the other hand, the contribution of secondary sector comprising manufacturing, construction and electricity & water activities improved from 27.26 per cent in 1993-94 to 33.66 per cent in 1999-2000 and fell to 25.36 per cent in 2003-04. It stood at 28.46 per cent in 2005-06. The service sector akin to the national level has become the major contributor to GSDP in Rajasthan. This has to be taken with a pinch of salt, as it is mainly informal activities that are contributing to the income from this sector. Rajasthan does not have a booming IT sector or trading/financial activities and nor does it have a population with commensurate education and skill levels (Singh and Sagar, 2004; Singh, 2005b).

It is also observed that by the turn of the century, manufacturing sector contributed 15.22 per cent to Rajasthan's GSDP at 1993-94 prices and this contribution declined to 13.35 per cent by 2005-06 (Table 5.3).[2] The declining share of manufacturing sector is ascribed to registered manufacturing sector as its share fell from 9.70 per cent to 7.62 per cent during this period. Thus, there are serious problems with regard to registered manufacturing sector and more so with large-scale industry in Rajasthan. The growth in GSDP is due to other sectors, it appears. It may also be added here that the marked slowdown in the industry and services sectors since the late 1990s has taken growth rates in these sectors almost back to that of the 1970s (World Bank, 2006). Growth in both these sectors has seen a significant deceleration. In industry, an intra-sectoral breakdown suggests that this may be mainly due to a slowdown in construction

2. In 1960-61, the share of manufacturing sector was 10.8 per cent with 2.03 per cent coming from registered manufacturing and 8.77 per cent from unregistered manufacturing at current prices (Singh, 1989).

activity and a decline in manufacturing growth. On the other hand, mining and quarrying, where Rajasthan has a strong comparative advantage given its rich endowment of mineral resources, saw a sharp increase in growth rates even in the 2000s when other sectors were faltering. For the services sector, the slowdown was largely due to lower growth rates in real estate and transport services. The share of high potential sub-sectors also remains disappointing.

Table 5.2

Distribution of GSDP by Sector (1993-94 Prices)

(Per Cent)

Years	Primary	Secondary		Services	Total
		Manufacturing	Others		
1993-94	33.98	12.27	27.26	38.77	100
1994-95	36.18	14.10	27.81	36.01	100
1995-96	33.58	15.04	29.10	37.32	100
1996-97	36.43	12.98	26.36	37.21	100
1997-98	34.01	14.49	28.61	37.38	100
1998-99	32.52	13.31	28.53	38.95	100
1999-00	27.49	16.61	33.66	38.86	100
2000-01	27.87	15.22	28.16	43.97	100
2001-02	31.69	13.48	26.38	41.93	100
2002-03	23.58	14.31	29.61	46.81	100
2003-04	32.24	12.23	25.36	42.40	100
2004-05	28.83	13.23	27.56	43.61	100
2005-06	27.74	13.35	28.46	43.80	100

Source: Directorate of Economics & Statistics (2004-2005) and (2005-2006), *Economic Review*, Jaipur.

A major disappointment in Rajasthan has been the modest contribution of mining and quarrying to GSDP, despite the state's abundant mineral resources. In 2003-04, this sub-sector contributed just over 3 per cent of GSDP in Rajasthan—compared to 14 per cent in Chhattisgarh and Jharkhand, and 8 per cent in Orissa. For rapid industrialisation, both national and state policies play a major role. A sound industrial policy with poor implementation would not yield any results. We have seen above that the Government was half heartedly pursuing industrial development in Rajasthan.

Table 5.3

Contribution of Manufacturing Sector in GSDP (1993-94 Prices)

(*Per Cent*)

Sectors	*1999-2000*	*2000-2001*	*2001-2002*	*2002-2003*	*2003-2004*	*2004-2005*	*2005-2006*
Manufacturing Regd.	11.17	9.70	8.10	8.38	6.90	7.53	7.62
Manufacturing unregd.	5.44	5.52	5.38	5.93	5.33	5.70	5.73
Manufacturing	16.61	15.22	13.48	14.31	12.23	13.23	13.35
GSDP (Rs. lakh)	5292020	5177032	5663550	5274655	6644133	6685283	7049094

Source: Same as Table 5.2.

Industries in the Organised Sector

This section reviews the industrial situation using Annual Survey of Industries information. Table 5.4 presents post-reform period changes in the industrial scene of Rajasthan. The number of registered factories in Rajasthan has observed an increase since 1992-93. However, the growth in number of factories is slower in the second half of the nineties compared to the first half of the nineties. Overall during the nineties the number of factories increased by 36.7 per cent. There was a significant reduction in growth of fixed capital, gross output, gross value added and net value added in the second half of the nineties and negative growth in employment. This happened after the 1994 Industrial Policy was announced by the state and the state having 300 industrial areas/estates, eight growth centres, nine mini-growth centres, three agro-food parks, apparel park, export zones and many other sectoral promotional centres. Overall (1992-93 to 2002-2003), except for negative growth in employment, all other indicators observed significant positive growth. These findings reinforce the argument put forth by Nagaraj (2005) that 1990s boom lasted only four years and employment in early 2000 is roughly the same as it was eight years ago at the national level.

Table 5.4

Some Industrial Indicators and Ratios

Items	1992-93	1995-96	2002-03	Per Cent Change in		
				1995-96 Over 1992-93	2002-03 Over 1995-96	2002-03 Over 1992-93
Factories (No.)	3839	4537	5248	18.2	15.7	36.7
Fixed Capital (Rs. Lakh)	772046	1201303	1355028	55.6	12.8	75.5
Employment (No.)	262958	293929	244265	11.8	-16.9	-7.1
Wages (Rs. Lakh)	96887	148898	170129	53.7	14.3	75.6
Gross Output (Rs. Lakh)	1258072	2145496	3311696	70.5	54.4	163.2
Gross Value Added (Rs. Lakh)	290514	472365	609148	62.6	29.0	109.7
Net Value Added (Rs. Lakh)	233315	388918	477799	66.7	22.9	104.8
Gross Output Labour Ratio*	4.7843	7.2994	13.5578	52.6	85.7	183.4
GVA Labour Ratio*	1.1048	1.6071	2.4938	45.5	55.2	125.7
NVA Labour Ratio*	0.8873	1.3232	1.9561	49.1	47.8	120.5
Gross Output Capital Ratio	1.6295	1.7860	2.4440	9.6	36.8	50.0
GVA Capital Ratio	0.3763	0.3932	0.4495	4.5	14.3	19.5
NVA Capital Ratio	0.3022	0.3237	0.3526	7.1	8.9	16.7

Note : *—Rs. lakh per worker.

Source: *Annual Survey of Industries*, Various Years.

In 1992-93 the 3,839 factories with fixed capital of Rs. 7,720.46 crore employed 2.63 lakh persons to generate gross output of Rs. 12,580.72 crore and created net value addition of Rs. 2,333.15 crore. In 2002-03, the 5,248 factories with fixed capital worth Rs. 13,550.28 crore employed 2.44 lakh persons to generate gross output of Rs. 33,116.96 crore and net value addition of Rs. 4,777.99 crore. The labour productivity as measured in terms of gross value added (GVA) and net value added labour (NVA) ratios have over the years significantly improved. When measured in terms of output, labour ratio it almost doubled. The labour productivity has been better during the second half of the nineties compared to the first half, though NVA per worker has observed a lower increase in the post

1995-96 period. Further, it needed Rs. 1.63 lakh of capital input to produce gross output worth Rs. 1.62 lakh in 1992-93 and Rs. 2.44 lakh in 2002-03. Similar is the relationship with value added indicators. This means that shift is towards more capital intensive industries (it is natural as no new technology is labour using) and it does not augur well for large booming labour market in Rajasthan (Singh and Sagar, 2004).

What is the situation across districts? We find that during 1992-1993 and 2000-01, Bharatpur, Bundi, Churu, Jhalawar, Kota, Pali and Tonk observed a decline in number of registered factories. The major gainers are Alwar, Ajmer, Banswara, Bhilwara, Chittorgarh and Jodhpur (more than 50 per cent increase in number of factories). The concentration of industrial units has not changed. Jaipur district, though observed a slower growth in the number of units, still account for 20 per cent of all industrial units of the state. The top five industrial districts in 1992-93 were Jaipur, Pali, Udaipur, Ganganagar and Jodhpur, accounting for 57.71 per cent of all units. In 2000-01, the top 5 industrial districts were Jaipur, Alwar, Udaipur, Ganganagar and Jodhpur accounting for 57.67 per cent of all units (similar was the situation prior to 1989, see Singh, 1989). Majority of the districts (14 of the 27) observed a decline in their share in factories. Thus, no major shift is visible at the district level and dispersal is marginal.

What is the structure of manufacturing sector in Rajasthan at the disaggregated level presently? The annual survey of industries data for the year 2002-03, shows that there were 5,248 registered factories, 27.52 per cent were manufacture of other non-metallic mineral products followed by manufacture of textiles (20.83%), food products & beverages (9.89%), manufacture of basic metals & fabricated metal products except machinery & equipment (6.19%) and manufacture of chemicals & chemical products (6.12%). These five industrial groups together accounted for 71 per cent of all enterprises and 73 per cent of employment, but 71 per cent of gross value added and 68 per cent of net value addition. These 5,248 enterprises thus, employed 2.44 lakh persons and added value of Rs. 6,091 crore and net value of Rs. 4,778 crore. This shows that the industrial structure is concentrated in a few manufacturing groups. These are traditional industrial groups with backward linkages in the state. This also indicates non-changing industrial structure and limited impact of opening up of the economy and the ineffectiveness of various policies and incentives that were provided or announced since the reforms. All this reinforces the above discussion on share of registered manufacturing sector in GSDP. It appears to be a paradox of Rajasthan's industrial development. This period has observed significant improvement in infrastructure (though progress in the power sector is slow).[3]

Textile Sector: A Case

It would be pertinent to articulate a major sector's issues that reflect the overall industrial scene in Rajasthan. Rajasthan, though known largely for its unorganised textile sector, is also the fourth largest producer of spun (synthetic and blended) yarn in the country, accounting for about 7.5 per cent of the national production (November 2004) and the fifth largest producer in the country of mill-made fabrics, accounting for 5.4 per cent of all-India output. The textile industry, including yarn and fabrics production, is the second largest employer in the state after mining and quarrying.

During the period April 2004-November 2005, Rajasthan's spun yarn production grew by about 9 per cent, compared to 6.6 per cent in the corresponding period in 2003-04. With the end of the Multi-Fibre Arrangement in January 2005 and the lifting of quotas on textile export from developing countries, Rajasthan, like the rest of India, can look forward to a significant increase in textile exports to developed countries. To exploit this potential, Rajasthan needs to improve the investment climate for textiles. Firms complain that they currently face the following key investment climate bottlenecks:

- High cost of power, which appears to be the single most important constraint to firm-level profitability and competitiveness, since firms cannot rely on power from the grid and have to install their own generators.

---

3. In 1991-92, the surface roads in Rajasthan were 2,846 kms of national highways, 7,098 kms of state highways, 3,467 kms of district roads, 12,808 kms of other roads and 21,176 kms of village roads and 2,239 kms of border roads with a total of 49,631 kms road network. However, in 2005-06, the corresponding figures were 5,603 kms of national highways, 10,109 kms of state highways, 6,513 kms of district roads, 19,828 kms of other roads and 69,058 kms of village roads and 1,11,111 kms of total road network. The road density still stood at 47.66 km much below the national level of 102.92 km in 2005-06 (DES, 2005-06).

- Connectivity to ports is another problem for these firms, particularly those that are export-oriented.
- Delays at ports have increased, and the waiting time for a container to enter the port is usually 8-10 days. This is largely because the number of containers reaching ports each month has increased almost ten-fold over the last three years even while the number of terminals has not kept pace with the increased volume.
- Water shortage raises costs, since water is a key input, and firms have to rely on private tankers in the water-deficient state.
- Rigid labour laws (most common problem articulated by very big industry), which make it difficult for the larger firms (employing more than 100 workers) to lay-off surplus labour and also to hire contract workers (World Bank, 2006).

The government needs to address these bottlenecks urgently. Firms, too, can take steps to better exploit the potential offered by the liberalised environment.[4]

Contract Labour and Skill Composition

The changing industrial profile is witnessing changes in nature and mode of work and nature of employment in India and Rajasthan's industrial scene is no different. In this section in order to throw some light on recent trends in skill composition of Rajasthan's manufacturing, we have estimated contract labour intensity and skill labour intensity. We define contract intensity as ratio of contract workers to total workers and skill intensity as a ratio of managerial personnel to total workers. Due to data limitations, the managerial

4. One textile company that is meeting the new challenge is Rajasthan Spinning, one of the leading manufacturers of polyester (along with Indo-Rama and Reliance). The company is making two big moves—capacity expansion and garment manufacturing—that makes it worth consideration in a deregulated scenario. It is expanding its yarn capacity by 60 per cent. What sets Rajasthan Spinning apart from the other two big polyester manufacturers is its forward foray into garments. Exports have been increasing, going up from Rs. 162 crore in 2002-03 to Rs. 250 crore in 2003-04, or 38 per cent of turnover; the company expects this to increase to 50 per cent by 2005-2006. At Rs. 54, the stock discounts its projected 2006-07 earnings 4.3 times. Unless high crude prices send raw material prices soaring and polyester manufacturers are unable to pass on these hikes, the stock looks tailored to deliver good returns. Other textile firms in Rajasthan could follow this example.

personnel is a total of persons in a factory having supervisory and managerial positions or mangers per worker. It is important to emphasise that the changing share of each industry group is an outcome of two-associated changes—changes in contract intensity and changes in the share of each industry group in total employment. Compositional changes in employment are captured in contract intensity and skill profile of manufacturing.

The Annual Survey of Industries data shows that in 1998-99, there were 1,73,779 workers in manufacturing sector in Rajasthan of which 36,732 were contract workers (21.1%) and this number went up to 58,327 in 2002-03 constituting 30.5 per cent of all workers (CSO, 2001; 2005). The number of workers grew by 9.9 per cent between 1998-98 and 2002-03 when contract workers grew by 58.79 per cent. This means that contract labour is increasing significantly in the recent times. In 1998-99, of the 36,732 contract workers, the highest proportion (32.1%) was in manufacture of glass and glass products; manufacture of non-metallic mineral products; followed by production, processing and preservation of meat, fish, fruit, vegetables, oils and fats; manufacture of dairy product, manufacture of grain mill products, starches and starch products, and prepared animal feeds; manufacture of other food products; manufacture of beverages industry group (11.7%) and spinning weaving and finishing of textiles; manufacture of other textiles; manufacture of knitted and crocheted fabrics and articles industry group (10.4%), 53.2 per cent of all contract workers. In 2002-03, these three industry groups had 62.8 per cent of 58,327 contract workers.

When we define contract intensity as number of contract workers in total persons employed, we find that industry group 16 (manufacture of tobacco products) tops the list of industries. This is because of *bidi* segment that is basically working on putting out system. Manufacture of coke oven products; manufacture of refined petroleum products; processing of nuclear fuel, agricultural and animal husbandry services activities, except veterinary activities and, manufacture of glass and glass products; manufacture of non-metallic mineral products are other industry groups that have high contract intensity. Across the board, contract intensity has gone up with the exception of five industry groups. This means that industries in Rajasthan have increasingly resorted to contract labour in the face of labour laws when any expansion was required. Regular direct labour is not hired. It could also be that the new firms resorted to contract labour more than older firms.

In case of skill intensity, it is high in manufacture of office, accounting and computing machinery group followed by manufacture of medical appliances and instruments for measuring, checking, testing, navigating and other purposes except optical instruments, manufacture of industrial process control equipment, manufacture of optical instruments and photographic equipment, manufacture of watches and clocks. These industry groups do use more skilled work force and professionals. But across the industry groups, only few have observed increase in skill intensity. This is to a large extent linked to high contract intensity. This means firms have resorted to contract labour/outsourcing when need arose for more labour.

Unorganised Manufacturing Sector

We have observed that unregistered manufacturing sector has a role to play in Rajasthan. In this section, we try to analyse the information on unorganised manufacturing sector. National Sample Survey Organisation in its 51st (1994-95) and 56th (2000-01) rounds, throws up information on unorganised manufacturing sector. At the aggregate level, Table 5.5 makes comparison by type and region, the size of unorganised manufacturing sector in Rajasthan. The estimated number of enterprises in 1994-95, in Rajasthan was 4.66 lakh constituting 3.2 per cent of such enterprises at the national level and this number went up to 6.24 lakh in 2000-01 recording a growth rate of 33.8 per cent. The share of Rajasthan at the national level in these enterprises also improved to 3.7 per cent. Further, the bulk of these enterprises (88.7 per cent in 1994-95 and 90.4 per cent in 2000-01) were own account manufacturing enterprises (OAMEs)[5] and this percentage is higher than the national proportion. In 1998-99, another 9.7 per cent were non-directory manufacturing enterprises (NDMEs)[6] and only 1.6 per cent were directory enterprises (DMEs).[7] The corresponding proportions in urban Rajasthan were 77.9 per cent,

5. OAME–Own account enterprise operates with no hired regular workers.
6. NDME–Non-directory establishment operates with less than six workers–household and hired.
7. DME–Directory establishment operates with six or more workers–household and hired.

19.0 per cent and 3.1 per cent. In rural Rajasthan, OAMEs were 94.4 per cent, NDMEs were 4.7 per cent and DMEs were mere 0.9 per cent. In 2000-01, 7.4 per cent were non-directory manufacturing enterprises and only 2.2 per cent were directory enterprises. The corresponding proportions in urban Rajasthan were 81.9 per cent, 13.9 per cent and 4.2 per cent. In rural Rajasthan, OAMEs were 95.4 per cent, NDMEs were 3.6 per cent and DMEs were mere 1.0 per cent. It is also observed that urban enterprises have recorded a higher growth rate of 43 per cent during the period compared to rural increase of 28.9 per cent.

Table 5.5

Estimated Number of Unorganised Manufacturing Enterprises: Rajasthan

Years	*1994-95*			*2000-01*			*Distribution in Total*		*% Increase*
	No. of Enterprises	*% Share*	*Share in India*	*No. of Enterprises*	*% Share*	*Share in India*	*1994-95*	*2000-01*	
OAME	286634	94.4	3.0	373334	95.4	3.4	61.5	59.9	30.2
NDME	14351	4.7	2.2	13951	3.6	2.2	3.1	2.2	-2.8
DME	2643	0.9	0.9	3964	1.0	1.6	0.6	0.6	50.0
Rural	**303628**	**100**	**2.9**	**391250**	**100**	**3.3**	**65.2**	**62.7**	**28.9**
OAME	126496	77.9	4.7	190145	81.9	5.3	27.1	30.5	50.3
NDME	30937	19.1	3.3	32369	13.9	3.0	6.6	5.2	4.6
DME	4983	3.1	1.4	9789	4.2	2.4	1.1	1.6	96.4
Urban	**162416**	**100**	**4.1**	**232303**	**100**	**4.6**	**34.8**	**37.3**	**43.0**
OAME	413130	88.7	3.4	563479	90.4	3.8	88.6	90.4	36.4
NDME	45288	9.7	2.8	46320	7.4	2.7	9.7	7.4	2.3
DME	7626	1.6	1.2	13753	2.2	2.1	1.6	2.2	80.3
Combined	**466044**	**100**	**3.2**	**623553**	**100**	**3.7**	**100**	**100**	**33.8**

Source: NSSO (1998a; b) and NSSO (2002b).

Table 5.5 reveals that own account enterprises during this period (1994-95–2000-01) have gained in share by 1.8 percentage points. This implies that shift has taken place towards family based enterprises. However, there is an increase in share of directory enterprises also. During this period, own account enterprises have increased by 36.4 per cent while directory enterprises by 80.3 per cent. The non-directory enterprise increased by 2.3 per cent only. This implies two things: one that expansion has taken place in case of own account enterprises with possibly two way process—new firms are also of this category and lower end non-directory enterprises have reduced to own account structure. Two, some non-directory enterprises have moved upwards to become directory enterprises and some new firms have directly entered at the directory level.

Table 5.6 provides information on the status of the enterprise over last three years. The information gives the owner's impression about the growth of the enterprise over the last three years. 12.8 per cent of the entrepreneurs had felt that their business activities have expanded over the three years preceding the date of survey. On the other hand, 11.1 per cent of the urban entrepreneurs had felt that their business activities have expanded over the three years preceding the date of survey. In case of rural enterprises, 13.8 per cent of the entrepreneurs had felt that their business activities have expanded over the three years preceding the date of survey. A large proportion, 54 per cent of the entrepreneurs had felt that their enterprises had stagnated during the last three years. A significant percentage of urban (52.8%) entrepreneurs had felt that their enterprises had stagnated during the last three years while this proportion was 54.7 in case of rural enterprises. Enterprises have been contracting too. 22.6 per cent of the entrepreneurs had felt that their business has contracted over the last three years and this percentage was 23.7 per cent in case of urban entrepreneurs and 22.0 per cent in case rural entrepreneurs in Rajasthan.

Table 5.6

Growth Status of Enterprises over the Period of Last 3 Years: 2000-2001

Growth Type	*Rural*	*Urban*	*Combined*
Expanding	13.8	11.1	12.8
Stagnating	54.7	52.8	54.0
Contracting	22.0	23.7	22.6
NA	9.5	12.4	10.5
All	**100**	**100**	**100**

Note: NA means unit is in operation for less than 3 years.
Source: NSSO (2002b).

Structural Ratios

How is the unorganised manufacturing sector performing in Rajasthan at the aggregate level? To understand it, we present certain structural ratios in Table 5.7. When we consider the output labour ratio, we find that in 2000-01, a worker produced output worth Rs. 47,111. In rural enterprises a worker produced output of Rs. 35,127 and in urban enterprises the figure was Rs. 63,022. So labour productivity is higher in urban unorganised manufacturing enterprises compared to rural enterprises. Besides, one worker produces Rs. 1.3 lakh worth output in directory enterprises when a worker produces output of Rs. 90,038 in non-directory enterprises and Rs. 28,212 in OAMEs. Output per worker in directory enterprises is 4.6 times that of OAMEs and 1.4 times that of non-directory enterprises. This ratio is 3.2 times between OAMEs and non-directory enterprises. Labour productivity is also higher in urban enterprises across the type of enterprise.

Table 5.7

Structural Ratios of Unorganised Manufacturing Enterprises: 2000-2001

Region/ Sector	*Output to*		*Value Added to*		*Fixed Capital to*	
	Employment Ratio (Rs.)	*Fixed Capital Ratio*	*Employment Ratio (Rs.)*	*Fixed Capital Ratio*	*Output Ratio*	*Employment Ratio (Rs.)*
Rural	**35127**	**1.41**	**17249**	**0.69**	**0.49**	**24930**
OAME	26627	1.13	15229	0.65	0.57	23518
NDME	81796	2.01	29585	0.73	0.36	40670
DME	101963	3.79	31690	1.18	0.31	26877
Urban	**63022**	**1.20**	**24504**	**0.47**	**0.39**	**52600**
OAME	31147	0.78	16875	0.42	0.54	39843
NDME	93688	1.32	34755	0.49	0.37	70985
DME	143487	1.86	40074	0.52	0.28	77058
Combined	**47111**	**1.28**	**2036**	**0.55**	**0.43**	**36817**
OAME	28212	0.96	15806	0.54	0.56	29243
NDME	90038	1.46	33169	0.54	0.37	61681
DME	129841	2.14	37319	0.62	0.29	60567

Source: NSSO (2002c).

Now, when we define labour productivity as value added per worker, then we find that per worker value added is Rs. 20,366 and it is Rs. 17,249 in rural enterprises and still higher in urban enterprises at Rs. 24,504. Across the regions, labour productivity is higher in directory enterprises than the non-directory enterprises and they in turn have higher labour productivity than the OAMEs. Also labour productivity is lower in rural enterprises across the type of enterprises compared to urban areas.

Capital productivity in unorganised manufacturing sector in 2000-2001 in Rajasthan was 1.28 implying that a rupee worth of capital produce Rs. 1.28 of output. The capital productivity is higher in rural enterprises compared to urban enterprises. Across the regions, capital productivity is higher in directory enterprises than the non-directory enterprises and they in turn have higher capital productivity than the OAMEs. Also capital productivity is lower in urban enterprises across the type of enterprises compared to rural areas. Now when capital productivity is defined as ratio of value added to fixed capital, we find that a rupee of capital investment added value worth Re. 0.55 and this ratio is 0.69 in rural enterprises and lower at 0.47 in urban enterprises. So the performance of rural enterprises across the type of enterprises is better than the urban enterprises.

It is also observed that value added to output ratio is 0.43 implying that for every unit of output value addition is 0.43 units. Here again rural enterprises have performed better than the urban enterprises with the exception of non-directory enterprises. The lowest ratio is found in the case of urban directory enterprises where a unit of output leads to only 0.28 units of value addition.

Finally, defining capital intensity as ratio of fixed capital to employment, we find that the aggregate ratio is Rs. 36,817 implying that to employ one worker, Rs. 36,817 worth capital investment is required. In rural enterprises, capital requirement is Rs. 24,930 compared to Rs. 52,600 in urban enterprises. This also means that urban enterprises are more capital intensive compared to rural enterprises. This is due to the size of the rural enterprises (as seen elsewhere in the chapter). In case of rural enterprises, we find that capital intensity is higher in non-directory enterprises *vis-à-vis* directory enterprises and the differences between own account and directory enterprises is not very large. In case of urban enterprises, we find that difference in capital productivity between non-directory enterprises and directory enterprises is not very huge though this difference is significant between own account and non-directory enterprises.

Firm Size

What is the size of enterprises? Table 5.8 shows that 53.1 per cent of enterprises were operating with one person and this proportion was 56.3 per cent in case of enterprises located in rural areas and 47.7 per cent in case of urban located enterprises. This was due to OAMEs mainly as 58.7 per cent were one person operated. The proportion of rural OAMEs is marginally higher than urban OAMEs. Another 30.6 per cent enterprises operate with two persons. This percentage for rural enterprises is 32.8 per cent and 27.0 per cent for urban enterprises. This means that unorganised manufacturing sector vastly (83.7%) operated with 1-2 persons. In case of urban located enterprises this proportion is 74.7 per cent compared to 89.1 per cent rural enterprises.

Table 5.8 shows that even in the case of directory enterprises 74 per cent have only 6-9 workers and urban located directory enterprises have higher proportion (78.1%) compared to rural located enterprises (63.6%). There are 35.5 per cent directory enterprises in rural areas that operate with 10-19 workers while this percentage is 20.5 per cent in urban locations. Overall this percentage is 24.9 per cent. This means that urban directory enterprises are relatively of smaller size compared to rural enterprises. In case of non-directory enterprises, 63.2 per cent have operated with 2-3 workers and urban located non-directory enterprises have higher proportion (65.7%) compared to rural located enterprises (57.5%). This means that the size of urban non-directory enterprises is smaller than rural non-directory enterprises. There are 42.5 per cent non-directory enterprises in rural areas that operate with 4-5 workers while this percentage is 33.9 per cent in urban locations. Overall this percentage is 36.5 per cent. This means that urban non-directory enterprises are relatively of smaller size compared to rural non-directory enterprises. Finally, there are few enterprises that have employment size of 20 plus across regions and types of enterprises.

Table 5.8

Distribution of Enterprises by Employment Size: 2000-2001

Region/ Category	*Employment Per Enterprise (No.)*									
	1	*2*	*3*	*4*	*5*	*6-9*	*10-19*	*20-49*	*50+*	*Total*
Rural	**56.3**	**32.8**	**6.3**	**2.0**	**1.6**	**0.7**	**0.3**			**100**
OAME	59.0	33.2	5.6	1.2	1.0					100
NDME		30.1	27.4	25.0	17.5					100
DME					0.3	63.6	35.5	0.6		100
Urban	**47.7**	**27.0**	**13.1**	**5.0**	**2.7**	**3.7**	**0.8**			**100**
OAME	58.2	28.2	9.6	2.7	0.8	0.5				100
NDME	0.2	28.4	37.3	19.5	14.4	0.2				100
DME	0.2			0.3		78.1	20.5	0.8	0.1	100
All	**53.1**	**30.6**	**8.8**	**3.1**	**2.0**	**1.8**	**0.6**			**100**
OAME	58.7	31.5	6.9	1.7	0.9	0.3				100
NDME	0.1	28.9	34.3	21.1	15.4	0.2				100
DME	0.1			0.2	0.1	73.9	24.9	0.7	0.1	100

Source: NSSO (2002d).

Contracting Firms

We have observed that industry groups resort to contract, but firms also work on contract for others. Table 5.9 gives information on the status of working enterprises working on contract basis by regions. It is found that about 13 per cent of the total manufacturing enterprises in Rajasthan have been estimated to be working at least some work on contract basis. The proportion of enterprises working on contract was higher in urban areas except for DMEs, but the regional difference between the NDMEs was rather small compared to OAMEs and DMEs. Considering all unorganised manufacturing enterprises in Rajasthan, one finds that 9.9 per cent work on some contract with 9.6 per cent such enterprises in rural areas and 10.3 per cent in urban areas. Thus, contract system is in place.

Disaggregated Scene

National Sample Survey Organisation has conducted various surveys of unorganised manufacturing sector over the years. Each survey has seen changing definitions/classifications and therefore at the disaggregated level we present the results of only 56th NSS round

Table 5.9

Enterprises Working on Contract: 2000-2001

Type	*Rural*	*Urban*	*Combined*
OAME	5.9	24.2	12.1
NDME	15.9	17.9	17.3
DME	45.1	24.4	30.4
All	**6.6**	**23.3**	**12.9**

Source: NSSO (2002b).

for the year 2000-01, which was the follow-up survey of the 1998 *Economic Survey*. However, it would be important to observe the unorganised manufacturing sector structure in 1994-95 separately. Table 5.10 shows that there were 4.66 lakh unorganised manufacturing enterprises in Rajasthan in 1994-95 that employed 8.72 lakh workers. Of these enterprises, 65.2 per cent were located in rural areas and the remaining 1.62 lakh (34.9%) in urban areas. The rural enterprises generated 59.9 per cent of total employment when 34.9 per cent urban enterprises employed 40.1 per cent of workers. Looking at the structure of unorganised manufacturing sector in Rajasthan, we find that 23.2 per cent enterprises were wood & wood products enterprises followed by 18.1 per cent repair services enterprises, 16.6 per cent manufacture of food products enterprises and 11.6 per cent non-metallic mineral products enterprises. These four industry groups constituted 69.5 per cent of all unorganised manufacturing enterprises in 1994-95 in Rajasthan and employed 65.6 per cent of all workers. Textile products, leather & leather products and other manufacturing industries were the other industry groups of some significance (21.9 per cent share). This means that unorganised manufacturing sector in 1994-95 comprised mainly of seven industry groups that had 91.4 per cent of all enterprises and 77.8 per cent of all employment.

It might be pointed out here that in rural areas non-metallic mineral products with 15.3 per cent enterprises employed 23.9 per cent of all workers. This is because all mines are located in rural setting and persons employed also come from rural areas. On the other hand, urban unorganised manufacturing sector was dominated by repair services (28.6%) followed by wood & wood products enterprises (15.6%), textile products (11.3%), other manufacturing industries (10.6%) and manufacture of food products (10.5%)—77.2 per cent of all enterprises. On the employment front these five industry groups employed 69.4 per cent of all workers (3.42 lakh). Thus, we find that there are some rural urban differences in structure of unorganised manufacturing sector.

Table 5.10

Distribution of Unorganised Manufacturing Enterprises and Employment by Industry: 1994-95

Industry	*Rural*		*Urban*		*Total*	
	Enterprises	*Employment*	*Enterprises*	*Employment*	*Enterprises*	*Employment*
Manufacture of Food Products	19.8	17.7	10.5	11.7	16.6	15.3
Beverages, Tobacco, etc.	0.0	0.1	0.3	0.3	0.1	0.2
Cotton Textiles	1.0	0.8	1.6	2.3	1.2	1.4
Wool, Silk & Man-made Fibre Textiles	1.5	1.7	0.3	0.9	1.1	1.4
Jute and Other Textiles					0.0	0.0
Textile Products	5.6	7.8	11.3	11.7	7.6	9.4
Wood & Wood Products	27.3	22.7	15.6	14.5	23.2	19.4
Paper & Paper Products	0.0		2.4	4.5	0.8	1.8
Leather & Leather Products	8.4	7.6	5.5	5.2	7.4	6.6
Chemical & Chemical Products	0.0		0.3	0.4	0.1	0.2
Rubber, Plastic & Petroleum	0.1		0.3	0.7	0.2	0.3
Non-metallic Mineral Products	15.3	23.9	4.6	5.2	11.6	16.4
Basic Metal & Alloys Industries	0.0		0.5	0.6	0.2	0.2
Metal Products & Parts	1.1	2.0	3.0	4.0	1.8	2.8
Machinery & Equipment Other than Transport Equipment	0.5	0.4	0.2	0.2	0.4	0.3
Transport Equipment & Parts	0.0		0.0	0.1	0.0	0.0
Other Manufacturing Industries	4.3	4.8	10.6	8.2	6.5	6.2
Repair of Capital Goods	2.4	1.9	4.4	6.1	3.1	3.6
Repair Services	12.5	8.6	28.6	23.3	18.1	14.5
Not Recorded Industries	0.1		0.0	0.1	0.1	0.0
All	**100**	**100**	**100**	**100**	**100**	**100**
Total (No.)	**303628**	**522668**	**162416**	**349136**	**466044**	**871804**

Source: NSSO (1998a; b).

As industrial classification has changed since 1994-95, we present below a disaggregated picture for the year 2000-01. Table 5.11 reveals that top six industry groups that have 87 per cent of all unorganised enterprises are manufacture of wearing apparel; dressing and dyeing of fur, manufacture of food products and beverages, manufacture of furniture; manufacturing, manufacture of wood and of products of wood and cork, except furniture; manufacture of articles of straw and plaiting materials and, manufacture of other non-metallic mineral products. In urban areas, top four industry groups *viz.*, manufacture of wearing apparel; dressing and dyeing of fur, manufacture of furniture; manufacturing, manufacture of textiles and, manufacture of food products and beverages account for 71.3 per cent of all urban unorganised manufacturing enterprises.

In rural areas, top five industry groups account for 84.6 per cent of all rural unorganised manufacturing enterprises and they are manufacture of wearing apparel; dressing and dyeing of fur, manufacture of food products and beverages, manufacture of wood and of products of wood and cork, except furniture; manufacture of articles of straw and plaiting materials, manufacture of furniture; manufacturing and, manufacture of other non-metallic mineral products. Thus, looking at the structure of unorganised manufacturing sector in 1994-95 and 2000-01, one finds the dominance is of five-six industry groups and these have backward linkages with the economy. This period has not observed any significant structural change in unorganised manufacturing sector of Rajasthan.

It is further found (Table 5.12) that industry groups *viz.*, manufacture of tobacco products; manufacture of textiles; manufacture of paper and paper products; publishing, printing and reproduction of recorded media; manufacture of chemicals and chemical products; manufacture of rubber and plastics products; manufacture of basic metals; manufacture of electrical machinery and apparatus nec and manufacturing of motor vehicles, trailers and semi-trailers are mainly urban in nature as majority of these enterprises are located in urban areas. In case of directory enterprises with the exception of industry group of manufacture of other non-metallic mineral products, all other industry groups are largely urban located. Among the non-directory enterprises, with the exception of cotton ginning, cleaning and baling; manufacture of tobacco products; tanning and dressing of leather;

manufacture of luggage, handbags, saddler, harness and footwear and; manufacture of other non-metallic mineral products industry groups all other are mainly urban based. In case of OAMEs, the scenario is quite mixed. It means that location of enterprises in rural-urban areas is determined by the availability of raw materials locally.

Table 5.11

Distribution of Unorganised Manufacturing Enterprises: 2000-01

Industry	*Rural*	*Urban*	*Combined*
1405	0.21	0.29	0.24
15	22.39	14.68	19.52
16	2.17	7.45	4.14
17	4.38	17.66	9.32
18	23.98	21.02	22.88
19	4.11	2.30	3.44
20	13.37	4.53	10.08
21	neg.	0.77	0.29
22	neg.	0.94	0.35
23	0.03	0.01	0.02
24	0.04	0.41	0.18
25		0.83	0.31
26	11.86	5.81	9.61
27	neg.	0.03	0.01
28	3.69	3.59	3.65
29	0.50	0.78	0.60
30			
31	0.26	0.49	0.35
32			
33		0.10	0.04
34	neg.	0.30	0.11
35	0.05	0.05	0.05
36	12.95	17.92	14.80
37		0.06	0.02
All	**100**	**100**	**100**

Note: For codes see Appendix A-5.1.
Source: Computed from NSSO (2002b).

Table 5.12

Distribution of Enterprises by Category

Industry	*Combined*		*OAMEs*		*NDMEs*		*DMEs*	
	Rural	*Urban*	*Rural*	*Urban*	*Rural*	*Urban*	*Rural*	*Urban*
1405	55.13	44.86	54.22	45.78	100.00			100.00
15	71.98	28.02	74.90	25.10	37.48	62.52	34.26	65.74
16	32.94	67.06	32.92	67.08	100.00		31.91	68.09
17	29.45	70.55	29.48	70.52	23.04	76.96	37.30	62.70
18	65.76	34.24	69.52	30.48	28.40	71.60	2.86	97.14
19	75.04	24.96	75.00	25.00	81.54	18.46	10.49	89.51
20	83.25	16.75	87.10	12.90	30.55	69.45	1.48	98.52
21	0.36	99.64		100.00	4.53	95.46		100
22	0.61	99.39		100.00	1.30	98.70		100
23	87.38	12.63	100.00			100.00		
24	14.94	85.06	15.92	84.10	13.37	86.63	7.52	92.48
25	0.14	99.86		100.00		100.00	1.25	98.75
26	77.47	22.53	79.12	20.88	61.68	38.32	68.58	31.42
27	17.20	82.80		100.00	32.32	67.69		100
28	63.38	36.62	75.20	24.80	27.78	72.22	2.64	97.36
29	51.95	48.05	69.06	30.94	15.13	84.88	16.00	84.00
30								
31	47.41	52.59	64.57	35.43	11.89	88.11	4.43	95.57
32								
33		100.00		100.00		100.00		
34	0.99	99.01		100.00		100.00	4.03	95.97
35	64.85	35.15	72.96	27.04		100.00		
36	54.90	45.10	59.18	40.82	16.53	83.47	29.56	70.44
37		100.00		100.00		100.00		100.00
All	**62.74**	**37.25**	**66.25**	**33.75**	**30.12**	**69.88**	**28.83**	**71.17**

Note: For codes see Appendix A-5.1.
Source: Computed from NSSO (2002b).

Some Structural Ratios: Disaggregated Level

This section presents labour productivity and value added per enterprise at 2-digit industry group level. The annual gross value added per worker was estimated to be Rs. 20,366 (Table 5.13). The highest value added per worker was estimated for industry group of manufacture of basic metals (Rs. 46,288) followed by industry group of manufacturing of other transport equipment (Rs. 46,095), industry group of publishing, printing and reproduction of recorded media (Rs. 43,086). The lowest estimated annual value added per worker was in case of industry group of manufacture of tobacco products (Rs. 5,453). The traditional Rajasthan's industry groups like wood & wood products, manufacture of textiles and manufacture of non-metallic minerals have lower labour productivity which is also lower than the state average. The difference in labour productivity of the lowest and highest is more than 8 times. This means that there are wide variations in labour productivity across industry groups.

Table 5.13 also reveals that labour productivity in case of directory enterprises (Rs. 37,319) is higher than non-directory enterprises (Rs. 33,169) and that in turn has higher labour productivity compared to OAMEs (Rs. 15,806). In case of directory enterprises the highest gross value added per worker was estimated for industry group of manufacture of electrical machinery and apparatus nec (Rs. 77,502) and the lowest in case of industry group of manufacture of tobacco products (Rs. 18,024). The difference between the lowest and highest labour productivity industry group is 4.3 times. In case of non-directory enterprises, the highest gross value added per worker was estimated for industry group of manufacture of coke, refined petroleum products (Rs. 56,600) and the lowest in case of industry group of cotton ginning, cleaning and baling (Rs. 9,800). This also appears to be due to technology and size of the enterprises. The difference between the lowest and highest labour productivity industry group is 5.8 times. In case of OAMEs, the highest gross value added per worker was estimated for the industry group of manufacturing of other transport equipment (Rs. 51,069) and the lowest in case of industry group of manufacture of tobacco products (Rs. 5,346). The difference between the lowest and highest labour productivity industry group is 9.6 times. There are quite a few OAMEs industry groups that have estimated gross output per worker of lower than Rs. 10,000. There are three OAMEs industry groups that have higher labour productivity than the non-directory industry groups (manufacture of electrical machinery and apparatus nec; manufacture of medical, precision and optical instruments, watches and clocks and; manufacturing of other transport equipment), while there are six non-directory industry groups that have higher labour productivity compared to directory industry groups. This shows that higher the firm size higher is the labour productivity, though there are some exceptions too. This would be due to technology used and location of enterprises.

Table 5.13

Gross Value Added Per Worker and Per Enterprise: 2000-2001 (56th Round)–Combined

	Gross Value Added Per Worker (Rs.)				*Gross Value Added Per Enterprise (Rs.)*			
Industry	*OAME*	*NDME*	*DME*	*All*	*OAME*	*NDME*	*DME*	*All*
01405	9776	9800	63028	11431	15479	49000	461019	19698
15	15520	31943	36559	18542	23568	94925	274293	31260
16	5346	20050	18024	5453	7776	74069	145392	7984
17	8137	24821	32885	15619	12926	84045	343868	33183
18	14926	29410	27993	18069	18001	88562	233113	25748
19	20073	35714	21251	21034	34474	122534	148755	37546
20	15762	33883	48876	18666	23184	93260	403410	29639
21	11146	17637	35143	21019	22234	79551	434161	67835
22	30530	30837	60561	43086	55717	90582	492821	148636
23	9192	56600	0	16187	23023	169800	0	41557
24	8709	47877	44917	25656	18207	177941	453450	73456
25	21757	39861	36739	32892	38839	127804	272151	95058
26	13334	37321	49565	20540	29587	132960	537350	53160
27	14850	51646	50461	46288	29700	188322	509153	200976
28	18443	35244	34620	24879	36192	128236	240985	60676
29	29108	37012	46882	35346	60325	148598	321633	104408
30		0	0	0		0	0	0
31	47031	26510	77502	43033	68149	69349	725105	86426
32	0	0	0	0	0	0	0	0
33	29956	15231	0	23572	31932	76154	0	38135
34	39601	24189	39927	35675	102143	88541	340470	156591
35	51069	36150	0	46095	51069	144600	0	61462
36	24141	38663	33246	27367	38985	133480	265634	54280
37	30836	31361	42920	32766	52343	89189	257520	80498
All	**15806**	**33169**	**37319**	**20366**	**24532**	**107298**	**331110**	**37442**

Note: For codes see Appendix A 5.1.
Source: NSSO (2002c).

It is estimated that in 2000-01, unorganised manufacturing enterprises on an average produced gross value of Rs. 7,442 and it was Rs. 3.31 lakh in case of directory enterprises, Rs. 1.07 lakh in case of non-directory enterprises and Rs. 24,532 in case of OAMEs (Table 5.13). So higher the size of the enterprises, higher is the value addition per enterprises. There are wide variations across industry groups in per enterprise estimated gross value added. The difference between the highest and lowest per enterprise gross value added is 25.2 times while it is 5 times in case of directory enterprises, 3.8 times in case of non-directory enterprises and 13.1 times in case of OAMEs. Also across the industry groups, the estimated gross value added per enterprise is higher in non-directory case compared to OAMEs and directory enterprises have higher estimated gross value added per enterprise compared to non-directory enterprises. These differences could be partially explained in terms of location of the enterprises. Thus, location does matter in generation of income. This is invariably due to the size of the enterprises. Household-based enterprises invariably operate at a lower scale.

The Small Scale Sector

The encouragement of small scale enterprises and village and rural industries had been an integral part of the industrial strategy in India. The literature identifies three types of policies towards small enterprise development- passive, protective and developmental (Kirkpatrick, Lee and Nixson, 1984). India has been in the protective mode. Small scale enterprise development can encourage the process of both inter- and intra-regional decentralisation—small scale enterprises can be located both in smaller urban centres and in rural areas. The establishment of small scale village enterprises is seen as an essential element in rural development *via* expanding employment opportunities, raising incomes and living standards and bringing about a more balanced and integrated rural economy. Small scale industries (SSI) played an important role as less capital-intensive producers of goods and providers of employment to labour thereby addressing the problems of reducing poverty and unemployment. Under the old policy regime, major support for promoting small scale industries was provided by the policy of reservation of economically viable and technically feasible items for exclusive manufacture in SSI sector. Indian policies on the small scale industrial sector have, by and large, centred on the concept of emergence and growth of individual firms (Kashyap and Shah, 1995).

As Rajasthan's industrial scene is dominated by small scale sector, it would be pertinent to undertake in-depth analysis to better understand what really is happening in the small scale sector and this may throw up some future policy directions. For this we look at the 2001-02 SSI census. Many important features are thrown up in this survey.[8] The total size of the small scale sector in Rajasthan is 4,41,572 units, or 4.20 per cent of all national enterprises are found in Rajasthan. The estimated number of unregistered SSI units in Rajasthan was 3,98,427 or 4.36 per cent of all such units at the national level. Within Rajasthan, the concentration of unregistered enterprises is in Jaipur with 34,499 in operation.

Nature of Enterprises

The survey reveals that 93.75 per cent registered SSI units were found to be operating perennially, while 4.88 per cent were seasonal and 1.36 per cent units were casual. In case of unregistered small scale enterprises, 95.39 per cent were perennial in nature with 3.38 per cent units operating on a seasonal basis and 1.23 per cent units were casual operators. The casual enterprises are relatively more prone to sickness. It finds that 36,847 units (4.15 per cent of all India figure) were closed and 34.22 per cent (12610) were located in rural Rajasthan and the remaining 24,237 (65.78%) were urban units. It is also revealed that 59.74 per cent rural registered SSI units were working compared to 50.2 per cent urban units. This shows that small scale units are more vulnerable in urban areas and it could be because of intense competition among the enterprises, higher capital requirement especially working capital, which may not be forthcoming easily.

The survey finds 86.71 per cent of registered SSI units' proprietary run with another 7.71 per cent being in partnership mode, 4.55 per cent with cooperative management, 0.17 per cent private companies and 0.86 per cent had other type of management.

8. It is argued that these censuses do not throw up reliable data and there have been definitional changes also across the censuses. Therefore, our analysis pertains only to the latest census. The removal of Inspector Raj has also complicated the registration process. This section therefore needs to be viewed in that light.

What are the activities these enterprises involved in? The survey revealed that of the 4,41,572 SSI enterprises, 23.89 per cent were rural manufacturing units with another 8.23 per cent units engaged in repair and maintenance and 24.30 per cent units were service units. In urban areas, 14.47 per cent enterprises were engaged in manufacturing while 9.13 per cent were repair and maintenance units and 19.97 per cent units were service units. In case of registered rural SSI units, 30.57 per cent enterprises were engaged in manufacturing/ assembly/processing while 1.01 per cent unit were repairing and maintenance and 12.14 per cent units were engaged in servicing activities. The corresponding proportions for urban registered SSI units were 40.56, 1.52 and 14.20 per cent, respectively.

Industrial Clusters

Recent experiences of some of the advanced economies suggest that product-specific spatial clusters of small scale units have demonstrated a high level of efficiency in responding to the new challenges of technology and market competition (Kashyap and Shah 1995). The survey found that in Rajasthan there were 38 clusters of registered SSI units having 6,664 units with 100 or more units producing same product/service in a district. The fixed assets of these 6,664 units stood at Rs. 447.06 crore and produced gross output worth Rs. 1,063.32 crore employing 26,454 persons. This means that per unit fixed assets stood at 6.71 lakh and gross output per unit at Rs. 15.96 lakh, but per unit employment of just 4.0. The capital output ratio is of 2.34. The capital intensity turns out to be Rs. 1,68,994 with labour productivity of Rs. 4,01,952. The survey found that in Rajasthan there were 31 clusters of unregistered SSI units having 30,263 units with 100 or more units producing same product/service in a district. The fixed assets of these 30,263 units stood at Rs. 97.30 crore and they produced gross output worth Rs. 122.12 crore by employing 48,756 persons. This means that per unit fixed assets stood at Rs. 32,150 and gross output per unit at Rs. 40,354 but per unit employment of only 1.6. The capital output ratio works out to be 1.26, much lower than that of registered SSI units. The capital intensity turns out to be Rs. 19,956 with labour productivity of Rs. 25,048. This shows that unregistered enterprises despite being less capital intensive have lower per unit employment compared to registered enterprises. Unregistered small scale enterprises are also less productive. Besides, most of these clusters are autonomous in nature rather than induced ones. In that sense these firms cannot reap economics of scale. Literature also argues that location, and physical infrastructure, other features like size, age and production concentration may also play a crucial role in influencing the efficient functioning of the firms within a cluster. The survey reveals that most of the working enterprises within the clusters are relatively new and size is small thereby rendering them inefficient and vulnerable.

Technology Use

These relationships could further be explained with the help of technology issues. It is reported that the small scale sector entrepreneurs largely use locally available technologies and technical know-how (Singh, 2006a). However, the survey showed that 1.28 per cent registered SSI units had obtained technical know-how from abroad with 4.88 per cent obtaining it from domestic collaborators and another 4.25 per cent from domestic research and development institution, special agency or organisation. In case of unregistered SSI units, the survey finds that 0.44 per cent units had obtained technical know-how from abroad with 4.64 per cent obtaining it from domestic collaborators and another 7.63 per cent from domestic research and development institutions.

Exports

The survey also throws up information on exporting small scale enterprises in Rajasthan and finds only 240 registered SSI units exporting goods worth Rs. 573.88 crore while 1,558 unregistered SSI units exporting goods to the tune of Rs. 16.39 crore. Thus, exports by 1,798 units (3.55 per cent of national units) touch Rs. 590.27 crore which is 4.16 per cent of all India SSI exports. It may be mentioned here that these figures appear to be under reported as there is high proportion not responding in the survey.

Gender and Employment Issues

Gender questions have also been raised by the survey. There are three categories of engagement/participation of women in small scale sector; some women are owners, some women are managers and some are employees. The survey reported that there were 29,785 SSI enterprises that were women managed and 36,371 were women enterprises. Data shows that SSI units employed 15,003 female workers in registered component and 46,065 in unregistered component. Thus 61,068 women workers found employment in SSI sector in Rajasthan constituting 7.04 per cent all women workers in SSI sector in India.

Rajasthan, thus, employed 8,67,608 persons in small scale enterprises that is 3.48 per cent share at all India level or per enterprise employment of 1.95. These enterprises contributed 4.84 to India's gross output with 4.27 per cent share in fixed investment in India. Thus, we find that women participation is only marginal in both the types of small scale enterprises. The women entrepreneurs in Rajasthan are far too little, given their total strength in the population. This has to do with the social-cultural factors, feudal nature of social relations and lower literacy levels among females in Rajasthan.

Khadi and Village Industries

Khadi and village industries have been an integral part of India's industrial development strategy, though lost some ground since the onset of reforms (Chadha, 2003). They were seen as an organic link between them and the people (Saith, 2000). Rajasthan has the conglomerate of traditional village industries including crafts and artisan industries. Rajasthan has performed reasonably well in this sector if one looks at the production and employment figures in case of both traditional and modern activities. At the state level, in 1990-1991 a total employment of 2.98 lakh was generated in the village industries and the major activity was leather (1.74 lakh persons were engaged in it).[9] The second most important activity is pottery (earthen pots are still in great demand during summers). It is followed by cane/bamboo activity. Under the joint forest management especially in the tribal areas of southern Rajasthan, bamboo cultivation was significantly increased and the civil society organisations have put self-help groups into bamboo manufacturing goods. However, of the various activities listed under village industries, only six are of any significance (leather, *ghani* oil, pottery,

9. The source of this information is State Khadi Board. The quality of data may be questionable but is an important source of at least part-time employment in rural areas, so we present some facts on this sector here.

fibre, cane and blacksmithy). All these have strong backward linkages in the economy. In 2001-02, total employment stood at 3.52 lakh, 18.41 per cent increase over 1990-91. Here the main activities are leather, pottery, blacksmithy, lime, cane, fibre, service units and textiles). The top six activities accounted for 92.11 per cent of all employment in 1990-91 while top eight activities accounted for 93.02 per cent employment in 2001-02.

This shows that traditional activities still hold sway over modern activities as far as employment generation in Rajasthan is concerned in village industries sector. Singh, 1997b did an extensive survey across Rajasthan covering all activities of village industries and reported that processing activities like food, fruits, soap, brass-copper, etc. are present in few districts only. At aggregate level leather activity predominates followed by pottery. The study also reported that traditional caste based occupations are still largely persisting. The traditional enterprises have lower labour productivity and one could ascribe it to low level of technology, poor quality of goods, low level of demand that gives lower output. The study also found capital productivity to be low in majority of enterprises. It must be mentioned here that these industries produce products that are consumed by low-income groups and hence have chronic deficiency of demand as Kurien (1978) articulated. Vyas and Mathai (1978) too held that the productivity is mainly dependent upon the skill and devotion of the workers. Singh (1997a) did find indications towards increase in size of the enterprises and the increase in employment (though mainly of family members).

Khadi sector has nation's emotions attached to it. It was seen as employment and income generator for the people in rural areas. Over the years not much diversification in the activities could take place because of systemic rigidities. In Rajasthan, the *khadi* sector pertains largely to cotton *khadi* and woollen *khadi*. Silken and poly sector is very small. The growth in the first half of the nineties (in terms of production/sales in values) is much higher compared to that in the second half of the nineties. It is rather negative across the board with the exception of poly sector. This scenario has varied explanations. For instance, the spinners do not want to spin because income accruing is too less for the time devoted to the activity (Singh, 1997a), remunerative alternatives are available, younger generation is not interested in spinning, *khadi* institutions are in bad shape. Many of them flout rule (only transactions in books take place rather than actual sales) as subsidy is linked to sales only and so on. Amber *charkha* technology was not helpful (this period saw more than 60,000 such *charkhas* lying idle—Singh, 1997a). If spinners are not willing to spin then weavers have not much to weave. The maintenance of *khadi* is costly. The attitude of salesmen at *khadi* outlets is indifferent. The outlets are mostly badly lit and product display is poor. The sale is only linked to seasonal rebate. The policy frame has been responsible for the sorry state of *khadi* sector in India and more so in Rajasthan. Unlike other states, modern rural industries have not really developed in Rajasthan.

Informalisation of the Economy

This section further addresses itself to the issue of informal component of Rajasthan's economy. Informal sector is characterised as consisting of units engaged in the production of goods or services that typically operate at low level of organisation, with little or division between labour and capital as factors of production and on a small scale. The production units in informal sector have characteristic features of household enterprises. The discussion here relates to 55th NSS Round Survey on Informal Enterprises.

Table 5.14 presents distribution of informal enterprises including manufacturing enterprises. The size of informal sector in Rajasthan in 1999-2000 was 18.48 lakh enterprises, which was 4.2 per cent of the national informal sector. It is also observed that vast majority of these enterprises (89.84%) were own account enterprises (OAEs) and the rest were establishments. About 58.2 per cent of enterprises are located in rural areas and 41.8 per cent in urban areas. Table 5.14 also shows that informal sector in Rajasthan is mainly consisting of three activities *viz.*, manufacturing (32.5%), construction (14.3%) and trading and repair services (35.4%)—82.3 per cent of all informal enterprises. The other activity of some significance is transport, storage and communications. Of the rural enterprises (10.76 lakh), 33.9 per cent were manufacturing enterprises followed by 32.1 per cent trading and repair services enterprises and 17.6 per cent construction enterprises while in urban areas of the total (7.72 lakh) enterprises, 40.2 per cent were trading and repair services enterprises followed by 30.3 per cent manufacturing enterprises and 9.8 per cent construction enterprises.

Table 5.14

Distribution of Estimated Number of Informal Enterprises by Regions and Type, 1999-2000 (55th Round)

Activity	OAEs			Establishments			Combined		
	Rural	Urban	Total	Rural	Urban	Total	Rural	Urban	Total
Manufacturing	33.91	30.42	32.59	35.41	29.93	31.28	33.98	30.33	32.46
Construction	18.31	11.98	15.91	0.80	0.09	0.26	17.56	9.80	14.32
Trading and repair services	32.43	38.50	34.74	23.44	47.59	41.62	32.05	40.16	35.44
Hotels and restaurants	2.87	3.28	3.02	5.62	5.38	5.44	2.99	3.66	3.27
Transport, storage and communications	5.61	6.40	5.91	16.61	4.71	7.65	6.08	6.09	6.08
Financial intermediation	0.00	0.20	0.08	0.00	0.09	0.07	0.00	0.18	0.08
Real estate, renting and business activities	0.61	2.41	1.29	1.92	3.86	3.38	0.67	2.67	1.50
Education	0.23	0.82	0.45	13.15	3.40	5.81	0.79	1.29	1.00
Health and social work	1.35	0.74	1.12	2.70	1.31	1.65	1.41	0.84	1.17
Other community, social and personal service activities (excl. domestic services)	4.67	5.27	4.90	0.36	3.66	2.85	4.49	4.97	4.69
All	**100**	**100**	**100**	**100**	**100**	**100**	**100**	**100**	**100**
Number	**1029786**	**630746**	**1660532**	**46423**	**141455**	**187878**	**1076209**	**772201**	**1848410**

Source: Computed from NSSO (2001).

Table 5.14 also shows that in case of 16.61 lakh AOEs, 62 per cent were located in rural areas and the remaining in urban areas. Again, of the rural enterprises (10.30 lakh), 33.9 per cent were manufacturing enterprises followed by 32.4 per cent trading and repair services enterprises and 18.3 per cent construction enterprises while in urban areas of the total (6.31 lakh) enterprises, 38.5 per cent were trading and repair services enterprises followed by 30.4 per cent manufacturing enterprises and 11.98 per cent construction enterprises. There were 1.88 lakh establishments and only one-quarter were located in rural areas while the remaining (1.41 lakh) in urban areas. The composition of establishment type informal sector in Rajasthan is significantly different from AOEs. For instance, at the aggregate level of the 1.88 lakh enterprises, 41.6 per cent were trading and repair services enterprises followed by 31.3 per cent manufacturing enterprises, 7.6 per cent transport, storage and communications enterprises and 5.8 per cent education enterprise—86.3 per cent of all establishments. Again, of the rural enterprises (46423), 35.4 per cent were manufacturing enterprises followed by 23.4 per cent trading and repair services enterprises and 16.6 per cent transport, storage and communications enterprises and 13.2 per cent were education enterprises while in urban areas of the total (1.41 lakh) enterprises, 47.6 per cent were trading and repair services enterprises followed by 29.9 per cent manufacturing enterprises and 5.4 per cent hotels and restaurants enterprises.

This analysis reveals that the structure of informal sector in Rajasthan is concentrated in three activities mainly and there are rural-urban and own account and establishment enterprise variations. In case of manufacturing enterprises, it clearly comes out that in Rajasthan, among OAEs rural manufacturing enterprises predominate while among establishments, it is urban areas manufacturing enterprises that predominate. This means that family-based manufacturing activities are of significant importance in rural areas and in urban areas it is relatively bigger enterprises that are in operation in manufacturing sector.

Employment in Manufacturing Activities

Informal manufacturing activities in Rajasthan employed 10.58 lakh workers and 57.2 per cent were employed with rural manufacturing enterprises. The remaining 42.8 per cent were urban manufacturing workers. These workers constituted 3.57 per cent of all India manufacturing activities workers and 35.9 per cent of all informal sector workers in Rajasthan. 71.1 per cent of all manufacturing workers were males with only 28.9 per cent female workers. In rural manufacturing activities of the total workers (6.05 lakh), 69.4 per cent were males compared to 73.2 per cent in urban manufacturing activities. This work force is both part-time and full time workers.

Some Ratios in Informal Sector

Table 5.15 presents annual per worker value added in the manufacturing activities. At the aggregate level the estimated value added per worker was Rs. 18,300 which is higher than the national average of Rs. 17,182. It is also found that estimated value added per worker in establishments (Rs. 28,773) is much higher than the value added per worker in own account enterprises (Rs. 15,657). In case of rural manufacturing enterprises, the estimated value added per worker was Rs. 14,818 that is much lower than that in case of urban enterprises (Rs. 26,088). The value added per worker in urban enterprises is much higher compared to rural OAEs and establishments. Thus, it is clear that family enterprises/home-based enterprises have lower labour productivity across regions. However, OAEs in Rajasthan have higher labour productivity compared to national average and obverse is the case of establishments. It may also be pointed out here that manufacturing enterprises generated value addition of Rs. 193.63 lakh of which 46.8 per cent was through rural manufacturing enterprises and 86.9 per cent of value added in rural manufacturing enterprises originated in OAEs compared to 52.3 per cent in case of urban manufacturing enterprises. At the aggregate level, 68.3 per cent of value addition was due to OAEs. The estimated value added in manufacturing OAEs was Rs. 132.28 lakh of which 58.8 per cent was due to rural OAEs while this contribution was 19.2 per cent in case of rural establishments to total estimated value added of Rs. 61.35 lakh. Thus, there are rural-urban and enterprise type variations in value added per worker in Rajasthan's informal sector.

Table 5.15

Value Added Per Worker in Manufacturing Informal Sector (Rs.): 1999-2000

Type	*Rural*		*Urban*		*Combined*	
	Rajasthan	*India*	*Rajasthan*	*India*	*Rajasthan*	*India*
OAE	14159	8963	18446	15585	15657	10768
Establishments	21398	22699	31340	35225	28773	31389
All	**14818**	**11157**	**22945**	**26088**	**18300**	**17182**

Source: NSSO (2001).

Public Sector

Public sector since the reforms era has begun, is perceived as a cause of all the ills in the economy and Rajasthan is no exception. Public sector enterprises in Rajasthan cover a wide range of activities like manufacturing (sugar, edible oil, chemicals, mining, etc.), infrastructure development (power, housing, transport, warehousing) and provision of services, credit or inputs (seeds, term loans, agriculture credit, etc.). The reform period has observed a number of initiatives over the past few years in order to improve their efficiency. The reforms include, *inter alia*, distancing the state government from the public sector enterprises, progressively reducing budgetary support, initiating the process of performance contracts or memorandums of understanding (MoUs), privatising or sale of loss making or unviable enterprise, management transfers, and strengthening those enterprises which are playing crucial role in the state's economy. However, if privatisation of the public undertakings is exclusively for reducing the fiscal deficit, then there is bound to be a tendency to focus on offloading heavy loss making enterprises as quickly as possible with much regard to long term consequences to such privatised units (Joshi, 2000).

During 1990-91, public sector enterprises in Rajasthan registered an aggregate loss of Rs. 83.62 crore. The financial performance did show significant improvement at the end of 1994-95 and 38 enterprises posted an aggregate profit (before tax) of Rs. 93.48 crore. A State Renewal Fund (SRF) has been set up for ensuring safety net for the workers of state enterprises. The objectives of SRF include providing assistance towards cost of retraining and redeployment of employees and to provide funds for compensation/voluntary retirement schemes affecting the employees as a result of restructuring or winding up or closure. In case of central government enterprises in Rajasthan, the value of assets was Rs. 2,219 crore in 1990-91 and it improved to Rs. 12,808 crore by 2002-03. The share of Rajasthan in the all India public enterprises assets stood at 1.71 per cent in 1990-91 and 2.44 per cent in 2002-03. The employees have however been around 30,000 plus throughout this period.[10] Per employee assets roughly were Rs. 0.13 crore in 1995-96 and Rs. 0.40 crore in 2002-03.

Industrial Relations

Industrial relations are important for investment climate. Rajasthan has observed peaceful environment over the years. Industrial peace is one of the necessities for achieving the desired level of productivity and production. However, since the onset of economic reforms, employer has become aggressive compared to trade unions. Man-days lost due to stoppage of work stood at 26,428 in 1991 and by 1995 the number was 16,290. It rose again till 2000 to fall to 23,767 in 2001 and finally rested at 29,695 in 2003. The major culprit in this changing situation is the Jaipur Metals Ltd. based in Jaipur that has seen continued hostile environment towards labour. However, Rajasthan has increased its share at the national level from 2.35 per cent in 1991 to 5.30 per cent in 2001 and then at 4.40 per cent in 2003.

Post-Reform State Policies

In the earlier phases of industrial development, Rajasthan was dovetailing the national policies as they brought resources to the states. States' initiative was missing. This is despite the fact that Rajasthan did not get adequate share in central investment in public sector investments. Lack of infrastructure and hostile physical environment had set in inertia. However, the early nineties saw some initiatives coming out of the corridors of power. The Industrial policy of 1994 was a major step forward. It aimed at an optimum utilisation

10. Upto June 2004, 9.33 lakh persons were employed with State public sector undertakings.

of available mineral, agricultural and other resources to increase the industrial production, creation of additional employment opportunities, reduction in regional imbalances, encouragement to entrepreneurship and augmentation of financial resources of the state. It gave due priority to *khadi* and village industries, handloom, handicrafts and small scale industries. The Mineral, Marble and Granite Policy of 1994 was also there to promote scientific exploration and exploitation of the State's rich minerals. The Industrial Policy 1994 had brought about a significant change in its investment climate, at least on paper. The Rural Non-Farm Policy of 1995 tried to focus efforts on growth and employment through rural industrialisation. With a series of policy initiatives it was thought that the State is poised for significant developments. The experience of implementing the State's 1994 Industrial Policy brought to light certain deficiencies and practical problems, which need to be redressed. There were areas like Infrastructure and Human Resource Development, which required even greater attention than has been accorded in the past.

The New Industrial Policy was introduced in 1998 as an exercise to reflect these developments and to launch new initiatives to take advantage of the emerging opportunities. The main objectives were to achieve global competitiveness by improving infrastructure, development of thrust sectors, simplification of rules and procedures, greater participation of private sector, setting up of Business Centres and Industrial Complexes, Development of Integrated Industrial Parks (IIPs) and Industrial Model Towns (IMTs). The Industrial Policy of 1998, thus aimed at making Rajasthan a preferred State for investment in the identified areas and to ultimately achieve global competitiveness. The policy lays special emphasis on accelerating the over all pace of industrial growth, increasing employment opportunities, improving productivity, ensuring sustainable development and strengthening the SSI, tiny and cottage industries sector.

The Investment Policy 2003, was introduced for encouraging industrial growth and investments in other sectors of economy like infrastructure and social sector, which will not only provide a major boost to the economy of the State but will also have all round impact leading to creation of additional employment opportunities and ultimately better quality of life for the people. The new policy is geared to provide SMART (Simple, Moral, Accountable, Responsive and Transparent) system of incentives and clearances to investors leading to better industrial growth, increased employment opportunities, sustainable development and investment in social infrastructure. The State through these incentives hopes to attract investors in all fields and especially in the areas like agro & food processing industry, glass, ceramic, cement, logistic based industry, textiles, leather, wool, dying, handicrafts, gem & jewellery, automotive, tourism, information technology, infrastructure development like park, road, urban and social infrastructure, bio-technology, etc.

These objectives can be achieved only when economic reforms result in creating a positive investment climate conducive to a dominant private sector role and that includes setting up state of-the-art infrastructure, capacity building in industry for global competitiveness, a level playing field with effective and transparent rules of fair play, augmentation of financial resources and efficiency-enhancing policy instruments. The strategy has to be growth focused and the new strategy envisaged development of clusters offering economics of agglomeration and thrust sectors. The highest priority has to be assigned to improving infrastructure and it has to take into account the resource endowment and the growth potential of each area. Special efforts are to be made for developing Government-Industry partnership in the implementation of the policy. The basic approach of all the initiatives is to encourage increasingly greater participation of private enterprise in the State's economic growth. The Board of Investment has been reconstituted as the Board of Infrastructure Development and Investment to ensure greater focus on industry-related infrastructure. It has to ensure formulation of perspective plans for different regions, inter-sectoral coordination and effective monitoring for timely provision of facilities in industrial areas. Based on the Memorandum of Understanding signed with Infrastructure Leasing and Financial Services Limited (IL&FS) and Housing Development and Finance Corporation (HDFC), a Project Development Corporation (PDCOR) has been set up in the private sector, with equity participation by the State Government. The company is to offer Investment Banking Reports on commercially profitable projects, tie up finances and offer projects for implementation to prospective investors. In important industrial areas of the State, establishment of Business Centres in the private sector is also to be encouraged. It was thus recognised that rapid industrialisation is necessary to bring about the desired increase in the State income. The industrial sector has to grow at a rate faster than the average rate of growth of the economy.[11]

Steps have also been taken to streamline clearances, simplification of rules and procedures, fixing of time limits for different clearances and setting up of committees at State and district levels to regularly monitor the pending cases and to ensure their speedy disposal. Government of Rajasthan has put in place the single window system to further simplify procedures. It has devised a single composite application form to make the task of the investor easier. It is expected that filling the form is all it would take for obtaining statutory approvals and clearances from various government departments and agencies. In pursuance of making the Single Window System truly effective, Rajasthan has changed the Rules of Business by setting up three empowered committees to take decisions to speedily clear investment proposals. Re-examination and refusal is out of the purview of individual department, once these committees take a decision. All decisions are to be taken by related departments within prescribed time schedules. In most of the districts the single window does function at all. The concept also appears to mean that each department has a single window rather than a single window facility for all entrepreneurial requirements.

Recent Industrial Investment Scenario

The thrust of the new industrial policy at the national level has been to enable entrepreneurs to take investment decisions based on their own commercial perception with a greatly reduced regulatory role of the government. Licensing stands abolished for most of the industries, and the entrepreneurs are only required to file an investment intention. The structure has also invoked response from foreign investors. Since the new industrial policy (NEP) aimed at making industries globally competitive, the process of foreign

11. It is a pity that research and development expenditure stood at Rs. 1,819.82 lakh in 1996-97 and it went up to Rs. 2,006.35 lakh by 1998-99; a 10.25 per cent increase as against 20.05 per cent at national level (IAMR, 2004).

collaboration through technology agreements was considerably simplified. In Rajasthan many steps have been taken to boost investment as detailed in preceding section. During past decade or so the government has set up Economic Development Board, Board of Infrastructure Development and Investment Promotion, Inland Container Depot at Bhilwara, Rajasthan Foundation and various committees to advise the State government on industrialisation processes. The ensuing discussion looks at the results of all these efforts.

Rajasthan has not been able to attract investment despite the liberal environment across the country. Of the total 26,466 approvals,[12] Rajasthan obtained only 1.30 per cent. In case of technical approvals that would bring new technology, the share of Rajasthan is mere 1.34 per cent and it is 1.28 per cent in case of financial approvals. This means that Rajasthan has not been able to attract foreign investment despite all the fairs, exhibitions and seminars abroad and in India. Rajasthan ranks tenth among all states in India. In value terms, the flow of FDI into Rajasthan was Rs. 29,112.11 million or US$ 752.29 million. It constituted only 1.16 per cent of all FDI that flowed into India during August 1991 and December 2004. The FDI flow registered at Jaipur RBI office from January 2000 to January 2006 stood at Rs. 18.76 crore or US$ 4.2 million and it was mere 0.02 per cent of national FDI figure. The investment climate in Rajasthan during August 1991 and December 2004 shows that a total of 2,662 IEMs (4.73 per cent of national share) were filed to bring in investment of Rs. 41,760 crore (2.93 per cent of national share) and would have created employment to the tune of 4,81,069 (4.42 per cent of national share).[13] In case of Letter of Intents (LoIs) and (DILs), during August 1991 and December 2004 a total of 97 (2.43 per cent of national share) were filed to bring in investment of Rs. 1,626 crore (1.42 per cent of national share) and would have created employment to the tune of 15,455 (1.79 per cent of national share). The total number of foreign technical collaboration

12. The break-up of this data is not available by industry. However, it does reflect the trend in investment attracted by the state and reflects on the investment climate created by policy changes within the state.

13. Between August 1991 and January 2006, 2,847 IEMs (4.51 per cent Indian share) were proposed with total investment of Rs. 47,371 crore (2.64 per cent Indian share) (see: *www.investrajasthan.com*).

cases approved has been 103 while 241 cases of FDI were approved amounting to investment of Rs. 2,911.2 crore.[14]

This is in sharp contrast to what was expected at the beginning of the reforms. The reduction in regulatory role to enable entrepreneurs to take investment decisions based on commercial judgement, the industrial investment was expected to get a boost. In fact prior to reforms, Indian industry often blamed licensing policy and subsequent bureaucratic red-tapeism as the main hurdle in their investment decisions. The initial bubble of enthusiasm burst very soon.[15] Rajasthan has always been adversely placed in terms of private initiative because of its natural location. Maharashtra, Gujarat, Uttar Pradesh and Tamil Nadu have cornered most of the investment proposals that have come up. Just poor infrastructure cannot be blamed for poor performance in attracting investment.[16] It is the mindset of the investor that determines the investment flow. World Bank (2006) also notes that there has been virtually no foreign direct investment in industry in Rajasthan. The key factors articulated for this are the usual legal and regulatory inefficiencies and red tape that restrict entry, exist and efficient operation of businesses, particularly of small and medium enterprises, insufficient access to credit, infrastructural shortages and slow urbanisation.

Finally, on the size of large companies, there are 90 companies listed as on March 2006 with market capital of Rs. 43,774.9 crore. The biggest company in terms of market capital is Hindustan Zinc and the smallest one is Richirich Agro with market capital of Rs. 1.13 crore. The private joint stock companies in 1997-98 were 1162 with authorised capital of Rs. 120.26 crore that has decline to Rs. 25.51 crore for 542 companies. There are only 101 such companies with authorised capital of Rs. 4.02 crore only. Public joint stock companies registered in Rajasthan in 1997-98 were 78 with authorised capital of

14. There are only 10 MNCs operating in Rajasthan that brought in technical backing. The major groups are Ericsson Telecommunication Ltd., MICO, GE Capital International Services and Gillette India Ltd.

15. The rate of implementation for the period August 1991 and March 1998 is 11.43 (numbers), 32.26 per cent for investment, and 11.74 per cent for employment (CMIE, 2006).

16. Mazumdar and Sarkar (2006), while developing an argument of urbanisation (population in metros) and FDI flow point out that in case of Rajasthan inflow of FDI per capita in metros is low, yet it shares the characteristics of the high FDI states in having a relatively high growth rate in the larger towns.

Rs. 49.23 crore that reduced to Rs. 12.65 crore for 23 companies. These are basically finance, real estate and business services companies; only 5 are in manufacturing with authorised capital of Rs. 0.55 crore. This also shows that Rajasthan has not performed well at this end of the industries. Finally, even the World Bank that is highly praising economic performance of Rajasthan reports that to date the record is that Rajasthan has failed in attracting private investment, it is only modest. It reports that what is of more serious concern is that private investment rates have been falling since the early 1990s (World Bank, 2006). Private investment stood at less than 6 per cent of GSDP in 2002-03 (15.7 per cent national), while public investment stood at 5.7 per cent of GSDP (6.3 per cent national).

Concluding Comments

Rajasthan has been moving very slowing on the path of industrialisation. Over the years, resources earmarked have been meagre and the private sector has not really invested due to a variety of reasons. The contribution of manufacturing sector in the state income has not shown any significant change over the years. The main culprit is the registered component of the manufacturing sector. There has been only marginal structural change also, in the industrial scene. The same set of industrial groups still predominates and the prominent ones are manufacture of food products, textiles, basic metals and chemical products. There has been significant improvement in the infrastructure and the policy regime has been made very favourable for investment in the reform era, not really effective at the ground level. Bureaucratic hurdles are still aplenty. Industry in Rajasthan is concentrated in National Capital Region.

There is a dominance of unorganised manufacturing sector with rural and own account enterprises having a significant role. Here also, the fall out/connectivity is visible of the large scale manufacturing. The small scale sector also is heavily relying on unregistered enterprises that have low productivity, use local know-know, low employment potential, clustered in few districts and have fewer women participation. There is sickness in the small scale sector. *Khadi* and village industries too are largely traditional activity based. There are all indications of informalisation of the Rajasthan's economy. Credit flow to industry has also slowed down, especially the small scale sector.[17] The manufacturing public sector is small and employs around 32,000 persons. Industrial relations have become employer friendly with man-days lost due largely to employers. There has been plethora of policy initiatives that have not got translated into investments. This may mean that in reality the prospective investor still faces age-old hurdles and is driven away as is visible from IEMs/ LoI filed and actual investments taking place. Rajasthan's strong economic performance during the 1980s and 1990s was largely driven by robust growth in the industry and services sectors. This growth was stimulated by a wide range of structural reforms introduced by the GoI in 1991 as part of a broader economic reform programme. However, much remains to be done to realise the state's potential more fully. A key thrust area of government policy, going forward, would to be on improving the climate for private investment and sound power sector. Infrastructure has improved but much more is required in terms of quality control of goods, standardisation to make products more competitive internationally. Special emphasis should be placed on sectors such as mining and quarrying, textiles, and tourism, where Rajasthan has a strong comparative advantage. Education sector also requires added attention as at macro level, education is linked to industrial development and economic growth (Singh and Sagar, 2004). The final word is that the industrial sector despite major initiatives and incentives has not taken off. In order to become a reality, the state has miles to go before it can boast of industrial sector of some significance.

---

17. In Rajasthan in 1990-91 there were 2.37 lakh accounts concerning industry and this number fell to 1.68 per cent in 2000-01 and the share in credit of industry in total bank credit fell from 37.57 per cent to 33.64 per cent during the same period (Singh, 2006b). Lending to the private sector is generally riskier and considerably more people and time are required for a bank to manage a portfolio to private sector loans than one of government debt and cash positions (Freeman and Click, 2006).

References

Chadha, G.K. (2003). *Rural Industry in India: Policy Perspectives, Past Performance and Future Options*, ILO-SAAT, New Delhi.

CMIE (2006). *Monthly Review of Rajasthan Economy*, Mumbai.

CSO (2001). *Annual Survey of Industries*, 1998-99, Volume 1.

———. (2005). *Annual Survey of Industries*, 2002-03, Volume 1.

Directorate of Economics & Statistics (DES) (2004-2005). *Economic Review*, Jaipur.

———. (2005-2006). *Economic Review*, Jaipur.

Freeman, Paul L. and Reid W. Click (2006). "Banks That Don't Lend? Unlocking Credit to Spur Growth in Developing Countries", *Development Policy Review*, 4 (3), pp.279-302.

Government of Rajasthan (undated). *White Paper on the State of Economy and Finances*.

———. (2005). *Draft Annual Plan: 2005-2006*, Volume I (Narrative), Planning Department, Jaipur.

———. (2006). *Draft Annual Plan: 2006-2007*, Volume I (Narrative), Planning Department, Jaipur.

Institute of Applied Manpower Research (2004). *Manpower Profile: India Yearbook 2003*, Concept Publishing Company, New Delhi.

Joshi, Gopal (2000). *Privatization in South Asia: Minimizing Negative Social Effects through Restructuring*, ILO-SAAT, New Delhi.

Kashyap, S.P. and Amita Shah (1995). "Induced Industrial Clustering and Efficiency: An Exploratory Study of Gujarat's Industrial Estates", *Journal of Entrepreneurship*, Vol. 4, No.1, pp.71-87.

Kirkpatrick, C.H., N. Lee and E.I. Nixson (1984). *Industrial Structure and Policy in Less Developed Countries*, ELBS, George Allen & Unwin.

Kurien, C.T. (1978). "Small Sector in New Industrial Policy", *Economic and Political Weekly*, March 4.

Mazumdar, Dipak and Sandip Sarkar (2006). "Poverty, Growth and Inequality in the Pre- and Post-Reform Periods and the Patterns of Urbanization in India: An Analysis for All-India and the Major States", in a Conference on *Labour and Employment Issues in India* "India: Meeting the Employment Challenge", July 27-29, New Delhi.

Nagaraj, R. (2005). "Fall in the Organised Manufacturing Employment", a paper presented in International Conference on *Employment and Income Security in India*, IHD, New Delhi.

NSSO (1998a). *Unorganised Manufacturing Sector in India: Salient Features*, 51st Round (July 1994–June 1995), August.

———. (1998b). *Unorganised Manufacturing Sector in India: Its Size, Employment and Some Key Estimates*, 51st Round (July 1994–June 1995), August.

———. (2001). *Informal Sector in India, 1999-2000: Salient Features*, 55th Round (July 1999–June 2000), May.

———. (2002a). *Non-agricultural Workers in Informal Sector Based on Employment-Unemployment Survey 1999-2000*, 55th Round (July 1999-June 2000), July.

———. (2002b). *Unorganised Manufacturing Sector in India, 2000-2001: Characteristics of Enterprises*, 56th Round (July 2000–June 2001), September.

———. (2002c). *Unorganised Manufacturing Sector in India, 2000-2001, Input, Output and Value Added*, 56th Round (July 2000–June 2001), November.

———. (2002d). *Unorganised Manufacturing Sector in India, 2000-2001, Employment, Assets and Borrowings*, 56th Round (July 2000–June 2001), November.

———. (2005). "Integrated Summary of NSS 55th Round (July 1999–June 2000), Survey Results on Informal Sector Employment in India", *Sarvekshana*, 88th Issue, Vol. 25, No.4 and

Vol.26, No.1, October.

Saith, A. (2000). *Rural Industries in India: Some Policy Perspective*, ILO-SAAT, New Delhi.

Singh, Surjit (1989). "Study on Industrial Structure: An Overview", in High Power Committee Report on *Strategy for Industrial Development in Eighth Five Year Plan*, Vol. II, Government of Rajasthan, Jaipur.

———. (1994). *Urban Informal Sector*, Rawat Publications, Jaipur.

———. (1997a). "Khadi Spinners and Weavers: Do they have any Future", *IDSJWP* No.96.

———. (1997b). *Performance of Village Industries in Rajasthan*, a report prepared for Khadi and Village Industries Board, Rajasthan.

———. (2005a). "Review: Rural Industry in India: Policy Perspectives, Past Performance and Future Options—G.K Chadha (2003), ILO-SAAT, New Delhi", *Indian Journal of Labour Economics*.

———. (2005b). "India and the Knowledge Economy: Overview and Global Context", *Indian Journal of Labour Economics*, 48 (4), pp. 803-820.

———. (2006a). *Rural Non-farm Sector in India: Experiences and Perceptions from the Grassroots*, National Bank for Agricultural and Rural Development, Mumbai.

———. (2006b). "Institutional Finance in Rajasthan: The Recent Trends" in R. Parthasarthy and Sudarshan Iyengar (eds.), *New Development Paradigms & Challenges for Western & Central India*, Concept Publishing Company, New Delhi.

Singh, Surjit and D. Sagar (2004). "Human Capital and Labour Market in Rajasthan", *Indian Journal of Labour Economics*, 47 (4), pp.789-806.

Vyas, V.S. and George Mathai (1978). "Farm and Non-farm Employment in Rural Areas: A Perspective for Planning", *Economic and Political Weekly*, Annual Number, February.

World Bank (2006). *Rajasthan: Closing the Development Gap*.

The author would like to thank Prof. R. Nagaraj for extensive comments on the first draft. I am also grateful to Prof. V.S. Vyas for allowing me to do a comprehensive paper.

Appendix A-5.1

Industrial Classification–Unorganised Manufacturing Sector 2000-2001

01405	Cotton Ginning, Cleaning and Baling
15	Manufacture of Food Products and Beverages,
16	Manufacture of Tobacco Products
17	Manufacture of Textiles
18	Manufacture of Wearing Apparel; Dressing and Dyeing of Fur
19	Tanning and Dressing of Leather; Manufacture of Luggage, Hand Bags, Saddler, Harness and Footwear
20	Manufacture of Wood and of Products of Wood and Cork, except Furniture; Manufacture of Articles of Straw and Plaiting Materials
21	Manufacture of Paper and Paper Products
22	Publishing, Printing and Reproduction of Recorded Media
23	Manufacture of Coke, Refined Petroleum Products and Nuclear Fuel
24	Manufacture of Chemicals and Chemical Products
25	Manufacture of Rubber and Plastics Products
26	Manufacture of Other Non-Metallic Mineral Products
27	Manufacture of Basic Metals
28	Manufacture of Fabricated Metal Products, except Machinery and Equipment
29	Manufacture of Machinery and Equipment nec.
30	Manufacture of Office, Accounting and Computing Machinery
31	Manufacture of Electrical Machinery and Apparatus nec.
32	Manufacture of Radio, Television and Communication Equipment and Apparatus
33	Manufacture of Medical, Precision and Optical Instruments, Watches and Clocks
34	Manufacturing of Motor Vehicles, Trailers and Semi-Trailers
35	Manufacturing of Other Transport Equipment
36	Manufacture of Furniture; Manufacturing nec.
37	Recycling

Source: NSSO (2002b).

6

Agricultural Development

Issues and Approaches

VIDYA SAGAR

Farm sector in India continues to be important determinant of the overall growth as well as for eradicating rural poverty. This is in spite of a fall in the share of agricultural sector in the State Domestic Product (SDP) from around 50 per cent during the early sixties to below 25 per cent during 2004-05. Agricultural sector continues to be important in the Indian economy generally and in the state's economy particularly, for two reasons. First, the fall in the sectoral share of SDP has not reduced the share of work force in this sector in the same proportion.[1] Second, the structure of consumption basket of the rural population has distinctly changed from the raw food basket (cereals, pulses, etc.) to the one based on processed food and non-food commodities.

A shift in consumption basket favouring processed food and non-food goods has two broad implications. Initially, it reduces the impact of agriculture on the overall performance of the economy. Accordingly, elasticity of non-primary SDP with respect to primary sector SDP has declined from 0.22 during 1961-1981 to statistically insignificant 0.08 during 1981-2005.

At a later stage, consumption of processed commodities tends to add, *via* the multiplier effect to the level of economic activity, thereby increasing/decreasing the level of income. To the extent such activities occur within the state, it contributes to the SDP and the employment. However, if a state continues to be a supplier of raw material such multiplier effect would not work on the income or employment within the state. A part of such commodities do not affect manufacturing activities of the state and hence any depression/upsurge in demand due to increased rural income from agriculture may not have any

1. Share of agricultural sector workers declined marginally in 2000-01 when compared to the corresponding figure in 1960-61.

multiplier effect within the state, which used to boost village/small town activities earlier.

It is possible to increase multiplier effect by encouraging food-processing industry within the state. However, impact of increased consumption of non-food items such as clothing, footwear, mechanised modes of travel, household furnishings, etc. would dampen or increase the multiplier effect depending on the comparative advantage of the state in producing such items. This broadly implies that the agricultural activity though still covering large part of rural employment, now weakly affects other sectors of the economy. Or there may not be a one to one correspondence between the performance of agricultural and non-agricultural sectors at the regional/state level.

In what follows, we shall evaluate performance of agricultural sector in the state since the first signs of economic liberalisation appeared during the early eighties and examine if changes in this sector during the last two and a half decades have put it on the road-map of growth, stability and sustainability. We shall restrict our analysis to crop husbandry.

Agriculture in Rajasthan, as in most semi-arid region of India is dualistic in nature. Issues related to dry land agriculture in large parts of arid and semi-arid Rajasthan are different from the issues related to irrigated agriculture. Ignoring the areas brought under canal irrigation, most of the western Rajasthan (west of Aravallis) historically, grew *bajra*, pulses and *guar* during *kharif* only, mostly as mixed crops, along with animal husbandry as a more stable contributor to the household incomes. It may not be possible to go into the details of the complex farming system of this region, but we addressed here one of the issues of the development of dry land agriculture, which may need some policy initiatives on the part of the state. In the remaining, we shall focus on the macro growth performance of the state, which relies more on irrigated agriculture.*

Section 1 examines the growth performance of the agricultural sector. Factors explaining growth during last two decades are discussed in Section 2. Diversification has emerged as a major theme

---

* Data used in the analysis has been taken from various publication of the GoR. These include for example *Agricultural Statistics* and *Statistical Abstracts* of various years published by Directorate of Economics Statistics & Planning Department, GoR.

for improving the income from agriculture in a macro food secure situation striving to develop in an open economic environment. Diversification in the past mainly attended to risk aversion rather than income enhancement, both for the rural economy as well as the agricultural sector. Section 3 discusses diversification in the state agriculture. Impact of various policy initiatives whether under economic reforms or earlier in shaping agricultural development in the state is discussed in Section 4. Finally, issues emerging from the analysis for a sustainable agricultural growth are discussed.

Growth story of the state's economy starts early during the eighties after a near stagnation in the state's economy during the preceding three decades. Growth in the Net State Domestic Product (NSDP) in primary sector, predominantly agriculture, is statistically insignificant both during the sixties and the seventies. When the entire period (1961-1981) is considered, primary sector has a growth rate of 2.8 per cent. Such growth in primary sector is comparable to growth in secondary and tertiary sectors at 3.3 and 3.6 per cent respectively. The overall growth in the economy at 3.1 per cent just equals population growth during this period, to result in a zero growth in per capita income in the state.

Table 6.1

Economic Growth in Rajasthan: 1960-61 to 1980-81

Net State Domestic Product	*1960-61 to 1970-71*	*1970-71 to 1980-81*	*1960-61 to 1980-81*
NSDP (Primary)	2.1 (ns)	1.4 (ns)	2.8
NSDP (Secondary)	2.3	3.9	3.3
NSDP (Tertiary)	3.4	4.6	3.6
NSDP	2.5	2.7	3.1
Per Capita NSDP	**0.1**	**-0.2**	**0.0**

Source: Sagar (2005a).

Growth and Structural Changes after 1980

From an insignificant growth in agriculture during the seventies, primary sector generally and agricultural sector in particular has a healthy growth of over 4 per cent during the eighties. Primary sector during this period has grown at the rate of 4.56 per cent. Within the primary sector agriculture and allied activities posted a growth rate of 4.03 per cent.

However, even in the high growth period, growth is uneven when the entire period (1980-81 to 2001-02) is divided into pre-reform period (1980-81 to 1990-91) and post-reform period (1990-91 and 2001-02). Agriculture shows significant decline in growth rate from 4.19 per cent during 1981-1991 to 2.41 per cent in 1991-2002. The growth rate of the forestry sub-sector declines from 18.23 per cent during 1981-1991 to 3.20 per cent in the following decade.

Till 1980-81, agriculture sector accounted for the largest share in GSDP. The share of agriculture and allied sector fluctuated between 56 and 65 per cent during 1960-61 to 1979-80. At current prices, the share of agriculture and allied sector peaked at 62.2 per cent during the triennium ending 1975-76, up from 56.4 per cent during TE 1961-1962. This happened primarily due to gains from the seed-fertiliser revolution of the agriculture sector, while other sectors stagnated. Its share declined to 52 per cent during TE 1979-80 and thereafter (Sagar and Ahuja, 1987; Sagar, 2005a).

Table 6.2

Sectoral Growth Rates 1980-81 to 2001-02

Sectors of the Economy	*1980-81 to 1990-91*	*1991-92 to 2001-02*
Agriculture (including A.H.)	4.19	2.41
Primary Sector	4.56	2.86
Secondary Sector	7.71	7.93
Tertiary Sector	7.77	7.21
GSDP	**6.5**	**5.8**

Source: Author's computation using GSDP series for Rajasthan.

Growth and Diversification in Agriculture

The state showed impressive gain in crop production during the last two decades. Growth rates of agricultural production during 1980-1981 to 2001-02 are shown in Table 6.3. Food grain production during this period observed average growth of 2.79 per cent annually, contributed mostly by the growth in crop productivity, as area under food grain had not shown any increase (Table 6.4). Large part of the

Table 6.3

Growth Rate of Crop Production in Rajasthan (1980-81 to 2001-02)

Crops	*1980-81 to 1991-92*	*1991-92 to 2001-02*
Kharif Cereals	1.10	4.39
Rabi Cereals	1.70	4.76**
Wheat	2.62	5.04**
Food grain	0.78	3.40
Kharif Food grain	1.65	4.01
Rabi Food grain	0.24	3.64***
Kharif Oilseeds	12.74*	6.81**
Rabi Oilseeds	16.73*	-0.15
Cotton	4.23	-0.29
Vegetables	14.52*	3.90
Condiments & Spices	7.52*	4.57**

Note: Estimated from the exponential growth function
* Significant at 1 per cent l.s.
** Significant at 5 per cent l.s.
*** Significant at 10 per cent l.s.

Source: GoR (1999; 2000; 2001).

Table 6.4

Growth Rate of Area of Crops for Two Sub-periods

Crops/Crop-Groups	*1980-81 to 1991-92*	*1991-92 to 2001-02*
Food grain	-0.99	-0.04
Kharif Cereal	-0.39	-0.99
Rice	-2.12	3.05*
Rabi Cereal	-1.36***	2.11***
Wheat	-0.59	3.47*
Rabi Food grain	-1.98	2.18
Kharif Oilseeds	4.32**	0.98
Rabi Oilseeds	13.44*	-1.07
Total Area	**-0.06**	**0.67**

Note: Estimated from the exponential growth function.
* Significant at 1 per cent l.s.
** Significant at 5 per cent l.s.
*** Significant at 10 per cent l.s.

Source: GoR (1999; 2000; 2001).

growth in food grain production was contributed by wheat alone. Wheat grew at the rate of 4.74 per cent annually during the reference period. Production of *kharif* cereals comprising mainly of coarse grains was stagnant but with large fluctuations. *Kharif* cereals were mostly un-irrigated and therefore, the production performance varied according to the quantity and the spread of rains in the respective crop zones. Except for marginal substitution in the areas bordering the predominance of major coarse cereals, inter crop substitution was minimal. This implies that the performance of major *kharif* cereals individually reflects the zonal patterns. The only *kharif* cereal showing statistically significant growth is *bajra*. The crop grew at 2.98 per cent during the period under study. *Jowar*, small millets and barley observed negative growth at the rate of -4.81 per cent, -4.97 per cent and -1.21 per cent respectively.

Other crops showing high growth during the reference period include oilseeds (10.37 per cent), cotton (5.21 per cent), condiments and spices (5.73 per cent). The growth in oilseed production was contributed mainly by rape and mustard (10.34 per cent), soybean (30.15 per cent) and castor seed (25.63 per cent).

When the entire period is divided into two sub-periods, which we may name as the pre-liberalisation and the post-liberalisation phase; asymmetry in the growth pattern emerges. The contrast in growth patterns of the two periods is evident when we compare statistically significant growth rates.[2] The decade of eighties may be considered as the one representing diversification in favour of the cash crops in the state. Healthy growth is observed in the production of both *kharif* oilseeds (12.74 per cent per annum) and *rabi* oilseeds (16.73 per cent per annum). The growth is contributed mainly by rape & mustard (18.44 per cent per annum) in *rabi* and soybean (44.07 per cent per annum) in *kharif*. Among other cash crops, cotton (4.23 per cent per annum), vegetables (14.52 per cent per annum) and condiments & spices (7.52 per cent per annum) also observe healthy growth. During the nineties, however, only *kharif* oilseeds and condiments & spices

---

2. Wide fluctuations in *kharif* production do not make it possible to compute significant growth rates over the short period of 10 years and very strong growth trend would be captured by the statistical technique of curve fitting. Only oilseeds production during the two sub periods shows relative stability. *Kharif* oilseeds observe statistically significant growth rate at 12.7 per cent and 6.8 per cent during the two sub-periods. Otherwise *bajra/kharif* cereals are statistically insignificant.

grow at the rate of 6.81 and 4.57 per cent per annum respectively. All other cash crops show a zero growth. In the food grain group, wheat shows an impressive growth of 5.04 per cent during the nineties. The trend of diversification of the eighties is thus arrested, during the economic liberalisation phase.

Growth in Crop Area and Shifts in Cropping Pattern

Contrasting growth patterns in crop area emerge for the food and non-food crops during the two sub-periods. Growth in gross cropped area (GCA) is statistically insignificant in both the periods because of the large annual fluctuations. The difference in cropping pattern during the two sub-periods, however, emerges rather sharper. During 1981-1992, GCA recorded no growth so that the direction of growth would indicate the changes in cropping pattern. Area under food grain during 1981-1992 declined while area under non-food grain crops grew. Non-food grain crops account for 33.09 per cent of GCA during the triennium ending 1982-83. Area under these crops grew at the rate of 0.8 per cent during this period. Prominent crops contributing to the growth in non-food area are *kharif* oilseeds (4.32), *rabi* oilseeds (13.44), cotton (2.6), condiments and spices (2.94), drugs and narcotics (10.62). This happened due to a favourable price environment along with availability of suitable technology (seed varieties).

The advantage in favour of oilseeds appears to have been lost after liberalisation when the country started importing edible oil on a large scale. This is discussed in some details later.

Growth in Crop Productivity

As pointed out elsewhere, the bulk of growth in agricultural production is contributed by the growth in productivity during 1965-1980. The trend continued in the state agriculture till 1990-91. Over the entire period of 1981-2001, agricultural productivity in the state had grown at the rate of 2.58 per cent. However, most of the growth in productivity occured during the eighties (Table 6.5).

The index of agricultural productivity observed a growth rate of 4.68 per cent during the decade ending 1990-91, as against a zero growth (statistically insignificant growth at 30 per cent) during the nineties. The pattern of growth, during the two sub-periods, holds even for the individual crops. Food grain, for example, observed a growth rate of 2.78 per cent during 1981-2001 but most of this growth is contributed by the high growth of the eighties (4.51 per cent per annum). Similarly, bulk of the productivity growth of the non-food crops (1.78 per cent) is contributed by the growth during the eighties (4.50 per cent). Within food grain, both the *rabi* and the *kharif* cereals have similar pattern of productivity growth. As against the growth rates of 6.57 per cent and 4.37 per cent respectively for *kharif* and *rabi* cereals during the eighties, zero growth is observed in both during the nineties. Overall growth rate, therefore, dilutes to 3.60 for *kharif* cereals and 3.32 per cent for *rabi* cereals.

Table 6.5

Growth in Crop Productivity

	Growth Rate		
	1981-1991	*1991-2001*	*1981-2001*
Food grains	4.51**	0.85	2.78*
Cereals	5.61**	0.73	3.34*
Kharif Cereals	6.57***	0.46	3.60*
Rabi Cereals	4.37**	1.18	3.32*
Pulses	1.29	0.31	0.87
Non-food Crops	4.50*	0.09	1.78*
Oilseeds	3.52**	0.72	1.27*
All Commodities	**4.68***	**0.52**	**2.58***

Note: *, **, ***Statistically significant at 1, 5 or 10 per cent or better.

Source: Based on the Index Numbers of Agricultural Productivity, GoR.

Growth of productivity of oilseed also drops to statistically insignificant levels during the nineties from a high of 3.52 per cent annually during the eighties.

What comes as a surprise, however, is the inconsistency of these numbers with the major productivity enhancing inputs, *viz.*, irrigation and plant nutrients. The Commission for Agriculture Costs and Prices (CACP) data on the input use is available for five crops in Rajasthan. These include wheat, barley, rape and mustard, *bajra* and maize. We discuss here the fertiliser use crop productivity interface using CACP data. During the eighties, all crops except rape and mustard observed negative though statistically insignificant growth in fertiliser use. Rape and mustard got a technological breakthrough during the beginning of the eighties and therefore fertiliser use grew from a low level. On the other hand, all the five cops observe high growth in fertiliser consumption during the nineties. The annual growth in fertiliser application in wheat, barley, rape and mustard, *bajra* and maize is observed respectively at 8.3, 16.2, 9.5, 19.7 and 4.3 per cent during the nineties. Yet growth in productivity is nowhere commensurate with the growth in fertiliser use. This is supported by the macro growth figures in fertiliser consumption (Table 6.6).

Table 6.6

Growth in Area and Fertiliser Consumption (1980-2001)

	Growth Rates	
	1980-1991	*1991-2001*
Net Irrigated Area	1.82	3.00
Gross Irrigated Area	1.50	3.36
Net Cropped Area	0.12	0.20
Gross Cropped Area	0.16	0.64
Fertiliser Consumption		
Kharif	11.19	8.95
Rabi	8.51	5.71
Total	**9.48**	**7.18**
Gross Irrigation Ratio (GIA/GCA)	1.34	2.70
Net Irrigation Ratio (NIA/NCA)	1.69	3.22
Fertiliser Consumption per GCA	9.31	6.49

Source: * Obtained by fitting Exponential Growth Function.

At the macro level, growth rate of irrigation ratio—both gross and net—doubles during the later period. The growth rate in fertiliser consumption, however, marginally declines to 7.2 per cent during the nineties from 9.5 per cent during the eighties. Besides, high growth in the use of critical inputs during the nineties, capital formation in agriculture also showed better growth during this period. The declining trend in agriculture sector capital formation at constant prices during the eighties is not only arrested but a strong growth is also observed during the nineties.

If all the components of rapid agricultural growth were present during the nineties, what explains a zero growth in productivity in individual crops, crop groups or aggregate?

Agricultural Policies and the State Agriculture

Although agriculture is a state subject, policies that seem to influence this important sector of the rural economy during the last two decades are primarily under the control of the central government. Price policy, mainly related to agricultural commodities but also related to important inputs such as fertilisers or power, has dominated the agricultural policy regime during the period under study. Similar is the case with the trade policy. Even within the domain of trade liberalisation, states have little say on imports even if it affects their farmers. Institutional credit is yet another area where the Central bank or NABARD designs broad policy parameters. Cooperative credit, which falls within the policy domain of a state, is in shambles in most areas. Fiscal policy is one area where the state exerts largest influence. We shall discuss these policies and their impact on agriculture below.

Agricultural Price Policy

Agricultural price policy in India sought to: (i) provide adequate incentive to the producer for a sustainable increase in production of food grain, (ii) evolve an agricultural production pattern in tune with the needs of the economy. The price policy was modified in 1980 when the balance between demand and supply of food grain was in sight (GoI, 1980), and again after the introduction of economic reforms in 1991.

Agricultural price policy of the early seventies has succeeded in its objective of enhancing the availability of food grain in India generally. However, large increases in procurement/Minimum Support Price (MSP), over and above the price recommended by the CACP contributed to both the expansions in area under the crop and its productivity. It is estimated that the price policy interventions have contributed 70 and 48 per cent of the growth in productivity and production of wheat during the nineties. Such contribution of price policy was far more during the nineties as compared to the eighties, when its contribution in the growth of crop production was modest

(Kumar, 2002). Kumar's analysis does not include the impact of prices on area substitution favouring wheat. A modest elasticity of crop substitution of 0.5 would increase the share and would substantially increase the contribution of prices on the production of wheat.

The predominant role, played by the price policy variables during the nineties, created certain distortions in agriculture sector. This resulted in supplies in excess of demand for the two cereals causing a pile up in buffer stocks. The resulting burden of food subsidies caused by an over-active price policy during the nineties affected investment in irrigation, stagnancy of resources for research and extension affected performance of agriculture (Hoda *et al.*, 2003).

We discuss below the role of price policy in shaping agriculture in the state. Figure 6.1 shows relative price movements in the prices of the three competing *rabi* crops, *viz.*, wheat, mustard and gram. Ratio of the wholesale price of mustard to wheat declined from 116 during 1990-91 to 57 in 2000-01 before recovering marginally subsequently.

Figure 6.1

Variation in Wholesale Prices: Rabi Crops

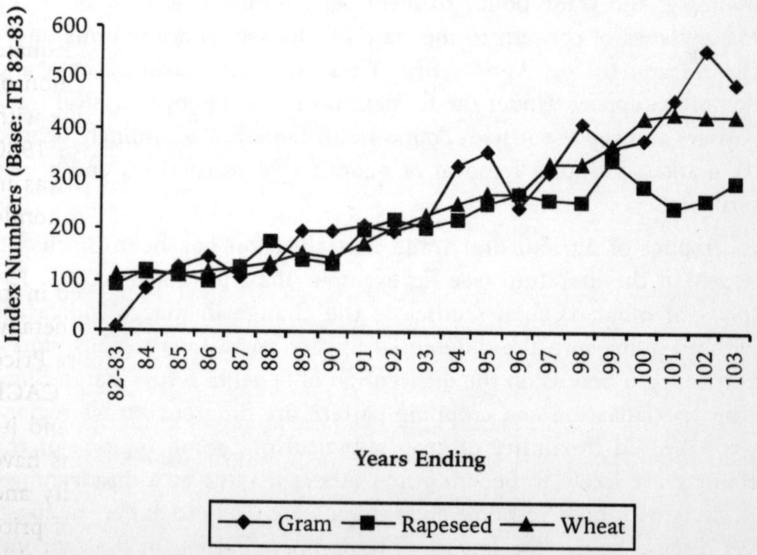

Source: Sagar (2005a).

Most of the area, under these *rabi* crops, is irrigated. However, because of the lower water requirement in mustard and gram, wheat does not directly compete with these crops unless the price ratio is overwhelmingly favourable to wheat. This is what happened during the nineties. The growing difference in the price ratio attracted larger area under wheat at the expense of other crops. Most of this area was taken away from the better-endowed regions under mustard, pushing its cultivation to marginal lands. It is important here to understand the differences in crop water requirement of the two crops. Water requirement of wheat in the state is estimated twice as that of water requirement of mustard. With a strong price advantage in favour of wheat, better-endowed areas for mustard were put under wheat, for which these were not the good areas. Mustard crop was further pushed to marginal areas by expanding groundwater irrigation to such areas. On the one hand, it increased production vulnerability and hence price variation. On the other, it substantially reduced the profitability of mustard.

Liberalising Agricultural Trade

As a founder member of WTO, India is committed to adjust its domestic and trade policy to meet certain obligations under WTO. Major issues of concern to the state like Rajasthan are reforms under the Agreement on Agriculture. These include market access and domestic support. Under the former, India is to remove physical trade barriers and replace it with bound tariff. India has accordingly opened its markets through removal of quantitative restrictions and a new tariff policy.

Impact of agricultural trade liberalisation has been discussed widely in the literature (see for example, Jha and Chand, 2002). The focus of most of such studies is the change in macro indicators without going into the differential impact on various regions/states. Our concern here is on the distribution of benefits across states. Since crop specialisation and cropping pattern are different across regions with limited flexibility of crop substitution, some regions of the country are likely to benefit while others may be at a disadvantage. Regions with poor resource endowments are likely to suffer the most. We discuss below, the impact of trade liberalisation on the economy of Rajasthan.

Public Distribution System, along with appropriate technology and related public policy initiatives helped farmers to shift to mustard cultivation during the late eighties (Sagar, 2000; Acharya, 2002). This crop requires low irrigation and hence suits well to the agro-climatic environment of the state. Rational diversion of resources towards mustard did help all size classes of farmers to increase incomes significantly. This also helped expansion of edible oil industry in the state.

Farmers in the state appear to have suffered the first shock of liberalised import policies when the country's import of edible oils started growing rapidly. Imports of edible oils increased from 200 thousand tonnes in 1992-93 to 2.1 million tonnes in 1997-98 and then to 4.4, 4.5 and 4.8 million tonnes in the subsequent three years. This happened due to: (i) removal of quantitative restrictions, (ii) customs duties progressively brought down from 65 per cent in 1994-1995 to 15 per cent in 1999-00, and (iii) a near halving of international prices of oils due to excess supply. Self-sufficiency in edible oils during 1992-2001 reduced from 97 per cent to 55 per cent. Imports of cheap palm oil during 1998-2001 badly affected the oilseed economy of the State by making mustard cultivation unviable for a large section of the farmers. The state had to procure mustard crop as the prices moved far below the minimum support price. At the support price, industry was not lifting the stocks of mustard seed.[3] Oilseed production in the state declined during this period from 3.8 mt to 2.0 mt. A part of this decline is contributed by the drought. But a significant part of the production loss is attributed to cropping pattern shifts. The resulting loss in income and employment in the farm sector was compounded as edible oil industry suffered heavily in the state. According to a memorandum submitted by Rajasthan Mustard Oil Industries Association, 90 per cent of the small industrial units have suffered. There is no denying that poor in Rajasthan, as elsewhere, were benefited by the fall in edible oil prices. However, if total employment and income effect of such a policy are taken into account, gains in welfare substantially get reduced. If a long-term perspective, where cost of providing alternative employment and/or reviving a sick industrial sector is considered, such policy may have resulted in net welfare loss.[4] It is generally agreed that international

---

3. Advertisements by NAFED were placed in local dailies for this purpose. (*Dainik Bhaskar*, January 18, 2002 and *Rajasthan Patrika*, February 26, 2002.

4. Jha and Chand (2002: 105-107).

prices of food products are more volatile than the domestic markets.[5] Already there are signs that edible oil prices have started increasing. Should the country prefer to import at higher prices or save domestic edible oil sector may be a matter of wider policy, but small economies or regions, which specialise in a commodity or two would need support from the centre to cope with such policies.

Jha and Chand have computed differential welfare gains from the trade of the important commodities. The authors compute loss/gain in welfare by the states for liberalising trade of individual agricultural commodities (Table 6.7).

Table 6.7

Net Social Gain from Agricultural Trade Liberalisation

(Rs. Per capita)

Crop	*Rajasthan*	*India*
Wheat & Rice	-25.6	2.1
Pulses	-62.3	
Edible Oils	-78.3	
Total	**-166.24**	

Source: Derived from Jha and Chand (2001).

As against consumers in India gaining Rs. 2.1 per capita, the state looses more than Rs. 25 per capita. In pulses and edible oils, the loss to the state is much higher at Rs. 62 and Rs. 78 respectively. Together the three crops imply a loss of Rs. 166 per capita or Rs. 930 crore for the population of 5.6 crore. The net welfare loss for Rajasthan exceeds Rs. 1,000 crores even when agriculture-industry linkages are ignored. If such impact is included the total welfare loss would be further higher.

Clearly, the impact of agricultural trade liberalisation has been adverse to the interest of the state. What Jha and Chand have estimated is the producers' welfare due to depressed prices to the cultivators. If one adds loss of employment along with the reduced supply and hence taxes to the state from the processing of oilseeds or

5. The Central Government, in the 2003-04 budget has announced a package for the coffee and cashew growers of the southern states, who have suffered from the decline in international prices of the two commodities. Such measures, on *ad hoc* basis or motivated by considerations of political economy, may significantly impact food security of a region.

other crops, the aggregate loss would be even higher. It is estimated that the state charges around 10 per cent on the purchased price of oilseed through such taxes as purchase tax, *mandi* tax, *daami* and sales tax. Other economic activities such as transport, village *daami* & brokerage, etc., further adds to the value. Finally, value added from the conversion of seed to oil (Rs. 100) gets distributed to labour and capital costs. All this amounts to over Rs. 200 per quintal. Applying this figure to the decline in production during TE 2001-02, implies a welfare loss of around 1,700 crores to the produces of the states.

It is pertinent to point out here that the state is not inefficient in producing mustard in India. The Cost data of the CACP shows an average yield of rape and mustard in Rajasthan at 12 Qt/ha. during 1998-2000, with 62 kg/ha. of fertiliser use and the labour input of 297 man days. Corresponding figures for the highest-yield state, *viz.*, Gujarat were 13 Qt with 111 kg of fertiliser use and 442 man-days of labour input. The Cost A2 of Cultivation in Rajasthan was Rs. 368/Qt as against Rs. 571/Qt in Gujarat during 1999-00. (Table 6.8).

Table 6.8

Cost of Cultivation/Production and Related Data of Principal Crops

(Rajasthan and the States with the Highest Yield of the Corresponding Crop)

Crops	*States*	*Cost (A2) of Cultivation (Rs./ha.)*	*Material and Labour Input*		*Yield (Qt/ha.)*
			Human Labour (Hrs./ha.)	*Fertilisers (Kg/ha.)*	
Wheat	Rajasthan	8192*	546**	106**	30**
	Punjab	10281*	304**	215**	45**
Barley	Rajasthan	6082*	540**	51**	21**
	U.P.	6719*	481**	69**	27**
Rape & Mustard	Rajasthan	4422*	297**	62**	12**
	Gujarat	7422*	442**	111**	13**
Soyabean	Rajasthan	4151@	408#	22#	13#
	Maharashtra	6195@	445#	54#	12#
	M.P.	5173@	407#	50#	12#

Note: * For the year 1999-00; @ For the year 1998-99; # Average of 1997-98 to 1998-99; ** Average of 1998-99 to 1999-00

Source: Various CACP Reports.

Impact of a stable and good price environment on crop production comes to a sharp focus with the state once again declaring MSP and procuring it at that rate. The state started purchase of mustard since 2003, at the MSP of 1,650/Qt. Minimum support price during the subsequent years was increased to Rs. 1,700 and Rs. 1,725 per quintal. This resulted in a further consolidation of area under mustard. As against the peak production of mustard at 2.6 million tonnes in 1996-97, the crop recorded an all time high of 4 million tonnes in 2004-05 and the advanced forecasts put it even higher during 2005-06. Production of all oilseeds has correspondingly increased from 3.8 million tonnes to over 5.5 million tonnes during 2004-05 and 2005-06 (See Sagar, 1996; Sagar, 2005; and Sagar 2005a for a fuller discussion on the impact of macro-policies on agriculture in Rajasthan).

Incongruencies in Agricultural Development

These developments have led to the first two incongruencies in agricultural development in the state. The first incongruency of agricultural development in the state is the dependence of farmers on public procurement when Indian agriculture has opted for the path of open trade policy under the WTO.[6]

The second incongruency is inability of the groundwater dependent agricultural growth pattern due to rapid groundwater depletion in arid and semi-arid regions of the state. We have discussed earlier about the zero growth in agricultural productivity during the nineties even though consumption of fertiliser and irrigated areas grow significantly during this period (Table 6.6). Growth in consumption of fertiliser and irrigation per unit of GCA at 6.5 per cent and 2.7 per cent must have reflected in the growth in aggregate productivity. This did not happen. A likely factor contributing to this was the agricultural price policy favouring wheat (Figure 6.1). This led to a 3.5 per cent annual growth in area under wheat without reducing the area under the competing *rabi* crop, *viz.*, mustard. What happened was that both mustard and wheat expanded to crop specific marginal areas. The expansion in area under wheat in the east of Aravalli range

---

6. Even though the chairperson of the Economic Advisory Council of the GoI, has argued for protecting the interest of small farmers, a proposed move to halve the import tariff on the import of edible oils from the ASEAN countries is not a move in this direction.

happened due to the substitution of mustard areas in favour of water intensive wheat, while area under mustard expanded to the west of Aravalli range (mostly arid). Such expansion in area under wheat did not create problem in areas served by surface irrigation (Chambal Command area of Kota Region and IGNP command areas of Ganganagar region in Figure 6.2). Since scope for expansion of surface water irrigation was limited, there was greater pressure to increase irrigation, both in the semi-arid and arid regions. Area under groundwater during the decade of the nineties increased by 80 per cent of what had been achieved till 1988. However, in the groundwater irrigated arid and semi-arid areas, this implied large withdrawal of groundwater over and above recharge capacity of the systems (Bharatpur, Jaipur and Jodhpur regions in Figure 6.2). Groundwater development in most of these areas became critical.[7]

Figure 6.2

Growth in Irrigated Area (Groundwater)

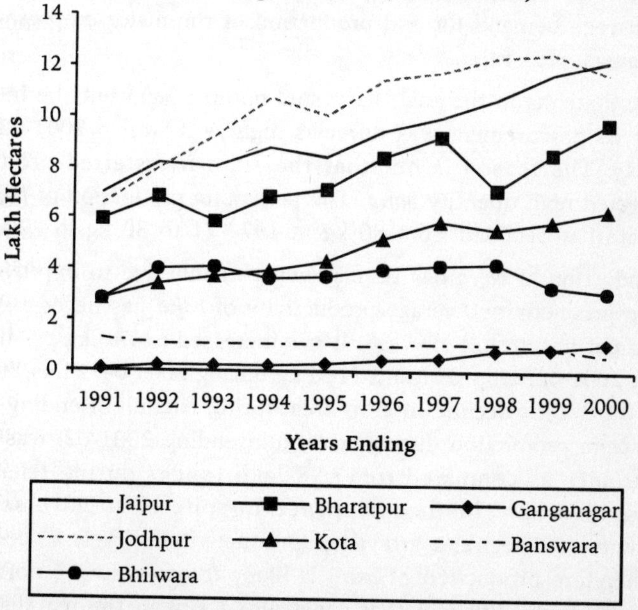

Source: GoR (various years), *Agricultural Statistics*.

7. Groundwater development is defined as critical if withdrawal exceeds recharge on a sustained basis, so that the level of groundwater declines continuously (see, GoR, 2004).

The groundwater department of the state estimates that 231 of the 238 blocks in the state have become critical. Price distortions appear to have led to agricultural development, which can not be sustained.

We have so far focussed on the issues related to irrigated *rabi* crops. We now shift our attention to the issues related to un-irrigated *kharif* crops which still cover over two-thirds of the GCA. The incongruency in *kharif* cultivation, mainly *bajra*, came to the fore during the *kharif* harvest of 2001-02, when farmers came on streets to press for the procurement of *bajra* during 2001-02. The crop output exceeded 38 lakh tonnes and the output of coarse grains exceeded 57 lakh tonnes during 2001-02. The year 2002-03, was the severe drought year and the output of coarse grains including *bajra* dropped to all time low of below 10 lakh tonnes. Production of *bajra* and coarse cereals during 2003-04 was 67 lakh and 93 lakh tonnes respectively.

A third incongruency has emerged in the dry land agriculture in arid and semi-arid parts of the state. And this relates to the growing gap between demand for and production of the major crop grown in these areas, *viz*., *bajra*.

The State, as in the past, harvested bumper *bajra* but the hue and cry for its procurement was never as high as it was in 2001-02 or it is today. The reason is not that the state has started producing unexpected high quantity *bajra*. The per capita production of *bajra* for the state has declined from 80 kg in 1970-71 to 30 kg in 2001-02.[8]

Production of *bajra* has been growing mainly due to improvement in crop productivity. Average productivity of *bajra* has never exceeded 550 kg per hectare till 1997-98. It has increased to 740 kg per hectare during 2001-02, crop year and 1140 kg during 2003-04. Thus, in spite of a 10 per cent decline in crop area during triennium ending 2001-2002, *bajra* production during triennium ending 2001-02, was 23.86 lakh tonnes as compared to 17.98 lakh tonnes during triennium ending 1991-92. This has happened in spite of an adverse price environment. The trend growth of productivity is likely to continue and therefore production of *bajra* is likely to grow during normal or good crop years. But will that constitute a glut in the market?

---

8. Such decline is primarily contributed by the decline in area under *bajra* and other coarse cereals since the eighties. In absolute terms, the area under *bajra* observes a declining trend. Average area under *bajra* has declined from 51.6 lakh hectares during triennium ending 1991-92 to 45.6 lakh hectares during triennium ending 2001-02.

Consumption Pattern Changes

The main reason for the glut in bajra production as far as markets are concerned, may be attributed to a major shift in consumption basket of food grains. According to 1973-74, the Consumption Expenditure Survey by NSSO, the share of coarse cereals in total cereal consumption during 1973-74 was 72 per cent in rural Rajasthan. This declined to 29 per cent during 1999-2000. Monthly per capita consumption of *bajra* had declined from 7.0 kg in 1973-74 to 2.4 kg in 1999-2000 in rural areas and from 2.5 kg to 0.4 kg in urban areas. Overall monthly per capita consumption of *bajra* declined from 6.2 kg to 1.9 kg during this period. This implies a decline in the consumption of *bajra* from 20.1 lakh tonnes in 1973-74 to 12.5 lakh tonnes in 1999-2000, in spite of a near doubling of population during this period.

There are number of reasons contributing to the change in food-basket. These include, growing incomes in rural and urban areas, availability of superior cereals such as wheat at competitive or lower price than *bajra* through the PDS or relief programmes besides greater reach and higher efficacy of the PDS and relief programms and wide variation in *bajra* availability due to recurring crop failures.

Table 6.9

Consumption of Cereals in Rajasthan

	Monthly Per Capita Consumption (kg.)				*Total Consumption (Lakh Tonnes)*	
	Rural		*Urban*			
	1973-74	*1999-00*	*1973-74*	*1999-00*	*1973-74*	*1999-00*
Coarse Grains	13.44	4.14	4.32	0.48	38.6	21.2
Bajra	6.98	2.42	2.52	0.37	20.1	12.5
Total Cereals	**18.76**	**14.19**	**12.97**	**11.56**		
Population (Lakh)	223	412	50	125		

Source: Derived from the NSS Reports.

Repeated crop failures in the state and the increasing role of public distribution system in providing access to wheat has, over years, reduced *bajra* consumption even in the bottom deciles of the income distribution. Earlier, coarse grains were consumed in rural Rajasthan, both by the poor and non-poor households in north, central and western parts of the state. Wheat and rice were the major cereals consumed in the higher income classes along with *bajra* which was consumed mainly in winter months. However, change in the food consumption was mainly due to increased availability of wheat at a competitive price, and also due to shortages in the availability of *bajra* caused by the wide fluctuations in its production. The PDS price of wheat for the poorer sections was kept below the market price of *bajra*. The Wheat Revolution experienced by the state during seventies and eighties along with central agricultural policy ensured lower prices for the wheat. In addition, greater palatability of wheat also ensured increased consumption of wheat.

The recurring droughts were accompanied with relief programmes such as the food-for-work programmes. These programmes, initiated by the State Government with support of the Central Government, provided additional wheat at cheaper prices. This, in turn, tilted the balance of consumption basket in favour of wheat crop. The shift in consumption got adequate support from the growing incomes, both in rural and urban areas of the state (Table 6.9).

With such a major change in the consumption basket against the coarse cereals generally and against *bajra* in particular, share of marketed surplus in *bajra* has increased steadily over the years. The divergence between demand for *bajra* and its supply is likely to grow further in the coming years and therefore, in a normal crop year or better, most of the produce would be marketed. If that happens, what can be done with the state's agriculture and what are the policy imperatives for doing so. One of the options would be to shift area under *bajra* to the competing crops for which there is adequate demand. Pulses, such as *moong, moth* and *chaula, guar* and sesame are the crops, which can substitute area under bajra in different agro-climatic sub-regions of the state. Pulses, being the leguminous crops, will also increase the soil productivity for *rabi* crops and release pressure on the prices of the pulses. A major difficulty with this option is the unfavourable economics of pulses cultivation in Rajasthan. It has been shown, in a number of studies, that farmers in India as well as in the state have generally been profit/price responsive for competing crops in an agro-climatic environment. Of the two components of profits, *viz.*, productivity and prices, impact of price changes has been studied in greater details. We discuss below the economics of pulses *versus bajra* production in the state to explore the possibility of shift in cropping pattern.

Economics of Crop Production

Bajra and *kharif* pulses are cultivated in an identical agro-climatic conditions and are largely un-irrigated. A comparison of relative productivity and relative prices shows that during last 20 years generally and specifically during last 10 years, the price of pulses has been increasing while its productivity is declining. During 1980-81 to 2001-02, prices of moong and moth, relative to *bajra,* have increased annually at the rate of 2.1 per cent and 2.6 per cent respectively, while productivity of pulses with respect to *bajra* has declined at the rate of 1.36 per cent annually. During 1991-92 to 2001-02, annual growth in relative price has been even sharper at 4.3 per cent and 5.3 per cent respectively for *moong* and *moth*. The decline in the productivity of pulses during this period is also sharp at the rate of 4.2 cent annually. The decline in relative productivity of pulses is contributed solely by a growth in *bajra* productivity rather than a decline in the productivity of pulses, which has been stagnant over the years. The average yield of bajra during triennia ending 1981-82, 1991-92 and 2001-02, is 1.6 Qt, 3.8 Qt and 5.2 Qt respectively. Corresponding value for *kharif* pulses is 1.2 Qt, 2.5 Qt and 2.2 Qt respectively (Sagar, 2003).

Is the spurt in relative prices of pulses adequate to support a cropping pattern shift in favour of pulses, individually or as mixed crop? We will discuss this along with other issues related to such a shift. First, let us examine changing pattern of farm income over the years. Unfortunately, not much information is available on the cost of pulses production in the state. We have some comparable data for the mid-eighties for *bajra* and *moong* (Directorate of Agriculture Rajasthan, undated). In addition we have comparable data for *moth* and *bajra* for Nagaur district for the year 1995-96 (Directorate of Agriculture, Rajasthan, 1998). Farm business income from *bajra* cultivation during 1981-82, 1982-83 and 1983-84 was Rs. 576, 728 and 710 per hectare respectively. Corresponding income from *moong* for the three years was Rs. 515, 616 and 654 respectively. The difference, between the two, varied between 10 to 20 per cent of the income from *bajra*. The 1995-96 figures of the farm business income from *moth* (Rs. 713) and *bajra*

(Rs. 2301) cultivation in Nagaur, though not exactly comparable to the above figures, show the kind of divergence emerging during the nineties (GoR, Undated).

Clearly, increase in pulse prices is not adequate to compensate for the growth of productivity in the competing crop *bajra* productivity and therefore, induce a change in cropping pattern. Besides, while crop productivity driven mainly by technology may be determined/ controlled within the domestic agricultural environment, profitability through increase in prices falls within the domain of political economy of imports in the liberalised agricultural trade environment. Farmers in the state have already suffered from liberalised imports of edible oils and pulses. This is one of the reasons why increase in price of pulses has been less than the expected corresponding to the stagnant domestic supply. Also, it is unlikely that the state exerts pressure on the centre for restricting imports. Nor would it be desirable for improving welfare of the consumers.

Figure 6.3

Index Numbers of Prices and Yield of Pulses Relative to Bajra

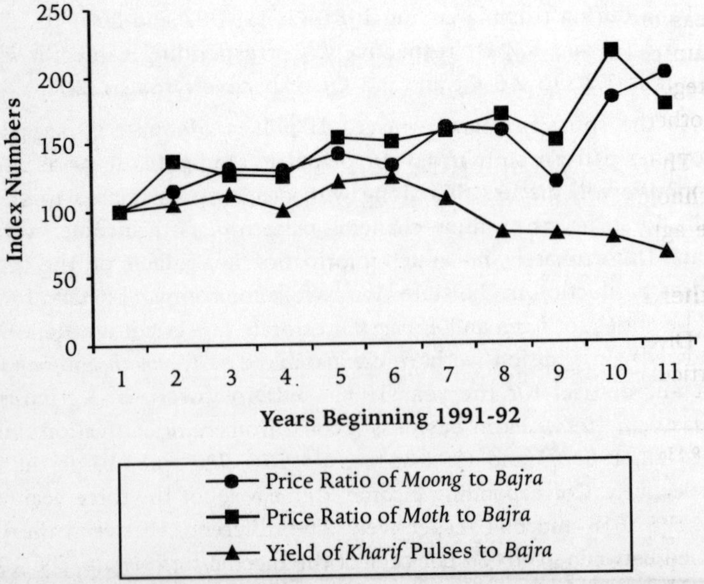

Source: Sagar (2003).

As mentioned above, in a large part of the state, *bajra* and pulses are grown together. The other crop competing for area under *bajra* is *guar*. If the crop pattern changes in favour of pulses it will also increase the soil productivity for *rabi* crops and release pressure on pulse prices.[9] A major difficulty with this option is the unfavourable economics of pulses cultivation as discussed above.

Second option is that the state continues to procure *bajra* for the management of the relief programmes and distribute *bajra* rather than wheat. This will also reduce the subsidy component considerably. However, low storage life of *bajra* is a major problem with this option. The low shelf life of *bajra* and related wastage may dilute whatever subsidy reduction advantage of the crop be. Besides, there are question marks on the sustainability of *bajra* as the food grain for public distribution or relief programmes. Once, the taste has changed in favour of wheat, it is unlikely that the beneficiaries of such programmes get paid in terms of *bajra* or other coarse grains, except for the real crisis situation.

It is possible to develop alternative uses of this crop. This includes, for example, a major shift in the farm economy towards livestock. Cultivation of green fodder for livestock in dry land arid areas or developing feed for poultry and cattle from surplus coarse grain could be one option. Developing products in the health food category such as roasts and puffs for the urban population could be another option. However, market for such products will be limited.

The only option for the state, in this case, is development of technology for pulse crops or other crops such as sesame that suits the agro-climatic condition of the *bajra* areas of Rajasthan.

Other Issues Related to Crop-sector diversification

Diversification of the farm sector generally and the crop sector in particular, is shown as the panacea for the agricultural problems of the

9. In the dry lands of north and eastern Rajasthan, *bajra* is cultivated mostly as mixed crop with *moth, chaula, guar* and sesame. The shift in cropping pattern in favour of pure pulse crops is unlikely because of a number of reasons specific to the farm economy of the region. These include risk minimisation in a region of high rainfall variation, and use of *bajra* residue as fodder for the livestock. But an increase in the ratio of crop mix is possible. A reduction in *bajra* area whether through pure cropping or mixed cropping will also be consistent with the demand for fodder for the cattle in the region. The population of bullocks is dwindling and the importance of cattle is gradually declining.

state. Such a view presumes that the produce of the farm sector has large demand and would be absorbed by the market economy at right prices. As discussed earlier, crop diversification initiated during the eighties failed to stand to the free market pressure during the nineties and the state had to provide support to sustain such diversification.

Within the crop sector, Jatropha[10] and castor, which have ready industrial use, besides a shift to the horticultural crops—fruits and vegetables, have been advanced to substitute the present cropping pattern. Such crops need to be individually evaluated with respect to the demand, the market infrastructure and water requirement before a push towards these crops is made. The agricultural scientists have advocated the case of Castor seed and Jatropha with large economic gains for the cultivators, quite for some time. The crops have yet to pick up in the state as reflected in the area under these crops. An understanding of why the farmers are not shifting to such remunerative crops may go a long way in diversifying agriculture in the state. Probably, processing facilities as well as the market for bio-fuels is not well developed.

Concluding Remarks

Agricultural policies pursued during the nineties have focussed mostly on the price policy with much less emphasis given to the non-price factors. Whether it was wheat and rice at the cost of regional specialisation in Rajasthan, for e.g., oilseed or whether it was to save bajra cultivators. Besides crop prices, input subsidies too have played a major role in agricultural policies. Such a policy conceals the true (social) costs of resources and has been found to result in/encourage inefficiency in resource use. This leads to uncompetitive crop production in a free trade economy (Chand, 2006).

The solution to dry land cultivation during *kharif* season lies either in a technology breakthrough in rainfed pulses, which are close substitute for bajra or promote a livestock based farming system in these areas. This involves dry land *kharif* production basket comprising green fodder, dry fodder and the surplus coarse grain converted as

---

10. Jatropha or *ratanjyot*, is a drought resistant perennial growing shrub, non-demanding, tolerant to extremes, suitable to tropical and non-tropical climate and considerable climatic changes, even up to light frost. It grows considerably easily and lives producing seeds for nearly 50 years.

feed for livestock/poultry. The coarse grain could also be marketed as health food after processing these as roasts or puffs in limited quantities.

These, however, remain short to medium-term responses to the problems facing the state's agriculture. A long-term solution needs to draw on improving the efficiency of resource use. On the one hand, this would require reallocation of crop area in such a fashion that the long-term sustainability of the crop system is ensured in every agro-climatic environment. On the other, continuous technology upgradation of the crops most suited to the agricultural environments of the state would be required.

Incongruency of this approach, however, lies in the fact that there might not be any long term solutions. Only short term responses to the impulses/signals of international markets dictated by the heavily subsidised and resource abundant agricultures of the first world. Such responses seek sustenance from the thin margins of the market economy. Such margins may be viable livelihood options in case of large holdings, but agriculture predominated by small and marginal holdings, provides the final incongruency to the globalised agriculture. More so where abundant availability of water is a constraint on crop/farm activity substitution.

References

Acharya, S.S. and D.P. Chaudhari (2002). *Indian Agricultural Policy at the Cross Roads*, Rawat Publications, Jaipur, pp.99-100.

Chand, R. (2006). "India's Agricultural Challenges and their Implications for Growth and Equity", presented at the Silver Jubilee Seminar on *Perspectives on Equitable Development: International Experience and What Can India Learn?*, Centre for Economic and Social Studies, Hyderabad.

Directorate of Agriculture Rajasthan (Undated), *Report on Cost of Cultivation and Production of Major Crops in Rajasthan (1981-82 to 1985-86)*.

———. (1998). *Report on Cost of Cultivation and Production of Major Crops in Rajasthan (1995-96)*.

Dainik Bhaskar (2002). January 18.

Governement of India (GoI) (1980). "Resolution dated March 5", Ministry of Agriculture, Department of Agriculture and Cooperation, New Delhi.

Governement of Rajasthan (2003). *Economic Review, 2002-03*.

———. (Undated). *Report on Cost of Cultivation and Production of Major Crops in Rajasthan (1981-1982 to 1985-86)*, Directorate of Agriculture, Jaipur, Rajasthan.

Hoda, A. and CSC Sekhar (2003). "Agricultural Trade Liberalisation, Poverty and Food Security—the Indian Experience", paper presented in the JNU-IFPRI seminar on *The Dragon and the Elephant: A Comparative Study of Economic and Agricultural Reforms in China and India*, India Habitat Centre, New Delhi, March 25-36.

Jha, D. and Ramesh Chand (2002). "Trade Liberalisation and Net Social Welfare", in S.S. Acharya, and D.P. Chaudhari (eds.), *Indian Agricultural Policy at the Cross Roads*, Rawat Publications, Jaipur, pp. 99-100.

Kumar, P. (2002). "Agricultural Performance and Productivity" in S.S. Acharya and D.P. Chaudhari (eds.), *Indian Agricultural Policy at the Cross Roads*, Rawat Publications, Jaipur, pp.99-100.

Rajasthan Patrika (2002). February 26.

Rathore, M.S. (2002). "Droughts and State Failure: Unwilling to Learn and Unwilling to Distribute", Institute of Development Studies, Jaipur, (*mimeo*), .

Sagar, V. (1996). "Agricultural Growth and Poverty: Emerging Issues in the Context of Structural Adjustments: Rajasthan", in G.K. Chadha and A.N. Sharma, *Agricultural Growth and Poverty: Emerging Issues in the Context of Structural Adjustments*, Indian Society of Labour Economics.

———. (2000). "Public Distribution System and Food Security in a Region of Large Agricultural Instability: A Case Study of Rajasthan", in T.N. Krishnan and N. Krisnaji, *Public Support for Food Security: Public Distribution System in India*, Sage Publications, New Delhi.

———. (2003). "Bajra Gluts and Medium-term Agricultural Policy for Rajasthan", *IDSJ Working* paper 135, November, Institute of Development Studies, Jaipur.

———. (2005). "Food Security in India", in V.S. Vyas (ed.) *Food Security in the Asian Countries in the Context of Millennium Goals*, Academic Foundation, New Delhi.

———. (2005a). *Macro-economics of Poverty Reduction in Rajasthan*, Indira Gandhi Institute of Development Research.

Sagar, V. and Kanta Ahuja (1987). *Rural Transformation in a Developing Economy*, Kumar Publications, Jaipur.

7

Sustainable Livestock Development in Rajasthan

Some Issues

SUNIL RAY

Introduction

The development discourse on livestock of the state seems to be taking an irresistible turn. While going beyond management practices, reproductive behaviour of animals and their productive contribution to the economy, it chooses to address whether the trajectory of livestock development that does not keep pace with resource regeneration can sustain. The state is unconcerned about it. It ignores the dialectics of production conditions of livestock in an agro-ecological context like that of Rajasthan. While ecological crisis, the state is grappling with, is not an exaggeration, the innate link between livestock reproduction and the stock of renewable natural resources has grown thinner. The gradual disappearance of the mixed farming system associated with it is pointer to weakened transformation of production conditions of livestock. It is in this context that one may like to redefine the terms of livestock development and seriously question some of them that exist at present and lends credibility to an obscurant and inappropriate policy approach of the state. Following this approach, state has found its major engagement mainly in the upscaling of production of livestock. It hardly takes cognisance of how the upscaling of reproduction of livestock is to be supported in the event of steady decline of the regenerative capacity of the renewable resources.

It draws one to a larger development discourse on the 'carrying capacity', what is addressed by many scholars in terms of exhaustibility of renewable natural resources (Perrings, 2005; Pernam, *et al.*, 1999; Chopra and Kadekodi, 1999; Dasgupta, P., 2001). However, while such a discourse is yet to gain a meaningful entry into intervention that the state designs for livestock development, sustainability of the latter remains a critical issue (Mishra, 2005). In other words, if term of livestock development is its sustainability, it must be specific to the carrying capacity of the land, both in terms of its physical unit and regenerative capacity of renewable resources, and, of course, the agro-ecological context in which it is sought. In that case, it is not the scale only at which animals are reproduced; one may be equally concerned about how composition of livestock changes and its implications for its sustainable development. It means that no compositional change is acceptable beyond a point where it tends to undermine livestock biodiversity or genetic variability of the animals (Mishra, 2005, Drucker, 2006). Any compositional change, which is inappropriate to the agro-ecological context, might weaken livestock production as a source of livelihood. In this case, sustainability is again a relevant issue to address. One may be a critic of the systemic response of the state and parastatal organisations to the emergence of inappropriate compositional change, if any. Then, the question that follows immediately is how does one conceive the role of the state and other intervening agencies to correct distortions that may bounce back overall development process of the livestock of the state.

The chapter intends to address these issues and argues why livestock development must be viewed as an integral part of the agro-ecological processes in the state. The chapter examines sustainability issue of livestock development in terms of carrying capacity of land *vis-à-vis* changing stock of animals. It then examines how the state had witnessed compositional shift of livestock over the years and its implications for sustainability. It also identifies gaps in the policy approach of the state and suggests the direction towards which it must improve and ensure sustainable development of livestock.

Capacity of Land and Sustainability

One may have reason to believe that livestock mobility can increase the overall carrying capacity within a region that assumes predictable environmental fluctuations (Behnke and Scoones, 1993). This has considerable influence on the herding practices designed to suit regeneration pattern of renewable resources. It also hints at sustainability of the resource base, which is one of the production conditions of livestock, by way of balancing environmental fluctuations and mobility of livestock. Problem arises if there is a mismatch between the rate of regeneration of the resource base and stocking rate of animals even if the latter is mobile. The difficulty with the reasoning of mobility that implies automatic adjustment is that it only banks upon the regeneration thesis, while it disregards the rate at which stock of animal increases. The regeneration of the resource base is invaluable especially when it ensures ecological resilience. One may argue that resilience of the rangeland is more than what is normally expected (Dasgupta, 2001; Chopra and Kadekodi, 1999). However, it does not necessarily mean that ecological resilience will never be threatened even if stock of animal increases. If the rate of regeneration of the resources falls short of the rate, at which stock of animals rises and the same repeats over a period, loss of resilience is more likely than ever. Hence, such an argument may not sufficiently help one to understand carrying capacity unless rate of regeneration of both is compared. Over and above, one must know the availability of the stock of land. For, a declining stock of land may automatically push carrying capacity of animals downwards even if regeneration of the resource base takes place at the optimum level. The availability of land for increased stock of animal *vis-à-vis* intensification of agriculture has a greater role to play to determine carrying capacity and therefore, sustainability of livestock development. It may influence livestock composition to change and stultify livestock biodiversity.

It is in this context that one must take cognisance of the agro-ecological changes that the state of Rajasthan has been witnessing in its fragile ecological system. The root of these changes is the demographic pressure of human population that seeks to generate more livelihoods to sustain. The immediate options are agriculture and livestock production. The relationship between the two is so much interwoven with each other that mixed farming was once considered an appropriate farming strategy to generate sustainable livelihood from both sources (Jodha, 2001). However, over the years, with rise in human population coupled with technology-centric agricultural development, mixed farming system gradually took a back seat. Apart from this, farming community increasingly brought large patches of uncultivated marginal and sub marginal lands under cultivation (Jodha, 2001). This had a negative contribution to the development process of livestock that was linked to the agro-ecological context of the state. At the same time, one must bear in mind that such a disruption never acted as a disincentive to the growth of livestock population. Both the sources of livelihood generation such as agriculture and livestock grew over the years, but their interlinkages were undermined. The result was obvious. It weakened the support base for livestock rearing in the state.

In order to examine how the trend of land use pattern in the state set apart less area for grazing and fodder collection, data were collected in respect of both gross cropped area and the types of lands that were used for animals (for grazing, collection of both green and dry fodder, tree lopping, etc.). We have taken four categories of land into consideration that is used by the rural community for livestock. These include barren and uncultivable land, other uncultivable land excluding fallow land such as permanent pasture and other grazing lands, land under misc. tree crops & groves and culturable wasteland (Nadkarni, 2002). We have not incorporated forestland into the calculation, since no data is available regarding the type of forest to which animals have access or from where fodder is collected. Despite this constraint, it is taken into consideration excluding the protected category of forest cover later in this chapter. However, this does not make any significant difference to the carrying capacity as estimated taking only four categories of land into consideration (Figure 7.1). Years have been chosen randomly only to gain insights into the changing trends of land availability for livestock and its implications for carrying capacity.

Figure 7.1 shows that land available (all four types of land together) for grazing and fodder collection for livestock gradually declined over the years since 1975-76. It declined from 11.60 million hectares in 1975-76 to 8.96 million hectares in 2001-2002. However, the gross cropped area of the state witnessed an increase during the same corresponding year from 17.60 million hectares to 20.80 million hectares with an exception during 1994-95 when it rose to 25.37 million hectares. It is here, one must underline that land available for grazing, etc. is estimated based on the information available from the secondary sources. Unfortunately, land, which is actually available in practice for grazing, etc. is never reported by the secondary sources. In actual practice, massive encroachment of common land is reported to have taken place in various parts of the state (Mahnot, 2002; Bhise, 2004; Ray, 1997). Based on this information, one can safely presume that the availability of land is still lower than what is indicated in Figure 7.1.

Figure 7.1

Availability of Land for Grazing and Fodder Collection

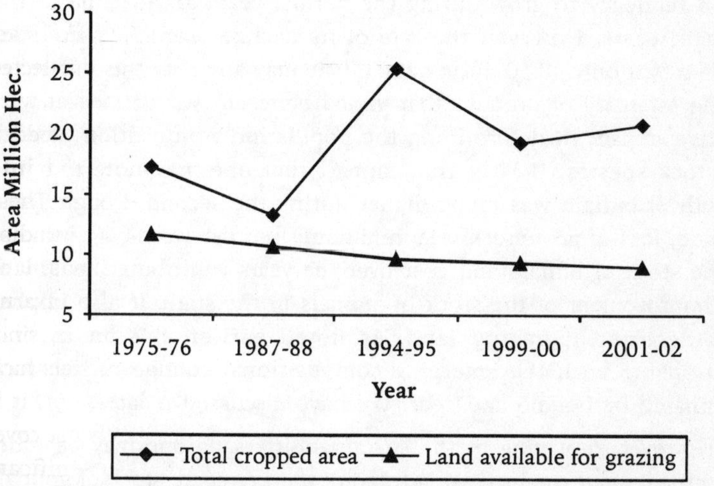

Source: *Statistical Abstract*, Various Years, Government of Rajasthan.

The pattern of land utilisation that emerged during the last three decades or so has serious implications for (1) sustenance of livestock development in view of shrinking carrying capacity of land and (2) livestock biodiversity *vis-à-vis* its compositional change. Although these issues are not exclusive to each other, it is important to address how carrying capacity declined over the years as a consequence of declining availability of grazing land and increased stock of animals.

Stocking Trend

In order to examine carrying capacity of the increased stock of animal, four major animal species are taken into consideration and converted them into standard cattle unit. They include cow, buffalo, sheep and goat. Other animal species reared in the state are horse and ponies, mules, donkey, camel, pig and rabbit. Altogether, they constituted only 2 to 3 per cent of the livestock population of the state.

Table 7.1 shows that that the stock of animal in terms of cattle unit increased from 26.83 million in 1972 to 38.40 million in 2003 with fluctuations in the stocking rates especially during drought years of 1988 and 2003. One may be interested to read the stocking trend in two different ways that are related to each other. First, stocking rate had a tendency to grow during the normal years and decline in the drought years. However, the rate of its decline was –2.29 in 1988, while it was only –0.60 during 2003. One may attribute this difference to the intensity of drought that varied between two periods and its relative impact in determining the population composition of each livestock species. It is in this context that one may note that the growth of buffalo was much higher during the second drought year. Besides, loss of goat stock was minimum. In other words, an increase in the stock of buffalo and goat over the years contributed mainly to the improvement of the stock of animals in the state. It also implies that decline in grazing land, as noted earlier, has an inverse relationship with the emerging compositional change of livestock dominated by buffalo and goat. We have discussed it later.

However, returning to the sustainability issue one may be more concerned about the increasing trend of the aggregate stock of animals notwithstanding its periodic decline due to drought. It is not the question of the number of livestock animals coming back to its original level after drought, and, therefore, designing an optimal strategy of herd management for yielding largest dividends as asserted by some (Chopra and Kadekodi, 1999). It may have some relevance to the present discourse. But, it must not lead one to think that stability in the carrying capacity is achievable through what one may call 'natural cycle'. For, stock of animals that increased more than the previous stock will automatically push down the carrying capacity.

Table 7.1 shows that the rate of growth of stock of animals grew annually at the rate of 1.16 per cent during 1972-2003. The growth rate of the stock was accompanied by the declining availability of grazing land. It finally led to the reduction in the carrying capacity of land. This is shown in Table 7.2(a) in terms of number of cattle units per unit of land area. Table 7.2(a) shows that the pressure of livestock on the same land area increased almost two folds in 2003 as compared to the same during 1972. During 1972, the number of cattle units was 2.31 per hectare of land. However, it increased to 4.33 cattle units in 2003 in the same land area in the state. In other words, 0.43 hectares of land was available (inverse of the former) per cattle unit in 1972. It declined to 0.23 hectare of land per cattle unit during 2003 (Table 7.2(b)). The zone wise analysis in this context further shows that land area available per cattle declined maximum in the arid zone—annually at the rate of -2.51 per cent. Next was the humid zone that witnessed a loss of carrying capacity annually at the rate of–2.07 per cent.[1]

Table 7.1

Annual Growth of Animal Stock and its Compositional Change (1972-2003)

(No. of Animals in Million)

Year	*Cow*	*Buffalo*	*Sheep*	*Goat*	*No. of Cattle Units*
1972	12.47	4.59	8.56	12.16	26.83
1977	12.90	5.07	9.94	12.31	28.60
	(0.68)	(2.01)	(3.04)	(0.24)	(1.28)
1983	13.50	6.04	13.43	15.48	32.82
	(0.92)	(3.66)	(6.20)	(4.69)	(2.79)
1988	10.92	6.34	9.93	12.58	29.24
	(-4.15)	(0.98)	(-5.86)	(-4.03)	(-2.29)
1992	11.67	7.78	12.49	15.29	36.16
	(1.33)	(4.15)	(4.69)	(3.98)	(3.16)
1997	12.14	9.77	14.58	16.97	39.57
	(0.79)	(4.67)	(3.14)	(2.11)	(2.98)
2003	10.85	10.41	10.05	16.81	38.40
	(-2.22)	(1.27)	(-7.17)	(-0.09)	(-0.60)
1972-2003	(-0.45)	(2.67)	(0.52)	(1.04)	(1.16)

Note: Figures in parentheses are annual compound growth rates. Cattle unit is estimated following the criteria of one cattle is equal to one cattle unit, one buffalo is equal to two cattle units, one goat is equal to 0.25 cattle unit and one sheep is equal to 0.25 cattle unit.

Source: Livestock Census, Various Issues, and Government of Rajasthan.

1. If forest area (excluding protected forest) is added to the area available for animals to graze and fodder collection, almost a similar declining trend is witnessed over the years with a marginal difference (not shown in Table). For instance, 0.42 hectare of land was available per cattle in 1977 in Rajasthan on an average; it declined to 0.26 hectare of land in 2003. In arid zone, it is estimated to have declined from 0.74 hectare of land per cattle during 1977 to 0.42 during 2003.

Table 7.2(a)

Carrying Capacity of the Number of Cattle Units Per Hectare of Grazing Land

Zone	*Cattle Units Per Hectare of Land*				
	1972	*1983*	*1988*	*1992*	*2003*
Arid	1.16	1.74	1.47	1.93	2.59
Semi-arid	5.20	5.81	6.10	7.18	9.04
Sub-humid	3.04	3.49	3.04	3.89	4.54
Humid	4.44	5.80	6.07	6.53	10.27
Rajasthan	2.31	2.93	2.73	3.32	4.33

Source: Estimated based on the data available from *Statistical Abstract* and *Livestock Census*, Various Issues, Government of Rajasthan.

Table 7.2(b)

Area Available Per Cattle Unit

(in Hectare)

Zone	*1972*	*1983*	*1988*	*1992*	*2003*
Arid	0.86	0.58	0.68	0.52	0.31
Semi-arid	0.19	0.17	0.16	0.14	0.11
Sub-humid	0.33	0.29	0.33	0.26	0.22
Humid	0.23	0.17	0.16	0.15	0.12
Rajasthan	0.43	0.34	0.37	0.30	0.23

Source: Estimated based on the data available from *Statistical Abstract* and *Livestock Census*, Various Issues, Government of Rajasthan.

Here, the relevant issue within the framework of the sustainability debate is: why is it that the stock of animals has a tendency to rise continuously despite declining availability of the grazing land? And, if quality dimension (grassland ecology indicating soil erosion and loss of grass cover, for example), which is also continuously deteriorating, is taken into consideration, then how does one account for increased stock and its sustainable development? A study was conducted recently in 11 villages of the state across all agro-climatic zones and examined the reason why farming community chooses to raise the stock of animals under the conditions mentioned above even during drought years (Ray,

2006). The study shows that increased human population reinforces the choice of the farming community to retain as many animals as possible even under the conditions of drought. The relatively higher rate of growth of population in the arid zone as compared to other zones provides a plausible explanation why animal stock increased in this zone and reduced carrying capacity of the land. The population increased at the rate of 2.59 per cent per annum in the arid zone during 1981-2001. This was higher than that of other zones, except semi-arid zone that witnessed the same at the rate of 2.61 per cent per annum during the same period. Table 7.2(a) shows that the same arid zone that witnessed highest growth of human population, experienced highest fall in the carrying capacity of land. This happened despite the fact that it had comparatively huge stock of common open land.

The study shows that the farming community is largely left with a limited choice in their struggle for livelihood generation in the fragile ecological conditions especially during drought or near-drought conditions. Either they have to choose wage labour in the non-farm activities or livestock rearing or both. The degree of importance being attached to both the sources of livelihood generation vary depending upon how households work out relative opportunity costs. Villagers treat livestock rearing as crucial since it plays a critical role in ensuring minimum livelihood in the most distressing conditions. In other words, the relative opportunity cost of livestock rearing scores lower. For, attached to it, is the hope that it will at least provide livelihood even if all other legitimate options are closed to the households.

In uncertainty brought by the fragility of the ecosystem, this norm works and encourages livestock population to grow concomitant with the rise in human population. It grows up to a point where the household looks for an optimal combination of livestock rearing and wage employment. Even if the average stocking rate is found to be low at the individual household level as a product of such combination, stocking rate of animal at the aggregate level rises along with the rise in human population. The continued vulnerability of the state to drought proneness did not impose natural control on the growth of stock of animals. However, it may do so only when the scarcity of resources in the shrinking pastures intensifies to such an extent that household will have to face declining impact of the animal stock at the given level of regeneration of the resource base.

It may be too difficult to visualise the intensity of the growing tension between resource depletion and increasing stock of animals for the entire state, as convincingly as one thinks, owing to diversity that exists at different layers of its regional profiles. In addition to the differences that exist in agro-ecological practices across zones, livestock composition differs, so are practices of livestock rearing (for example, more than 60 per cent of sheep is reared in the arid zone, while other zones of the state do rest of the stock. Similarly, buffalo rearing tends to dominate cows wherever milk production is commercialised.). Despite such differences, the same study, mentioned above, shows that dependence of the household on common resource base was low but significant for maintenance of his/her livestock unit (Ray, 2006). The estimation of the average livestock unit per household was based on 635 households that were surveyed across all agro-climatic zones. It appears that 1.27 cows, 1.16 buffaloes, 1.57 sheep, 4.88 goats and 0.63 bullocks constitute average livestock unit at the household level. The quantity of fodder, both green and dry, and treeloppings that were collected from the uncultivated land including common and private land and the agricultural by-products that were not purchased during the concerned drought year (2002-03), were converted in money terms at local prices. This is done to gain some insights into the extent to which farmers depend on the unpaid inputs to feed livestock collected from their local resource base. This is shown in Table 7.3.

The average annual gross value from livestock unit per household[2] in the drought year was estimated to be Rs. 12,960.64. However, potential cost, as shown in Table 7.3, was Rs. 18,057.20. One must bear in mind that this estimation does not include cost equivalence of grass being grazed in money terms. If this were added, potential cost would be much more than what is shown here. As mentioned earlier, household actually paid only Rs. 7,123.16 (39.44 per cent) of the estimated annual potential cost towards feed and fodder. However, household never paid in practice for the rest of the estimated cost of Rs. 10,934.03 (60.56 per cent). This makes the basic difference to

2. This exercise was undertaken based on the survey of 635 households across all agro-climatic zones. The annual gross income from livestock was estimated, based on the sale of animals and animal products. The animal products that are used for household consumption are also taken into consideration for estimating gross value by way of imputing their prices at the prevailing market rates. Similarly, cost of fodder (green and dry) and treeloppings collected from the village commons and private lands are estimated, based on the ongoing local market prices.

sustainability of livestock at the household level. It gives an impression that livestock sector is not in deficit. For household is able to generate gross surplus to the tune of Rs. 5,837.48 per annum (Rs. 12,960.64–Rs. 7,123.16) purely from monetary point of view. However, one may argue that it may run into deficit if scarcity value of the resources is actually paid.

Table 7.3

Average Estimated Cost of Feed and Fodder of Livestock Per Households Per Annum

a. Not Purchased	Rs.
1. Agricultural By-products	6128.06 (33.94)
2. Collection of Green and Dry Fodder	
A. Private Land	3350.19 (18.55)
B. Common Land	1455.78 (8.06)
Total (a)	**10934.03 (60.56)**
b. Purchased	
1. Agricultural By-products and Others	5246.44 (29.05)
2. Concentrate	1876.72 (10.39)
Total (b)	**7123.16 (39.44)**
Average Potential Cost Per Household	18057.2 (100.00)

Note : Figures in the parentheses are percentages of the total estimated expenditure.
Source : Estimated based on the data available in the research report on "Institutional Reforms for Alternative Ecologically sensitive People Friendly Development Interventions", 2006, Institute of Development Studies, and Jaipur.

The feed and fodder worth Rs. 10,934.03 are collected from two sources that include: (1) own agriculture and (2) natural resource base of the village (private + common). Now, if the household is to pay the same amount in reality,[3] livestock economy may reach the

3. Although value of agricultural by-products is considered unpaid, actually it is not so. Investment is made in agricultural production. If this is taken into account, the unpaid value of agricultural by-products becomes lower than what is shown in Table 7.3. It then raises relative scarcity value of natural resources collected from both common and private lands.

point of collapse. For, the estimated cost for maintenance of the same stock of animal would be 39.32 per cent more than the gross annual income. It will be further higher if the cost of grass due to grazing is taken into consideration. It is this unpaid scarcity value of the resources that does not allow stock of animal to decline. While one may like to emphasise on agriculture's contribution (both paid and unpaid inputs together) and its positive implication for livestock sustainability, contribution of the natural resource base (collection of green and dry fodder) is no less important. It contributes to the tune of 27 per cent of the total estimated cost (Table 7.3). Villagers never pay for these inputs. However, if the unpaid scarcity value of resources goes beyond a tolerable limit, stocking rate of animal is bound to decline. The rise of this unpaid scarcity value may affect composition of animal stock also. In such a situation, households may prefer those animals that fetch more income than expenditure and do not depend much on village pastures.

Compositional Shift

Related to the discussion on compositional shift, one may be more concerned whether such a shift has taken place at the expense of livestock biodiversity in general and genetic variability in particular. It is argued that sustainable production system of livestock needs to be designed in a way that animal genetic resources (AnGR) are not endangered. In order to orient AnGR conservation policy, Safe Minimum Standard (SMS) is advocated (Drucker, 2006). However, the present analysis does not intend to cover these aspects although they remain critical to the discourse on sustainability of livestock development. It is important to recognise that the state is endowed with a wide range of genetic variability of livestock. May it be cows or sheep? While indigenous cows have seven descript breeds along with non-descript breeds, sheep has eight descript breeds. The major concern, here is to examine the trend of compositional change of livestock and its implications for sustainability. While composition of livestock is determined broadly by the stock of agro-ecological inputs and the extent of commercial gains, the former one plays primary role.

One of the significant trends, Table 7.1 shows, is that the growth of buffalo was continuously positive and remained almost stable during the last 30 years or so. Its stock increased from 4.59 million during early 1970s to 10.41 million in 2003. It grew at the rate of 2.67 per cent per annum. Contrary to it, stock of cow witnessed a decline since 1980s. It declined at the rate of –0.45 annually during the period concerned. The increasing incidence of replacement of cows by buffaloes definitely indicates compositional shift in favour of buffaloes. Even in the driest part of the state, the arid zone, witnessed its steady growth during last 30 years. The story of other zones was not different from that of the arid zone. For instance, the study that was conducted a few years ago shows that the annual growth rate of the stock of breedable cows was consistently negative in the semi-arid zone, while it was consistently positive in respect of breedable stock of buffalo (Ray, 2004). The stock of breedable buffalo of the total breedable animals (cows and buffalo) was 37.65 per cent during 1983 and that of indigenous cow was 62.16 per cent. However, it was 54 .0 per cent in respect of buffalo and 46. 0 per cent for cows during 2003.

The hybridisation programme that was initiated to improve the stock of breedable cow was of little significance in practice. It did not count much on the efforts made by the government and other non-government organisations. According to some estimate, only 0.55 per cent of all breedable cows were crossbred during 1993-94 (Ray, 2004). It increased to 0.96 per cent in 1997 and 2.42 per cent in 2003. In this regard, the state is found to be lagging far behind the major milk producing states of the country. What needs to be underlined here is that, while Rajasthan is the third largest milk producing state in the country, it holds 13th position in terms of progress of its hybridisation programme on indigenous cows (Government of Rajasthan, 2004-05). This, however, does not suggest that efforts need to be made to scale up the programme. All that it shows is that the contribution of the breed improvement programme in respect of cows to improve milk production in the state was insufficient.

Needless to mention, the extent to which livestock keepers gain from livestock (both monetarily and non-monetarily) has a decisive influence on compositional change. This becomes increasingly important as scarcity of natural resources grows. This is mentioned earlier. The relevance of this issue here is that acceptability of the breed improvement programme for cows among the livestock keepers is much lower than what is expected. It is lower mainly due to low commercial value of cow milk and more important, scarcity of natural resources. Additionally, over the years, the state had witnessed a steady rise of mechanisation of agriculture that reduced the importance of bullock for cultivation (Kurup, 1997; Ray, 2004). Of course, this programme suffers from serious operational deficiency (Ray, 1999b).

However, what needs to be stressed is that acceptability of milch buffalo is more than improved breeds of cows despite scarcity of natural resources or declining carrying capacity of land. Apart from suitability of this animal in the harsh climate, there are other reasons for preferring buffalo to cow rearing. The most important among them is the higher fat percentage in buffalo milk that fetches more income to the livestock keepers in addition to higher average milk productivity as compared to that of cow. Thanks to the growth of organised dairy industry in the state, that pays price for milk in terms of fat percentage. These factors together reinforce acceleration of the stocking rate of buffalo. One must take note that its average milk productivity increased by little more than 1 kg per day per buffalo in 2003-04 as compared to what it was during 1960s (Figure 7.2). During 1962-1965, it was 3.02 kg per buffalo per day, while the same was 4.29 kg in 2003-04. The milk production per cow was 2.12 and 2.79 kg per day during the corresponding years.

If the present level of production of milk of both cow and buffalo is optimum (not shown here), sustainability of livestock development, as the present trend shows, is supported more by the stock than productivity. One may doubt whether such stock-led livestock development would sustain in view of the declining carrying capacity of land as discussed earlier. Hence, efforts need to be made to bring about a shift in the trend more towards the rise in productivity. In order to achieve comparatively higher level of productivity of the existing stock of animals, local base of renewable resources needs to be improved. The same study, as mentioned above, shows that in several places in the state, village communities renovated their community institutions, improved regenerating capacity of their resource bases and brought about breakthrough in milk production in particular and livestock development in general (Ray, 2006).

Figure 7.2

Average Milk Productivity

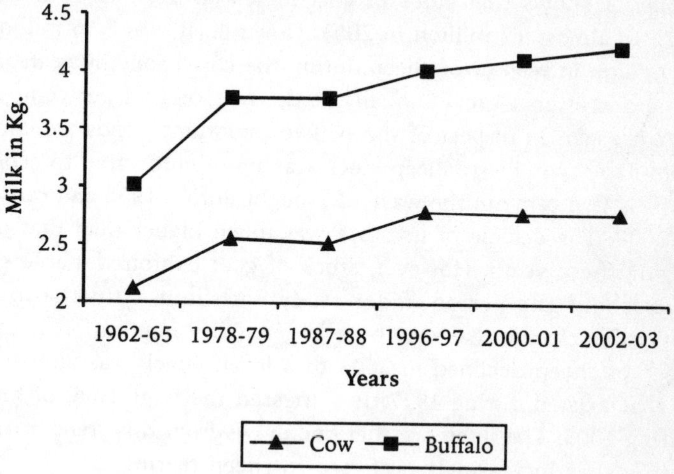

Source: Administrative Report, 2004-05, Directorate of Animal Husbandry, Government of Rajasthan.

In addition to the above, one must be concerned about how share of the milch animals in the natural resource bases *vis-à-vis* the share of non-breedable and non-descript livestock could rise. The state is endowed with a huge stock of non-descript cows (70 per cent of the total cattle population) with low average milk productivity. Similarly, 57 per cent of its stock is non-breedable. Both these together generate a negative surplus when one takes into account the amount of pressure it creates on feed and fodder availability leading to reduced overall, livestock productivity (Shah *et al.*, 1996). The higher stock of these animals competes for resource inputs but does not fit much into the enhancement of household welfare. While one may seek introduction of Safe Minimum Standard for conserving animal genetic resources, attempt may be made to see that the share of the productive animals in the resource base does not shrink. One must not trivialise the issue of accumulation of the stock of unproductive animals that brings negative pressure on productivity of the livestock economy and reduces the prospect of sustainable development of livestock.

The trend analysis of the compositional change of small ruminants indicates, almost a similar pattern in that one variety of livestock was preferred increasingly more than the other during last 30 years or so. Table 7.1 shows that stock of goat increased from 12.16 million in 1972 to almost 17 million in 2003. However, it was 8.56 million and 10 million in respect of sheep during the corresponding years. While the stock of goat grew annually at the rate of 1.04 per cent, it was 0.52 per cent in respect of sheep. Two important trends are emerging from Table 7.1. First, sheep stock was more vulnerable to ecological distress that came in the wake of drought during 1988 and early years of 2000. The decline of its stock was much higher than that of goat during these years. However, stock of goat exhibited stable growth throughout the period under study with minor fluctuation. The noticeable change that may have larger policy implication is that the stock of sheep declined in 2003 to a level, which was almost same, as that existed during 1977. It witnessed the largest fall of its stock during 2003. The inference that one draws from this trend analysis is that goat is increasingly preferred to sheep rearing.

The study, as mentioned earlier, reveals that 482 of the total sample households of 635 (76 per cent) had goat with an average flock size of six goats. Contrary to it, only 47 households (7-8 per cent) kept sheep with an average flock size of 20 sheep. Besides, the average holding of goat by the non-poor is more than the poor household is. For example, average holding of goat per non-poor household is 7.7, while it is 5.6 per poor household. However, in the case of sheep, the average holding per poor household is 21.4, while for non-poor it is 18.6 (Ray, 2006). In other words, poor households prefer sheep to goat rearing.

While it is difficult to say whether the same trend will continue, its implications for sustainability of sheep husbandry pose formidable challenge. It is in this context that one may mention about the forces that have been undermining the prospect of sheep husbandry in the state. The first impediment that strikes herd size of sheep is the deteriorating condition of the village pastures in the state associated with the declining carrying capacity, as discussed earlier. The study conducted by IDS in late 1990s revealed that the western Rajasthan, where sheep stock was concentrated maximum with 65 per cent of the total stock, was facing a permanent crisis of flock management owing to degradation on the one hand, encroachment of pastureland on the other (Ray, 1997). While grazing land and its conditions determine production conditions of sheep stock and its by-products, shrinkage of both affect economics of sheep husbandry practice adversely. The decline of production of grazable biomass, continuous loss of vegetation cover, falling short of protein due to the lack of mixed type of herbage containing both leguminous and non-leguminous forage and grasses have weakened the production conditions (Ray, 1999a). The net effect that one may discern, is the decline of productivity of sheep in terms of raw wool (Ibid). So much so, it created a scarcity in the local wool market. The irony is that wool markets of the biggest wool producing state, the state of Rajasthan, are increasingly filled with the imported wool.

In such circumstances, migration is found to be the easy way out. Although sheep migration is a process that cannot be reversed, its increasing scale with low cost effectiveness (Kavoori, 1991) coupled with inter-state problems and disputes (Bharara, 1989), continued to be a matter of serious concern. It means that the sheep rearers, beyond a point, may not accept the process, where the relative opportunity cost begins to increase. However, one must bear in mind that the incidence of migration of sheep oscillates depending upon the intensity of the internal crisis of the grazing land. For instance, total number of sheep migrated (including permanent and temporary migration) during 2002-03 was 2.61 million. It declined to 0.86 million in the following year and during 2004-05, it was 2.55 million (Government of Rajasthan, 2004-05). In any case, it never exceeded 25 per cent of the total stock of sheep of the state. It suggests that one must concentrate more on strengthening the internal production conditions including improvement of the huge stock of renewable natural resources that the state is endowed with, while addressing sustainability crisis of sheep husbandry.

The hybridisation programme (cross-breeding with exotic breed) and commercial gains that lend support to the production conditions of sheep directly and indirectly, failed to make significant dent in arresting the decline of sheep population. While hybridisation programme was never given a central place by the sheep rearers in their local sheep husbandry practices, exploitative market for raw wool and animal, that continues to operate unchallenged pays too little tc the sheep rearers to widen their choice for sheep rearing (Ray, 1995). What is true for sheep is almost equally true for cows in the overall analysis of compositional shift of livestock in the state. For instance, in both cases hybridisation programme (with exotic breed) left much to be desired. Similarly, economics of rearing of these animals is no longer an important source for the livestock keepers to prefer these animals to others.

If the trend on compositional shift continues towards buffalo and goat, it may have serious development implications for the state. First, there may be a gradual loss of livestock biodiversity, which is interwoven, with the agro-ecological conditions of the state. Second, command over livestock resources especially large animals may shift towards the non-poor, for poor cannot afford to own buffalo and, third is squeezing of choice of animals to rear. The last one is immensely important for the poor who have the tradition of rearing cows and small ruminants including sheep in the state. Their sustainable livelihood is drawn largely from these animals through the sale of animals and fibre in the case of sheep and using animal byproducts for self-consumption in the case of cows. If these practices shrink in the absence of any alternative, it will have an adverse impact on the household economy of the poor. More particularly, its spillover effect will hit employment opportunities significantly that are provided by the raw wool-processing sector to the skilled and semi-skilled poor workers. While these issues are intrinsically connected with the larger development goals, one must recognise their growing incompatibility with the compositional shift of livestock, the state had witnessed during last few decades or so.

Policy Reforms

Such an incompatibility on the one hand, and, the weak production conditions on the other, is the source of threat to sustainable development of livestock that the state cannot dispense with. At the same time, one has no reason to expect much from the obscurant and disintegrated policy support of the state to reduce vulnerability of livestock development process to unsustainability. Of course, several development programmes including providing livestock services are implemented by the state. However, one does not know how poor cost effectiveness of these programmes with built-in incomprehensibility could support livestock development to sustain (Ahuja *et al.*, 2000). This programme-oriented approach, which is palliative in nature, may allow one only to seek for a trade off between options within a limited set. It is yet to provide adequate space for meeting the sustainability crisis that originates from both supply (resource base) and demand management (market) sides. This suggests that state must follow a pragmatic approach and seek reforms of its livestock policy.

One may suggest several ways to reform the existing approach of the state. However, what is fundamentally important is to recognise first, the inseparable link between livestock and agro-ecological practices. This has been missing all along in the state-led discourse on sustainability issue of livestock development. No policy exists to regenerate huge stock of pastureland the state is endowed with, improve its carrying capacity and utilise it on a sustainable manner for livestock development. State, as a development facilitator, must have a decentralised approach to implement it. It must come to terms for pastureland development with the renovated institutional practices at the community level (Ray, 2006).

The second most important aspect of the policy reforms is related to the breeding policy that needs to be revised in consistent with the agro-ecological conditions of the state. While the hybridisation programme initiated by the state with exotic breed in respect to both cow and sheep witnessed failure in each successive year, one does not understand why selective breeding programme continued to be pushed to the periphery of breeding policy. The selective breeding is not only conducive to the local environment and able to adjust to the local feeding conditions, but also, it raises productivity. However, one may be dismissive of selective breeding if a responsive and stable system of supplying feed and fodder development programme is absent. It is here that one seeks to integrate breed improvement programme with the development of village pastures by the village community within an institutional framework in collaboration with the state, if necessary. A renewed emphasis for revamping breeding policy (selective) of the state is needed to improve the quality of the stock with more productive animals than the ones that dominate the present stock.

The third important policy concern is marketing of animals and their byproducts. No doubt, state has created better conditions for marketing of large animals (through animal fairs) and their by-products (through dairy development). However, policy response in respect of small ruminants is too weak to destabilise the intermediary system that constantly deprives the rearers of their due share in value added. One of the reasons why sheep rearing became less appealing from demand management side was lower value addition from the entire practice. The creation of a few physical infrastructures for marketing of wool does not make any difference to the intermediary system. It is here that the state must seek a new management regime and, accordingly, evolve the marketing policy that will facilitate the sheep rearers to generate sustainable livelihood. The decentralisation approach may hold the key to such policy, in that formation of cluster is an important strategic component. Each cluster must have a Common Facility Centre (CFC), which has to be formed by the sheep rearers themselves within an institutional framework. One seeks a real integration of all activities including shearing of wool fibre and its preliminary processing, standardising, storing and selling, implementing breed improvement programme, selling animal, veterinary care etc. under the agies of CFC (Ray, 1997). In the case of marketing of milk and milk products, it is true that the state has achieved considerable improvement as far as harnessing marketing potential of the domestic market is concerned. However, one is yet to see how policy response could stand the test of global competition under WTO regime (Bhattacharya, 2002).

The fourth and the last policy component are livestock services and their delivery system. The objective is to deliver livestock services of improved quality in a cost-effective manner. It will not only facilitate sustenance of rich stock of animals with higher productivity but also it may reduce pressure on state's budgetary resources. It appears that large percentage of budgetary resources are required to meet salaries and benefits of the veterinarians, technicians and maintenance, leaving very little funds for other recurring needs such as drugs and veterinary supplies (Ray, 2004; Ahuja *et al.*, 2000). Besides, market structure of livestock services is highly distorted. All these create scarcity value of the services high enough to exclude the poor from accessing them. In view of this, there is a need to reevaluate and reorient the strategy of the service delivery system that exists at present. The state may like to promote commercialisation of those services that have no externalities, and leave those that have externalities to the public sector. It is in this context that one might seek combination of services from both the government and private institutions. It may work in different ways including: (1) fostering grater financial autonomy to veterinary institutions and artificial centres, (2) creating an enabling environment for private practioners and (3) evolving a regulatory framework to ensure service quality (Ahuja *et al.*, 2000).

Conclusion

In the context of poverty redressal, availability of sources for livelihood generation matters significantly to the poor. Logically speaking, degree of vulnerability to impoverisation rises, as the availability of sources of livelihood generation becomes scarce. This provides a perspective to understand how imperative it is, to emphasise on the sustainability issue of livestock development in the state. For, it stood the test of all crises and remained active in providing alternative source of livelihood generation to all including the poor and non-poor, in fragile agro-ecological conditions of Rajasthan. While one should not ignore its development implications for the state as a whole, one must seek for a different management regime to ensure sustainable development of livestock in the state. This new management regime needs to be guided, apart from strengthening marketing institutions on competitive lines and emphasising on productivity of livestock, more by the principles of sustainable growth of natural resources. It means that no development policy of livestock can be conceived devoid of revival of degraded natural resource base of the state and its sustainable growth. It might lend incredible strength to this sector to turn into an invincible source of income and employment generation in general and poverty alleviation in particular, in the state. A horizontal integration of the rural communities, civil society organisations and the state may be a step to begin with, to achieve this goal.

References

Ahuja, V. *et al.* (2000). *Agricultural Services and the Poor, Case of Livestock Health and Breeding Services in India*, Indian Institute of Management, Ahmedabad, The World Bank and Swiss Agency for Development and Cooperation.

Behnke, R.H. and I. Scoones (1993). "Rethinking Range Ecology: Implications for Range Management in Africa", from Cousin, B. (1996). "Livestock Production and Common Property Struggles in South Africa's Agrarian Reform", *The Journal of Peasant Studies*, Vol. 23, No. 2/3, January/April.

Bharara, L.P. (1989). *Socio-Economic Aspects of Livestock Migration and Pastoral Nomadism in Drought-prone Areas of Rajasthan in Livestock Economy of India*, Oxford and IBH Publishing Co., Indian Society for Agricultural Economics, Bombay.

Bhattacharya, S. (2002). "Entwining of Trade Policy with the Environmental Standards: A New Form of Non-tariff Barriers", in N. Reddy, S. Singh and D. Arora (eds.), *Political Economy of WTO Regime, Some Aspects of Globalization and Governance*, Rainbow Publishers, New Delhi.

Bhise, S.N. (ed.) (2004). *Decolonising the Commons*, National Foundation for India, New Delhi and Seva Mandir, Udaipur.

Chopra, K. and G. Kadekodi (1999). *Operationalising Sustainable Development*, Sage Publications India Pvt. Ltd., New Delhi.

Dasgupta, Partha (2001). *Human Well-being and the Natural Environment*, Oxford University Press, New Delhi.

Drucker, Adm. (2006). "An Application of the Use of Safe Minimum Standards in the Conservation of Livestock Bio-diversity", *Environment and Development Economics*, 11; 95-126.

Government of Rajasthan (2004-05), *Administrative Report*, Directorate of Animal Husbandry, Jaipur.

Jodha, N.S. (2001). *Life on the Edge, Sustaining Agriculture and Community Resources in Fragile Environments*, Oxford University Press, New Delhi.

Kavoori, P. (1991). *Pastoral Transhumance in Western Rajasthan-A Report on the Migratory System of Sheep*, Institute of Development Studies, Jaipur.

Kurup, M.P.G. (1997). "Cattle Numbers and Drought Animals", in *Dairy India*.

Mahnot, S.M. (2002). *The Maru Gochar Yojna: A Proposal*, The School of Desert Sciences, Jodhpur (Rajasthan).

Mishra, S.N. (2005). "Sustainable Livestock Development in India", in C.H.H. Rao, B.B. Bhattacharya, and N.S. Sidharathan (eds.), *Indian Economy and Society-in the Era of Globalisation and Liberalization*, Academic Foundation, New Delhi.

Nadkarni, M.V. (2002). "Commons, Development and the Poor", in D.K. Marothia (ed.) *Institutionalising Common Pool Resources*, Concept Publishing Company, New Delhi.

Perman, R., Yue Ma, J. Magilvray and M. Common (1999). *Natural Resource and Environmental Economics* (Second Edition) Pearson Education Ltd., England.

Perrings, Charles (2005). "The Economics of the Environment: Lessons from Ecology" in N. Sengupta and J. Bandyopadhyay (eds.), *Bio-diversity and Quality of Life*, Macmillan India Limited, Delhi (The Indian Society for Ecological Economics).

Ray, Sunil (1995). "In the Shadow of 'Kotris', An Analysis of Wool Markets of Rajasthan", *Economic and Political Weekly*, November 25.

———. (1997). *Natural Resources, Organisations and Technology Linkages*, Rawat Publications, Jaipur.

———. (1999a) "Declining Production Conditions of Raw Wool, Analysis of Emerging Conflicts in Sheep Husbandry in Rajasthan", *Economic and Political Weekly*, Vol XXXIV, May 15.

———. (1999b). "Livestock Services in Rajasthan" in the Workshop Procedings on *Commercialization of Livestock Health and Breeding Services*, Vinod Ahuja (ed.), Indian Institute of Management, Ahmedabad.

———. (2004). *Dairy Industry in Rajasthan—Problems and Prospects*, Institute of Development Studies, Jaipur, (Monograph).

———. (2006). *Institutional Reforms for Alternative Ecologically Sensitive People Friendly Development Interventions*, Institute of Development Studies, Jaipur (A Research Report).

———. (2006). "Institutional Renovation for Pastureland Development in a Village of Rajasthan", in R. Parthasarathy and Sudarshan Iyengar (eds.), *New Development Paradigms and Challenges for Western and Central India*, Vol. II, Concept Publishing Company, New Delhi.

Shah, T. *et al.*, (1996). "Draft Policy Approach Paper", *National Livestock Policy*, Government of India.

I am extremely grateful to Ajay Garg and Jagdish Sharma for their help in writing this paper. Thanks are due to Prof. S. N. Mishra for his useful comments on the draft of this paper.

III

Beyond Economics

8

Civil Society in Rajasthan

Initiative and Inhibitions

PRADEEP BHARGAVA[1]

Replacing the domination of circumstances and chance over individuals by the domination of individuals over chance and circumstances.

— Karl Marx

We begin with a basic premise that civil society is primary to a functioning democracy that helps realise human rights while deepening democratic consciousness. For example, challenging the dominant feudal and communal forces thriving on hate and discrimination would require an understanding and belief in capability of people to deliberate and their potential capacity to do things to realise their freedom. Civil society helps people to 'do'—to define their agency, choice, independence and self-determination. Yet another face of civil society is to bring relief and help to people. Seeing the utility, desires and satisfaction of people, civil society helps them to 'be' through increasing their welfare and happiness. This is achieved through a variety of activities and building networks of relationships.

Both faces of civil society, i.e., to 'do' and to 'be', are interrelated and often conflate into one another. The processes are very different. The former lays emphasis on building capacities of people to exercise their rights in the given domain, making them aware of both rights

1. The author is thankful to a number of civil society organisations in Rajasthan with whom he interfaced for several years, and learnt from their experiences. In this chapter I have been able to cover only a fraction of my learnings and a very large number of organisations with whom I interacted closely do not even find a mention in the chapter. The NGO Centre at the Institute of Development Studies, Jaipur provided opportunities for dialogue with a number of civil society organisations on issues of current interest. Many faculty members, including the author provided academic support and a forum for civil society advocacy. I am thankful to V. S. Vyas, Harsh Sethi, Rajiv Gupta and M. S. Rathore for their critical comments and/or discussing several issues raised in this chapter. I also thank Manju Balana for research support and comments on the chapter.

and duties, and building a democratic consciousness. The latter provides people the much needed help in managing natural resources, and increasing their incomes by involving them in economic and social activities. Both processes may, however, involve building organisations of people. Though processes are disparate, goals remain largely the same—freedom from want, i.e., fulfilling the basic needs of employment, food, water, shelter or freedom to realise one's human potential for education and health, freedom from fear and injustice, freedom of participation, expression and association and freedom for decent work.

In this chapter our purpose is to analyse the role of civil society in Rajasthan in helping people 'do', their limitations and successes, and problems they encounter. A number of civil society organisations that help people 'be', have successfully implemented projects with support from the government, and national and international donors. This chapter gives an assessment of how much or how little civil society has been able to achieve people 'do' in building a democratic consciousness and how. It first explores how the state-civil society interface changed in the wake of decline of state institutions. It then analyses three major successes to the credit of civil society, the right to information, the right to work, and the right for decentralised management of water. The first two are being realised by working not against the state but creating a space for dialogue and consensus, considered to be hallmarks of civil society. Chapter also analyses the lack of social movements among women and the Dalits and presents the face of a negative civil society. It then presents the universal or narrow perspectives of civil society organisations as reflected in their own discourse.

State and the Civil Society

The national movement in India symbolised the values of freedom and democracy, self-determination and self reliance, equality and social justice, service to the poor and to society at large—together synthesised in the Gandhian concept of *Swarajya*. Not only did the national movement provide an opportunity to build a powerful institutional structure, it also permitted quite a large role for voluntary effort and autonomous institutions outside the state sector. The emerging state, on the one hand, provided a rule bound administrative and judicial structure, and a non-partisan planning machinery, and at the same time the space for civil society for informed criticisms and debate to address the social reality of a highly dispersed and decentralised society, on the other (Kothari, 1988).

But in the princely states of Rajasthan, the national movement was not as strong as in other parts of the country and the feudal bonds of the princes, though broke after Independence, the feudal consciousness persisted.[2] However, the feudal bonds were "a decenteredness of hierarchy in a centralised mode of authority... but they took care of base and grassroots incorporating the sub-cultural identities and ethos" (Singhi and Joshi, 1995), and to this extent these bonds had a character of religious tolerance. Like in other parts of the country, where the civil society has participated in sociocultural transformation, national reconstruction and nation building, Rajasthan also had the *Sarvodaya* Movement, the *Khadi*, the cooperatives and the adult education movement in the 1960s and 1970s that laid a foundation for secular voluntary action.

India as a whole witnessed a decline in state institutions of democracy and erosion of the legitimacy of the state[3] in the 1970s in the wake of the emergency. This made room for parochial identities, caste and communal groupings.[4] When institutions get eroded, the victim is autonomy of individual, individual right to equal citizenship and exclusion from decision-making apparatus and participatory democratic framework. As the state failed to guarantee these, and instead functioned as an instrument of sub-serving dominant sectional interests only, non-state associations and voluntary mobilisation became important. In the wake of Jai Prakash Narain's Sampurna Kranti movement, new social formations began to emerge in the

2. Folk, Faith and Feudalism shows the interaction of feudalism and modernity in Rajasthan. A number of articles in this volume are a testimony to the continuing feudal consciousness in the state through environmental wisdom, patronage and folk performers, etc. See Singhi and Joshi (1995), and also Singh (1993).

3. The emergency, 1975, threw the old institution out of gear, decline of Congress Party as the basic institution of the system was displaced by bureaucracy and personal charisma.

4. Kothari (1988) says that in a way this was inherent in the process of change. A particular institutional apparatus in course of time proves to be a drag and an obstacle to social change: the colonial bureaucracy, the rule-enforcing and adjudicating machinery and the planning apparatus become too rigid and too conservative to permit new social formations to emerge and produce a just and humane society in the face of massive demographic, social and psycho-cultural shifts.

country. This was the time when the voluntary sector or the NGOs in Rajasthan emerged as an effective 'third sector' after the government and the private sector and engaged itself in community development. The Seva Mandir in Udaipur, the Social Work Research Centre (SWRC) in Ajmer, Urmul in Bikaner, Cecoedecon in Jaipur, and Gramin Vigyan Vikas Samiti in Jodhpur emerged as initiators of NGO movement in Rajasthan. Interestingly, the majority leadership of these NGOs, barring Seva Mandir, hailed from states other than Rajasthan.

The political turmoil in the late 1970s provided an opportunity to build democratic consciousness and mobilisation for realising human rights, social reform and social justice. However, barring a few small groups,[5] NGO foci were on to complement and supplement the state initiated development activities, such as supply of basic services: primary school buildings, teachers, drinking water, school feeding programme, health clinics, agriculture and livestock, etc. Some NGOs responded to the development needs of the people and put their thrust on natural resource management and livelihood.

The 1980s witnessed proliferation of NGO activity, which was supported by international organisations and donors: UN agencies, bilateral agencies, private foundations and international non-government organisations in all possible areas of welfare mentioned above. The impact was positive, and appreciated, especially when seen in contrast to failure of state institutions to deliver. NGOs provided a mechanism of delivery of services at low costs, efficiently and effectively and in many cases through community participation to foster sustainability of development programmes. The international donor opinion showed inclination for participation of NGOs, the Rajasthan state also sought favour of their greater involvement in government programmes: watershed development, water and sanitation, health, education, drought mitigation.

Small experimental initiatives of NGOs were substantially scaled up. For example, the Barefoot College experiment of the SWRC, Tilonia was scaled up to the Shiksha Karmi Programme, the Women's

5. These were mainly youth organisations, such as the Rajasthan Democratic Student's Front (RDSF), Student's Federation of India, All India Democratic Youth Federation, Democratic Youth Federation of India, All India Student's Federation, which were opposing emergency during that period. The leadership associated with these organisations later joined several professions like journalism, and acted as opinion leaders for civil society.

Development Programme was also based on learning from SWRC, Tilonia and other NGOs.[6] The Bodh innovative schooling method in poor urban areas was scaled up to Janshala schools.[7] These programmes built an interface of the NGO, state and academics. Initially successful, these programmes reported setbacks in a few years time. One of the main reasons was that these programmes were built on voices from the grassroots and asked the state to yield to the demands from that level. Responding to voices from below on a sustained basis was beyond the extant capacities of the state, and the programmes collapsed, at least in spirit. The experiments proved that a Leviathan state works with an iron hand likes uniformity in norms, rules and regulations, and discredits flexibility or diverse opinions. The *fait accompli* of other programmes with an interface with NGOs in the 1990s and 2000s has been similar or even worse. The state fails to even recognise the comparative advantages of working together with NGOs,[8] far from taking benefit of them. They would like the NGOs to be an extended arm of the government (or even contractors), which a few refuse, but there are many who would succumb to such a treatment and invariably join hands with the rentier class within the state.[9] There were also complaints of malpractices among NGOs from the other side.

The state in some ways wanted to control the emerging 'third force'. It took on the responsibility of training NGOs, rather than learning from them. 'Government Sponsored NGOs', such as Aravali were set up (Registered Societies managed by civil officials) to establish linkages and capacity building of Civil Societies and NGOs. Though the Aravali had carried out a number of projects with varying degree of success, but taming the NGOs in this manner was to create an extended arm of the bureaucracy.

---

6. The Shiksha Karmi Programme took over schools in remote areas where regular teachers would not go and replaced them with local teachers who were trained by NGOs and helped them innovate in teaching. The Programme has been merged with the Sarv Shiksha Abhiyan, a national programme for education. The Women's Development Programme has been described and analysed elsewhere in this volume.
7. For an evaluation of Janshala see Bhargava (2004).
8. A number of monitoring reports by the Institute of Development Studies of the District Poverty Initiative Project, funded by the World Bank, have brought home this point.
9. The experiences of NGOs involved in the Jal Yatra have been mixed. Some of them have expressed reservations on how they were drawn into the campaign and that the yatra failed to address the core issues surrounding water. See Chaturvedi, (2006) and Rambabu (2006).

The NGO action gained momentum in 1990s and there are NGOs perhaps in all conceivable sectors: basic and adult education, health and family welfare, women and child development, environment protection and sustainable development, and so on. They have expanded into counselling, training, educational studies, capacity building, advocacy, and also research.

Panchayati raj is a vital tool for institutionalising citizen participation in the development process. In continuation of the state's legacy of community-based initiatives, Rajasthan took major strides in extending democracy through decentralisation. The Panchayati Raj Institutions (PRIs) have been strengthened in the state by introducing significant changes in the legal framework governing the PRI regime.[10] But only some of these have been put into practice. *Panchayati raj* by itself is too limited an approach, which is also, in the absence of a sociopolitical movement at the grassroots, subject to manipulation by entrenched interests.

The 1990s witnessed an active judiciary at the call, mainly of the human rights organisation and the rise of the institutions of the local governance. Together with voluntary bodies they provided the means for accountability of the authorities components of the polity, *viz*., the police, the army, the bureaucracy and the ruling party or coalition.

Realising Right to Information, Right to Work and Right to Water

Right to Information

The civil society in Rajasthan will always be remembered for the Right to Information Act. The architect of this Act was the Mazdoor Kisan Shakti Sanghthan (MKSS).[11] The Right to Information is now a comprehensive law covering, perhaps, all spheres of government functioning. All government departments have made a mandatory provision for making available information on demand. Their website

---

10. The commitment of the State Government towards *Panchayati raj* could be ascertained from the second round of elections to the PRIs. Undeterred by a general strike by government employees, the State Government went ahead with *Panchayats* elections, completing the process successfully. This could however be seen as strengthening the political base of the political parties than as real transfer of power.

11. The MKSS is led by a trio of Aruna Roy, Nikhil De and Shankar Singh. Aruna Roy received the prestigious Magsaysay Award for her role and contribution for furthering the cause of right to information.

carries a subhead of right to information and guides the user on how she could exercise the right in the respective departments. But all this has been achieved after a long protracted struggle in a small cluster of villages where the MKSS was working for people's rights, and among other things monitoring public works programmes. The MKSS is constituted of mainly agricultural and casual labourers most of who work in public works programmes. When they became aware of their right to speak against the large embezzlements that occurred in public works, the foundation of the Right to Information Act was laid.

Public works, as is generally known are a hotbed of corruption:[12] muster rolls are fudged with names of persons who have not worked, the wage payment is less than what has been entered therein, and the material used in the work is substandard and that too over invoiced. When the MKSS decided to demand copies of muster rolls and the account of money spent, they were rebuffed at all quarters: they had no business to see government accounts, and how dare they interfere in government functioning and secrecy. But this was the beginning of the MKSS movement for the people's right to information in the mid-1990s. The entire local administration and the elected representatives at all level were up in arms. The MKSS members were even physically attacked at places where they demanded these accounts.

One single slogan: *Hamara Paisa, Hamara Hisaab* (Our money, Our Account), of the right to information movement carried in it the essence of democracy. First, it was expression of a right to freedom of speech and expression. Second, the claim that the money in government treasuries is of the people and that they are entitled to have an account of their money signals a warning (to all those who wish to keep people at a distance in a democracy) of people's direct participation in governance with responsibility.[13] Third, that the due wages, earned by one's blood and sweat be received as part of fundamental rights under Article 21 of the Constitution—the Right to Life and Liberty. Lastly, the slogan proclaimed the arrival of the last person in a functioning democracy.

---

12. The MKSS describes the functioning of the government machinery as lethargic and corrupt that plagues the development machinery of the country (MKSS, undated).

13. Astha has carried this idea still further by setting up a Budget Analysis Research Centre, which analyses the state government budget and informs people how much money budgeted for them has actually been spent and on what.

This 'functioning democracy' manifested in *Jan Sunvai*, where photocopies of all expenditures were read out before the public in the presence of government officials and public representatives. In their own analysis of the *Jan Sunvai*, the MKSS finds that it serves five purposes: it informs the public, shares concerns with officers, critiques government policies, empowers people, and holds the authorities accountable (See MKSS, undated).

The Right to Information movement has now emerged nationally as a force against corruption in the public space.[14] Individuals who do not have recourse for a just deal and are not prepared to pay a rent for public service could perhaps use it as a tool in the future.[15] It was a long struggle to obtain the Right to Information Act, but it is even a longer and harder struggle to realise the right and make people (do) ask for the right by educating and empowering them to break the silence.

Right to Food, Right to Work and the Civil Society

Civil society in Rajasthan could be credited to a very large extent for the enactment of the National Rural Employment Guarantee Act, being implemented in all states in the country. But this came about after almost a decade of people's struggles and movements to claim their rights for food and work.[16] This section analyses various aspects of the movement, which is still active and vibrant.

People of Rajasthan (as also several other states in the country) went through consecutive droughts during the period 1988-89 through 2002-03,[17] i.e., *Samvat* 2055-2060. The drought of *Samvat* 2059 was recorded as one of the severest in the last one hundred years. Livelihoods were at stake and even life was threatened. In some areas even hunger deaths were reported. The state thus had an obligation to meet and help the affected people in times of such calamities.

---

14. The role of intellectuals and opinion leaders including the forum at the Institute of Development Studies, Jaipur was quite significant.

15. In the fight against corruption spearheaded by MKSS in Jaipur city in July 2006, an individual who refused to pay a bribe to get her passport was waiting for the last 8 months. Simply on seeking information for reasons of delay in her case, she received the passport in three day's time.

16. The Institute of Development Studies, Jaipur provided academic support to the movement.

17. In these years more than 60 per cent villages in the state lost 50 per cent or more *kharif* crops sown in that year. The year 2001-02 was not a major drought year.

There was a very large demand for employment in the drought period. It exceeded the opportunities available by almost a thousand per cent, i.e. in a village of 500 households only 50 got an opportunity to work at any given point of time and in the remaining households not a single person got employed. People's desperation levels were so high that very often they get into quarrels to be enrolled at the famine relief work site. This dismantling of social capital in the village is of major concern as it fractures the social relationships, which could be difficult to rebuild. Migration to urban areas did not solve the problem. In Jaipur alone where 200-300 labourers gathered at a single *chaukti* in search for employment, no more than 90 were able to find work (data provided at a symposium on *Need for Employment Guarantee Act in Rajasthan*, IDS, July 7, 2001).

At the village level, the processes of providing employment were *ad hoc* or at times by rotation. The spatial distribution of works and programmes was driven not by well thought of needs based planning but the politico-economic interests of the ruling elite. Besides, who got employed was determined by a number of factors including caste, relationship with the *sarpanch* or any other factor that could push the interests of an individual. In these circumstances the likelihood of the poor to get work was quite low, far from being guaranteed. The system brought only partial relief to people. Then wages received were far from the minimum guaranteed wages and corruption was generally reported.

A number of civil society organisations in Rajasthan, most of which came together under the banner of the Rajasthan Akal Sangharsh Samiti, campaigned for the implementation of the right to work through guaranteed employment to all those who demand work in the rural areas of the state. A right has a dimension of universality and does not exclude anybody. Even in normal times there are many households whose demand for employment remains unmet.[18] Thus the claim to provide work was made onto the state.

An unprecedented mobilisation of workers happened during the relief works in the state, especially in areas where civil society had

---

18. According to the current daily status of unemployment, 16 crore man-days of unemployment are reported in rural areas of the state in a year (1999-2000). The state does make provisions of employment through public works to the tune of 5.5 crore man-days per annum. In the absence of public works the unmet demand would have been at least 21.5 crore man-days per annum. Thus rural development works are meeting almost a quarter of demand for employment.

been actively supporting the workers, demanding additional jobs, ensuring payment of minimum wages, preventing corruption through social audit and networking with other organisations doing similar work. A number of demonstrations were held in various parts of the state, mainly in southern, western, and the capital city.[19] A very radical programme of educating through theatre and other modes of communication was also adopted by more than one organisation.[20] Work was now no more articulated as an individual need but also a common good that is workers' right. The demand by rural workers for Right to Work announced their arrival on the political stage. They proclaimed that their demand should be an irrevocable part of the political agenda.

The movement inspired the People's Union of Civil Liberties (PUCL) Rajasthan to submit a writ petition to the Supreme Court of India[21] asking three major questions: Starvation deaths have become a national phenomenon while there is surplus stock of foodgrains in government godowns. Does the right to life mean that people who are starving and who are too poor to buy food grains free of cost from the state from the surplus stock lying with the state particularly when it is lying unused and rotting? Does not the right to life under Article 21 of the Constitution of India include the right to food? Does not the right to food which has been upheld by the apex court imply that the state has a duty to provide food especially in situations of drought to people who are drought effected and are not in a position to purchase food?

As a result of the ongoing proceedings, the Supreme Court has been issuing orders calling upon government agencies to ensure proper implementation of schemes meant for the poor. These schemes are: Employment Assurance Scheme which may have been replaced by a Sampoorna Grameen Yojana, Mid-day Meal Scheme, Integrated Child Development Scheme, National Maternity Benefit Scheme for

19. It goes to the credit of the state that a number of various Senior Secretaries of the Government of Rajasthan spent hours at the workshops held at the Institute Development Studies, Jaipur to listen to various grievances and tried to resolve them to their best abilities.

20. The MKSS team led by Shankar Singh used the traditional folk tools of communication in Rajasthan and transformed the erstwhile feudal character of songs, puppetry and theatre into a progressive and radical discourse. The group's artistry has a finesse that appeals the masses.

21. The petition was filed on April 16, 2001 by Kavita Srivastava on behalf of the PUCL.

pregnant women below the poverty line, National Old Age Pension Scheme for destitute persons of over 65 years, Annapurna Scheme, Antyodaya Anna Yojana, National Family Benefit Scheme and Public Distribution Scheme for below poverty line (BPL) and above poverty line (APL) families.

The verdicts of the Supreme Court came as a great support to the people's movement for their right to food and work as they got linked to the Right to Life. The movement, thus empowered, prepared a draft Employment Guarantee Act (EGA), 2003 for Rajasthan[22] drawing lessons from the Maharashtra's Employment Guarantee Scheme. The civil society movement for right to work influenced preparation of the draft Act in a manner that would strengthen the bargaining power of all those demanding work: ensuring employment when needed and where. It advocated, first, for decentralised planning and devolution of powers in Rajasthan (it envisaged the *gram panchayat* rather than the *panchayat samiti* as the main implementing agency at the village level), and second, for stronger mechanisms for transparency and accountability at all levels (*gram sabhas* were expected to conduct 'social audits' of the projects taken up within their jurisdiction). The draft Act was discussed at various forums of civil society organisations across the state.[23]

Public work schemes such as the Jawahar Rozgar Yojana or the Pradhan Mantri Rozgar Yojana have had for several years been handed down as grants, more as a benevolent gesture. Testimony to this is the fact that employment schemes invariably bear the name of the benefactor. When the demand for Right to Work gets articulated it demarcates that autonomous space of action where rural workers proclaim equality with any other individual or group.

The civil society movement in Rajasthan reverberated to other states in the country and a Right to Food Campaign emerged at the national level. It took the synergy of the movement in Rajasthan

---

22. The draft was prepared by a group of concerned citizens, initially convened by members of the Right to Food Campaign in collaboration with Mazdoor Kisan Shakti Sangathan (MKSS), Rajasthan and Professor Jean Drèze. The draft aimed to safeguard the right to work by providing guaranteed employment at the statutory minimum wage to all adult persons who volunteered to do unskilled manual work in rural areas of the State of Rajasthan.

23. The Institute of Development Studies organised a dialogue with policymakers, academics and civil society organisations on Right to Work on June 14 and June 15, 2004. See Bhargava *et al.*, (2005).

forward and recreated the proposed Rajasthan Employment Guarantee Act into a National Employment Guarantee Act, which finally began to get implemented in February 2006.

The initial reports of the implementation of the Act are both heartening and at the same time discouraging. While people are realising the right by asking for employment and also getting employed, the attitudes of officials at the ground level have not changed much. They still look at it as a relief programme and their rent seeking attitude has not dissipated. Workers are not getting paid minimum wages. The worst thing is that they are not protesting. A few civil society organisations are protesting on their behalf.[24]

Right to Water

In 1985, the Tarun Bharat Sangh (TBS), identified water as the main problem in rural India and concluded that without augmenting water as a resource, no effective development could take place. For rapid progress, they have to rediscover traditional methods of rain-water harvesting. Since then, local people have built over 4,000 water harvesting structures with the support arranged by the TBS. A geographical area of 6,500 sq. km. comprising 750 villages has been turned into 'white zone' from 'dark zone' over the years. Water harvesting has been instrumental in reducing the ill-effects of drought as well as floods. At least five rivulets, which were dry during the last 50 years, have become perennials. A water parliament has also been constituted for the Arvari rivulet.

The achievements of the TBS are by no means small. The distinguishing feature is that social cultural values, local wisdom and a balance between human and natural resource development circumscribe the *praxis*. The strategy has five distinct features: inclusion of all in the community without exception, building on collective wisdom, collective enforcement of decisions, individual responsibility to carry out collective community decisions, and use outside help only as a catalyst for guidance. The processes got initiated in a manner that the *gram sabhas* and water parliament began planning on futuristic basis, evolving out of the needs of the communities.

24. A demonstration against poor implementation of the National Rural Employment Guarantee Programme was held at the Statue Circle, Jaipur on June 23, 2006 where about 500 workers and civil society organisations were present. The point is that a few protests are reported at *panchayat* or district level.

The right to decentralised water management, as emerging from the *praxis* of the TBS could be one priority area for the civil society in the persisting drought and depleting water levels in Rajasthan. Learning from the successes of Right to Work and Right to Information, the civil society needs to define the right to water and ensure that collective action and responsibility for decentralised water management is possible.

The Unfinished Agendas of the Civil Society

Women's Movement

Civil society in Rajasthan has also grown with the women's movement. While women participated in the national movement, but the impact thereafter was almost nil. Not a single woman got elected in the first Vidhan Sabha. Women's movement in Rajasthan in 1980s thrust forward by addressing issues related to violence against women in a predominant patriarchal society. The movement was not to replace existing patriarchal hegemony with matriarchal hegemony but was a humanitarian movement for justice and equality (Roy, 2006).

The global call on women to raise their own issues also reverberated in Rajasthan and women started raising their voices in various forums across the state. Questions pertained to the status of women, their traditional roles and norms, the unequal relationships within homes and in the community and work place, the discourse in folk, songs, and idioms. This was also the time when many civil society organisations were engaged in the formation of Self-Help Groups and other organisations of women. The SWRC raised voice against non-payment of minimum wages, an issue subsequently decided by the Supreme Court. The Women's Development Programme (WDP), a collaborative effort of the Government and the NGOs was initiated and addressed issues relating to economic empowerment, concientisation, and some extent opening up gender issues in the community. The civil society and government programmes like WDP played a significant role in strengthening the movement and brought the learning to the national attention. The movement, however, was short lived for reasons explained earlier. As the global thinking shifted from women to gender, the state and the academia in particular, engaged in gender sensitisation of government and non-government functionaries. Gender sensitisation campaigns and workshops, however, could not replace the women's movement, and perhaps halted it to an extent.[25]

On the other hand, the women's movement raised issues of violence against women. The movement raised issues of gender violence through public demonstrations, petitioning and lobbying against/around incidents like Bhanwari Rape, Roop Kanwar *Sati* and sexual harassment at workplace, which compelled governments to acknowledge inequities of gender and address these through law and policy. Advocacy by various women's groups led to setting up of the National and State Commissions for Women in 1999 for addressing violations of women's human rights; formation of the national and state policy for women; the increased representation and participation of women in urban and rural local government institutions called PRIs following from the 73rd and 74th Amendments to the Indian Constitution; amendment in the *Sati* Act, 1987, and a Supreme Court ruling against sexual harassment of women in the work place.[26] The successes were manifold. Nevertheless, the energies of movement shifted from addressing the questions of freedom of women and helping them realise these through their own initiatives to working for institutional changes in laws and government policies.

An authoritative study, *AAdhi Abadi ka Sangharsh* (Jaitley and Sharma, 2006) concludes that the women's movement has ebbed in the state. Women's groups get together on specific events but there are no organised attempts to revive the movement and draw a common strategy for this purpose. Agreeing with the authors, we are of the view that the movement requires a civil society consciousness to work not only in the spaces provided within the state structure but also in the community to attain democratic values and equality.

25. Gender concerns are undoubtedly for equality but the programmes for gender sensitisation were mainly for government functionaries or in some NGOs for grassroot workers. And to an extent these have been successful in creating the desired sensitivities. Those engaged directly or indirectly in women's movement were also the front runners in sensitising programmes. Energies shifted from organising women and the movement to gender sensitising the general publics. In that sense, gender sensitisation is a poor substitute for women's movement.

26. In the Vishakha *vs.* State of Rajasthan case the Supreme Court specifically defined Sexual Harassment to prevent sexual harassment at work place.

Some problems related to women have accentuated. The juvenile sex ratio has worsened, mainly due to female foeticide. Early marriages and pregnancies are still a norm in the larger part of rural Rajasthan. Atrocities on women are daily news items in local media. With economic growth new avenues for women's employment open up and gender relations can be renegotiated. Yet the dominant patriarchal mindsets may take time to change, especially when civil society does not make a frontal attack to challenge and change it. Other than women, another exploited class is of the Dalits in the state and their situation is even worse and has attracted little attention of the civil society in the state.

Freedom from Discrimination: Dalits, Sawarns, and a Weak Civil Society

Civil society in Rajasthan has largely failed to enable Dalits[27] to live a life with dignity. While contempt, hatred, oppression and coercion of the Dalits by the *sawarns* manifest in subtle discrimination at homes, schools, hospitals, tea stalls, public places, water sources and marriage celebrations, instances of aggressive open oppression make headlines in local newspapers almost daily. The contemptuous practices of untouchability and impurity may have reduced with growing urbanisation and a developing economy, the mindsets have hardly changed. The civil society in general, barring a few voices in response to reports on atrocities, has remained silent.

Dalit children in schools confront discrimination early in life,[28] which they internalise for the rest of their lives. Their self-worthiness in schools is largely influenced by the ascribed potential that the teachers believe these Dalit students possess. The pedagogy, the school environment, the curriculum, both the evident and the hidden, are mannered with understated references to the status and dignity of the Dalits. Dalit children, therefore, miss the opportunity of self-construction in schools through a process of looking within to arrive at a point of looking beyond. The exposures received inward or outward—make the recipients passive rather than active. The village

27. The word Dalit is being used to mean the people of untouchable origin and victims of discriminations and oppression. Untouchability is a notion of defilement or impurity

28. A study by Vishakha has documented the discriminations against Dalit children in schools. See Vishakha (2003).

community, in the absence of a vibrant civil society,[29] remains a silent observer to intergenerational transmission of passivity resulting from violation of human dignity and basic human rights.

Passivity among Dalits encourages blatant atrocities on them.[30] Dalit ownership and cultivation of land is challenged by the dominant castes and at times they are forcibly alienated. Disputes relate to land reforms and distribution of surplus land,[31] irrigation rights, use of common pastures and community land, and allotments of house sites. The animosity may take many forms; stealing or damaging of crops is a common feature. Land cultivation by Dalits is also resented due to reduction in the pool of agricultural labour.[32] Dalits borrow from moneylenders within their village or the vicinity and prolonged indebtedness in several instances results in bonded labour or near bonded labour situations, wherein their position to bargain for a wage is considerably reduced. Any assertion of their right usually results in atrocity.

Rajasthan has one of the highest crime rates against the scheduled castes and the scheduled tribes[33] in the country. In an incidence of violence, the village community tries to limit the case within the boundaries of the village so as to reduce any possibility of disrupting the social fabric of the village society. In many places, the village community takes pride in 'resolving' such cases and settling within the village without punishing the culprits. In this manner Dalits are

29. Efforts by the Sarv Shiksha Abhiyan to create a civil society organised in the form of village education committees who would make the community own the school could be seen in this perspective. The Vishakha study finds that the Dalit communities in most villages do not perceive schools as a public good (Schools are a public good meaning that all children would have equal access to the school without discrimination) or as their own. Among Dalits, the most marginalised generally distant themselves from schools. This is not surprising as most parents never went to schools themselves, and if they did must have suffered more ignominy than their children.

30. The National Commission of SC/ST has identified several reasons for disputes between the high castes and the low castes.

31. The Government of Rajasthan adopted the Rajasthan Imposition of Ceilings on Holdings Act, 1973 that gave preference to landless labourers, particularly the SC in distribution of surplus land. Accordingly, until March 1987, of the total land distributed the SC received 33 per cent. Process of land reforms has not been implemented properly due to animosity with traditional land owning classes, especially if the land distributed is fertile or irrigated.

32. One-fifth of all SC workers are agricultural labourers. Among all agricultural labourers around 33 per cent are SCs.

33. The Annual Reports of the Police Department have reported 6,679, 5,915, and 5,465 cases registered of atrocities against SC/ST for the years 2000-03.

denied justice. Such a negative civil society has sustained and there is little attempt to break this cauldron of injustice.

When Dalit victims do try and break the village cauldron by reaching out to law enforcing agencies, they find the collusion of dominant forces and state institutions difficult to breach. The case of a Laxman Singh Jatav (See Box 8.1) shows that atrocities are committed on petty issues like payment of due wages and refusing to work, the collusion among the accused, community, police, other institutions of society such as hospitals, and the state itself. Even organised civil society organisations such as the People's Union of Civil Liberties are not able to go very far to seek justice as the main witnesses turn hostile due to pressure of the victims and the community at large. And all that the civil society organisations are able to do is to seek more 'compensation' for the victims.

The Home Department accepts its institutional failure (GoR, 2005) but finds itself helpless in the face of the witnesses turning hostile and admits the institutional failures such as the improper registration of cases and summons not being sent on time.[34] Accepting the fact that there is a culture of denial in the police and the judiciary who would like to make believe that no atrocity has taken place,[35] and while proper functioning of state institutions could reduce crime rate and bring justice to the victim, and punishment of the culprit, the absence of a strong civil society needs to be underlined, which would transform the social relationships in a manner that such crimes do not happen in the first place.

34. The high incidence of corruption reported in police and lower levels of judiciary is also an impediment in the achievement of justice. A number of studies and reports state that the local police officers charging anywhere between 100 to 300 rupees from the victims for entering the police station and many times that sum if you want to move on your complaint. They take money from both the sides and whoever pays more wins the case. So even if the Dalit shell out a majority of their earning to get the case registered they may actually loose it if they pay less than the accused. This can be achieved by tampering with the evidence and delaying the whole procedure.

35. This attitude is also reflective of the wider perception, which was reflected in the recent stand of the Indian government at the 'World Conference on Racial Discrimination' at Durban where it refused to acknowledge the existence of any form of discrimination in Indian society. The culture of denial is reflected in the tardy implementation of the measures to ensure justice to these people.

Box 8.1

A Dalit's Search for Justice

The village Guthakar of Bharatpur district has about 300 families of Gurjars and only 10 of the Jatavs (Scheduled Castes). Laxman Singh, a Jatav in the village worked for the Gurjars. In June 2000, the Gurjars asked him to work on the construction of their house, which he refused. He asked them to pay the 1000 rupees that were due to him from a previous work. This angered the Gurjars and there was violent confrontation between them. He tried to file a complaint in the police, but the police officers (some among them were Gurjars) refused to entertain the complaint, instead they abused him for daring to register a case against the Gurjars. The police reportedly told the Gurjars that they would be protected even if they killed Laxman. Further, the police went to Laxman's house, threatened and abused him. His brother was also treated similarly when he asked for his wages. The Gurjars were so angered by these cases that they pledged to take revenge, which they did. Laxman was beaten so severely that his legs had to be amputated. The hospital authorities refused proper treatment and were later bribed into falsifying the medical reports.

The case was not investigated properly and even the high-ranking officers were slack in performing their duties. The investigating officer did not record the names of all persons involved in the crime in the F.I.R. The main accused was arrested only after a period of three months but he was soon released on bail within 3-4 days. The Circle Officer helped the accused by not noting down the testimony of the witnesses. The accused on the contrary abused Laxman and disgraced his wife. A Final Report (FR) was put on Laxman's case and he and his family had to leave the village as a result of terror of the accused. Subsequently a number of other Jatav families also left the village.

Laxman Singh also did not receive any compensation from the state government under the Chief Ministers relief fund or from the disability fund. The family could not return to the village. This issue was raised with the Chief Minister of the state several times by Bhagwan Singh, the victims themselves, and the People's Union of Civil Liberties (PUCL). However, the Chief Minister told that he was helpless in face of the fact that Laxman's father himself has said that Laxman's injuries were not due to the attack by the accused but due to an accident while mining stones. In reality his father was forced to turn hostile. Subsequently some compensation was given to Laxman but the amount is measly in comparison to what Laxman and his family had to go through. The National Dalit Rights Commission demanded higher compensation for Laxman. Further, it is not only Laxman and his family that had to suffer but his supporters, including Bhagwan Singh also faced backlash.

Source: The Centre for Dalit Human Rights, Jaipur.

Realising Freedom from Discrimination: The Civil Society Action

Historically, there have been some social reform movements in the state but they were limited in scope and have had little enduring effects.[36] Presently, a few organisations are working for the Dalit cause, these include the Ambedkar Mission, the Ambedkar Krantikari Vichar Manch, Dalit Sahitya Academy, Unnati and the state bodies—the National and the State Human Rights Commission. There are some instances of civil society organisations taking up issues of Dalit atrocities as and when they occur.[37]

A Centre for Dalit Human Rights[38] (CDHR) has recently been set up with two major objectives: (a) to enable Dalits to speak out for their rights without fear and use the legal system to their advantage; and (b) to strive towards elimination of all forms of political, social, and economic oppression arising as a result of caste discrimination. The CDHR has been able to make the Dalit issues significantly visible in Rajasthan by exposing the complicity of the state with dominant castes to perpetuate caste discrimination, apart from creating some awareness among Dalits. It has raised issues with Human Rights Commissions, Women's Commission, etc.

Civil Society Course for Future Action

Constitutional and legal provisions to realise freedom from discrimination are in place. The accountability of upholding the constitutional provisions rests with the state, but the civil society could play a pro-active role, systematically and strategically: monitoring atrocities, preparing independent database, awareness generation, legal and financial support to victims, and highlighting cases through public interest litigation. They could engage with the government in formation of vigilance committees at the district level

---

36. In the year 1923, the Arya Samaj, initiated efforts for educational, social and religious reform with the sweeper community in the state. The Harijan Sevak Sangh formed by Gandhi during the national movement worked among the untouchables within the state. The other movements include opposition of bonded labour of the Dalits by the Prajamandal. A number of caste organisations such as the Marwarh Lok Parishad, Marwarh Mehtar Sudhar Parishad and Rajputana Mehtar Sudhar Parishad worked towards the welfare of their respective castes.

37. Dalits were not allowed to sit on a cot in mixed caste villages. The Khetihar Mazdoor Sangathan, Bhadesar, Chittorgarh fought against the practice in the form of 'khat andolan' and to some extent has been successful at least in the Chittorgarh district.

38. The CDHR is hosted by a voluntary organisation, Cecoedecon.

to look into the atrocities and violation of rights, monitoring the conviction rates, forcing the government to open the closed cases especially those resulting in false reports and other kinds of advocacy work. Some organisations are already working in this direction but the agenda for social change has to be larger.

In Rajasthan, Dalits are spread all over the state. In most places their density is low and they maintain a hierarchy within them. In this sense the Dalits do not have a single identity as they have acquired in Maharashtra (Kamble, 1998).[39] The first task of a movement against discrimination of Dalits would be bringing the castes together to a common identity.

The Dalit agenda should perhaps aim at withering away of the caste phenomenon through a democratic consciousness. This can be achieved first by believing that it is achievable. It would require belief in the identity of the individual and the dignity of every human being. In Rajasthan, the goal is far on the horizon as caste based organisations claim for a share in political and economic power. The good behaviour of these castes with the well-off Dalits is a mirage and should not be interpreted to mean that raising the economic standards of the Dalits would lead to social change. The notions of purity and pollution are far deep rooted and requires a larger social reform movement in the state, but there is no civil society group even in its infancy to initiate this.

An Analysis of Civil Society Discourse

Civil society's own discourse about themselves reflect their perceptions of action. These are given in their Mission Statements or objectives. We analyse below four of these.

Seva Mandir's mission statement[40] calls for free and equal citizenship in the particular contexts of the people in their own

---

39. From the turn of the 20th century Maharashtra has been the site of the most radical Dalit assertions in the country. See also various articles in *Seminar* (1998).

40. Seva Mandir's mission is to make real the idea of society consisting of free and equal citizens who are able to come together and solve the problems that affect them in their particular contexts. Seva Mandir's work on strengthening the natural resources based on village level people's institutions, comprising all residents of the village, which are the locus of planning, implementation and management of this intervention. The strategic focus is on developing the capabilities of these institutions through training and workshops so that they may become self-reliant.

communities. The organisation invests in "creating...common resources for people to come around, and norm-based village institutions that foster principles of good governance." Their Mission is very clear that they build capacities of communities to deal with internal threats. What about external threats that also limit the freedoms and equity in citizenship? And these threats are many. The Jan Jangal Zameen Andolan for rights to tribal on their own and forest land, the Mansi Vakal that threatens to inundate many villages, forest policy, issues of migration and so on are not on the agenda of Seva Mandir. Their partial success in natural resource management and building village institutions, that ensure equity, could partly be attributed to them ignoring the external threats. Nevertheless, such organisations have helped people to 'be' and realise to some extent their freedom from want and freedom of association, albeit at a local level.

On the contrary, is the philosophy of the Tarun Bharat Sangh that takes into account both internal and external threats to manage water so that people's needs are met; and the responsibility of such management is seen as a 'civilisational concern':

> Those civilisations which conserve and manage water with responsibility are successful in surviving. Those who do not understand this and believe in claims of ownership alone face scarcity and are forced to indulge in conflict. In this process people suffer, their sense of community is weakened, and credibility of their governments lowered...Consequently responsibility for the management of water so that people's needs are met, is not an individual responsibility either of a person, a nation or any particular culture or religion, but a collective civilisational concern; a responsibility that must bind all together. There are today multiple and complex forces tearing apart this commonwealth... People are sandwiched between antagonistic global, national and local interests. As arguments for the marketing and trading of water gains credibility at the expense of community solidarity and collective interests, people loose their sense of involvement and governments become party to private interest. There is consequently a civilisational choice ahead of us.
>
> — Rajendra Singh, in a communication to Kofi Annan

The TBS builds on collective community solidarity to manage water and interface with state and private interests. It universalises the issue of water and calls it a civilisational concern. It involves people to do, to protect their collective interests from all antagonistic forces. It is in this context that they critique the state water policy for not committing to decentralisation of water management, and on the contrary intending to have complete control through legislation and regulations. See Rathore (undated) for details. Many other civil society organisations have criticised the state water policy.

We quote here from discourses of two prominent civil society organisations, the Prayas and the Mazdoor Kisan Shakti Sangathan (MKSS). Both discourses underline the relation between people and the state and seek redressal within the spaces provided by the state, invoking the rights perspective. The MKSS has the contours of struggle for livelihood well defined in the organic relationship with the state,

> Prayas believes that instead of providing direct services, people from the vulnerable sections of the society should be mobilised to demand from the Government what is rightfully theirs according to the constitutional rights of every Indian citizen. Prayas works to generate awareness of human rights and enable people to seek redress for violation of their rights.
>
> —(Prayas: *www.prayaschittor.org*)

> In this (Right to Information) campaign, the analysis and paradigm of struggle has been defined organically and collectively by a group of ordinary people. Many of whom live day to day, looking for daily wage work. For whom abstractions like 'Rights' mean nothing and can only define their existence in the context of hunger or lack of it, illness or good health, work and unemployment. They have in this struggle defined their livelihood and their right to live in terms of their organic relationship with the state, and their birthright to hold it accountable.
>
> —(Roy, undated)

The organisations like Prayas and MKSS have empowered people to 'do' and make them aware of both their rights and duties to build a democratic consciousness.

The above discourse reminds us of the national movement, which was anti-colonial but did not make a frontal attack on feudalism, which ensured that feudal attitudes and consciousness remain intact. Similarly, it is evident that these movements work within the spaces provided in the state, are not anti-state, and creating space for dialogue and consensus is considered hallmarks of the civil society. In this manner, they provide means to the people to challenge the exploitative and dominant interests in the state, and also succeed in making institutional changes through advocacy at the national level. But in the absence of a mass base they fail to build peoples' power that could contest the existing state.

In sum, we generally agree with Chandhoke (2006) that (a) civil society groups have succeeded in expanding the domain of policy-making and implementation; (b) these campaigns do not address inequality and unfreedom—restructuring existing structures of power and forging new and equitable structures of social relations, which require building a mass base; and (c) the state is no longer seen as the object of political contestation but as the provider of social goods. Chandhoke asks, has politics, we are compelled to ask, come to be subordinated to public policy? Has the rights bearing citizen been reduced to being the consumer of goods and services? And does civil society, rather than being autonomous, actually function within the terrain charted out by the state? Does the state, therefore, continue to stand squarely at the centre of things? The concern of Chandhoke is valid that civil society campaigns fall short of people's movements.

Conclusions

We have seen both faces of civil society in Rajasthan to 'do' and to 'be'. The first face of civil society in Rajasthan that helps people to 'do' has been successful in building new institutions and programmes where people could define their agency and reach out to the state with dignity. Organisations working towards this goal have often taken a confrontationist stance against the state but have also maintained a dialogue with them, (an activity supported by the Institute of Development Studies, Jaipur). But building capacities of people to actually work towards self determination is a larger agenda. The campaigns to build new institutions are not the same as people's movements.

The other face of civil society that helps people to 'be' works more in collaboration with the state. Seeing the utility, desires and satisfaction of people, the civil society helps them to 'be' through increasing their welfare and happiness. This is achieved through a variety of activities and building networks of relationships. They have worked with people to help them realise their needs and wants within their local communities. They have made important landmarks in civil society, the community, and the country.

There are many civil society organisations that would not fall into these compartments. To be and to do conflate into one another and are not separable. However, democratic consciousness could be built if and only if people do, i.e. when they realise their rights and work towards achieving them fully.

The approach of civil society is largely of advocacy, protest and initiative (Vyas, 2003) and there are major successes as well in Rajasthan. However, there remains a large unfinished agenda of social transformation. And the unfinished agenda is long and exasperating. The civil society efforts to build a democratic consciousness, where there is freedom from discrimination, freedom from fear and injustice and a more equal and just society, still remain on the margin or there is a big and frightening silence on their part. The near absence of social reform and peoples' movements in the state shows that chance and circumstances could dominate for a long time in a feudal, patriarchal and casteist[41] mindset of the people in Rajasthan.

41. Several caste-based organisations exist in Rajasthan. They run educational and charitable institutions across the state trying to improve the conditions of their caste folk. They have varied traditions and work towards providing an identity to their caste. The flip side of many of these '*panchayats*' is that they are currently undemocratic, often of self-designated 'elders' with vested interests to protect. Many of these in recent years are advocating for their caste to be included in one of the constitutional reserved categories of Other Backward Castes and the Scheduled Castes to take advantage of the positive discrimination policies of the state. These caste *panchayats* are also part of the civil society that mediates between the people and the state. But with a parochial character they generate more of negative externalities. There is very little research on these organisations and their inter-relations with the civil society discussed in this chapter.

References

Bhargava, Pradeep (2004). "Evaluation of Janshala in Rajasthan", Institute of Development Studies, Jaipur, *(mimeo)*.

Bhargava, Pradeep, C. Gupta, and Sarthi Acharya (2005). "Entitlement to Work: The Crossroads of Employment Guarantee", Institute of Development Studies, Jaipur, *(mimeo)*.

Chandhoke, Neera (2006). "The Taming of Civil Society", *http://www.india-seminar.com*.

Chaturvedi, Satyen (2006). "Jal Abhiyan Yatra Sirf Rajnitik Pahel", *Soch Pani Kee*, No. 19, June.

Government of Rajasthan (2005). *Annual Report of the Home Department*, Government of Rajasthan, Jaipur.

Jaitley, Mamta and Prakash Sharma (2006). *AAdhi Abadi ka Sangharsh*, Rajkamal Prakashan, Patna.

Kamble, Ramesh (1998). "Dalit Interpretations of Society", *Seminar*, No. 471.

Kothari, Rajni (1988). *State Against Democracy: In Search of a Humane Governance*, Ajanta Publications, New Delhi.

MKSS (undated). "Grassroots Experience and the Perspective of People's Struggle to Access Information", Mazdoor Kisan Shakti Sangathan, (mimeo).

Rambabu (2006). "Jal Abhiyan Yatra Sirf Rajnitik Pahel", *Soch Pani Kee*, No. 19, June.

Rathore M.S. (undated). "Pro-poor and Gender Sensitive State Water Policy–NGOs Perception on Water Resource Management in Rajasthan", *Research Report* No. RR-156, Institute of Development Studies, Jaipur.

Roy, Aruna (2006). "Bhoomika" in Mamta Jaitley and Prakash Sharma, *AAdhi Abadi ka Sangharsh*, Rajkamal Prakashan, Patna.

———. (undated). "Survival and Right to Information", *Gulam Rasool Third Memorial Lecture*, Mazdoor Kisan Shakti Sangathan, *Mimeo*.

Singh, Hira (1993). "Classifying Non-European, Pre-Colonial Social Formations: More than a Quarrel Over a Name", *The Journal of Peasant Studies*, Volume 20, Number 2.

Singhi, N. K. and Rajendra Joshi (1995). *Folk, Faith and Feudalism*, Rawat Publications, Jaipur and New Delhi.

Vishakha (2003). "Exclusion and Inclusion in Education in Rajasthan", Jaipur, *(mimeo)*.

Vyas, V.S. (2003). "Weakening Roots of Democracy and the role of Civil Society", Dr. Mohan Singh Mehta Memorial Lecture, *Occasional Paper* Number 1, Tata Dhan Academy, Madurai.

9

Local Governance through *Panchayati Raj*

P. R. SHARMA and ANITA

Introduction

Decentralisation and participation have become distinct features of governance as well as planning. Decentralisation provides space for the people and their organisations to assert their interests and make the system more sensitive to the local development problems. Democratic decentralisation is a meeting point of consensus for liberal as well as radical political opinion. This received a lease on life with the 73rd and 74th Constitutional Amendments. The objective of this paper is to map the evolution of Panchayati Raj Institutions (PRIs) in Rajasthan since the beginning and the unfolding process of their empowerment. In the process, it critically looks at important provisions contained in various Government notifications, orders and circulars.

The Evolution of PRIs

Village *panchayats* were central to the ideological framework of Indian national movement. Gandhiji had called village *swaraj* as a complete republic where village *panchayats* would be based on perfect democracy and individual freedom (Gandhi, 1942). *Panchayats*, in one form or the other, have been an integral part of rural sociopolitical life in Rajasthan. Between 1939 and 1948, seven princely states of Rajasthan passed resolutions accorded statutory recognition to the *panchayats*. Later, the Rajasthan State Legislative Assembly consolidated the *panchayats* at the state level and enacted Rajasthan Panchayat Act, 1953. A *tehsil panchayat* at the intermediate level and district boards at the district level were constituted through this enactment.

The Union Government launched the Community Development Programme and the National Extension Service Programme in 1952 and 1953. However, these programmes could not meet with the expected success and could not involve people in the rural development works. A committee under the Chairmanship of Shri Balwant Rai Mehta was constituted in 1957, which recommended a three-tier *panchayati raj* system at village, block and district levels across the country. It laid down the foundation stone of *panchayati raj* in India, as the accelerated pace of constituting PRIs in all states was an outcome of recommendations of the Mehta Committee report, favouring democratic decentralisation through statutory elected bodies (GoI, 1957). During this stage, the term "Panchayati Raj" came into vogue conceptually as a process of governance. "It refers to a system organically linking people from the *gram sabha* to the *lok sabha*" (Mathew, 2000).

Rajasthan was the first state in India to inaugurate *panchayati raj* on October 2, 1959, when the then Prime Minister of India Pt. Jawahar Lal Nehru kindled its lamp at Nagaur in Rajasthan. Pt. Nehru hailed the system as "the most revolutionary and historic step in the context of new India...democracy at the top would succeed only if built from below (Nehru, 1959)". The then Union Minister for Community Development, Mr. S. K. Dey announced that *panchayati raj* as we now visualise will, therefore, mean progressive increase in competence from the ground upwards and corresponding transfer of responsibilities from the centre to the ground. If one wishes to climb higher, one must reduce the burden of avoidable weight on his shoulders. In this regard the Article 40 of the Directive Principles of the Indian Constitution states that the state should take steps to organise village *panchayats* and endow them with such power and authority as may be necessary to enable them to function as units of self-government (GoI, 1950). This implies grassroots democracy and 'Power to the People.'

Pre-73rd Amendment: PRI Scenario in Rajasthan

Panchayati raj functionaries gained importance in rural areas since 1959. Many local development works like drinking water wells, *panchayat* and school buildings, *gram sevak* quarters, village roads, culverts, drains were constructed as per local needs and aspirations of the villagers. People's participation was significant with 50 per cent contribution coming from the village community. People offered *Shram Dan* (voluntary labour) in many cases. Extension officers from departments of agriculture, animal husbandry, industries, co-operation, education, social-welfare, etc. all were placed at the disposal of *panchayat samiti*, which was like mini-government at the block level. There was great enthusiasm and team synergy at the intermediate *panchayats*. Even Chief Minister and Chief Secretary gave much importance to *panchayati raj*. District level officers including the Collector attended monthly meetings of *panchayat samiti* and quarterly meetings of *zila parishad*. The Chief Minister gave greater importance to the *zila pramukh* compared to the District Collector. State posted IAS officers as Block Development Officers. Several block chiefs/ *pradhans* rose to become MLAs. *Pradhans* also became Ministers and *pramukh*(s) ascended to Chief Ministership. In certain quarters, however, Panchayati Raj Institutions were perceived as a constant threat to political authority of state level leaders, who tried to weaken *panchayati raj* in the state. However, this initial euphoria did not last long. *Panchayati raj* system lay dormant in India and Rajasthan for decades together till the early 1990 when the Government of the day brought in amendment in the constitution.

Second generation *panchayats* led to withdrawal of departmental extension officers from *panchayat samitis*. Besides, various other developmental agencies like Small Farmer Development Agencies (SFDAs) and District Rural Development Agencies (DRDAs) came into existence for initiating rural development and employment generation and implementation of poverty alleviation programmes.[1] Funds also started flowing directly to such agencies by-passing the *panchayati raj*. This was a step towards weakening of *panchayati raj*. *Panchayati raj* was also weakened by irregular elections of these bodies; elections were not held between 1965 through 1978. This period saw Block Development Officers (BDOs) as administrators in *panchayat samitis* and Collectors as administrators in *zila parishads*. In 1978, only *Panchayat* elections were held. The subsequent elections were held in 1981 and in 1988. In 1991, *gram sevaks* became administrators in

1. Canal Area Development (CAD) in Bikaner, Chambal, Kota and Mahi, Banswara; Desert Development Programme, Drought Prone Area Programme, Border Area Development Programme (BADP), Tribal Area Development Programme (TAD), etc. began to be implemented through DRDAs or concerned departments.

panchayats, BDOs in *panchayat samitis* and Collectors in *zila parishads*. These bureaucratic administrators continued till 1995 when constitutional amendment made it compulsory to hold elections every five years through State Election Commission.

Constitutionalisation of Panchayati Raj

Though *panchayati raj* was the state subject, yet Union Government took the initiative to make *panchayati raj* system a part of Indian Constitution by passing 73rd Constitutional Amendment Act in 1992 (GoI, 1993). "The amended Constitution requires the states to constitute *panchayats* as institutions of self-government not only for villages, but also at intermediate and district levels. Consequently, there will henceforth be three strata of government: the Union, the States and the *panchayats*. A more radical change is difficult to visualise (Mukarji, 1993)."

This amendment was enacted to rejuvenate PRIs through provisions for holding regular elections every five years, for which responsibility was cast on State Election Commissions rather than the State Governments. Reservation of seats of members and chairpersons of *panchayats* at village, block and district levels was made mandatory. Revival of local self-governance has been a major initiative for empowering weaker sections of the rural society. One-third seats for women and seats in proportion to population for Schedule Castes (SC) and Schedule Tribes (ST) were reserved so that weaker sections of society get empowered and mainstreamed in grassroots democracy. State Finance Commission was to be constituted every five years to strengthen the financial position of PRIs and suggest share of state tax revenues to be shared between the state and PRIs. The recommendation of State Finance Commission regarding devolution of powers, administrative control over functionaries and transfer of budget provision to PRIs are not mandatory. Since devolution of powers and finances was left at the discretion of State Governments, the states continue to procrastinate and lack the political will to empower PRIs. These changes are seen as the harbinger of rural development by tuning the development programmes to suit the needs of local population. Local self-governance is thus an effective strategy for poor and the backward to access greater equality in the development pie. This means that the transformative 73rd

Constitutional Amendment is still not implemented in full spirit. This entails that states have met the legal requirements of the constitutional amendment without, in any way, devolving funds, functions and functionaries, which is inescapable. Therefore, literature that shows weaknesses in the functioning of these bodies reflects, not on decentralisation itself, but on its stunted implementation (Vyasulu, 2003). However, almost a decade after the implementation of PRI Act, it is possible to evaluate gains from this people oriented development initiative.

Devolution of Powers to PRIs in Rajasthan

In pursuance of the constitutional mandate, Rajasthan Panchayati Raj Act, 1994 was enacted in April 1994 (GoR, 1994). Prior to promulgation of the Constitution (73rd Amendment) Act, Panchayati Raj Institutions in Rajasthan were governed by Rajasthan Panchayat Act, 1953 and Rajasthan Panchayat Samiti and Zila Parishad Act, 1959. Many amendments were necessary in both these Acts in the wake of the mandatory constitutional provisions contained in the Constitution (73rd Amendment). To overcome this, Rajasthan preferred to promulgate a unified Act known as Rajasthan Panchayati Raj Act, 1994 and in the process the earlier State Acts stood repealed.

Enactment of the Act in itself was not seen as an end in itself by the government. Devolution of powers and functions was considered necessary. As a background to the amendment, a High-powered Committee headed by a Development Commissioner in August 1993 was set up to suggest powers and functions alongwith resources to be entrusted to PRIs consequent upon the Constitution (73rd Amendment) Act. It recommended merger of *panchayati raj* and rural development departments. It was also for PRI's administrative control over all the concurrent officers concerned with rural development at district and block levels. It allocated Schedule I, Schedule II and Schedule III for functions to *panchayats*, *panchayat samitis* and *zila parishads* respectively. It was provided in Sections 50, 51 and 52 of the Rajasthan Panchayati Raj Act, 1994 that *panchayat*, *panchayat samiti* and *zila parishad* shall exercise powers mentioned in Schedule I, II and III respectively, but subject to such conditions as may be specified by the Government from time to time. It was a dereliction of state's duty that in spite of legislative provision, the state government could not specify the conditions for a period of over five years, mainly because political will was lacking. Pretext being given was that the PRI-elected representatives are new, let them gain some experience. A subsequent committee headed by a Development Commissioner in May 1999 recommended transferring of 16 subjects (of the 29-included in XI Schedule of the Constitution) to Panchayati Raj Institutions. The State's Cabinet approved it in January 2000. Thus, an ordinance was issued that devolved some powers on PRI's for the first time. A village monitoring committee headed by a *sarpanch* exists for recommending disciplinary action and transfer of village level employees on account of absence from duty.[2] A cabinet sub-committee can only review a decision of transfer carried out at the recommendation of village committee. This has definitely increased the power and status of *sarpanch* among village level officials. Devolution of powers to *panchayat* is a continuous process. In this process the government of Rajasthan took several steps effective since June 2003.

Administrative Powers

The Rajasthan Panchayati Raj Act's amendment of January 2000 provides for *gram sabha's* control over functions and functionaries of various social and development institutions. Village level officials are expected to attend *gram sabha* meetings, get attendance verified and leave sanctioned from *sarpanch* and inform him of their tour programmes. These are significant departures from the previous regime. However, the task force in January 2001 found that departments were hardly complying with these directions. The officials of revenue, medical and health and women and child departments though have been attending *gram sabha* meetings, they still do not get approval of tour programmes etc. from the *sarpanch* as required.

The State Cabinet on January 2, 2000 placed village extension workers of agriculture, animal husbandry sub-centres with staff, staff of 'D' class fisheries tanks, *khadi* supervisors of industries department, assistant engineer and junior engineer (PHED) in District Rural Development Agency, chief medical officer, doctor in-charge primary

2. These village level officials are *Patwari*, Teacher, Auxiliary Nurse Midwife (ANM)/Multi-Purpose Worker (MPW) of Health department, *Gram Sevak*, *Anganwadi* Worker and *Ayurvedic* Compounder.

health centres, sub-centre staff, *anganwadi* workers and Child Development Project Officers (CDPOs) of Integrated Child Development Services (ICDS) and staff of social welfare hostels under PRIs control.[3] However, owing to change of political regime and bureaucratic resistance, administrative control of functionaries and finances remained under the control of respective departments. Though fresh orders were issued in June 2003 for transfer of funds and functionaries, still BDO and Chief Executive Officer (CEO) only counter signs the salary bills. The budget control continues to vest in respective departments. On the matter of penalising the transferred staff for minor offences, PRIs have been devolved some powers without amending the relevant rules.[4] Government has stayed the transfer of staff of Public Health Engineering Department (PHED), Food and Civil Supplies, Public Works Department (PWD). This testifies to the half-baked overtures to empower the PRIs in Rajasthan.

Gram panchayats on paper (since 2003) has power to construct and maintain *haat* markets hitherto under the domain of Agriculture Marketing Board; the actual transfer of power has not taken place yet. *Panchayats* also now have powers to construct and maintain tanks with capacity of irrigate up to 80 hectares, while to construct and maintain tanks with capacity to irrigate up to 300 hectares *panchayat samitis* get pro-rata budget. To accomplish these tasks, one assistant engineer of the sub-division has been placed under *zila parishad* and one junior engineer along with support staff placed under *panchayat samiti*. To facilitate this, PRI concerned is required to pass a resolution for taking over the tanks.

District Fisheries Officer too is under *zila parishad*. Besides, since September 2003 the staff also has been divided among districts having 'A' class fishery tanks. Also since June 2003, an assistant engineer of PHED with staff has been placed under *zila parishad* control and a junior engineer with staff placed under *panchayat samiti* control. However, actual transfer of the staff has not been affected yet.

---

3. As per recommendations of the Committee and approval of the Chief Minister of Rajasthan, the then Chief Secretary issued order No.F.4 (66) PR/PC/2002/565, Jaipur, Dated 19.06.2003 regarding partial transfer of powers to PRIs against the 29 subjects listed in XI Schedule of the Constitution.
4. Functions of 18 departments and funds and functionaries of about half of these departments were transferred in June 2003 to PRIs in Rajasthan.

Gram panchayats would now not only select *anganwadi* workers, but also supervise *anganwadi* centres, lady supervisors and Child Development Project Officers (CDPO). *Sarpanch* is expected to not only exercise effective control over distribution of nutrition material to Below Poverty Line (BPL) beneficiaries but also prevent pilferage and mis-utilisation. On the ground level, ANM and *anganwadi* workers now regularly attend *gram sabha* and *panchayat* meetings. However, CDPO is still acting independently of BDO though officially placed under the control of *zila parishad*.

Patwari has been made the main assistant in proceedings of Finance and Taxation Standing Committee of *gram panchayat* since June 2003 and has been attending *panchayat* meetings, getting mutation attested by *panchayat* but his administrative control and resultant loyalty continues to rest with revenue department rather than the PRIs.

Gram panchayats now are expected to supervise operation of Fair Price Shops. *Sarpanch* has the authority to check distribution of articles and verification of the registers. The licensee dealer will now submit the account of receipt/distribution, etc. of materials to *gram panchayat* and send monthly information directly to the *panchayat samiti*, which in turn would send them to the District Supply Officer (DSO), effective since June 2003. BDO now does send monthly consolidated report to the DSO.

Block Education Officers and District Education Officers have been placed under the control of *panchayat samiti* and *zila parishad* respectively. Director, Elementary Education has now to deal through *zila parishads* rather than departmental officers. Powers of transfer and Rajasthan Civil Services Rule 17 CCA (Classification, Control and Appeals Rules) regarding transferred teachers will vest in Administration and Establishment Standing Committees of *panchayat samiti* and *zila parishad*. Recruitment of teachers also has to be done through standing committee of *zila parishad* effective June 2003. Thus, PRIs have been delegated complete administrative control over elementary education, though periodic technical directions has to be followed by them regarding syllabus, examination, holidays, etc., as issued by the Administrative Department. The real situation is totally at variance from what the issued orders entail; education department has usurped all the powers in violation of the orders.

All the activities of agriculture/agriculture extension hitherto performed by agriculture supervisor have now been transferred to *panchayat samitis* along with agriculture supervisors and assistant agriculture officers. One Assistant Director (Agriculture) with staff has been placed under *zila parishad;* though activities are still being implemented by the department. All the activities of soil conservation and watershed also stand transferred to *zila parishads*. Director is now part of rural development and *panchayati raj* Department, though subordinate staff is still under the control of the department.

All the activities executed by District Social Welfare Officers at the district level have been transferred to *zila parishads*. District Level Probation Officers/Social Welfare Officers, Assistant Directors/ Deputy Directors will work under *zila parishads*. *Gram sabha* selects eligible beneficiaries for old age, widow or handicapped category pensions and BDO sanctions them now. *Zila parishad* is now expected to approve the list of all the applicants desiring benefit under Prime Minister's Rozgar Yojana (PMRY). Besides, proposals for small industries will now be placed before concerned standing committee of the *panchayat samiti*. It is expected that the draft list of potential industries prepared annually by Industries Department should be discussed in standing committee meeting and all suggestion to be incorporated.

Zila parishad now has the jurisdiction of decision/relation of villages in respective districts for consideration of Renewable Energy Development Authority (REDA) for supply of non-conventional energy-based electrification. Concerned *zila parishad* will select villages in respective districts for electrification and forward the list to electricity corporation for action.

Since August 2003, DRDA has been renamed as Rural Development Cell of *zila parishad* and the 6th standing committee has been constituted as 'Rural Development Committee' of *zila parishad* through a Government Order. However, the act and rules have not been amended. District Women Development Authority (DWDA) and Small Farmer Development Agency (SFDA) have also been merged with *zila parishad*. *Zila pramukh* is chairperson of all bodies. Now a CEO controls all the activities of rural development and *panchayats* at the district level and a Principal Secretary and Minister at the state level.

Financial Powers

It is heartening that three types of financial powers have been devolved on PRIs besides the above mentioned administrative powers. The complete rights are given to PRIs for use of income generated at the level of PRIs themselves. Further, a *gram panchayat* has power to issue administrative and financial sanction up to Rs. 2 lakh under Rule 176(1) and 214(1) of Rajasthan Panchayati Raj Rules, 1996 (GoR, 1996). Further, Finance and Taxation Standing Committee constituted under Section 56 has *panchayat samiti* has the right to sanction Rs.2 to 4 lakh from own income of a *gram panchayat*. The power to sanction Rs.4 lakh and above vests in the *zila parishad* or Finance and Taxation standing committee constituted under Section 57. This is subject to resolution of *gram sabha* and technical sanction as per Directory for Rural Works, 2002 effective since June 2003. The above delegation of financial powers for use of own resources is practicable only in case of PRIs having own income from farms, shops, tanks or other natural resources, etc. It is an affirmative step towards self-governance of PRIs.

Rights of recovery of irrigation tax and its use also now vest with PRIs. Since June 2003, it is maintained that *gram panchayat/panchayat samiti* will undertake maintenance/repair works on priority out of funds received under Sampoorna Grameen Rozgar Yojna. The grassroots picture is entirely different with little been handed over to PRIs.

Besides, the control of 'D', 'C' and 'B' class fishery tanks has been transferred to *gram panchayats, panchayat samiti* and *zila parishad* respectively. Concerned PRI can now auction and use auction income. However, PRIs have to maintain these tanks with the income generated. Auction notices are being issued by respective PRIs. *Panchayat samitis* have control over installation and repair and maintenance of hand pumps, tanks and piped-water supply schemes, the budget to this effect would be transferred to them. Besides, the *sarpanch* will now verify the salary of the hand pump *mistri* (mechanic). PRI can now organise agricultural fairs, but the financial compliance still has not been implemented.

Under new dispensation, BDO/CEO now countersigns salary bills of the agriculture officers. All firewood, fodder and minor forest produce related income in forest and non-forest area is now PRIs income, but has to ensure compliance of concerned forest acts and rules and departmental circulars. In case of *tendupatta* the income net of administrative expenses stands transferred to PRIs.

Thus, as per spirit of 73rd Constitution Amendment-functions, functionaries and funds have begun to be transferred to PRIs. In reality the progress is very slow in many instances to render these institutions of self-government effective. Transfers, attendance, sanction of leave and tour approval powers shall vest in the PRIs.[5] Disciplinary Action Power regarding minor penalty up to stoppage of two grade increments has also been vested in PRIs. However, *status quo* is maintained with regard to budget-drawing and disbursing officers for salary. State government will allot budget to department, but as per activities transferred, budget for the same has to be transferred to the concerned PRI. The concerned *zila parishad/panchayat samiti* has the administrative and financial sanctioning authority now. This transfer of budget clause is yet to be implemented in practice.

Finally, keeping the spirit of 73rd Constitution Amendment, the state of Rajasthan has slowly begun to empower PRIs by devolving the functions, functionaries and funds in small measure after a lapse of 10 years.[6] PRIs do have the potential to become institutions of self-governance, provided-in situation intensive and sustained training of elected representatives and transferred officials is ensured, to inculcate a positive, proactive and responsive attitude; alongwith devolution of four Fs -i.e., functions to be transferred with functionaries, funds and the freedom to function.

Capacity Building

In the wake of the 73rd Constitutional Amendment, the number of elected representatives in the three tiers of PRIs has increased drastically. With the proviso of rotational reservations in place every

5. Order of Chief Secretary to Government of Rajasthan, regarding transfer of powers to PRIs: 2003 No. F-4(66)P.Raj/PC/2002/565, dated 19.6.2003, issued by Panchayati Raj Department, Government of Rajasthan; in compliance of which-concerned Departments, Secretaries were directed to issue detailed administrative orders, after getting them approved by the Chief Secretary by 26.6.2003.

6. *Panchayati Raj Sansthaon Ka Sashaktikaran*: 2003, compendium of Government Orders issued by different departments between 19.6.2003 to 19.7.2003, compiled by Indira Gandhi Panchayati Raj and Gramin Vikas Sansthan, SIRD, Rajasthan, Jaipur.

five years election rounds of PRIs, more than 80 per cent persons who enter these local self-governance institutions expectedly change in each election. Resultantly, the capacity building effort for training of newly elected leaders is a continuing challenge.

Training Mode

It became quite clear, after the first innings of PRI elected leaders that training of PRIs, if restricted to an institutional mode would render the task of reaching 'Training for All' an impossible endeavour (see Anita, 2000; 2004). As the number of elected leaders was 1.20 lakh in the Rajasthan PRIs, decentralised training system appeared to be a pragmatic alternative (Anita, 2005b). It propelled the Rajasthan government to embark upon streamlining the training system for capacity building of PRIs through adopting a systematic and scientific approach to training from 2000 onward with Indira Gandhi Panchayati Raj and Gramin Vikas Sansthan as a nodal training agency. The financial support was provided by state, national and international agencies. Since 2000 series of training of all levels of PRI representatives have been held. Innovative modules have been developed and replicated (Anita, 2005a).

Impact of Training

It is important question whether how efficient and innovative is the training programme, it has to effective. Has PRI training made any impact? To assess the impact of the training, a study was launched in 270 *gram panchayats* of 70 blocks in 30 districts. The pedagogy used involved in-depth interview guides, focus group discussions, semi-participant observation and peer-review as tools. It was found that (Anita, 2004) the role clarity and self-confidence amongst trained *panchayat* leaders had increased universally, the prevailing mindset of 'development means construction' has been broken and the desired unlearning achieved. Training appeared to have inspired fresh learning on human development issues, enhanced understanding of human development goals that led to a shift of priorities towards improving water and sanitation access, food security and social security schemes. Training also led to efforts made for universalising elementary education, especially through enrolment of girls, focus on poverty reduction, improving access to healthcare, especially, mother and child health, immunisation services and management of seasonal diseases became visible in development decision-making of *panchayats*. Greater gender sensitivity is being shown which is more inclusive by including the felt needs of village women in *panchayat's* development planning and practice. The study found women *panchayat* leaders were visibly perceived to be more articulate and assertive compared to their male counterparts. There are initiatives being taken to eradicate social evils such as giving up *purdah/ghoonghat* (custom of veiling by women leaders), child marriage, alcoholism and domestic violence/sexual violence. Team synergy appeared to have increased across elected members and officials (amongst *sarpanches* and secretaries) hitherto a tension-ridden relationship. Efforts are afoot to initiate greater transparency and social audit process of *panchayats* accounts in fortnightly *gram panchayat* (GP) meetings and quarterly *gram sabhas*. The study found that there is a demand for continuous six-monthly/yearly refresher training. The follow-up of continued resource support has become almost universalised, evidencing the value of training perceived by PRI-elected leaders and their official counterparts. In sum, Rajasthan has established its credentials in professional handling and nurturing of the challenge of building capacity of *panchayats* for effective local self governance, committed to prioritising human development, through mass-scale training cascades for *panchayat* leaders and officials.[7]

Government of India has provoked the federating process of Elected Women Representatives (EWRs) in Panchayati Raj Institutions. Even after 12 years of the enforcement of the 73rd Amendment, invoking the revolutionary change of feminising grassroots polity by bringing in lakhs of elected women in local self governance, these elected women representatives still experience

---

7. The case study of IGPR&GVS efforts leads the handful of Institutions facilitating Development Communication in Rajasthan. It is included amongst the 50 pioneering development communication resources of South Asia, documented in the UNICEF Directory for South Asia (2006). Rajasthan's model of training led by IGPR&GVS supported pilot project in Sawai Madhopur district (2004-06), focusing on capacity building of *panchayats* for population, health, RCH and gender-sensitive governance is another trail-blazer, setting an example for replication countrywide, especially, in the states under the National Rural Health Mission strategy. Under this pilot experiment, after the joint training of *panchayat* & health functionaries, *panchayats* have been empowered to conduct their own village HDI-surveys, analyse the deficits and prepare the village health action plans with technical support of local NGOs, acting as Panchayat Resource Centres and overall guidance of IGPR&GVS (Anita, 2006).

vulnerability of atomisation, isolation and male- dominant subversion of political cultural milieu. To facilitate the process of federating elected women representatives across party, caste, class lines to help improve their collective bargaining and negotiating positions in governance platforms, Rajasthan has launched the 'Panchayat Mahila Shakti Abhiyan' in partnership with Ministry of Panchayati Raj and the National Commission for Women. A core committee comprising of women activists/ feminists, NGOs, EWRs did evolve a draft charter of demands on behalf of EWRs (GoI, 2005a). As a follow-up, regional workshops and NGO-led federating/networking processes are underway to proactively help elected *panchayat* women to forge their collective platforms for action and advocacy. In fact, on the capacity building front of PRIs, Rajasthan has emerged as the model state to have actively followed in letter and spirit the 27 resolutions adopted on the theme of capacity building and training of *panchayats* at the VII Round Table Conference (GoI, 2004).

Civil Society and PRI Empowerment

Right to Information is an issue which has gained considerable importance in recent years. More and more people are beginning to feel the need for greater access to information, which hitherto been in the exclusive domain of the government, even though it relates to the well- being of the individual or the public at large. Growth of democratic values have led to the feeling that the government must be made transparent and accountable in order to make democracy meaningful. People's participation is central to good governance. The Right to Information is also being viewed as a possible potent instrument for minimising corruption and inefficiency in government. *Jan Sunwai* is the tool being employed to impart greater transparency to the system.[8]

---

8. *Jan Sunwai* is also part of a broader movement for the people's right to information. It is an example of the tools that can be used to assert the right of all citizens to transparent and accountable government (Sharma, 2001). In the current climate of pervasive corruption, the right to information is one opportunity for ordinary citizens to break out of the vicious circle of collective apathy and individual hopelessness. *Jan Sunwais* are vibrant platforms in village democracy. As details are read out from copies of the official records of works undertaken by a *panchayat*, assembled villagers are asked if they confirm them. One by one, they come forward to testify to fraud from what they

contd...

Rajasthan-based civil society groups and NGOs such as Mazdoor Kisan Shakti Sangathan (MKSS), People's Union of Civil Liberties, Seva Mandir, Astha, etc. have definitely earned a name and fame through *Jan Sunwais* and other public hearing/social audit interventions regarding development works executed at *panchayat* level.[9] Inhabitants of the concerned villages participate in these meeting and question the elected representatives and functionaries in the presence of NGOs and government officials. Such public hearings help expose cases of corruption, fund misappropriation and other malpractices indulged by the representatives and functionaries. In some cases these meetings turn into people's courts with the guilty being suitably punished on the spot.[10] The story of unlettered labourers in a remote village of Rajasthan demanding the right of access to muster rolls during the mid-1990s has become an unforgettable part of the history of the right to information (RTI) movement in India. This and other movements launched for food security, environmental protection, consumer rights, protection of habitats from illegal mining and justice for people displaced by development projects finally resulted in the framing of comprehensive RTI legislation now applicable throughout the country (GoI, 2005b).

The RTI Act enacted by the central government in June 2005 became fully operational on October 13, 2005. Under this law, any citizen can seek information from any public office starting from President down to the *gram panchayat*. Articles 321-328 of Rajasthan Panchayati Raj Rules, 1996 are related to RTI. Use of the Right to

---

...contd...

have actually seen happening or not happening. Women do not hesitate to testify. Nor do the labourers in parched clothes; and all in the presence of powerful sarpanches and local bureaucracy, (MKSS, 1994-2000). *Jan-Sunwai* has three objectives viz., public review and audit of development works; exposing corruption and building responsive democracy by making elected representatives accountable for misuse of public money. *Jan Sunwai* is an effective medium to arouse popular awareness for Right to Information. Their success derives from the culture of face-to-face panchayat democracy made accountable to the moral sense of the village community. Since the object of *Jan Sunwai* has been social audit of works and verification from muster rolls, hence such *Jan Sunwai* is generally organised for a cluster of 4-5 *panchayats*. Many local people have been mobilised in this process with the campaign for Right to Information. These efforts ultimately culminated in announcement by the Chief Minister of 'Right to Information Act' in 2000 and issue of Rules on January 26, 2001.

9. This has especially happened in districts of Ajmer, Rajsamand, Pali, Bhilwara and Dungarpur. *Jan Sunwai* or *Lok Adalat* has been an initiative taken by the Mazdoor Kisan Shakti Sangathan in Ajmer, Bhilwara, Pali and Rajsamand districts since 1994.

10. The guilty have been made to return the money appropriated and give public apology.

Information (RTI) Act can ensure that *gram sabhas* and the elected bodies of *gram panchayats*, and the intermediary and district levels plan, prioritise and implement development schemes properly, in the best public interest and with peoples' ratification.

NGOs in tribal areas, particularly in Udaipur district *viz.*, Seva Mandir, Vanvasi Kalyan Parishad, Jan Jangal Jamin Andolan, Astha and Panchayat Sanstha Sangh have been making efforts to popularise the concept of tribal self-governance as pronounced by the Bhuria Committee and the Panchayat Extension over Scheduled Areas Act (PESA), 1996. Now since Rajasthan Government has enacted a separate law in 1999, for tribal sub-plan area, efforts of local NGOs will bring more fruit and strengthen tribal *gram sabhas*.[11] However, modalities are yet to be worked out.

Social Audit for Empowerment of PRIs

The concept of social audit is premised on the principle that in a democracy the decision-makers should account for the exercise of their powers and that these powers are used as far as possible, with the consent and understanding of all concerned in the best public interest. Social Audit is a democratic process of ensuring public accountability through a systematic demand of information by the community in response to the works/programmes that have already been implemented by the People's Implementing Agency or the state or the civil society for the development of that particular area/ community. In particular, it aims to involve all the stakeholders in the process to measure work performance, in order to achieve improvement as well as to report accurately on what has been done. Social audit empowers the voiceless to question and seek answers. It builds a social platform for the marginalised, from where they learn to demand their rights. It helps to prevent corruption by displaying the accounts and expenditures. It ensures public accountability and social justice by strengthening grassroots level democracy; especially, addressing its socioeconomic domain by creating social pressure groups through harnessing social capital.

---

11. UNNATI in Jodhpur, PRIA and The Hunger Project in Jaipur have also been organising a network of NGOs to strengthen *gram sabhas*, as well as, Dalit and women elected *sarpanches* to build their confidence and enable them to exercise powers invested in *panchayats*.

Panchayati Raj Institutions (PRIs) cover most of India's rural population, where *gram sabhas* act as platforms for people's participation, to raise demands and to ensure transparency and accountability in the responses of *panchayats*. *Panchayati raj* can spearhead local economic development with social justice. PRIs can more effectively deliver initiatives like the Sarva Shiksha Abhiyan (SSA), National Rural Health Mission and National Rural Employment Guarantee Act, provided the functionaries and funds and the freedom to implement local need-based plans is given in their control.[12]

The most appropriate institutional level for social audit of ongoing *panchayat* Initiatives is the *gram sabha* (GoR, 2000). In most states, *gram sabhas* are given the mandate to supervise and monitor the functioning of *panchayat* elected representatives and government functionaries and examine the annual statement of accounts and audit reports of *panchayats*. These are implied powers indirectly empowering *gram sabhas* to carry out social audits in addition to other functions of participatory development planning, prioritisation and concurrent review of all social sector schemes and not merely Rural Development Schemes. Members of the *gram sabha* and the village *panchayat*, intermediate *panchayat* and district *panchayat* through their representatives can raise issues of social concern and public interest and demand an explanation on use/misuse of public money, public works, services and public servants/development functionaries. Thus, social audit is a regular and effective institutional mechanism to promote the culture of transparency and accountability in local governance institutions through the *gram sabha*.

States should enhance *gram sabha* powers to make them effective instruments of participatory decision-making and ensuring accountability of PRIs for local development. An agency can be set up to look into complaints of local mal-administration. Development functionaries found guilty of violating established norms for local

---

12. The Indian Constitution envisions *panchayats* as statutory institutions of local self-governance. The subversive tendencies in delaying devolution of full-scale powers to PRIs would derail the process set in for sustained development of rural areas. The true power should be with the people rather than with donor agencies and civil society networks and the state should not become a party to it. Capacity building and programme implementation funds of social sector and poverty reduction projects should be implemented by *panchayats* who are constitutionally empowered to sustain the twin goals of economic development and social justice rather than NGOs/CBOs. Article-243(G) is nothing short of developmental and constitutional myopia, befogging the vision of state governments.

development planning should be punished. It is important to ensure that the rural poor are given due protection when they wish to stand up to speak against any governance misconduct on part of elected leaders or officials of *panchayats*. Finally, prime need of the hour is to make the most effective use of resources and expertise available with the government, as well as, NGOs. Both these actors need to pool their efforts to ensure maximum utilisation of resources, to be invested and synchronised in capacity building and conscientisation of Panchayati Raj Institutions.

Conclusions

The state of Rajasthan has made wide range of changes in its approach and functioning of PRIs. To recapitulate there has been devolution of functions, functionaries and funds and it has become the greatest strength and an opportunity for empowerment of PRIs by enabling actual hands-on experience of grappling with governance issues at the local level. All the respective departments have issued clear orders in writing and partially staff has also been transferred, except in case of PWD, PHED and Food and Civil Supply and Forest, for carrying out assigned tasks. Organic linkages between respective PRIs have also been restored through amendment in the Rajasthan Act, in 2000. Limited autonomy for expenditure from own resources has been given to encourage PRIs to raise resources for expenditure as per local needs, without permission from state government. Income flow from irrigation and fisheries tanks is expected to enhance financial viability of PRIs to some extent. The merger of DRDA, DWDA and Fish Farmers Development Agency (FFDA) in *zila parishad* and placing the services of various District Level Officers (DLOs) at the disposal of *zila parishad* by making non-official *zila pramukh* is step in the right direction. Full delegation of administrative powers to make PRIs as controlling authority can increase the effective delivery of services at the village level. One can see the direct control over women and child development, nutrition programme, fair price shops, agriculture extension, animal husbandry centres is also an opportunity for PRIs to execute need-based programmes of health and nutrition, agriculture and animal husbandry, food security etc. These administrative orders require full implementation in letter and spirit to empower PRIs.

On a positive count, the fact that now the *gram sabhas* can be held over a period of 15 days instead on a fixed single day/date should go a long way to improve the attendance of officers and attract significant the local residents to participation. Since local problems will expectedly be attended to by local officers would ensure greater people's participation. *Gram sabha* has been empowered to select beneficiaries for rural housing, pension for aged, widow and handicapped or selection of BPL families. It can also do social audit of PWD works, rural development works, quality of social services, human development, deficits approval of annual income and expenditures of *panchayat* and also issue utilisation certificate for works undertaken by *panchayat* and keep surveillance of the quality of works. Political participation by way of reservation of more than 50 per cent seats of chairpersons of PRIs for women, SC/ST/OBC is also a great opportunity for marginalised sections of community which can be encashed by building their capacity on priority level. Effective capacity building programme of elected representatives and official functionaries would go a long way to enhance their knowledge and skills in organisational and administrative aspects of good local self-governance with a focus on human development concerns.

There is no doubt that plethora of steps have been initiated to empower PRIs. However, lot needs to be done to enable PRIs to play a proactive role in social development. There is need to overcome lack of political and bureaucratic will to expeditiously devolve functionaries and funds with regard to transferred subjects. Recommendations of Cabinet Sub-committee have yet to be approved by the full Cabinet. In absence of *panchayat* secretariat[13] and competent staff, mere transfer of multifarious functions will not suffice. Besides, capacity building of government functionaries performing multifarious duties is also necessary. As surplus staff has been absorbed[14] as *panchayat* secretaries, they require intensive training in office management, accounting procedures and record maintenance. There is a dire need for PRIs to have its own cadre of *panchayat* secretaries. Financial constraint to meet local developmental demands raised in *gram sabhas* is another impediment in effective functioning of PRIs. There is also

13. Administrative Reforms Committee did recommend it.
14. These are *nakedars* of local bodies, forest guards, mechanics of PHED or work-charge persons of PWD.

need to improve the low performance of *panchayats* in generating own resources.[15]

District Planning Committee is still ineffective at the district level because they have neither any untied funds nor power of execution and monitoring. These are yet to be devolved on it to operationalise the district plan. The district plans drawn along sectoral lines at present do not include the ward/*gram sabha's* development priorities. Thus, true decentralised planning for development is still a distant dream.

Finally, looking at the developmental history of planned development in India, it emerges clearly that our planning for development has been beset with the ills of centralised goals and target-setting by diktats of central or state governments. As a result fiscal planning has been mired in allocation of budgetary outlays and expenditures and not geared to monitoring of outcomes.[16] Without any doubt, *panchayati raj* is the largest experiment in decentralised governance on the human planet. The state has to play a proactive role to further the cause of decentralisation and strengthen it. It has to remove all the hurdles being created by vested interests. The pitfalls need to be avoided. Fully empowered *panchayats*, administratively and financially, can go a long way to develop rural India truly with people's participation. If the essence of democracy is that people make their own informed developmental choices, then fully empowering the PRIs to function as autonomous local self governance institutions is the first bold step required in the direction of sustainable human development. To this end, the time has come to remove all the roadblocks in the process. The future of rural development in India lies in strengthening the third stratum of governance, the PRIs, not merely in form but in true functional spirit, as decreed by the Constitution.

---

15. *Panchayat* should utilise its powers for imposition of taxes, fees/penalty, different administrative fees to be charged as per rules of 1996, rates of house tax, water cess rates, tax on commercial crops as laid down in the Panchayati Raj Rules, 1996.

16. Today there are about 30 lakh elected representatives at all levels of the *panchayat*. These members represent over 2.4 lakh *gram panchayats*, about 6000 intermediate block Panchayats and over 500 district *panchayats*. This third tier of governance in the Indian polity cover over 96 per cent of India's 5.8 lakh villages and nearly 99.6 per cent of the rural population (PRIA, 2001). In Rajasthan, there are 1.2 lakh elected representatives at all levels of the *panchayats* who represent over 9189 *gram panchayats*, about 237 intermediate block *panchayats* and over 32 district *panchayats*, thus covering total rural population.

References

Anita (2000). *Report of Training Needs Assessment of PRIs,* Rajasthan, IGPR&GVS, Jaipur.

———. (2004). *Report of Training Needs Assessment of PRIs,* Rajasthan, IGPR&GVS, Jaipur.

———. (ed.) (2005a). *Panchayati Raj Prashikshan Modules,* Rajasthan, IGPR&GVS, 2000 (First Edition); 2002 (Second Edition); 2005 (Third Edition), Jaipur.

———. (2005b). *Summary Report of Decentralized Training Campaign for PRIs: Rajasthan Experience,* IGPR&GVS, Jaipur.

———. (2006). *A Comprehensive Report of Pilot Project for Capacity Building of PRIs on Population, Health, RCH and Gender Issues,* IGPR&GVS, Jaipur.

Gandhi, M.K. (1942). "My Idea of Village Swaraj", *Harijan,* July 26.

Government of India (1950). *Directive Principles of State Policy,* Constitution of India.

———. (1957). *Report of the Team for the Study of Commnity Projects and National Extension Service,* Chairperson: Balwantray Mehta, Committee on Plan Projects, National Development Council, New Delhi, November, Vol. I.

———. (1993). *The Constitution (Seventy Third Amendment) Act,* 1992, The Gazette of India Extraordinary, Part II, Section I, April 20.

———. (2004). *A Compendium of Resolutions of the Seven Round Tables: 2004 (July-December),* Ministry of Panchayati Raj.

———. (2005a). *Panchayat Mahila Shakti Abhiyan,* Udaipur, Rajasthan Declaration: 2005, State Level Consultation of Women PRI-Representatives, April 23-24.

———. (2005b). *Right to Information Act, 2005,* Gazette of India Extraordinary, October 13.

Government of Rajasthan (1994). *Rajasthan Panchayati Raj Act*: 1994, The Rajasthan Gazette Extraordinary, April 23.

———. (1996). *Rajasthan Panchayati Raj Rules*: 1996, Rajasthan Gazette Extraordinary, December 30.

———. (2000) *Rajasthan Panchayati Raj Amendment Act*: 2000, Rajasthan Gazette Extraordinary, May.

———. (2002). *Right to Information Act,* 2000, Rajasthan Gazette Extraordinary.

Mathew, George (2000). "Panchayati Raj in India-An Overview", in *Status of Panchayati Raj in the States and Union Territories of India,* Institute of Social Sciences, Concept, New Delhi.

MKSS (1994-2000). *Campaign for Right to Information.*

Mukarji, Nirmal (1993), "The Third Stratum", *Economic and Political Weekly,* May 1, pp.859-62.

Nehru, Jawahar Lal (1959). Quoted in the *Hindustan Times,* New Delhi, October, 3.

PRIA (2001). *The State of Panchayats,* Samskriti, New Delhi.

Sharma, P.R. (2001). *Decentralization through PRIs: A Case Study in the Context of Rajasthan,* Ph.D. Thesis, MDS University, Ajmer.

Vyasulu, Vinod (2003). "Decentralization, Democratization, Finances and the Constitution", in *Panchayats, Democracy and Development,* Rawat Publications, Jaipur & New Delhi, pp.148-77.

10

Tracing the Journey

Reflections on Doing Women's Studies[1]

KANCHAN MATHUR and SHOBHITA RAJAGOPAL

'Women's studies' at one level, can be seen as an academic response to the larger concern for `justice' in society—for according an equitable status and dignity to women. This view rests on a realisation that our society has, over a very long period, sustained a systematic injustice to women. The radical departure in our approach is to credit an increasingly large 'group of women' with the possibility of being researchers—of inquirers and reflectors of their own reality. If this position is accepted the addition to the existing body of knowledge would be qualitatively different. The central value in this possible framework for research is that of demystifying the 'professionalism' vis-à-vis knowledge, giving a clear recognition to the faith that the right to know must be for all. It must be accompanied by creating conditions, which would allow the possibility to acquiring knowledge for those who have, so far, only been treated as `objects' of knowledge. Women's studies, therefore, should create an occasion to do economics, political science and sociology in a manner in which the social reality is not only 'studied' but also 'altered' in an essential sense.

— Jain, 1986

Introduction

The journey into women's studies at Institute of Development Studies (IDS) began when a group of women researchers with similar concerns came together and began questioning the processes which led to women's subordinated status in society as well as examining and redefining those mechanisms through which subordination is legitimised, taken for granted and internalised as personal destiny. The effort was to analyse how research and action can lead to changing existing realities within the context of development policy and practice.

---

1. We gratefully acknowledge the critical inputs given by Dr. Sharada Jain on an earlier draft of the paper.

In 1984, the Women's Studies Unit (WSU) comprised three members belonging to different academic disciplines and age groups.[2] The younger members were enthusiastic but brought with them their fears, inhibition and anxieties. They were hopeful that they would learn as well as contribute to the understanding of women's studies *albeit* in a small way. One more member joined in 1987 increasing the size of the core group to four. Others joined for shorter periods ranging from one to three years.

Our collective experiences led us to venture into unfamiliar areas. In the initial years the mode was exploratory. The effort was to develop a methodology, discover the core areas, design the content and identify the target group as well as issues. Women's Studies was interpreted as creating fresh knowledge on women's issues by reflecting, questioning and contributing significantly to the existing body of knowledge.

The present chapter reflects on the journey on doing women's studies at the Institute of Development Studies over the past two decades and more. It traces the evolution and the various phases of the work. It dwells on our attempts and achievements as well as on the failures and continuing challenges. The chapter is divided into four sections. It first focuses on the main assumptions guiding the initial years of our work and the learning emerging from a combine of action and research. It then highlights the shift in understanding development policy and practice from a gender perspective. It also elaborates on some of the dilemmas faced in establishing women's concerns in the larger context of state policy and practice. The concluding part of the chapter looks at the road ahead.

The Beginning

When we began working, the development indicators in Rajasthan were particularly unfavourable to women. Sex ratio was 919 women to 1,000 men, women's literacy rates were as low as 11.42 per cent compared to 36.30 for men, the literacy rates among scheduled castes (SC) & scheduled tribes (ST) women was abysmally low at 2.69 and 1.20 respectively. As many as 82 per cent women workers were

---

2. Dr. Sharada Jain envisioned the WSU in 1984 and was later joined by Kavita Srivastava and Kanchan Mathur. Shobhita Rajagopal joined in 1987.

engaged as agricultural labour but they had practically no ownership rights and had little opportunity to improve their functional skills (GoR, 1984). It was evident that most development efforts had 'bypassed' women. It was also clear that the Unit's work would have to be located against a feudal patriarchal backdrop wherein women's roles, mobility and choices were severely curtailed. Taking into account the harsh terrain in most parts of the state where women have to forage for fuel, fodder and food crisis adding to their vulnerability would also be essential.

The questions that stared us on the face, therefore, were related to the continued subordinated status of women and the forces that sustained this subordination and denied them access to crucial resources. Any effort to transform the condition and position of women would require addressing a larger number of women across categories of caste, class, age and marital status. It was pertinent that the research brings the voices of the rural marginalised and deprived centre stage.

Science and Technology Workshop

The first workshop organised by the Women's Studies unit in 1984 was on Science and Technology for women at the behest of the department of Science and Technology, Government of Rajasthan. The multi-disciplinary group of participants were drawn from diverse backgrounds: Government of India, Planning Commission, Government of Rajasthan, NGOs as well as academicians and activists from different parts of the country. This was in line with the IDS approach to understanding the problems of development from a holistic perspective rather than pursue research within the straight jacketed points of view of particular disciplines and specialisations. It was felt that be it in the field of education, health or of economic activities, women are treated as onlookers, and recipients of technology. This workshop attempted to establish that women must be made participants in the process of technology choice, rather than mere recipients. One of the main issues raised at the workshop was the relationship between technology, women's work and drudgery. It became apparent that it is plausible that technology per se has no gender bias but decisions regarding technology do contain such a bias (IDS, 1984).

The workshops also clearly established that there was a need to open communication channels between planners or 'doers' and the target group and to involve people in the process of planning. This led us to explore the various ways in which development planning can include a woman's perspective and involve them as equal partners in the process of development. The learning from this workshop became the basis for designing and planning the Women's Development Programme.

Breaking the Hiatus between Action and Research

As the work evolved, the content of research and the methodology to be adopted became clearer. It was realised that the processes adopted should be such that the gap between thought and action is minimised. Facilitating women to seek their own knowledge was seen as an 'action' step. It was also felt that when rural women begin looking at their ownselves and plan for development, the hiatus between research and action would break as the women themselves became researchers. Therefore women's narratives provided textures of the situation and the process of 'naming' the experience led to understanding the various dimensions of subordination.

The above understanding formed the basis of our involvement with the Women's Development Project (WDP) in the year 1984 when the project was still being designed.

Box 10.1

The Women's Development Project

The Women's Development Project (WDP) was one of the first initiatives for women's development and empowerment in India. The project attempted to reach rural women through eliciting partnership between the state government, NGOs and academics. It registered a clear recognition that a fresh approach to women's development was needed. Despite the fact that serious attempts were being made to divert 'benefits' to women, it was apparent that their condition had continued to be that of subjugation and deprivation. The project, therefore, called for a shift in focus. Instead of stressing upon creation of delivery mechanisms, it was an attempt at strengthening the receiving components.

Source: IDS (1986).

The project took into account the experiences of a number of women's groups/activists from all over the country. The leadership trainings of rural women conducted by Social Work and Research Centre (SWRC), Tilonia in Ajmer district of Rajasthan in the year 1980 provided the background on which the programme was formulated.

WDP's point of departure can be seen in making a shift in attention from 'delivery mechanisms'—that so far had looked at women as objects of compassion and welfare—to a serious attempt to strengthen the so-called recipients. The *sathin* or the village level change agent was the key player around whom all the WDP activities evolved. She was responsible for the formation of women's forums at the village level and discussing issues related to their development. She was supported in all such activities by the block level worker i.e. *prachetas,* and functionaries of IDARA (Information Development and Resource Agency) and Project Directors of the District Women's Development Agency.

The trainings in WDP sought to demystify the process of women's subjugation by unpacking the multiple power relations that have a bearing on women's lives. In each training issues related to the various aspects of the government delivery system i.e. water, forests, famine relief works, public distribution system, health delivery, harassment of women and the systemic corruption were discussed to assess the efficacy of development interventions and their impact on women's lives. The trainings helped them to evolve strategies to transform the development agenda at the local level. They also aimed at strengthening the self-confidence of women and enhancing their collective capacities for the transformation of their own lives. The experiential trainings created a climate of questioning, reflecting, sharing, choosing, seeking and discovering, through listening and talking and attempted to initiate a revised positive perception of women's identity and self-image leading to a change in social image of women (IDS, 1986).

For many of us these trainings were the first experience of living with rural women and experiencing a process of self-discovery. We recognised that women lived with multiple identities based on gender, caste, class, age, marital status and that at different points of time and in different contexts a particular identity could be more prominent and oppressive than the other.

The WSU facilitated the process of participatory evaluation and monitoring in WDP, which was an integral component of every stage of activity in the programme. In the spirit of 'learning by doing', monitoring and evaluation was interpreted as 'shared reflection' that was to be woven into each of its processes, be it a training programme or a village meeting or a workshop for subsequent planning. This approach leant itself to constantly revising the programme strategy through information and knowledge acquired through group based reflection. Monitoring and evaluation, in turn, gave a concrete content to the notion of participation (IDS, 1986). In the initial years of the project, members of the WSU participated in each activity of the project—be it at the village, block, district or state levels. There was close involvement in conducting training programmes, documentation, providing field level support and policy level interventions. The information generated through this participation acted as a feedback for ensuring and facilitating effective monitoring as well as corrective action.

Box 10.2

Collective Action

One of the first empowering experiences of collective action in WDP was the case of attempted rape of Vimla Rana taken up by the *sathins* in village Bhateri in Bassi *panchayat samiti*, Jaipur district, in 1986. In the case the *sathins* questioned the decision of the *jati panchayat* to punish the culprit without the involvement of the woman survivor of rape.

In this case active support was provided by WSU in mobilising support of not only the State level agencies including the state IDARA, the Additional Director of the DWCD, *sathins* and *prachetas* from some neighbouring districts and members of women's groups from SWRC, Tilonia. A major show of strength meeting was held at the village level, which led to an expression of solidarity with the rural women.

The meeting succeeded in establishing that the onus of guilt should be borne by the culprit and not by the woman who is raped. It also helped WDP functionaries to articulate a woman's perspective on rape and raised a serious question on the notion of justice itself. The understanding that emerged was that rural men and women have their own notions of justice that need to be understood and recognised. The notion of justice for the *jati panchayat* or for the legal system, which is male dominated and for the woman who has been raped varies considerably.

Source: Mathur (2004).

At this stage there was also constant interaction with state government officials especially the Directorate of Women and Child Development. Any new incumbent was initiated into the philosophy and working of the project by WSU. This built a relationship of trust amongst the unit members and the bureaucrats leading to a quick response to suggestions made from time to time.

As the programme evolved the *sathins* raised issues relating to education, health, environment, wage-employment and empowerment of women and girls. Our involvement in many of these struggles at the local level provided important learnings. The process of recording, analysing and reporting field level observations helped in reinforcing what is worth doing and how it should be done. Further, IDS also organised a series of evaluation meetings and workshops, which also helped the WDP group to critically reflect on their processes and make necessary changes. Hence rather than providing hindsight wisdom, the effort was to give a simultaneous feedback in case corrective measures were needed in the programme.

In September 1987, when Roop Kanwar, an 18-year-old Rajput girl of village Deorala in Sikar district was forced to immolate herself on her husband's funeral pyre, the incident shocked the public at large as also women's groups in Rajasthan and throughout the country. It brought to the fore the deep-seated belief system that had been left untouched by the so-called education system. It was felt that there was a need to explore the backdrop of our social reality to ensure that no more Roop Kanwar's were burnt on the pyre in the future.

A series of dialogues were organised in various districts of Rajasthan to elicit the perceptions of a cross-section of people from urban/rural or educated/uneducated backgrounds. At one level, strong outbursts of emotion continued to accompany the positions and counter positions that provoked the Deorala incident. The point of serious concern was the glorification and the support of the incident by some *Rajput* youth who declared it as a matter of religious and communal pride. The climax of the horror story, in fact, did not lie in Deorala but in the elitist distant quarters. It was from the urban educated elite that the oft-repeated question came, "Did Roop Kanwar commit *sati* of her will or was she forced?" (Jain, Misra and Srivastava, 1987).

In direct contrast was the response of *sathins* of the programme who, in the short span of three years, had an opportunity to vocalise their thoughts in collective forums (Mathur, 2004). The overwhelming response of the *sathins* was that it was a clear case of murder. They responded that:

Box 10.3

Sathin's Responses to Deorala Episode

- Roop Kanwar could have been saved if her family members and villagers had wanted her to live.
- No woman gives away her life happily, even those who have committed *sati*. The thought of leading the life of a widow appears hopeless and makes her take this decision.
- Only the rich women can afford to commit *sati*. Who would look after the children if a widow in a poor household died. She has no option but to work and live for them.

Source: Srivastava *et al*. (1988).

The level of analysis offered by the rural women was far too sophisticated. While all of them were planted firmly in a common belief system they were able to move from the specificity of the case to the larger issue of women's subordination in society. This and many similar interactions were published in leading journals to initiate a larger public debate and questioning.

The women's protest movement that followed brought together women's groups, both at the local as well as national levels. It asserted that religion, state and caste cannot be used to exploit women. The women's rally of over 3000 participants marched through the streets of Jaipur reaffirming that the issue was that of women's dignity and identity. It emerged that violence against women had to be kept central to the development discourse and for an understanding of development paradigms.

By the 1990's it was evident that there was need to bring in fresh challenges leading to revised roles in WDP by reviewing the programme in its entirety i.e. its organisation, content and direction. This became necessary in the context of emerging discontent and cracks at various levels. The WSU and State IDARA undertook this exercise with the aim of consolidating the existing strengths within the programme and arriving at future possibilities. It was felt that the knowledge of certain processes in WDP—'what had succeeded' and what did not would help design a more focused project. An attempt was made to document the extent and nature of human resource generated in the programme. The *sathins* and *prachetas* assessed their work and also identified areas in which they wanted to work in the future. This review put together as a document "WDP Emerging Challenges" was presented to the state government for planning the next phase of the programme.

The report put forth several suggestions: The role of the *sathins* would undergo a significant change and the focus at the village level should be on group building. Instead of having one paid worker in each village the programme should provide inputs and support to village women to enable them to participate effectively in village level forums. The report also highlighted the need for the formation of a team at the block level. The dual structure at the district level was also to become one unit (IDS, 1991). The WSU members and State IDARA functionaries participated in several rounds of discussions with the state government officials on the basis of this document to re-design the project structure but with little success. A lack of political will was clearly apparent.

In September 1992, the gang rape of *sathin* Bhanwari in village Bhateri, Jaipur district revealed starkly the vulnerability faced by poor, rural, low caste women and presented a serious challenge to development interventions. In this case, as in the case of Deorala episode, two parallel positions gained ground; one held by people from the village and caste leaders who basically questioned the authenticity of Bhanwari's story and the other espoused by social activists, many sensitive bureaucrats, researchers and others who were outraged by the violence meted out on Bhanwari (Mathur, 1999).

The members of the Unit along with state IDARA and others were closely involved in documenting and widely disseminating the case to garner support for the movement against the injustice meted out. The facts of the case were extensively shared highlighting the implications of the episode both within and outside the state and succeeded in eliciting support from women's groups/activists and women and men from all walks of life and from different parts of the country. The protest movement gained momentum as several protest rallies were organised in Jaipur and other districts culminating in a large 'show of strength' meeting at Jaipur attended by an unprecedented number of people. Bhanwari and other rural women spoke about their experiences of rape and violence. It was the first time that a public articulation of the issue of rape took place—something that was hitherto unheard of in an erstwhile feudal state. Though a long struggle for justice ensued with small victories the experience also exposed the complexities of the judicial system and how it denies justice to women. Bhanwari's struggle and fight for justice became a personal struggle for many of us closely involved with the case. A sense of disillusionment set in when all the accused were finally acquitted. The backlash and reactions in this case clearly pointed out that women would have to face extreme violence if they questioned entrenched power relations. However, one significant outcome of this long battle was the Supreme Court judgement against sexual harassment at work place in August, 1997 popularly known as the Vishakha judgement.[3]

The Women's Development Programme started as an experimental project in which an attempt was made to turn the notion of development 'on its head'. Moving away from centralised policy planning and top-down policies for women's development, it placed its priority on providing support to the needs and demands articulated from the village itself.

The WDP experience clearly validated that:

- Poor non-literate rural women given space and support, can reflect, articulate and challenge injustice.
- They can emerge out of a situation of powerlessness and assume a greater degree of control over their lives.
- They can develop skills of communication, mobilisation and reflection and grow to become 'leaders', and
- Catalysing change would necessitate a change in self-image leading to a change in social image.

Between 1984 and 1991, the unit members were primarily involved with the WDP. However, the unit also undertook many other research projects. One of the early researches looked at the functioning and impact of Development of Women and Children in Rural Areas (DWCRA), a study of child care services in the state was taken up as part of a larger collaborative project with CWDS, New

3. As defined in the guidelines, sexual harassment includes such unwelcome sexually determined behaviour such as physical contact, a demand or request for sexual favours, sexually coloured remarks, showing pornography and any other unwelcome physical, verbal or non-verbal conduct of a sexual nature.

Delhi. A process review of SWRC Tilonia's famine relief activities highlighted the need for incorporating values of justice, honesty and equality in relief activities implemented by the state. The Situational Analysis of Women and Children in Rajasthan provided an in depth understanding of the status of women and their access to crucial resources. The study on Situational Analysis of Women in the Indira Gandhi Nahar Project (IGNP) clearly revealed that the coming of the canal had not brought any positive change in the lives of women and had sharpened gender inequalities. Several documents/reports related to WDP were also brought out. All these different studies helped us further our understanding on issues related to women's development and empowerment.

In 1987, some of the unit members also got involved with the Shiksha Karmi Project (SKP), an innovative educational intervention to address factors sustaining educational backwardness in the state. The programme demonstrated that if the educational services offered enjoyed community support, even 'ordinary' persons (not having requisite formal qualifications), if given opportunity, training and support can rise to a high level of performance and contribute to social development in a significant manner.

Box 10.4

Objectives of Shikshakarmi Project

SKP sought to reach the unreached by developing appropriate institutional responses and aimed at universalisation of education in remote areas of Rajasthan. The main objective of the project were:

- to identify and train voluntary education workers from among the village community—*shikshakarmis*—who would be requested to run primary education day and/or night centres in selected villages;
- to establish, with active involvement of NGOs and voluntary organisations, a training and support system adequate to sustain and promote the role of *shikshakarmis* (GoI, 1986: 9).

The unit's role in the SKP was similar to the role in WDP—participatory monitoring and evaluating partners. Participatory evaluation in SKP found a strong reinforcement through a simple and effective intervention i.e. the creation of a forum for review, dialogue, problem-solving which met every month after each major training programme. The information generated through these exercises acted as feedback ensuing and facilitating effective monitoring (Rajagopal, 1999). This project represented a design and an implementation strategy for providing quality education in distant areas of the state. Many of the factors that constrained girls' education like distance of schools, timing of classes and lack of female teachers were addressed in this project. A number of research studies were carried out on the academic achievement of children, night schools, status of *mahila shikshakarmis* and role of NGOs in the SKP. These reports were shared with the state government functionaries as well as other NGO partners in the project.

The long experience of linking with WDP and researching on women's issues helped us reflect, introspect and question existing inequalities at a personal level. In the development context it gave insights into designed interventions for women's empowerment i.e. that development programmes have to develop rather than be 'implemented' and that there was a need for continuous critical reflection at every stage of planning and implementation. It also affirmed the possibility of rural women's participation in development processes as equal partners as well as their ability to raise their voice against existing patterns of unequal social relationships, which had cast women in subordinate roles.

Our involvement in WDP and SKP crystallised into long term focused areas of research i.e. violence against women and education for girls.

At another level, our active involvement with the Indian Association of Women's Studies helped us link with a larger network of academics, researchers and activists from different parts of the country. This involvement has continued to date.

The learnings of WDP also became the basis for designing the Mahila Samakhaya Project. A series of meetings were held at IDSJ to discuss in depth the various gaps and areas of dissatisfaction within WDP. The *mahila samakhaya* was initially implemented in 6 states of the country, later expanded to 14.

From Women's Studies to Gender and Development

The foray into mainstreaming gender into development policy and practice began in the early 1990s. The experience of analysing issues related to women's subordination and subjugation created a strong base for further understanding gender issues in development.

In 1993, the Gender Planning Training Project (GPTP) was initiated as a joint collaboration between the Government of India and the British Overseas Development Agency with the aim of developing a training resource capacity by drawing on trainers and potential trainers from diverse agencies: government training institutions and departments, academic institutions and NGOs. In terms of its approach, strategy and content, this project constituted a landmark of sorts in the entire experience of gender training in India. This project spanned a period of three years from 1993-1996. Three faculty members from IDSJ participated in this capacity building process and contributed their own experiences of working in the development sector as well as on issues related to women's development.

For the Unit members the GPTP provided an opportunity to understand and reflect on concepts of gender, gender relations and the use of various gender analytical frameworks. It also helped take forward gender training as a useful and strategic tool for addressing institutional and policy changes within the government. This project attempted to ensure that gender training was not used just to sensitise people but to develop an integrated gender focus on both the personal as well as professional fronts for individuals from different agencies.

As part of our commitment to the project we undertook a series of gender trainings of development planners and practitioners, both government and non-government officials using the social relations framework. The latter involves an analysis of different rules and norms that structure gender power relations, the ways in which practices are shaped and resources allocated and the basis on which women and men are permitted entry into or excluded from participation and power in the institutions of the household, community, market and state.

An important element of the gender workshops has been the use of participatory processes, which have facilitated the sharing of both subjective and objective experiences, as well as given the space to address the personal dimensions of social change. These have led participants to shed their inhibitions and share the unconscious biases that have shaped their childhood. Personal narratives of events and incidents that have influenced their lives by virtue of their being women or men also created an understanding of systemic discrimination within society.

Gender sensitisation entails changing a series of gender regimes and addressing a whole range of complex factors that impinge upon social relations. The experience also revealed that gender training by itself without a broader base of support within an organisation has limited potential especially if gender aware perspectives are not part of prior processes by which core competencies within such organisations are acquired. In other words, unless gender training programmes become part of an integrated package, they are unlikely to change mindsets which have taken roots over several years of gender blind or biased processes (Rajagopal and Mathur, 2001). However, a major gap has been the inability to make a realistic assessment of change processes through training within bureaucratic institutions. This has led to a fair amount of stagnation and frustration.

Along with gender training programmes, using a gender lens became intrinsic in all our work related to education, violence and health and disaggregating poverty and gender. A gender perspective was also fed into all the other projects of the Institute related to natural resource management, economic and social policy issues and poverty. Alongside critiquing state policies and programmes from a gender perspective was part of the advocacy role. In March 2000, the State Policy for Women was announced by the Government of Rajasthan highlighting the critical areas for strategic interventions. While the policy combined a number of women in development approaches i.e. welfare, equality, anti-poverty and empowerment to a large extent it remained a women specific policy. It also remained silent on the role of men in initiating change and did not focus on the interconnecting relations between women and men (Rajagopal and Mathur, 2000).

However, our experience of mainstreaming gender indicates that there is significant policy pressure to create an environment for equality and social justice at the national and state level. There is also a clear advocacy for gender issues among civil society, donors and governments. But the phenomenon of 'policy evaporation' i.e. a tendency for policy commitment to gender equity to be lost, reinterpreted or heavily watered down in implementation is also visible (Standing, 2004). The operational confusion and lack of analytical clarity in mainstreaming gender at various levels continues. In many a case gender mainstreaming has simply been reduced to ensuring that women participate in a development agenda that has already been decided upon.

Influencing the Development Agenda: Challenges and Dilemmas

Taking stock of our work over a period of two decades is not easy, especially when the journey has been interspersed with major highs and lows. While there were phases of extreme excitement, euphoria and elation, there were also periods of frustration, anguish and disillusionment.

The WSU was one of the first Women's Studies Units to be set up in Rajasthan. Its location in an ICSSR supported social science research institute also indicated an acceptance of Women's Studies as an important area of inquiry. The ICSSR programme at that point in time emphasised the study of women belonging to the poorer and less visible section of society and stressed that the purpose of women's studies was to renew the debate on the women's question. It was therefore necessary to get information on existing condition of women and also to look into causes of discriminatory practices, attitudes and beliefs that impede women's contribution to development policies.

The early years saw a vibrant atmosphere in the unit. Seminars, discussions, conferences and meetings were an intrinsic part of academics and research was conducted amidst all these sets of activities. The emphasis was on networking with scholars and activists from different parts of the country and abroad which enabled us to gain insights into women's struggles and arrive at a common understanding of issues related to women's development and empowerment in a wider frame. The unit also provided space for interaction with students and researchers from other institutes. Networking with NGOs was central and their experiences informed our work and discourse on a sustained basis. Mobilising support around both the Deorala and the Bhateri incident and other such events gave further momentum to the unit's work.

However, our association with the Women's Studies Centre at the University of Rajasthan did not materialise into a long-term relationship. This was largely due to the fact that the Women's Studies Centre was ridden with its own set of problems: understaffed with lack of strong leadership and not having a central research agenda.

Collective work was a core value and all the members were oriented to teamwork though there was recognition for individual perspectives. This was seen as imperative for generating new knowledge on women's issues. Austerity was valued and there was an ethos of 'sharing'.

As time progressed several challenges and dilemmas were thrown up. Shared consciousness gave way to the question of individual pursuits and identities. The camaraderie experienced in the initial years gave way to breakdown in relationships and a feeling of mistrust. Probably this was inevitable and also a reflection of the external currents in the women's groups/movements.

By 1993, two colleagues had left the institute. A gap in leadership resulting from the retirement of the senior most colleague in WSU led to several changes. The struggle for gaining academic legitimacy in a research institute also proved to be a great challenge.

Gradually the action/research mode and partnerships with the women's movement reached low ebb. Group work and collective writing were accorded low priority. Increasing pressure for raising institutional grants led to undertaking research studies that were donor driven or state sponsored. The changing donor vocabulary and language of development has also influenced the research agenda.

Today an uneasy relationship between quantitative *vis-à-vis* qualitative research continues. Creating a gender sensitive value system and inculcating a feminist consciousness continues to be a challenging task.

Conclusion: The Road Ahead

Shifting the position of the poor, marginalised women from the margins to the centre by including their voices in planning processes and thereby altering the notion of development planning itself has guided our engagement with research and advocacy. Looking back, influencing the development agenda was and remains a central part of our work.

It is paradoxical that despite almost two and half decades of planning and innovative interventions, development indicators show that the position and condition of women in the state is vulnerable.

While some gender related development indices have improved in the last decade i.e. adult sex ratio and literacy, other indicators are not so encouraging.

- Rajasthan made considerable progress in improving its literacy status in the last decade. According to Census of India 2001, the overall literacy rate rose to 61.03 per cent as compared to 38.55 in 1991. Women's literacy more than doubled from 20.44 per cent in 1991 to 44.34 per cent in 2001. The cumulative gains of various innovative educational programmes like—the Women's Development Project (WDP), Shiksha Karmi Project (SKP), Lok Jumbish (LJ), District Primary Education Programme (DPEP) and Total Literacy Campaigns (TLC) have been widely recognised as contributing to this improvment.

The continuing dilemma *vis-à-vis* girls education is that education has not necessarily led them to question existing social norms, values and belief patterns. Women and girls continue to be seen in their roles as wives and mothers within their families and society. The struggle to strive for an educational system that can enable girls/ women to negotiate from a position of strength and which can lead to recognition of selfhood continues.

- The Census of India 2001 recorded the overall sex ratio in Rajasthan as 922 compared to 910 in 1991. Most of the districts in the state have shown an increasing trend from 1991 to 2001. However, the increase in overall sex ratio conceals a very high and significant decline in the sex ratio in the age group 0-6 years. The child sex ratio in the state was recorded as 909 in 2001 compared to 916 in 1991.

Practices of female infanticide, female foeticide and strong son preference in most communities are factors contributing to this imbalance. Modern technologies like amniocentesis are used for sex selective abortions and have exacerbated discrimination against the girl child. The above scenario is indicative of the low value and discrimination against the girl child in a state where patriarchal norms and practices continue to operate.

- Issues related to violence against women and girls have gained public articulation and increased visibility in the recent years. There is a strong movement to combat violence against women/girls. Organisations like Mahila Atyachar Virodhi Jan Andolan (MAVJA) and the setting up of Mahila Salah evam Suraksha Kendras in different districts have also helped to provide support to women survivors of violence.

Recent studies at IDS reveal that violence against women continues unabated and is manifested in more brutal forms than earlier. Trafficking of young girls from the state is a crucial area of concern. Several communities sanction sex work in Rajasthan, which makes women more vulnerable to trafficking. The subordination of women, along with the social construction of their sexual identities makes them more vulnerable to this form of exploitation. Ostracising women by naming/labeling them as *dakan/dayans* is common in the state. Other social practices like *kookri, nata, bemail vivah* (mismatched marriages) continue to add to women's vulnerabilities.

- Recent reports of the state government reveal that there is a decline in infant and maternal mortality rates as well as improvement in overall healthcare provision, which have led to improvement in women's health status.

However, ground realities continue to show that girls are often discriminated against in the distribution of food and nutrition. The low value accorded to women and girls and restrictions of mobility often results in poor access to healthcare services and a lack of information of reproductive health issues. The 'culture of silence' around reproductive health issues prevents them from accessing information related to their own bodies.

- The number of women at various levels in local governance has increased and there is a greater visibility of women in public forums, which have been dominated by men since long.

A serious gap confronting women in these institutions is the lack of support structures especially for women entering these structures for the first time. Institutions of local governance continue to be patriarchal in nature and in practice.

In the current context of the state a number of policy commitments to gender equality have been proclaimed. The setting up of the State Commission for Women, State Policy for Women, gender component in state programmes and projects and gender sensitisation of government officials are positive interventions. Gender budgeting exercises have also been initiated in the state. The next Human Development Report is to focus on women.

The relationship between women and development policy remains complex. It is hoped that our research will continue to engage with the complexities of the politics of gender on a sustained basis in the quest for a gender just society.

The ongoing quest for theoretical issues at the WSU include the more covert forms of gender-based violence, body politics and sexuality, redefining education and women's equality and women and voice. Some of the areas that need greater clarity and further exploration include reinterpretation of the institution of marriage and family, the notion of equality in a dynamic social context, use of 'power' by women and understanding the new forms of feminist analysis and practices as well as second generation issues and multiple sites in which gender relations operate.

References

Government of India (1986). *The Shikshakarmi Project*, Project Document, Department of Education, Ministry of Human Resource Development, New Delhi.

Government of Rajasthan (1984). *Women's Development Project*, Department of Rural Development and Panchayati Raj, Government of Rajasthan, Rajasthan.

Institute of Development Studies (IDS). (1984). *Workshop on Science and Technology for Women*, Jaipur.

———. (1986). *Exploring Possibilities: A Review of the Women's Development Programme*, Institute of Development Studies, Jaipur.

———. (1991). *WDP-Emerging Challenges*, Institute of Development Studies, Jaipur.

Jain, S. (1986). *On Doing Women Studies*, Institute of Development Studies, Jaipur.

Jain, S., N. Misra, and K. Srivastava (1987). "Deorala Episode: Women's Protest in Rajasthan", *Economic and Political Weekly*, Volume XXII, Number 45. November.

Srivastava, Kavita *et al.* (1988). "Rural Women Speak", *Seminar*, No. 242.

Mathur, K. (2004). *Countering Gender Violence: Initiatives Towards Collective Action in Rajasthan*, Sage, New Delhi.

———. (1999). "Emergence of Violence as an Issue in WDP of Rajasthan in Institutions, Relations and Outcomes", N. Kabeer and Ramya Subrahmanian (eds.), *Kali for Women*, New Delhi.

Rajagopal, S. (1999). "Closing the Gender Gap in Education in Institutions, Relations and Outcomes", N. Kabeer and Ramya Subrahmanian (eds.), *Kali for Women*, New Delhi.

Rajagopal, S. and K. Mathur (2000). "Women's Empowerment as State Benevolence", *Economic and Political Weekly*, Volume 33, Number XXXV, August 12-18.

———. (2001). "Gender, Organisations and Change: Lessons from Gender Training of Community-level Education Workers", in Ranjani K. Murthy (ed.), *Building Women's Capacities: Interventions in Gender Transformations*, Sage, New Delhi.

Standing, H. (2004). *"Gender, Myth and Fable: The Perils of Mainstreaming in Sector Bureaucracies", IDS Bulletin*, Volume 35, Number 4, October, pp.82-88.

11

NGOs and Academics

JYOTSANA RAJVANSHI

Background

Role of NGOs in accelerating the process of development has been rooted in a specific sociopolitical context and inspired by the emergence and continuity of social reforms, social changes and political movements. It is an established fact today that NGOs play a major role in the development of the society in addition to filling the gaps in service delivery system. In general terms, development implies structural changes fundamentally altering power relationships among the social classes. The overall objective and role of NGOs in development research have been to analyse the nature and functioning of present—local, national and international structures and to reveal how social forces might be instrumental in changing them. It includes the improvement of not only of material things, but also of human beings, particularly as much as the community is able to rise above the level of absolute poverty and also to fulfil basic needs. Community should be able to participate in decision making processes in all fields of life—socio-cultural, economic and political. Community should not be handicapped from participation in decision making and availing their rights by reasons of poverty, lower social status or a state of political marginalisation. Moreover, ideas of the role of NGOs in development have been changing over the years with the changing needs of the community from economic growth to growth with justice, participatory development, gender equality and equity, self-sustainability and adopting rights based agenda. The activities of development organisations i.e. government organisations (GO), business and self-help groups are also changing with the changed concept of development. The strategies of development oriented NGOs during its four to five generations have been visualised. The sequence of term during generations was relief and welfare, community development, sustainable system development, people's movement and peace building. The scope has been shifted from individual and family, to village, region or nation, national and global and community and global. The NGOs role in these generations has changed as doer, mobiliser, catalyst, activist and educator. The chief actors are also changing i.e. NGO, NGO plus community, relevant public and private institutions, networks of NGOs and people, NGO plus academicians plus researchers plus activists (GoI, 2002).

In the context of democratic decentralisation, civil society at the village level acquires three distinct functions *vis-à-vis* the state. It could act as an agency of the higher levels of government in implementing various development programmes, respond to the policies and programmes as they impinge at the local level, disseminate useful information and perform watch dog function and it can take proactive role (Vyas, 2000). The NGOs roles are useful in better outreach, cost efficient for delivery of programmes, community mobilisations for participatory approach and micro-planning, management and implementation of development programmes. NGOs role has also been recognised as they have intrinsic strength to be the main catalyst of social change and increasing participation of the community in decision making for their development. NGOs can be referred as social action groups. In the context of development NGO's activities and constructive work is the only development path in furthering progress of the nation and nation building.[1] Constructive work is basic and abiding activity. NGOs and Community Based Organisations is one of the five horses of the chariot for nation building in addition to the Central Government, the State Governments, the Panchayati Raj Institutions (PRIs) and the Private Sector.[2] NGOs mainly focus on *sangathan* (organisation), *sangharsh* (agitation) and *samrachna* (constructive work). In this way voluntary action, can be defined as *'Janshakti'* i.e. community's power.[3]

There are wide and diversified developmental research theories and strategies in various parts of world, nation and the state on role

1. One of the main teachings of Gandhiji.
2. Hon'ble Prime Minister Shri Atal Bihari Vajpayee during the All India Conference on the Role of the Voluntary Sector in National Development on 20th April, 2002.
3. Ibid.

of NGOs in development. NGOs in the present study have been considered as the organisations working with the community. At Institute, as a social sciences research and development institute, NGOs role has been viewed for a better understanding of the developmental processes, leading to better results in the field.

The chapter portrays the genesis and journey of NGO Centre of the Institute, the evolution and range of its operations, modalities of action, the constraints and challenges faced and consequences of involvement with NGOs, GOs and other agencies. The chapter explains the journey of NGO Centre from one step of growth to another, expansion of activities, etc. A brief review of the Institute history to find out the involvement of NGOs from its beginning and the key objective of NGOs resource centre reveals that the Institute mainly confined to social, economic, cultural and political issues and take up problems of research transcending social sciences with involvement of NGOs/VOs (voluntary organisations). For the last 23 years particular attention has been given to the study of processes, the impact of trickle down effects of growth with participatory efforts of VOs with respect to the marginalised sections of the society. It has provided a platform to NGOs, helped them build capacity, and undertook research and policy advocacy in the sector.

The Institute is a social sciences research institute. One of the key approach of the Institute is to generate knowledge on development processes through research studies and make timely interventions through dissemination of knowledge so generated. The studies cover macro initiatives and policy environment, development strategies, planning processes, their trickle down effects, direct government intervention and efforts of voluntary non-governmental organisations. The Institute's research efforts include theoretical analysis (in-built as well as explicit), applied studies (the output becoming input into policies, programmes or trainings) and adaptive studies (operational researches, training and sensitisation programmes). From its beginning the Institute maintained close contact with NGOs working towards socioeconomic development of Rajasthan. After few years of the foundation of the Institute the NGO Centre was established with a view to maintaining close contacts with NGOs and local organisations for pursuing a better understanding of development processes, to provide a forum for reasoned debate on issues concerning them and their dialogue with policy planners, experts and thinkers, as well as to strengthen and facilitate the development efforts of NGOs by way of training their personnel and information sharing. The specific activities pursued by the NGO Centre in this area include advocacy, skill development, networking and undertaking research studies related to voluntary initiatives and PRIs. To give adequate information to NGOs on vital aspects, researches are conducted and trainings are provided to NGOs on relevant issues. Researchers at NGO Centre took particular care to design and disseminate the studies in a manner to be used by those NGOs or social groups and social forces working for development. NGO Centre made critical assessments of what is being done in the field by the GO or NGO on the similar type of agenda or issue.

The Beginning

During early years of the foundation of the Institute (i.e. in 1982-1983) a seminar on the "Role of Voluntary Agencies in Development" was planned (IDSJ, 1983). During 1984-85, a shift was made in the objectives of IDSJ. One of the key objectives added was that the development research should attempt to identify those classes and groups excluded from, and discriminated against, by existing social institutions and trends. The Institute also recognised the role of VOs in 1984-85, in a project (Social Inputs in Area Development). During 1985-86, one of the objectives of the Institute was described as, "to monitor, evaluate and appraise development projects carried out by the governmental and non governmental agencies, with a particular references to Rajasthan" (IDS, 1985: 2). During these years gender cell of Institute did some work in association with NGOs in Rajasthan. Gender cell of the Institute was involved in *Mahila Mela* at Tilonia, for conceptualisation of the format of *mela*, discussion sessions on wages, employment, and legal issues as well as the analysis of empowerment process. Research support was given for writing the report on the wage study undertaken by SWRC Tilonia. During 1986-87, a study on condensed course for women, Rajasthan, was conducted by two faculty members which reflects a linkage with NGOs, in relation to their involvement in the Central Social Welfare Board scheme.

Participation of faculty of the Institute in other areas (other than gender cell) at or outside the Institute programmes on seminars, workshops, lectures, discussion and publications at or by IDSJ never focussed on NGOs or VOs till the year 1990. Very few efforts were made to identify the role of NGOs as an agenda of research. In 1987-1990 a major shift in the Institute's activities[4] was seen. Some relevant training programme for the first time were geared. The key areas for action emerged, i.e. the training of NGOs and policy related training. Besides strengthening these traditions an element of dynamism was added in all the activities of the Institute during 1990-1991.[5] The Institute decided that instead of organising training in routine or ad hoc manner, the groups of trainees should be clearly identified. Accordingly, two groups were identified for major concentration: the policy analysts and the NGOs. First of all in collaboration with FAO's Production Economics Services a workshop to develop training materials for a course on "Use of Micro Level Data for Macro Policy Formulation in Agriculture" was organised. Similarly a course on land relationship was specially designed for and offered to NGOs for providing adequate information on vital aspects of land legislation and implementation. In pursuing its central objective, namely a better understanding of the developmental processes, the Institute maintained close contact with NGOs working towards socioeconomic development of Rajasthan. This concept, until recently, has been selective both in terms of the voluntary agencies involved and the project (purpose) for which it was established.

To systematise interaction with the NGOs, a development dialogue with relevant public/on chosen developmental themes as an important part of its mandate as research and training was organised in January 1990. A representative group of voluntary agencies was invited in order to:

- elicit their voices on the concept of development; and
- explore the possibilities of a symbiotic relationship between academics and NGOs.

Among the questions addressed were: (i) What should be the basis of development? (ii) How has environment affected development

4. Prof. V.S. Vyas, Senior Advisor, Agriculture and Rural Development, The World Bank was invited by the Chairman of Institute to join as Director of the Institute.
5. M.M.K. Wali Chairman, Institute of Development Studies, Jaipur, 1991 noted this point.

process? (iii) What is the relationship between people and the voluntary agencies?

There was a great deal of self-evaluation and introspection by the voluntary agencies of their own work and their changing relationship with the people. Expectations from research institutions like the Institute of Development Studies, Jaipur were also discussed at length. On the latter, an expectation that was voiced by the participants was that IDSJ could provide both, forum for reasoned debate on issues of concern to NGOs and also undertake to make information on selected themes available to the NGOs. The themes to be chosen by the NGOs were expected to be those where lack of information constrained action. On the training side the efforts to concentrate on the 'under trained' sectors, particularly NGOs started showing results. The evidence for that is provided by the desire of numerous NGOs of Rajasthan to use IDSJ as a referral centre. NGO Training and Resource Centre was established in 1991-92. A programme on "NGOs Training through Information Exchange" was visualised by the then Director and two faculty members. This thought provided an opportunity to systematically consolidate and expand our knowledge base on micro-level situations, as well as participate in the theoretical debates on NGOs, the voluntary sector and their relationship with the government and funding organisations. It also evolved new concepts and modules of training and dissemination of information to the rural people. Consequently, a plan of activities was formed. Based on the experiences of the programme and other learning experiences IDSJ submitted a proposal to IDRC and Ford Foundation. Initially IDSJ was sanctioned grant for a period of three years for conducting training programmes and setting up a data bank. The NGO Centre was, entrusted with the objectives of, (i) training the NGO workers for empowering them, (ii) preparing a directory of NGOs in Rajasthan and (iii) acting as a resource centre for NGOs.

Subsequently, with the financial grants from Ford Foundation and IDRC, the Institute embarked on a series of programmes for conducting trainings, workshops, seminars etc. for NGOs, and setting up a data bank. The researchers at the NGO Centre are concerned with multidisciplinary key development issues. Based on the informed assessment an attempt is made to bridge the gap between ground realities or practices and macro initiatives. A distinguishing feature of the NGO Centre is to help design interventions for grassroot organisations that are concentratedly attempting to cope with the problems of deprivation in a specific area.

Sharing Platform and Policy Advocacy

One such theme suggested by the participants pertained to land relation. Consequently, a pilot training programme with NGOs for the understanding the technicalities of land legislation and administration was conducted. It was also a unique opportunity for the resource persons to learn about field-level realities and the genuine voluntary efforts towards change. The participants unanimously endorsed the concept of such training and made suggestions with regard to themes and conduct of future programmes.

The second training programme on "Land Relations" was organised in March 1992. The objective behind this second training programme was to initiate the creation of an information network amongst the NGOs, government officials and academicians working on land issues with the purpose of increasing understanding of laws and procedures. The outcome was the translation and transmission of these laws and procedures to the people affected by them and logically follow its demystification.

In the sequence of above given suggestions by NGOs, the next issue was on Forest Laws, "Forests: People's Access and Rights." Most of the NGOs working in the south eastern districts of Rajasthan discussed on policies and laws concerning forests at the national and state levels; and the related issues of the law and the concept of Joint Forest Management (JFM). Sub-group discussions on issues identified as concerns for future programmes—included the Aravalli Regeneration Project, national parks and sanctuaries, and traditional systems of forest management. The tone and content of the discussions during the workshop suggested that the experience that has been gained by the faculty in conducting such programmes has enabled fruitful interactions to take place. It was also agreed after an intensive discussion with NGOs that there should be some coordination at the regional level between NGOs working on similar issues.

Capacity Building and Policy Advocacy

With a view to sensitisation of the NGOs as also to develop course material for future NGOs, a seminar on the then current topic on "Theory and Practice of Secularism in India" was organised. NGOs, eminent academics and thinkers discussed: (i) Theory and Evaluation of Concept of Secularism, (ii) The Practice of Secularism, (iii) Communal Violence, and (iv) Foundations and Vision of Pluralism. Participant NGOs felt that they were now better informed about the macro issues involved in the politics of communalism and could now relate more meaningfully to the local level communal tensions.

It was the time that Government was contemplating amendments in the *panchayati raj* law in the wake of the constitutional amendment. The approach of the Institute has been to generate knowledge on development processes through research studies and make timely interventions through dissemination of knowledge. A series of training programmes on *panchayat raj* with a difference, with grass root activists, NGO representatives and ex-*panchayati raj* members of Rajasthan, to foster enthusiasm among them were organised. This subject was chosen not only because there was a demand from the NGOs but also because as Rajasthan State would be amending its *panchayati raj* law on the basis of the changes in the constitution and election would be held soon. The NGO Centre had a group of people who having a wealth of experience on this subject and therefore it was felt that suggestions could be given apart from providing a forum on this subject. The main objective of this training was to understand the concept of Democratic Decentralisation, important provision of the act and the vision that exists in the *panchayati raj* system, especially in the context of the 73rd constitutional amendment.[6] In order to have a holistic understanding of the issues concerned care was taken. Due to heterogeneity in experience and levels of formal education of the NGO participants, an attempt was made at working simultaneously with different methodologies.

Effort was also made to organise suitable materials for providing information, the participants to use in longer terms. As well as the participant NGOs were supported in-groups to develop programmes

6. This training had a 40 per cent participation of women, over 65 per cent of the total participants were from the village level, and more than one-fifth was ex-*panchayati raj* members which included women members.

to work in their villages. This process reflects the participatory technique used for providing information and also supporting implementation, as to how they would work on this subject at the village level. It left many with desire to know more, and finally it raised questions for NGO centre in terms of how it should rethink its role of providing ongoing support to the information needs of the participants. During the year the nomenclature of NGO centre was changed to NGO and Panchayati Raj Centre.

Similarly, a platform on 74th Constitutional Amendment and Urban Administration: Role of NGOs in Urban Administration besides other relevant issues of the act was provided to NGOs, elected representatives of the Urban Bodies, officers concerned with urban administration and development and faculty members of the institute.

Both these programmes had an encouraging response from the participants. The 73rd and 74th Constitutional Amendments being very important for the new pattern of *panchayati raj* (rural local bodies) and municipal administration (urban local bodies), these were lively discussions on the various aspects of *panchayati raj* and rural development and urban development and administration with definite conclusions and recommendations.

The Next Step

The NGO Centre was further strengthened by addition of an associate fellow, a research officer and an information officer in addition to NGO centre coordinator during 1996. The action also got academic and action support from institute's faculty and resources. Beginning with small faculty and sparse resources the NGO centre developed over a period of time. Because of strength of researchers a number of national and international agencies asked for collaboration research on issues of importance. These collaborative projects provided excellent opportunities to the faculty for interaction among scholars, policy makers, NGOs and community to generate research base and knowledge, since NGOs have always been seen by NGO centre as partners in development process.

Building Capacity of NGOs and Establishing their Interlinkage with Funders

A large number of NGOs were facing the problems on project

formulations and related issues for getting funds from funding agencies. The NGOs were taught and provided information and material on registration of the organisation (as society or trust); accounts and audit; income tax; foreign contributions regulation under Foreign Contribution Regulation Act (FCRA) and project formulation in the workshop held at IDSJ. Apart from these aspects the role and contribution of NGOs in development was discussed. The participants were informed that NGO centre is continuously in touch with the voluntary agencies in the state and having a continuous dialogue with the NGOs.[7] During these programmes the experts observed that NGOs have been actuated mainly by considerations of service to the society. There is no alternative to voluntary action, if we want development in real sense,[8] politics and constructive work should not be mixed.[9] Further, "Information is power in the modern age and dissemination of necessary knowledge and information to NGOs becomes very valuable."[10] NGOs should have frank and free discussions. The conditions for success of voluntary organisations depends on transparency of NGOs in their decisions and accounts and the necessity of good relations and mutual understanding between Government machinery and NGOs is necessary.[11] Moral values and transparency and democratic traditions in the working of NGOs should be maintained.[12] Such aspects gave a further direction to NGO centre for developing interlinkages with NGOs.

The NGOs and sponsoring organisations demanded to provide detailed, clear and unambiguous guidelines to enable NGOs to formulate viable projects. Various funding agencies and government representatives told about their specific needs for project formulation.

---

7. NGO Centre is lending support to them in a number of ways, such as, action research, information sharing, gender sensitivity, advocacy, support and capacity building, project formulation, institution building, support in innovations and various action programmes, networking and linkages, publications, etc.
8. I.S. Kavadia IAS, during the programme mentioned this.
9. Shri Shriram Gotewala former State Minister for LSG and Town Planning and presently Chairman, Jaipur Rural Health and Development Trust at IDSJ, 1996.
10. This was opined by Prof. V.S. Vyas, Director, IDSJ.
11. Shri L.C. Gupta, Retd. IAS and Coordinator NGO & PRI Centre, IDSJ, 1996.
12. Shri Ajay Mehta of Seva Mandir, Udaipur.

Regional Programmes: Sharing Information and Capacity Building

It was observed and also NGOs demanded organising separate workshops and training programmes for subjects like accounts, income tax and FCRA as also for organising regional level meeting of the NGOs, so that greater number of NGOs are able to participate and take advantage of information dissemination. Several regional meetings of NGOs were organised in collaboration with Government and NGOs in selected districts of Rajasthan. NGOs were informed about the setting up of Council for Advancement of People's Action & Rural Technology (CAPART) and other such type of regional offices and urged the NGO's to take advantage of their programmes/projects. Regional programmes reflected mutual understanding and goodwill between Government machinery and NGOs. The NGO representatives came out frankly with their problems and difficulties and suggestions. These regional level programmes provided a forum for NGOs in Rajasthan in resolving problems of importance to the state. The GO and NGO representatives appreciated this initiative from the Institute and suggested that there should be some committee at the District level to look after the NGOs and an open forum to share their experiences.

The NGO Centre has put into practice the empirical researches and participated actively in framing state policies, e.g. state child policy, health policy, water policy and others. This shows the importance of autonomous social sciences research institute operating at the state level.

The response of the NGOs has been very good all along. The level of participation in the programmes was sufficiently high. There were no problems in carrying out the activities. In fact there was always a demand from the NGOs to continue these Programme at regular intervals. Another important activity *viz.*, the evaluation and assessment form an essential part of every programme conducted by the NGO Centre at the Institute. The participating NGOs apart from giving out their assessment and evaluation of the programme were encouraged to give their suggestion for future courses/programmes.

NGO Sector Research

The study of NGOs in Rajasthan on their structure, operation and vision (1999) covering 450 NGOs brought out useful role of NGO and PRI Centre of the Institute. The study substantiated the higher level of credibility of the IDSJ through acceptance of its effective role both by the PRIs/NGOs and the State Government. The study revealed that the NGOs in Rajasthan have different origin, nature, size, functions and sources of funds. Their distribution across the geographical area is not uniform; some districts have a high density, while a few districts have a very small number of NGOs. The NGOs in Rajasthan are developing inter- linkages with other organisations and NGOs due to various reasons within the state and outside state also. In recent years the number of NGOs have risen very sharply and many factors have contributed to their emergence in large numbers. The study analyses the structure of NGOs in view of the different concepts, definitions, characteristics, pattern of funding and origin of NGOs. In the study, the duration of operation of NGOs has been linked with the problems of NGOs. Their future areas of operation have been analysed and linked with their ongoing activities to find out the modifications in the trend of NGOs. To assess the accountability and credibility of an NGO in the community an effort has been made in the study to find out their working system mainly through discussions with them.[13]

Another study on the assessment of NGOs in Rajasthan working with women and children was conducted. The assessment and observation report of project reveals that almost all the districts have more than 70 per cent NGOs with the objectives of welfare including that of education and health of women and children. Foreign agencies allotted various projects of health, education and empowerment of women to NGOs.

Operational area reflects that approximately 80 per cent NGOs are working only in rural areas, whereas 20 per cent carry out their activities in rural and urban areas both. Hence, more emphasis in future programmes was given to provide trainings to NGOs on specific issues based on rural problems. NGOs networking programmes based on mutual relationship were started for dissemination of information, exchange of technology, legal aspects, project preparation work on a 'give and take' basis.

13. The commonalties and differences in NGOs on the issues of age, objectives, profile, operational area, sources of funds, relationship with other organisations and problems and challenges have been spelled out.

Networking of NGOs on Nutrition and Health Issues

Besides this, faculty accumulated a useful corpus of information and knowledge about the nutrition and health status of women in Rajasthan. After a lot of discussions with GO and funding agency it was decided to establish a networking of NGOs for reducing malnutrition among women and children in rural Rajasthan. This also emerged during the experiences of other action research projects. The project was undertaken to prevent malnutrition through promotion of basic health care, feeding practices and community empowerment in prevailing socioeconomic conditions in 10 per cent villages of Bikaner district in Rajasthan in coordination with UNICEF Rajasthan. The basis for planning was situation analysis, needs assessment in a state level workshop and planning by NGOs through PRA in villages. Strategies were framed keeping in mind enriching the knowledge levels of the beneficiaries, NGOs and GOs regarding health and nutrition so as to bring changes in their practices. The programme was handed over to the community and district authorities after achieving the targets. This challenging initiative was taken to assess the feasibility of a blend of bottom-up and top-down approach in improving health and nutrition status of women and children in rural area. The results have shown a drastic change in nutrition and health indicators (status) of women and children in target group and nearby area also.

Documentation and Providing Information

Two compendia of schemes of different Government departments were prepared to provide information to NGOs and also GOs. For a greater involvement of voluntary organisation in the field of women and child rights a data base of NGOs in a format in the form of resource directory of NGOs has been prepared. Earlier in the year 1996, NGOs' information on relevant issues was collected and a directory was published containing information of 350 NGOs of different districts of Rajasthan. The directory proved to be database of NGOs information in brief. Subsequently it was updated in 1999. It contained of 452 NGOs working in different areas. Since then many more NGOs have entered the field during last five years. NGOs dealing specifically with programmes/services for women and children, NGO centre, with UNICEF support, compiled a Directory within a short period of time printed by UNICEF for instant use. A brief of funding organisations is also given in the resource directory for providing information to NGOs, etc. The information given in the directory can be used as a resource base to initiate a process of dialogue between the needy, community and helplines to share the issues with a view to reaching out to the needy women and children in the society.

Advocacy and Research Support on Child Rights

Several NGOs at Rajasthan are working for betterment of children with the support of various funding agencies especially UNICEF. NGO centre supported NGOs in this area, undertook researches on status of children and facilitated the implementation of child related activities. Capacity building of NGOs and sensitisation of representatives of allied departments has been done by NGO centre for practising child rights in reality. Networking of NGOs was made to share their experiences and faculty of NGO centre played role of leader of the group of "Children in Special Protection Measures" during formulation of state child policy. Advocacy initiative on child rights and gender issues were taken up with several NGOs to implement in their area. For the advocacy of child rights and sensitising Government and NGO representatives, a campaign on National Initiative for Child Protection sponsored by Ministry of Social Justice and Empowerment, Government of India, (MSJ&E, GoI) was initiated to ensure that every child has a childhood by translating rights into reality. A number of training programmes were conducted with NGOs to explore the strategies for putting this agenda into action.

Another programme based on translating child rights into action is CHILDLINE: Research Support and Monitoring. It is a partnership platform bringing together the MSJ&E, GoI, UNICEF, the Department of Telecommunications, street and community youth, non-profit organisations, academic institutions, the corporate sector and concerned individuals. For the purpose of providing services to children in distress, conducting outreach programmes, monitoring and research, the Institute of Development Studies has been identified as the nodal agency for Childline, Jaipur. It functions with a network of collaborative agencies and support agencies and the Social Welfare

Department, GoR. Childline 1098—a phone number that spells hope for millions of children across India—India's first 24-hour, toll free, emergency phone service for children in need of aid and assistance. In last five years Jaipur Childline has built its different identity at national, state and district level. NGO centre efforts are aimed at generating a deeper understanding of the rights and needs of children everywhere.

NGO Centre is always keen to extend support and provide social justice to the marginalised section through operational researches and social action. One such programme Juvenile Justice Care and Protection Act-2000 was taken into consideration intensively with deprived children, children in need of care and protection and in conflict with law. It was framed and operationalised with a network of NGOs, allied department and functionaries, media etc were also sensitised for making them child protectors.

Assessment and Evaluation Studies of NGOs

Topics of research and action research were taken up on availability of projects and funds for evaluation studies of education, health etc. One of the studies was to increase efficiency of NGOs working and advocacy on the issues of health to combat the problem of HIV/AIDS, the corrective and remedial measures for suitable changes and improvements in the strategies and activities. The project specific factors, strengths and weaknesses of NGOs and the factors responsible were identified to benefit the ultimate target group, NGOs and also GOs. The department appreciated the study, recommendations and assured for implementation of some recommendations. Another study on Concurrent Evaluation of Family Health Awareness Camps in Alwar District was conducted. Appropriate suggestions to improve the services of camps were given on the spot, to Medical Officers, Chief Medical Health Officers (CMHO) and at State level Officers.

Other Studies with Weaker Sections

The activities of the NGO and PRI Centre had taken special care of the weaker sections, such as members of the Schedule Caste/ Scheduled Tribes (SC/ST), Other Backward Classes (OBCs), minorities, people living in the slums and rural areas, tribal and desert areas, etc. Above all, programmes for women and adolescent girls received priority in the centre. The thrust has been on the NGOs, who serve the deprived people, deprived areas and less endowed and less empowered people in the state. A survey of traditional crafts to assess the nature and extent of microenterprises, to identify the factors responsible for their status and to suggest measures for improvement in their economic status was done. Itinerant and Training-cum-production, Module of training were framed and suggested to the concerned authorities. The role of NGOs and NGO Centre was recognised in the context of making the receiving system alive and preparing the neglected sectors of society to participate more actively in the process of social development and make fuller use of GO schemes.

From Need-based to Rights-based Approach

A shift from a needs-based approach to a rights-based approach was witnessed in the scenario of NGOs in Rajasthan. The NGOs stand up as a peer group with their own ideas for innovations and development strategies. Some of them have engaged in social movements and work towards realising the rights of the marginalised and strengthening democracy and citizenship. It is in this perspective that the NGO centre has undertaken to redefine its objectives and strategies for future action. Accordingly participation in rights based approach campaign has been done by some faculty members to support NGOs in Rajasthan. Mainly it has been done on the issues of right to food, right to education, right to employment etc. The linkage between rights and participation, practices and the approaches for powerful forces for change adopted by the NGOs have been understood and the faculty held discussions with social scientists, activists for a better approach.

NGOs in Rajasthan have played a major role in creating a discourse on economic, social and cultural rights when they realised the lack of political will on the part of the state to address the issues of the marginalised. People's Union for Civil Liberties (PUCL) played a significant role in initiating and promoting new discourse on civil liberties. Faculty on individual basis participated in the campaigns of PUCL at Jaipur, and in social audit, public hearing and *pad-yatras* organised by NGOs in Rajasthan. The movement for the right to transparent and accountable governance stressed the people's right to know and asserted the right of the people to participate in governance. The series of *Jan sunvais* (public hearing) and social audits, initiated by the MKSS in Rajasthan in 1994 is a well-known example of a process of mobilisation that combined rights based approach with people's participation.

Social Change and Development: Role of NGOs—A Study

Over the last decades NGOs have gained recognition and some NGOs have developed a high degree of depth and stability. Looking at the success and failure of an organisation, which depends on several important features, has been key focus of the study on "Self-Assessment and Institution Building Among NGOs". The organisational structure and role set within NGO has been emphasised as a cause of concern for the development of NGOs.

Constraints and Challenges

The constraints and challenges facing the NGO Centre can be classified into external and internal factors. Internal constraints are lack of resources: human and financial which restricted the task of the centre. NGO centre planned to produce booklets containing information about significant aspects of legislation and administrative procedures on relevant issues, in simplified language, for use by NGO grassroots workers and village people but could not prepare these booklets due to engagement in other projects of faculty and lack of resources. The external challenges are legal and administrial which were faced by the centre during implementation of action research and evaluation projects due to bureaucratic nature and internal organisational problems. The weak motivation and poor perception of NGOs work at community level is another constraint.

The challenges faced by the NGO Centre are relating to sustainability and the relevance of building civil society. The geographic distribution of NGOs shows a neglect and relative absence in rural areas. Regrettably, the action research studies at NGO Centre also show a limited involvement of local communities in the design, conceptualisation, planning, implementation, monitoring, evaluation phases of the programme/project cycle prepared by NGOs. There is weak involvement of staff in planning and decision making, and a lack of staff development strategies. NGOs still do not adequately monitor, learn, or share lessons from inside or outside their walls. NGOs have trouble in formulating good proposals, and most failed to develop plans and mechanisms for sustainability. The role of the community in project identification, implementation and maintenance was lacking. Whenever community and NGO workers were asked about these issues, they didn't show much knowledge, which affected the programme results.

The code of accountability for NGOs regarding their finance, data accuracy and decision making process is very much lacking. Some NGOs remain poor in documentation of their practices and experiences; sharing of lessons also is limited. As a result weaving these lessons into policy formulation and programming initiatives by NGOs has been limited.

Due to the commercialisation of NGOs where staff is used with commercial and not non-profit motives supposed to loose credibility and trust of community for NGOs (Estellt, 1997). Most of the NGOs are unclear about networking, coordination and cooperation practices. Knowledge about right to information, rights based agenda and social audit is lacking among NGOs. Lack of clear vision amongst some NGOs inevitably leads to confusion in roles and responsibility of an NGO in society. Information about various schemes is not proper to NGOs. The NGO staff was provided training on several relevant issues of related project. Exit of such trained staff is another major problem. Some NGOs had stopped functioning or changed their office address but they do not inform the concerned agencies.

Some NGOs have their main office in other states, their branch offices are operating at district level. The information about that NGO is lacking at such offices due to unavailability of full information at branch office.

Conclusion

If we look at the journey of NGO Centre activities, we find that during the early years of IDSJ, the NGOs were provided research support through documentation of activities and programme planning. The training of NGOs, community leaders etc. on identified issues was started after a few years. Simultaneously, the research findings were taken into consideration for planning of programmes, training and documentation with NGOs participation. Action research projects were taken as the next step at the centre. To put it in a nutshell, the IDSJ and the NGO Centre has played the following roles in relation to the NGOs, *viz.*

1. Providing a platform to the voluntary organisation/NGOs.
2. Helping them build capacity.
3. Researching the voluntary/NGO sector.
4. Undertaking policy advocacy for the sector.

During early years, a seminar on the "Role of Voluntary Agencies in Development" was planned but programmes with NGOs or VOs were not focussed till the year 1990. A Development Dialogue with relevant publics on chosen developmental themes as an important part of its mandate as research and training was organised. This thought provided an opportunity to systematically consolidate and expand our knowledge base on micro level situations, to bridge the gap between ground realities or practices and macro initiatives. Consequently, a plan of activities was formed. Based on the experiences of the programme and other learning experiences IDSJ submitted a proposal to IDRC and Ford Foundation. Initially IDSJ was sanctioned grant. After that for sharing platform for policy advocacy mainly on Land relations, forest policies, etc. NGOs were invited. Capacity building and policy advocacy was done during the programmes and had an encouraging response from the participants. The 73rd and 74th constitutional amendments being very important for the new pattern of *panchayati raj* (rural local bodies) and municipal administration (urban local bodies), these were lively discussions on the various aspects of Panchayati Raj and rural development and urban development and administration with definite conclusions and recommendations. Aspects like Building capacity of NGOs and establishing their interlinkage with funders gave a further direction to NGO Centre for developing interlinkages with NGOs. Regional programmes: sharing information and capacity building programmes provided a forum for NGOs in Rajasthan in resolving problems of importance to the State.

NGO Centre has put into practice the empirical researches and participated actively in framing of policy, for example state child policy, health policy, water policy and others. NGO sector research has been done as the NGOs in Rajasthan are developing inter- linkages with other organisations and NGOs due to various reasons within the state and outside state also. NGOs Networking programmes based on mutual relationship were started for dissemination of information, exchange of technology, legal aspects, project preparation work. Networking of NGOs on nutrition and health issues, a challenging initiative was taken to assess the feasibility of a blend of bottom-up and top-down approach in improving health and nutrition status of women and children in rural area. The results have shown a drastic change in nutrition and health indicators (status) of women and children in target group and nearby area also. Under Documentation and providing information two compendia of schemes of different Government departments, data base of NGOs in a format in the form of resource directories of NGOs has been prepared. Advocacy and research support on child rights has been done by networking of NGOs, a campaign on National Initiative for Child Protection and Child Line: Research Support and Monitoring. Programmes on Juvenile Justice Care and Protection Act-2000 were taken into consideration intensively with deprived children, children in need of care and protection and in conflict with law.

Assessment and evaluation studies of NGOs were conducted to increase efficiency of NGOs working and advocacy. A shift from a needs-based approach to a rights-based approach was witnessed in the scenario of NGOs in Rajasthan. The NGO centre has undertaken to redefine its objectives and strategies for future action mainly on the issues of right to food, right to education, right to health, right to employment, etc.

NGO Centre has been lending support for documentation, monitoring and providing research and technical support and also for ensuring effective networking and training of organisations associated with the allied system. Information is strength hence the laws related to the target group are also discussed with NGOs, Judicial and law experts. Such programmes were problems solving and enhancing knowledge base of beneficiaries and faculty also. The conceptual and theoretical debate was inbuilt in such type of programmes. The output of such studies and programmes had policy implications at immediate operative level as well as for long term formulation of development policies and their implementation. Immediate operative level was with allied departmental functionaries, committees, boards, judiciary etc.

Long term perspective was for extensive participation in formulation of various state policies with a full participation of NGOs and the field level experts.

The training programmes for NGOs and community has been conducted for last 23 years to disseminate information as well as to learn from the process of information sharing. Although the training programmes conducted were many times demand driven, the knowledge gained through different studies was applied to make the programmes informative and more useful to the participants.

The purpose of conducting such programmes is not only to provide a platform to initiate discussion/debate on development issues but also make attempt to resolve problems NGOs face both at conceptual and operational level while participating in the development programmes in rural areas. These types of programmes reflected better outreach to the unreached and better information and building synergy between research and training by incorporating learnings from research. NGO centre has kept the notion of sustainability in mind mostly in framing the programmes. The outcomes are:

- Sensitising the policy makers to the realities at the grassroots level.
- Constant interaction with NGOs/GOs/academics and PRIs.
- NGOs influencing the policies of the state for development of people.
- Useful publications and documentation of themes relevant to people.
- Better professionalism amongst NGO functionaries.
- Promotion of various organs helpful in having a civil society.

Consequently, we can analyse that NGO Centre's role at three different levels; micro policy, macro policy and norm setting. Assessment of the problem and approaching the community is micro policy, the larger campaign goal is macro policy and norm setting is persuading the public that are immoral and threat to real development of society. It can be concluded by the analysis and implementation of programme, NGOs are facing structural impediments caused by the hierarchical division of society, economic inequalities and gender social relations. GOs should set up open sharing forum and mechanisms at the state, district and block level for GOs and NGOs to have a dialogue for collaborating and other programmes to establish more synergy. To strengthen NGOs a lead NGO for each district or block is needed to promote and support smaller NGOs. The learning practices should have the dimensions as appropriate and supportive systems, organisational linkages and relationships, programme effectiveness. The staff should have the technical skills, knowledge, qualities and approaches to be more effective.

NGO's do not work in isolation. A collaborative autonomy between other development organisations and NGOs can lead to a social change. The mission to bridge the gap between micro realities and macro initiatives; reflecting the concern for the vulnerable sections, transparency and efforts for sharing with NGOs has provided a place of honour among the community of researchers as also among the users of its researches. As NGOs, individually and collectively, we need to constantly improve our work at the micro and macro levels, and strengthen the link between the two. The capacity building including trainings on specific issues and others is needed for NGOs.

The NGO Centre at IDSJ can look back with a sense of satisfaction with regard to its roles and consider itself poised for still deeper and wider involvement with the voluntary/NGO sector.

References

Dantwala, M.L, Harsh Sethi and Pravin Visaria (1998). *Social Change through Voluntary Action*, published by Sage Publication, New Delhi.

Estellt, James (1997). "Whither the Third Sector? Yesterday, Today and Tomorrow", *Voluntas* 8:1-10.

Government of India (GoI) (2002). *Report of the Streering Committee on Voluntary Sector for Tenth Five Year Plan 2002-2007*, Planning Commission, January.

Gulhati, Ravi, Kaval Gulhati, Ajay Mehra and Janaki Rajan (1995). *Strengthening Voluntary Action in India*, published by Konark Pvt. Ltd.

Institute of Development Studies (IDS) (1983). *Annual Report*, Institute of Development Studies, Jaipur, p.2

———. (1985). *Annual Report*, Institute of Development Studies, Jaipur, p.2

Planning Commission (2002). *Report of the Steering Committee on Voluntary Sector*, for the Tenth Five-year Plan (2002-07), Government of India, January.

Vyas, V.S. (2000). "Ensuring Food Security", *Economic and Political Weekly*, Vol. XXXV, No.50, December 9.

12

Rajasthan: A Mosaic of Culture

VARSHA JOSHI

Different scholars have defined culture in different ways. According to some scholars culture is a complex totality, which includes knowledge, belief, art, law, customs and all other abilities and habits which man acquires as a member of the society. Where as others say that culture is made up of a series of factors, objects and attitudes brought together during the passage of time that give it its specific features which form the basis for its values, objectives and out-look on the future. Rajasthan has many things to offer under the umbrella of culture; whether it is language, clothes, music, traditions, food, etc. As Lodrick says, "The desert, the dress of the people, are certainly elements of a specific environmental setting, cultural traditions and social structure have all played a significant role in shaping the character of modern Rajasthan" (Lodrick, 2001: 2). This paper confines itself to few cultural aspects of the Rajasthan, which are dying out due to various factors.

Rajasthan as a Region

In order to understand Rajasthan's social customs and traditions, we need to keep in mind some aspects of the history of the state. The *Rajputs*, among the most known warrior class of India, started emerging on the political scene of Rajasthan from the 7th century onwards and gradually acquired a distinct political identity. By the beginning of the 13th century, the *Rajputs* had created a network of states by both migration and invasion throughout present day Rajasthan. In order to expand their territories and gain military strength *Rajput* chiefs entered into matrimonial alliances with each other. Rajasthan also had two *Jat* states of Bharatpur and Dholpur and the Muslim principality of Tonk. *Rajput* chiefs up to 1947, thus, continuously ruled Rajasthan, almost entirely. The boundaries between individual princely states, however, continuously fluctuated until the 15th century, as the *Rajputs* constantly fought each other for the expansion of their territories for defense. In the two years following 1947, most of the princely states of erstwhile Rajputana merged into what became present day Rajasthan. With the end of these princely states certain sociopolitical and economic patterns also changed drastically, though certain traditions and deeply rooted attitudes carried forward. Though it needs to be emphasised here that: "*Rajput* culture is not the same thing as the culture of Rajasthan. The state is culturally variegated and *Rajput* traditions are only one element in a regional mix of cultures associated with castes and other groupings" (Babb, 2004: 16). Apart from the *Rajput*, Muslims and the *Jat* who were ruling in various parts of Rajasthan, the other important group we find in Rajasthan is the traders of the region.

Rajasthan can be divided into geographical regions not only by the physical features of the state, but also by various other features like dialect, cropping patterns, and style of clothing. The state had three major crop zones—*bajra, makki* and *jowar* (Millet, Maize and Sorghum). The food habits of the people in these zones depended on the crops grown in the area (Joshi, 2000: 4). Even in present times food continues to be an important determinant of not only the social status but is also instrumental in marking differences between cultures, serving to strengthen group identities. The livestock population also was in accordance with the agricultural pattern; in the desert there was sizeable sheep and goat population while in other regions cattle and buffaloes were/are found. Similarly, each caste had a distinct dress code and could be identified by it; whether it was the style of wearing turban or the colour and design of the *ghagras* (long skirts) worn by women. The motifs of the dress also were signs of identification of the castes. In Rajasthan, the yearly cycle of the people was also determined by the agriculture production cycle of the region. For instance, marriages took place once the harvesting was over. The festivals and fairs were also celebrated in accordance with the agricultural production cycle. The prominent crops grown in the *bajra* zone, which comprised of Marwar, Bikaner and Jaisalmer and

Shekhawati region, were *bajra* (millets), *moth* and *moong* (green pulses). The historical records also reveal that wheat was also grown in this region wherever irrigation facilities were available.[1] It is said for this region that though for food there is only *moth*, *matira* (watermelon), *bajari* (millet) and *khurat* (a thorny grass) yet the people of this region are healthy and strong—such is our Thar land (Chundawat, 1961: 115).

The contribution of *Rajputs* to Rajasthan's life extends beyond their political and social histories. *Rajput* courts were important centres for promotion of literature and the arts. The contribution of *Rajput* courts in the field of architecture cannot be undermined—whether they are forts, water reservoirs, gardens, temples, etc. In fact the castes, which were working in close knit with the *Rajput* households, adopted the lifestyles of their rulers. The best example is of the *Mussaddis* (*Oswals*) who adopted the *purdah* system and the architectural style of their *havelis* was also based on the *Rajput* architecture. The various accounts of the feudal lords whether in the form of *Bahis* or *Yadhasthas* reflect the continuity of traditions and normative structure at the level of values. It was through ceremonies, festivals and various rituals—coronation, birth, marriage, death or festivals like *Dushera, Teej* and *Gangaur*, the religio-politico-economic values of the Rajasthan feudal system were reinforced. Celebrations of festivals in the village provided occasions for inter-caste meets. For instance, if we take the example of *Holi*, a major spring festival, the entire village community joined the celebrations of *Holi*; the *Balai* fixed the central pole of holi fire, the *Brahmin* performed the worship, while the agricultural caste lit the holi fire, and the *dholi* beats the drum (Chauhan 1967: 104).

Western Rajasthan has had a tradition of collectively working on each other's farms at the time of ploughing of agricultural land, sowing, weeding, harvesting, etc. This collective work was called *lah*. There are different types of *lah*. The person on whose farm *lah* was done, provided three meals a day to all those involved in *lah*. Collective work was not only limited to agricultural work, it was done for animal work also, and was called *lav*.

---

1. The revenue rates of the state also determined the cropping pattern. For instance, wheat cultivation carried a higher rate of revenue to be paid compared to millets or small millets. Rich grew wheat and poor peasants grew inferior grains (*Nainsi Ki Khyat*).

In the village society, all occupational caste groups had an interdependent relationship with their patrons. According to Komal Kothari three terms were in use for the relationship between patron and those who provided them with services *viz., birat, ayat* and *jajmani*. When technical services are provided (as in case of Carpenter) it is either *birat* or *ayat*. *Birat* is hereditary while *ayat* is contract service. These two are barter, based on share of crop or some other economic benefit rather than cash. *Jajmani* on the other hand is used for non-physical services such as of musicians and priests (Kothari, 2001: 206). These relationships are hereditary and strict rules govern the relationship between the *jajman* and the *jachak*. The most important fact is that each caste not only has its importance in the society but also earns due respect from their *jajmans*. For example, the *damami* earned certain privileges and respect from their rulers. Similarly, the sweepers, lowest in hierarchy, also were given due respect by their patrons. A unique feature of Rajasthan has been that each occupational caste has three names—one, which is respectful, the second which is general and third which is demeaning. For instance, a leather worker would be respectfully addressed as *Meghwal*, the neutral term is *Bhambhi* and is despairingly referred as *Dhed*.

Composite Culture

The cultural openness of Rajasthan is revealed by the art, architecture, literature, costumes, ornaments, food habits, recreation and other modes of life of the people in general, and of the rulers in particular. Rajasthan has had a privilege of being secular in its traditions right from early medieval times. In fact, in Rajasthan there is a term that is used for secular traditions and is termed as *ganga-jamuni* culture. The best example of this tradition has been the *Kayamkhanis* of Shekhawati region. *Kayamkhanis*, though being converts, retained their original *gotras* and married outside their own *gotra*. Despite the fact that *Shekhawats* defeated *Kayamkhanis*, they gave them their due respect and made them stay in Shekhawati. They also gave *Kayamkhanis* responsible posts in the feudal set up.

The *Sufi* culture is another example of secular traditions of the state. The shrine of Hazrat Moinudin Hasan Chisti at Ajmer, which attracts devotees from all faiths, is one of the best illustrations. The *Medis* of Gogaji Chauhan (also known as Goga Pir) at Dadwera and

Gogameri are visited by both Hindu and Muslim devotees. The temple of Gogade Pir has a Muslim priest. During the medieval times we find that apart from the *Sufi* movement, Rajasthan also witnessed a social reform movement. These social reformers preached against existing caste and class hierarchies, superstitions, orthodoxies, religious tolerance and social evils. Baba Ramdeo, Dhanna, Jambhoji, Jasnathi, Harinath Niranjani, Laldas, Dauduyal (Chandra, 1992: 34-5), Rajjab, Mira, Charandas are some of the well-known social reformists. On the basis of the preaching of these saints it can be said that they popularised certain teachings which were not only relevant in the medieval context but also in the contemporary world. Both Hindus and Muslims visit the shrine of Baba Ramdeo (1352-1385). Similarly, Laldas Meo (16th century) was basically from Islam but his devotees are both Hindus and Muslims. His religious sect still exists and on specific days his devotees collect together and sing religious songs composed by him.

Bhairav was the local God for all castes and communities; usually Bhairav is worshipped on the outskirts of the village, as it is believed that Bhairav protects the village. Even members of Jain community used to worship Bhairav as a protector of the village. Bhairav has also been accepted in the Jain religion and Nakoda Bhairav is the best example of this. At Nakoda temple along with Shantinath, Bhairav is also worshipped and is visited by both the Hindu and Jain communities (Singh, 1994). The Jain temples have non-Jain priest. Similarly, at the time of the completion of a Jain temple and *Murti Sathpana* (installation of the idol) there are elaborate feasts, in which people of the entire village/town are invited. It is an occasion when a piece of cloth is tied on the tallest tree of the village, and all the villagers of the area who come under the visual contact of the cloth are invited for a collective feast. This ceremony was called *Phera Chunri* feast.

The tribal culture is also secular. The traditional *Bhil* culture is drawn towards Jainism. If a *Bhil* makes a promise at Rikhabdeo Kaishriyaji (Jain shrine), he would fulfil it. On the persuasion of Colonel C.K.M. Walter, the Mewar resident, about 400 representatives (*gametis*) of the *Bhils* in a meeting at Rikhabdeo agreed to stop torturing a woman suspected to be a *dakan* (witch) and in case such a crime is committed, by any one, the person has to surrender to justice. This agreement is engraved on *agat* (stone) shrine of Rikhabdeo (Vashishtha, 1997: 7).[2]

In the political arena too, we find that even though the *Rajputs* had ousted the tribes and acquired their land yet they did not completely oust the previous rulers. The Kachahawas of Amer defeated Minas and ousted them as rulers. But the Minas were appointed as guards of the royal treasury. Even the Maharna of Udaipur after defeating the *Bhils* made a compulsory tradition that the *raj tilak* of the Maharana would be first done by the *Bhil Sardar*. It is said that Doongarpur is named after the Doongar *Bhil* who was defeated and killed by Rawal Vir Singh who in order to please the wives of Doongar *Bhil* named Doongarpur after their husband's name.

Besides, irrespective of the caste and religious differences among the craft producers as well as their clientele, it posed no problems in their dealings with each other. For example, till today the sacred thread known as *Mauli* used at the time of religious rituals by the Hindus, is produced by Muslim dyers. Similarly, the symbol of *Suhag* of Hindus—the ivory bangles are made by Muslim *Chudigarhs*. The *Manganiyars*, who are *Sunni* Muslims, sing for Hindu families who are their *Jajmans*. Muslim *jogis* have sung oral epics called *Shivaji Ka Byyarla* and *Narsiji Ka Bhaat*. Interestingly, in Rajasthan there was a tradition that on the occasion of *Muhaaram* during the procession of *Tazia* young Hindu children and even adults go underneath the *Tazia* for blessings. This was considered good omen to protect themselves from bad evils.[3]

The examples of composite culture are also found in the literature and the language of the state. For example, *ajrakh* is one such word, which is used today for a form of block print in blue and red colour. *Ajrakkh* in Arabic means blue colour. This block print

---

2. A *Bhil* woman, generally old and haggard was castigated as a *dakan* (witch) who inflicts pain, disease or death upon human beings especially children or cattle. Usually a *Bhopa* did the declaration of a witch.

3. There is an interesting story linked to Rawala Tazia of Shahpura (Mewar). The ruler of Shahpura, Nahar Singhji was an ardent *Arya Samaji*. A group of *Arya Samajis* once approached him to ban the *puja* offered at the Palace temple, as well as the participation of Shahpura Rawala Tazia in the annual Moharrum procession. To this Nahar Singhji remarked that being an *Arya Samaji* was his personal matter. The state of Shahpura, however, was duty bound to participate in the beliefs and practices of its common people, and as such, no ruler could impose his own religious beliefs on the people (Chundawat and Hooja, 1994).

cloth was exported to Arab countries. Due to the blue colour it was called *Ajrakh* in those countries. In Rajasthan too, this particular style of printing began to be recognised by the same name. This particular style of printing, which is still prevalent, is done in Jaisalmer, Barmer, Kutch in Gujarat and Sindh (now in Pakistan).

Similarly, in some parts of north-west India, Greek coins were in circulation. These coins had a Greek female goddess by the name of Nana inscribed on one of the sides of the coin. Because of this particular coin, in Rajasthan coins were called *Nana*. A poet mentions that, *"jas rahey jasi thakara nana naha rahant"* (Thakur after death you leave behind your glory/fame not money (Singh, 1994: 2). *Nana* here means money.

Folk Oral Traditions

The oral tradition of the state is another interesting area of research, which is basically the life and blood of the commons. There were a number of institutional mechanisms, which ensured a regular flow of transmission of the oral traditions, customs, practices, and social and cultural norms. Unfortunately, these mechanisms of carrying forward have either broken down or weakened considerably. The rich oral traditions of the state encompass thought processes of a large section of society. It refers to value and meaning which people attribute to their social relationships. Though oral traditions may not be historically accurate but are mystified through relevant mediation of folklore and converted meaningfully into a purposeful discourse. It is people's wisdom, which incorporates the local socio-geographical and even economic situations. It is the repository of the wisdom of the common man, which is conveyed to people from generation to generation. Though it may differ from one area to another, yet on close study, some similarities will be found. The practice and production of these forms of oral tradition, however, has almost got paralysed now as its practitioners consider it non-remunerative and moreover, there is a loss of patrons of these forms of culture and traditions. The same applies to *Bat Sahitya* (folk stories).

If we look at the folk songs of Rajasthan we find that a number of styles of folk song singers has diminished considerably. For instance, the *Mand* style of singing today is on verge of extinction. This is mainly due to the fact that the *Damami* singers who used to sing this particular style were unable to transfer the knowledge to the younger generation. With end of feudalism the *Damami's* were facing economic hardships and the younger generation was shifting to other sources of income generation that did not acquire the hereditary skills. Interestingly, after feudalism ended most of the artisans survived on *Lata,* or *Kuta* or *khadka,* which the cultivators used to give to them but this also did not last long. Similarly, *Mushak* singers of Mewat have also virtually extinguished.

Folk songs were largely creations of women. The songs were created on and for different occasions and very often they were spontaneous reaction on a particular occasion or a setting. Marriage songs and songs on other occasions like *lori, bidai, jawai, kaman, gangaur, teej,* etc. were all composed by and sung by women. Women in spite being uneducated were worldly wise. They had immense knowledge about the *puranic* traditions, climatic conditions, historical events etc. Unfortunately a big cultural heritage, which has not been recorded and preserved, is of *Samuhik gana* (collective singing). *Bhanat* is another form of collective singing done at the time of *lah*. There are religious, historical, social and reformist songs (*Amalido* is one example of this kind), which were sung, in a particular style.

Interestingly, in Rajasthan there exists a feudalistic style (*rajwari geet*), rural or common people and tribal form of singing and dancing. Folk songs were composed on different situations and festivals as well as reaction to any political situation. For instance, in 19th century Maharaja Ram Singh II concluded a treaty with the British on salt. A rumour was spread in Jaipur State that salt will now become very expensive and will not be readily available in the market. As reaction to this women composed a song:

Mahraey to raja bhola ey
Sambhar to deney angreja ney
Mahara tabra mangey ey
Roti tikhi loon kee

(Our ruler is so innocent that he has given away Sambhar to the British
Our children are demanding *chapattis* made of bitter salt).

There is a famous folk song, which acknowledges the gesture of a ruler as protector of women. This song is sung in praise of a ruler who saved women from abductors. In the spring of 1492 A.D., soldiers from the army of neighbouring Nagore abducted 140 maidens from their village near Mertia. The ruler of Marwar, Rao Satal, was immediately informed and he promptly set out to rescue the girls despite a *Rajput* tradition of not engaging in battle after sunset. In the ensuing battle, Satal killed the commander-in-chief of the Nagore army, Gudhla Khan and beheaded him. The pierced and slashed head was then carried as a triumphal trophy by the rescued maidens who marched it through their village as a symbol of their untarnished honour. Rao Satal himself died that night of the wounds received in the battle. It is in commemoration of the event that an annual festival is still held in Marwar during the month of March (the exact date being decided according to the lunar calendar). At sunset, on the appointed day, young married girls make their way to the local potter's home to get earthen pot, which is riddled with holes. The girls place an oil lamp in the *matka* (earthen pot) and the procession wends its way through the streets with the pot held high midst a chanting of a folk song *Gudhla Ghoomelaji* (*gudhla* will spin). After sunset the pot is taken to the nearest lake and gently cast away. The riddled pot symbolises the head of Gudhla Khan, and the festival acknowledges the long-dead king (Satal) who lost his life in the protection of his subjects (in this case 140 virgins).[4]

Similarly, songs also depict the social relationships within family. For instance, in a folk song a sister says that on the occasion of *Holi* when she visits her brother's house, the brother would get *lapsi* (sweet porridge made of wheat and jaggerry) made for her, whereas the sister-in-law (brother's wife) will make her a *bajra-ka kichda* (porridge made of millets).

holi ka din char, bai ey
begi ajaey pavani
mahoro beer randhevey bai key lapsi
mahari bhawaj bajario ko kheech raey.

Folk Dances

The feudal dancing was more sophisticated in its form than the rural and tribal forms. This could be attributed to the forms of *purdah*

4. Interview with Rani Laxami Kumari Chundawat, dated October 20, 1994.

imposed on the feudal women. Similar differentiation was present in the singing style also. The tribals did not believe in seclusion of women, both men and women danced together. In fact among the Garasia tribals, 400-500 men and women dance together on the same rhythm. The actions of folk dances performed by the common women were largely based on the daily household chores they performed. The best example is that of *Tera Tali* which has all the actions that a woman does in daily household work like churning the butter, etc.

Folk Proverbs

Local proverbs (*kahavatey*) are another powerful mode of expression. This was a reflection of the local wisdom of the people. These proverbs throw light not only on the social systems but also on the agrarian and geographical, caste relationships, political conditions etc. Each region of the state had its own proverbs reflecting on the local context. For instance, if we look at the proverbs related to agriculture they throw light on the condition of rain, appropriate sowing time, what particular things should be looked at while purchasing of animal, etc.

Akha teej ke dina, guru rohini sanjot
Sahdeo joshi khawat haey, nipjey mal bhot! (Joshi 1979: 152).

(If on *Akha teej* day *Rohini* and Thursday are together then the crop would be immense i.e. there will be good rainfall).

Ashad poonam dina, nirmal ugaey chand
Koeye sindh koeye malwey jayaen katsee fhand (Joshi, 1979: 152).

(If on a *Ashad* full moon day (falls in the months of June/July) the moon rises, it is the sign of famine, than people will have to migrate to Sindh or Malwa).

Kartik thehra, teen Ashad! (Joshi, 1979: 153).

(In the month of *Kartik* (November) sowing should be done on the 13th day of the lunar calendar, in *Ashad* (June/July) it should be done on the *teej* (third day).

Similarly, on the climatic condition of the state it is said:

Jin bhuayen panng pivana, kair kantala runkh
Akae fhogey chajadi, dhdha bhagee bhukh (Chundawat, 2002: 59).

(This is a land which has snake which bite you while sleeping, where you have thorny bushes of *kair* (Capparis Decidua), and trees like *akh* (Calotropis Procera) and *Phog* (Calligonum Polygonoides) provide shade and *chappattis* made of grass seeds end your hunger).

Even in the *Dhola Maru* narration, number of couplets mention about the scarcity of water and hardships faced by women in Rajasthan.

Balu, Dhola, desad, jeuen pani kuveyen
Kum kum varna hathada, nahi sun dhada jayen!

(Hey *Dhola* burn such a place/country where you have to fetch water from the wells located at distance, Where tender soft hands find it difficult to take water out from the wells).

Similarly, there are numerous proverbs, which throw light on the caste relationships, food habits and various other political and social aspects of the society.

Folk Theatre

Rajasthan has had a culture of folk theatre for a long period. The first written plays known as *khayals* have been identified as early as 18th century. The three main popular *khayals* are *Kuchamani* of Nagore district, *Shekhawati* of Chirawa and *Ali Bakshi* of Alwar district. The *Shekhawati Khayal* is performed by the *Mirasis* who are basically classical singers and therefore this particular *khayal* has intricate singing. Being *Ranas* they used to sing for the Shakar Pir Baba at Narwar. *Kuchaman Khayal* is more of a folk theatre and the plays are based either on religion or historical events, for example, Amar Singh Rathore, Durgadas, Goga Pir and Jagdev Kankali. Ali Bakshi was a convert *Chauhan*. He was a *Nawab* of Mandawar in Alwar district. This *Khayal* is based on *Krishna Bhakti* and he used to sing devotional songs in particular style. Unfortunately, this art died with Ali Bakshi himself. Though after his death very few members of the group performed it, there is now no one who could sing this form.

Crafts

Rajasthan has a rich tradition of handicrafts. Tie and dye, block printing, wood crafts, blue pottery, pottery, stone work, embroidery, weaving and jewellery making etc. are some of the leading crafts of

Rajasthan for centuries. References to artisans and the craft practiced by them are found in the epigraphs, sculptures, documents and the rich oral tradition of the region. The East India Company records also refer to the textiles printing of Rajasthan.

Each craft was practiced by a particular caste. Within a caste, because of the skill being imparted on a hereditary basis, some families were able to develop the skill to the level of art and become master craftsmen. Some skills were practiced by more than one caste, like weaving was done by *julahas, balahi-bunker* as well as *kolis*. Within the same occupational caste also there was differentiation on the basis of specialisation. Such as the carpenters were known as *Suthars* and *Khatis,* each practicing a different branch of woodwork.

In Rajasthan, the craftsmen were not only involved in production but enjoyed a special place in the society. Their craft endowed them a place in the rituals and ceremonies performed even in the elite households. For instance, a *Maniharan* (bangle maker) was invited to put on the *suhag ka chura* to the newly wed and give blessings to the new bride in the *Rajput* households.

Indian artisans have been considered to be independent commodity producers with the artisan's family acting as a unit of production. As a result women and children also actively participated in the process of production. Thus, the classical concept of village community was in existence in Rajasthan. The artisan family was the unit of production except when the artisan was hired by some agency for a specified job. Within this broad framework there were two categories of the artisans: (i) artisans living in a village, supplied goods and services to the village clientele on a customary basis in lieu of which they received the share of village produce. With passage of time these customary ties got crystallised as *jajmani* system as understood in the context of Maharashtra, and (ii) Some craftsmen were engaged by the state and the elite to work in their *kharkhanas,* set up to meet their conspicuous demand (Sethia, 2003: 251). They received daily allowance as wage. However, some of the highly skilled artisans were engaged by the state and the *thikanas* on a permanent basis and were given land grants and extended various privileges as patronage. Consequently, they came to enjoy a higher status within their own caste members who were providing services to the village community. A common thread in the two categories is that artisans had a dependency relationship with promoters of crafts. According to Bhadani, craft production for the market seems to have been largely organised in two forms; first as domestic industry in varying degrees of association with agriculture; and, secondly, as full-fledged autonomous production mainly in towns" (Bhadani, 1999: 360). The historical evidence clearly indicates that members of the craft community also continued agriculture with their own caste occupations.

Since demand for craft was governed primarily by the local needs, each area had its special designs and patterns reflecting the local specific requirements. Local customs, festivals and rituals governed these requirements. Several folk songs and proverbs portray the demand for the various goods produced by the artisans. This phenomenon can be observed very clearly in the case of different types of head gears (*phagh-phenta*), *saris, odhanas, lahengas* dyed and printed for different occasions. Similarly, designs and patterns were made differently for specific castes.

Thus, it is clear that the demand for the various items was created primarily by the community patronage extended to the local artisans. Therefore, the local demand was stable and regular while the external demand was incidental and fluctuating.

The tools and raw materials used by the artisans were simple, locally manufactured and owned by them. Most of the cloth used by the dyers and printers was produced locally. The natural dye products such as indigo, *al, kasumal,* etc. were locally produced. In some cases the *neelgars* and *rangrez* were engaged in cultivation and processing of indigo and *al*. Use of locally produced raw material enabled the artisans to carry on production in spite of slow means of transport.

Although, craft production was widespread and not confined to a few centres, by the 17th century certain towns in Rajasthan had become well known for a particular style of craft. For instance, the Sanganer was known for its *bhandej* (tie and dye) and block printing. There are references to its product being sent to the wider markets.

Contribution of Women to *Rajasthani* Culture

Women in Rajasthan have held a peculiar position in the society. If on one hand, the birth of a girl child goes uncelebrated, on the other hand, they are deified also. Being a feudalistic society with restrictions imposed upon them, women in this society have had to live in specified cultural norms. Acts which are today recognised as acts of violence e.g. *Sati, Jauhar, Purdah* and child marriage were the norms of medieval society, which women of that time were conditioned from childhood onwards to believe as being the established behavioural norms of practice and not as acts of gender violence.

The overt forms of violence prevalent in the different sections of the society ranged from abduction to selling of females and rape. Unfortunately much less importance has been given to record the history of ordinary people, due to which we do not find recorded instances easily. The *thikana* records for this purpose have been found very useful as they show that the instances of violence were not only reported in the *thikanas* but the state authority intervened to solve the cases. On the study of Bedla, Mandalgarh and Karera papers of Mewar (Joshi, undated), it was found that large number of cases of rape (interestingly such cases were termed as *cham chori* in Mewar district), abduction, breaking of engagements from the boy's side and selling of females were reported from various castes and tribes like the *Dholi, Bhangi, Teli, Meena, Soni,* etc. (*ibid.*). For instance, *Parwana* issued from Bedla *thikana* to Shah Sadalal Lodha of Gangrar in the year 1874 indicates that a *Bhangi* from Kapasan had reported that a *Bhangi* from Gangrar has abducted his wife. There are records of Maharana Mewar, which throw light on the strict actions taken by the state against violence against women. In the year 1854, Maharana Mewar had taken out an order for all the *Thikanas* (fiefdom), *Khalsa* villages, *Patels* and *Patwaris* that, "if any body is found abusing a woman as a *dakan* (witch) and being violent towards her, will be imprisoned for five months and will be considered as murderers. Even those *Bhopas* will be punished who identify a woman as *dakan*. Those *Thakurs* and *Kamdars* who do not inform the Maharana about such untoward and insulting event will also be punished. The orders should be followed strictly (Joshi, undated (a))."[5]

---

5. Whereas in Kota region cases have been found in 18th century where *dakans* were handed over to the state. The state used to penalise these *dakans* (see Sethia, 2003 and Tod, 1914).

Similarly, there are innumerable examples of breaking of engagements from the boy's side. There has been a major lacuna of information regarding the reasons for breaking engagements, as they have not been recorded. However, a few records do mention that due to migration of the boy's family during famine, they did not keep in touch with the bride's family.

Here, it will not be out of place to mention that in cases of severe famine or if a child was orphaned, the female child was left outside the main gates of the local chief's fort. The community had the confidence that the abandoned child would be taken inside the fort, cared for and brought up within the fort. By this act the parents and relatives of the female child would absolve themselves from the sin of killing a girl child.

In spite of living a secluded life women kept in touch with a wider public through their cultural activities. The *Zenanas* of *Rajput* ruling houses were not only political arenas; they were also cultural arenas. Literature was one area where *Rajput* women have contributed. Some of the queens have written volumes of religious texts (Joshi, 1994: 128-29). Apart from keen interest in literary activities, *Rajput* women also manifested an interest in religious foundations of various kinds. They had built them from their personal funds which was called *hath kharch ki jagir*. It was just not temples, which they had built, but also artificial lakes and *bavdis* (water reservoirs), which were used by the entire village. Such constructions were not just limited to the *Rajput* women only, women from other caste groups also got temples, water reservoirs (*bavdis*), wells and gardens constructed (Singh, 1998: 158).

The royal households were also patrons of music and dance and even though this was for their own personal entertainment; it gave rise to court music. The bigger states had their *patar khana, akharas* or *gunjan khanas*. They also patronised fine arts. For example, the Sisodia *Maharani* of *Maharaja* Anup Singh of Bikaner during 1698-1700 is known to have patronised her painting atelier (Joshi, 1994: 130). This was certainly one of the ways by which these women came out from private to public sphere.

Another major contribution of women to the folk culture of the state is the *Mandanas*, the folk art. They were not only well versed with the motifs and designs but also knew that on what occasion or festival which design needs to be drawn. The women also transfered this art from generation to generation. In fact from the designs and motifs of the *Mandana*, one is able to identify that to which region the daughter-in-law of the house belongs; Each region had certain local specific designs.

Folk songs, dances, folk art and even *Rajasthani* cuisine, which is a major contribution of women to the cultural heritage of the state, was also one of the ways of forms by which women living in seclusion were able to express their feelings. Here it will not be out of place to mention the contribution of Mira to the reformist and religious movement of the medieval Rajasthan. In order to understand Mira's life it is necessary to look at the notion of an ideal woman in a Rajput society. An ideal Rajput woman is one who accepts the decision of the family regarding her marriage. After marriage she is devoted towards her husband (*pativrata*) and his family, who follows the patriarchal norms of the society and lives in feudal set up and performs *sati* on the death of her husband. She thereby shoulders the responsibility of maintaining and upholding the honour of both the natal and conjugal family (See, Jain & Sharma, 2002: 4648). Along with it follows the restriction imposed on her mobility and seclusion in purdah. Her indifference towards her husband and passion for Krishna is seen and understood as adulterous by her marital family, especially by her brother-in-law and father-in-law. Mira ignores the claims of *suhag*. She designates *jag suhag*—a marriage with a mortal as *Mithya*—as 'useless' and illusionary. The rejection of marriage, alongside the honour of the family, of clan (*kul*), and the bonds of kinship, is in effect a rejection not only of their educative and organising functions, but also of the whole social order within which they are enmeshed. Further, the break with domesticity is a rejection of the primary domain where sexuality is customarily regulated. Mira's claim is substantive when she says:

Sati no hosya giradhar gassiya, Mahara man mohe ghannami
Jeth bahu ko nato na ranaji, her sevak they swaami

Giridhar kant, Girdhar dhani mahaaree, Maat, pita boi bhai
Thaey thaare man mahaare Ranaji, yon kahey Mirabai.

Though Mira's mendicancy breaks the mandatory seclusion of the upper caste *Rajput* widows (*Ab kahe ki laaj saajn, pargat ho naachi*), like many other renouncers, she breaks with 'outer', 'ephemeral' social systems of kinship and political power only to join the community in another capacity—as critic and commentator. She clearly rejects the caste system and its notion of pollution by accepting Raidas who was a *chamar* (leather worker) as her religious *guru* (teacher). The degree of `real' choice available to Mira is still unclear—whether she rejected the court or was she pushed out? The songs sometimes present Mira's choice of Krishna as a product of her own will. In one of the songs, she resists the persuasion of her brother-in-law to give up wandering in the company of saints: it destroys the honour of the family (*kul ko daag lagai chai bhahhi ninda ho rahi bharey*), a women from such a family demeans it by dancing in public (*Bada ghar thaey janam biyo chai nachio de de taari*), so she must return to the palace, and to her ornaments, etc. She refuses to do so and says that *sadhus* and *sants* are her family.

Mira may have chosen to break the feudal relation. She may have been forced to break with it or she may even have felt herself broken by it. Yet, if the feudal relation crumbles in her personal practice, in some ways her songs recover it both figuratively and as idealist and as recompose it's ever–present 'necessity' as choice. It is because of this that Mira for a very long time was not accepted in her conjugal clan and was considered dishonour for Mewar. It is for this reason that Mira was not accepted within her community. Even Tod in his famous Annals and Antiquities mentions of Mira in a very indifferent manner "Meera *Baee* was the most celebrated princess of her time for beauty and romantic piety" (Tod, 1914: 232). Lindsey Harlan in her work on religion and *Rajput* women has shown that within the *Rajput* women Mira is accepted as a *'bhakt'* and not a *pativrata* (Harlan, 1992). Though some women interviewed by Harlan admire Mira as a courageous women for "Mira had to be brave, they say, in order to withstand social criticism and cruelty from her husband's household." On the other hand, some women believe that, "Mira's courage allowed her to see God, just as Padmini's courage allowed her to liberate her husband (Ibid)."

Among the other castes also, Mira is accepted as a devotee of Krishna rather than as a woman who gave up the structured patriarchal social norms. All her writings are seen and sung from a devotional aspect. Her criticism of the existing social norms is neutralised and her devotion towards Krishna is what is extremely significant. This is acceptance of her devotion and silence on her reformist attitude is primarily because of the belief of the people in conventionally laid down norms for women.

Culture and Tourism

Rajasthan has had a rich culture of fairs and festivals and also dance and music. The royal courts have played a major role in patronising the cultural traditions of the state. Some of the festivals were confined to the State *Durbars* (royal courts) only but certain festivals have been celebrated with the community. The best example is the *Ganguar* and *Teej* festivals, which are basically women's festivals. Interestingly, festivals like *Dusherra*, which were basically court festivals were political in nature have now become oblivion. The festivals of *Teej* and *Gangaur*, which were celebrated with larger community, are still being celebrated in the same tradition. These in fact have now become State festivals where they are made tourist attractions. The other important feature in this context is the heritage hotels. This shift from castle to heritage, apart from commercial incentive, has helped the families to preserve and maintain the familial property. These properties might well be lost, constitute a major element of the historical, architectural and cultural inheritance of Rajasthan (Taft, 2003: 133).

Along with some good acts of preservation of cultural heritage certain negative impacts are also coming to force. It is at this juncture when one finds that combining tourism with culture can be at times dangerous. Since culture at the hands of tourism becomes a commodity for sale and thus tends to be distorted to meet the demands of tourists. The folk artists are at time presented in a very poor manner. The traditional songs and dances have become tourist oriented. The Haksar Committee has mentioned in its report that, "manifestations of folk art and culture must not be considered as museum exhibits for satisfying exotic interests. Their subordination to the laws of commercial 'mass culture' is a threat against which it is necessary to provide an institutional protection and support." (GoR, unpublished: 152).

Conclusions

Rajasthan has a rich cultural tradition. Despite many variations within the region, a common identity has continued to evolve due to historical circumstances. This further emphasises the need for the developmental interventions to recognise the existing continued culture and traditions of the society and the state at large. Historically speaking the Rajasthan's culture and society had two levels, the elite and the popular. The unique feature of these two levels of culture was complimenting each other, commonalties and variations. The *Rajput* polity also played a vital role in maintaining the balance between different cultural levels of the region.

With modernisation, the society has not been able to preserve our cultural heritage—whether it is architecture, folk art, literature, etc. With the onslaught of external influences, the people are culturally today not strong enough to withstand the invasion of foreign cultures and fall an easy prey to them. The state needs to give a serious consideration to having a cultural policy instead of simply commercialising it for tourism purposes. Culture certainly cannot be taken as mere entertainment form. It is an integral part of the society and must be used as a tool for social changes. There is a need to recognise and to own our rich cultural heritage. The state should emphasise on preservation of popular culture through museums and cultural centres located in each zone. The museums should reflect on the day-to-day life of the people of the state—whether it is social institutions, craft, etc. The cultural policy needs to emphasis on dissemination, documentation and preservation.

The author would like to thank Dr. Pratibha Jain, Ranbir Sinh, Rani Laxami Kumari Chundawat and Dr. Madhu Sethia for their comments on the initial draft of the chapter.

References

Babb, L.A. (2004). *Alchemies of Violence: Myths of Identity and the Life of Trade in Western India*, Sage Publications, New Delhi.

Bhadani, B.L. (1999). *Peasants, Artisans and Entrepeneurs*, Rawat Publications, Jaipur.

Bhati, N.S. (ed.) (1974). *Nansi Ki Khyat*, Rajasthan Shodh Santhan, Jodhpur.

Chandra, Savitri (1992). "Akbars' Concept of Sulha Kul, Tulsi's Concept of Maryada and Dadus Concept of Nirpekh: A Comparative Study" in *Social Scientist*, Vol. 20, No.9-10, September-October.

Chauhan, B.R. (1967). *A Rajasthan Village*, Vikas Publishing House, New Delhi.

Chundawat, Rani L.K. (ed.)(1961). *Rajasthani Doha Sangrah*, Rajasthan Sanskrit Parisad, Jaipur.

———. (2002). *Rajasthani Doha Sangrha*, Jagdish Singh Gehlot Shodh Sansthan, Jodhpur.

Chundawat, Rani L.K. and R. Hooja (1994). "A Co-mingling of Communities and Cultures: Anecdotes and Traditions of Rajputana", Paper presented at the Seminar on *Composite Culture of Rajasthan*, Institute of Rajasthan Studies, Jaipur.

Harlan, Lindsey (1992). *Religion and Rajput Women: The Ethnic of Protection in Contemporary Narratives*, University of California, Berkley.

Govt. of Rajasthan (unpublished). *Haksar Committee Report*.

Jain, Pratibha and S. Sharma (2002). "Honour, Gender and the Legend of Meera Bai", *Economic and Political Weekely*, Vol. XXXVII No. 46.

Joshi, Laxamilal (1979). *Mewar ki Kahavatey*, Krishna Brothers, Ajmer.

Joshi, Rajendra (undated(a)). *Vigat*, No. 14, Document 112: 56, University of Rajasthan, Jaipur.

———. (undated). *Vigat*, Nos. 15, 16, 17, 18 & 19, University of Rajasthan, Jaipur.

Joshi, Varsha (1994). *Polygamy and Purdah among the Rajput Ruling Houses*, Rawat Publications, Jaipur.

———. (2000). *Changing Food Habits in Rajasthan*, IDS, Jaipur.

Kothari, Komal (2001). "Musicians for the People", in Karine Schomer *et al.*, *The Idea of Rajasthan*, Vol.1, Manhohar Publications, New Delhi.

Lodrick, Deryck O. (2001). "Rajasthan as a Region" in Karine Schomer *et al.*, *The Idea of Rajasthan*, Vol.1, Manhohar Publications, New Delhi.

Schomer, Karine, Joan Erdman, Deryck O. Lodrick and Loyd Rudolph (eds.) (2001). *The Idea of Rajasthan*, Vol.1, Manhohar Publications, New Delhi.

Sethia, Madhu (2003). *Rajput Polity: Warriors, Peasants and Merchants*, Rawat Publications, Jaipur.

Singh, Chandramani (1994). "Rajasthan ki Samanvit Sanskriti", unpublished Paper presented at the Seminar on *Composite Culture*, Organised by Institute of Rajasthan Studies, Jaipur.

———. (1998). "Madhyakalin Rajasthan: Striyon ka Sanskritik Yogdan", in Pratibha Jain and Sangeeta Sharma (eds.), *Bhartiya Stri*, Rawat Publications, Jaipur.

Singh, Surjit and Varsha Joshi (eds.), (2003). *Institutions and Social Change*, Rawat Publications, Jaipur.

Sinh, Ranbir (undated). "An Approach Paper to Cultural Policy", Samantar, Jaipur.

Taft, Frances (2003). "Heritage Hotels in Rajasthan", in Singh and Joshi (eds.), *Institutions and Social Change*, Rawat Publications, Jaipur.

Vashishtha, V.K. (1997). *Bhagat Movement*, Shruti Publications, Jaipur.

Tod, James (1914). *Annals and Antiquities of Rajasthan*, Vols. I & II, Reprint, Routledge, London.

Index

H

I

Z